Violent Crime in North America

Edited by Louis A. Knafla

Westport, Connecticut
London

Library of Congress Cataloging-in-Publication Data

Violent crime in North America / edited by Louis A. Knafla.
    p.   cm.
    Includes bibliographical references and index.
    ISBN 0–313–31027–0 (alk. paper)
    1. Violent crimes—United States—History. 2. Violent crimes—Canada—History.
    I. Knafla, Louis A., 1935– .
HV6789.V59   2003
364.15′0973—dc21   2003052892

British Library Cataloguing in Publication Data is available.

Library of Congress Catalog Card Number: 2003052892
ISBN: 0–313–31027–0

First published in 2003

Praeger Publishers, 88 Post Road West, Westport, CT 06881
An imprint of Greenwood Publishing Group, Inc.
www.praeger.com

Printed in the United States of America

The paper used in this book complies with the
Permanent Paper Standard issued by the National
Information Standards Organization (Z39.48-1984).

10   9   8   7   6   5   4   3   2   1

Contents

Preface   ix

Introduction   xi
Louis A. Knafla

Chapter 1   State, Community, and Petty Justice in Halifax, Nova
              Scotia, 1815–67   1
              Greg Marquis

Chapter 2   Making "Docile Bodies": Prison Science and Prisoner
              Resistance at the Minnesota Reformatory, 1889–1920   31
              Alexander W. Pisciotta

Chapter 3   Violent Crime on the Western Frontier: The
              Experience of the Idaho Territory, 1863–90   53
              Robert G. Waite

Chapter 4   The Wendigo Killings: The Legal Penetration of
              Canadian Law into the Spirit World of the Ojibwa
              and Cree Indians   75
              Sidney Harring

Chapter 5   Sexual Assaults in Calgary, Alberta, between the Wars   105
              David Bright

Chapter 6   Creating the Peace: Crime and Community Identity
              in Northeastern British Columbia, 1930–50   131
              Jonathan Swainger

Chapter 7   Capital Punishment and the Death Penalty in the
              United States. A Selected Bibliography   155
              Dennis Wiechman

BOOK REVIEW ESSAY   195

Genocide as Government through Murder: A Review of Recent
Contributions
              By Augustine Brannigan and Kelly Hardwick

Christopher Browning, *Ordinary Men: Reserve Police Battalion 101 and the
Final Solution in Poland, New Afterword*

Irving Louis Horowitz, *Taking Lives: Genocide and State Power*

Daniel J. Goldhagen, *Hitler's Willing Executioners: Ordinary Germans
and the Holocaust*

James Turner Johnson, *Morality and Contemporary Warfare*

Iris Chang, *The Rape of Nanking: The Forgotten Holocaust of World War II*

Chris Hitchens, *The Trial of Henry Kissinger*

Norbert Elias, *The Civilizing Process*

Gary Jonathon Bass, *Stay the Hand of Vengeance: The Politics of War Crime
Tribunals*

BOOK REVIEWS   211

Julius R. Ruff, *Violence in Early Modern Europe 1500–1800*
              By Sara M. Butler

J.M. Beattie, *Policing and Punishment in London, 1660–1750: Urban Crime
and the Limits of Terror*
              By Jennine Hurl-Eamon

Peter Oliver, *"Terror to Evil-Doers": Prisons and Punishments in Nineteenth-
Century Ontario*
              By Greg Marquis

Clive Emsley, *Gendarmes and the State in Nineteenth-Century Europe*
              By Simon Devereaux

David Philips, *William Augustus Miles (1796–1851): Crime, Policing and
Moral Entrepreneurship in England and Australia*
              By Mary Clayton

Maurice A. Martin, *Urban Policing in Canada: Anatomy of an Aging Craft*

Philip Rawlings, *Policing: A Short History*

Rob C. Mawby, *Policing Images: Policing, Communication and Legitimacy*
              By Rod Martin

Ideology, Crime and Criminal Justice: A Symposium in Honour of Sir Leon Radzinowicz, ed. Anthony Bottoms and Michael Tonry
       By Mary Beth Emmerichs

John Phillip Reid, *Patterns of Vengeance—Crosscultural Homicide in the North American Fur Trade*
       By Jonathan Swainger

Index   233

About the Editor and Contributors   245

Preface

Violent Crime in North America features seven original essays on the history of violent crimes and punishments in North America in the nineteenth and twentieth centuries as well as a major bibliography on capital punishment and the death penalty in the United States. It also contains a long book review essay on 8 books dealing with global terrorism, and reviews of 11 individual major works on the history and ideology of crime and criminal justice that have appeared from the end of the 1990s. The introduction outlines the issues and themes that are contained in the essays and the reviews. A comprehensive index identifies all subjects, names, and places in the volume. The subject index headings include all references to the general areas of corrections, courts, crime, crimes and offenses, criminal law, economics, government, the human condition, law, police and policing, professions, religion, social relations, violence, and war, to enable the reader to locate material that might otherwise be difficult to find in a collected work.

Introduction

Louis A. Knafla

Violent crime has caught the imagination of contemporary society, if not in the statistics presented. We are living in an era when the media insist on placing crime reports on page one or at the top of the hour; it does not seem to be able to report enough of it. The historical record, however, does not appear to bear out this preoccupation with violence. We do not, for example, live in an age of "ubiquitous violence" that was manifest in the military, civil institutions both legal and extralegal, and was rife in the form of interpersonal, group, popular, and organized crime in earlier centuries. Julius Ruff's *Violence in Early Modern Europe, 1500–1800*, provides insight into that time. The book, which Sara Butler has called a masterful history, describes an age in which violence was common, attaining its height in the sixteenth century and then declining over the next two centuries as European elites began to reform human behavior through the "civilizing process."[1] That process is still with us today. It is bringing to an end traditional forms of social violence and violence in local communities through expanded institutions of government and police, positive law and professional courts, more rational forms of proof, and a pluralistic society.

What often interests us is not merely the act of violence, but the thought process behind it: the rationale, or mens rea, its roots in the individual self and in the structure of society. Witness, for example, the ageless popularity of crime novels and criminal biographies. There is, however, no single vision of how to deal with violent crime. The three most relevant models for North America are the European, U.S., and Canadian models. The Europeans, first of all, use a different language: crime, criminals, prisons, and prisoners; not offenses, offenders, corrections, and inmates. Their ambitions are modest, based on the supposition that crime is a fact of life, that "reform" is problematic, and that most prisoners will not be corrected. Americans tend to believe that crime is something to make war against, that criminals are different people, and that they should be contained in a massive prison system until their errors are rent out of, or die with them. Canadians, on the other hand, believe that crime is not a major problem, and when it is committed they still have faith in rehabilitation. Prisoners are seen as having a disease that can be eradicated by good governance.

What has changed is the recognition of new violent crimes in the late twentieth century: child abuse, wife beating, and (at the turn of this century) terrorism. These have changed our definition of violent crime, as previously they were unreported. The prosecutorial energy to deal with them has come from the increased role of the central state in identifying serious crime rather than the interests of corporations, local communities, and private individuals. Much of this, however, has been at the expense of the working class, the poor, and the unemployed,[2] as well as ethnic minorities, Aboriginals, and women: groups previously referred to as "marginal" in society.[3]

The dangers that have engulfed modern society are addressed by us as subjects of legislation, which is how we deal with them. According to John Pratt's path-breaking study of governmentality,[4] dangerousness, through legislation, was conceptualized and responded to in Australia, New Zealand, Canada, the United States, and the United Kingdom from the late nineteenth century in social, political, and economic contexts. Part of the growth of modernity, its history and regulation, is underpinned theoretically by the concepts of risk and governance. In the nineteenth century habitual criminals, especially repeat property offenders, were regarded to be more serious threats than violent offenders against persons. Regulation was marginal because of the relationship of the state to the individual: the state's duty of care was minimal. A shift in mentality from the physicality of property to the physicality of the body at the turn of that century changed people's conception of dangerousness and gave rise to a new prosecutorial zeal of crimes against the person, the more violent, the more the machinery of the state was placed at its disposition.

In the United States, as in Western Europe, recorded rates of violent crime decreased significantly over the course of the nineteenth century as those nations developed into urban and industrial societies, and then rose slowly in the early twentieth century.[5] The concern, however, with crimes against the person, as well as crimes and public order and the state, in the United States led to a new common law definition of protecting oneself from danger which, in consequence, led to more violence akin to its Anglo-Saxon past. Enshrined in law by the Supreme Court, the "no duty to retreat" rule provided that one who sensed imminent danger could fire the first shot before being harmed.[6] As the American frontier moved from east to west, that rule became part of the American vision of frontier justice.

The American concern for dangerousness extended into how communities, states, and the courts handled their convictions of offenders. On one hand, the rise of vigilantes to defend person and property from violent acts in the absence of trusted legal institutions created a form of extralegal criminal justice. But as Christopher Waldrep has demonstrated from an exhaustive study of the records in one locale, eventually, in the course of time, people resorted to the courts.[7] While "justice" in terms of retribution was less final in the hands of courts, state-sponsored executions were eagerly sought and accommodated. And when public executions became unpalatable, private ones replaced them so that they would not be abolished.[8] Eschewed by other "western" countries, capital punishment has grown as part of American culture since its reintroduction in 1976.[9] The concern for controlling dangerousness continues, however, as the country still imprisons more persons per capita than any other nation except, perhaps, Russia.[10] It also uses private enterprise to manage the perpetrators of dangerousness, while convict labor thrives.

Canada, in contrast, has been coined the "peaceable kingdom." Current scholarship, however, has put aside that concept. Violence has, indeed, deep historical roots. A major collection of essays, *Violence in Canada*, which is just going into its second edition, posits that Canada is more violent than Australia, New Zealand, and Western Europe.[11] From the violence of the early fur trade era, the British conquest of Quebec and expulsion of the Acadians in Nova Scotia, to the rebellions of the late 1830s, and an era of imaginary criminals in the popular press, 1880s–1930s, the country's history is marked by sensational trials often reported as representative of a morally unfit and criminal class. But on the ground, a world of petty crimes and confidence schemes, often linked to gambling, alcohol, drugs, and prostitution, persisted in the first century of confederation. In agricultural communities, sexual violence toward farm women by the hired hand has been documented, while cities were often the center of sin and seduction. Thus communities and courts can be viewed as sites of violence between male and female, Natives and immigrants, employers and workers, husbands and wives, with the criminal law often serving a hegemonic function in the settlement process.[12]

In nineteenth- and early twentieth-century Canada, as in the United States, race and class were instrumental factors in determining who was prosecuted and who was convicted.[13] Single women, Natives, and minorities were singled out. But domestic violence was swept under the carpet and seldom prosecuted, because legislators, magistrates, and judges considered the family to be beyond the purview of the courts. The early twentieth-century increase in Canada was in crimes of public order and morality, as a result of the emergence of large transient populations in urban centers. In Ontario, Canada, the decrease was most significant in cases of violent assault. And the defendants who were most socially and economically marginal suffered the most.[14] In Toronto, Canada's largest city, the more prosecutions for a particular type of crime, the lower the rate of conviction, except for the case of minority men accused of violating White women. Nonetheless, serious crime comparatively was large in the country's landscape. For capital offenses, the rate in Canada for the 1951–84 period was 2.2 per 100,000, the third highest rate among OECD countries.[15]

More recently, two types of violence have received a disproportionate amount of media attention: sensational murders and public protests in which both demonstrators and the police engaged in violence. Some of the more salient of these incidents were in Ontario and Quebec. The legacy of Marc Lepine's shooting of 27 women, 14 of whom died in December 1989 at Montreal's École Polytechnique, remains in and perhaps pervades the Canadian consciousness. Others include the November 1997 protests at the APEC conference in Vancouver, which culminated in a long political battle on the right of the state to terrorize citizens participating in peaceful protests, and the October 1998 nonviolent protest in Toronto where the police responded in a heavy-handed manner with arrests involving in what many commentators, observers, and participants considered unnecessary force. Later, in June 2000, five hundred protesters appeared at the Ontario Legislature to protest government cutbacks. Not only were stones, bricks, and garbage pails thrown, but a firebomb as well. The police responded in riot-type fashion. In April 2001, during a Summit of the Americas meeting in Quebec City, riots by protesters similar to those that took place in 1999 in Seattle during globalization talks were responded to by riot police. More recently, the meeting of the World Trade Organization in Montreal in July 2003 to liberalize trade was beset by street protests that led to violence. Every day, somewhere in Canada, someone is shot. Usually the cases involve people who know each other, rarely are they strangers.

VIOLENT CRIME AND NATIVE PEOPLES

In the early periods of Canadian history, European Canadians perceived the crimes of Aboriginals in terms of "a discourse of savagery" that typed Aboriginals as a barbaric "Other," forging a colonial identity that structured future relations that still bear their scars today.[16] The scars of Aboriginal questions, steeped in politics and sovereignty, are global in scope.[17] In Canada Aboriginal homicides remained both prevalent and spontaneous down through the twentieth century. This is manifest in the fact that 75 percent of Native offenders charged with homicide were found guilty of at least manslaughter, with the percentage higher in mixed-race than in Native communities.[18] In the United States an analysis of nineteenth-century Supreme Court decisions revealed how the Court went beyond the law with "inverted doctrines" to erode Indian tribal sovereignty.[19] This process was repeated in Canada, as revealed in the chapter by Sidney Harring.

"The Wendigo Killings" explores the spirit world of the Ojibwa and Cree

Indians in northern Canada at the turn of the twentieth century. A series of cases from 1885 to 1906 established at common law throughout the British Empire the doctrine that common law had jurisdiction over Natives regardless of their lack of exposure to it. Thus Natives who killed the cannibal spirits clothed in human flesh that entered bodies (wendigos) to kill family members were subject to trials that lacked proper translation, competent legal counsel, or knowing jurors. They were also subject to prosecution for murder or manslaughter and sentenced to prison or hanging. Not even the common law defense of justified killings was employed. The trials revealed improbable allegations, problems of evidence, distorted interpretations of tribal customary law, and a department of Indian Affairs dedicated to the extermination of Native custom. The result was Natives' distortion of homicide cases to conceal wendigo killings to preserve their cultural beliefs.

VIOLENT CRIME IN THE EARLY TOWNS AND CITIES

Greg Marquis's chapter, "State, Community, and Petty Justice in Halifax, Nova Scotia, 1815–67," questions the view that criminal law was used primarily as a tool of the state to defend interests of the privileged classes at the expense of lower ones, women, and minorities. Examining police and court records for the city of Halifax, he finds a weak and disorganized state that placed law and order in the hands of part-time community amateurs who served as night watchmen, constables, and JPs. Most criminal prosecutions in the early nineteenth century were launched by private citizens, representative of all classes as Allen Steinberg has shown for colonial American cities.[20] And by 1864, one-third were still private prosecutions, including most of the cases for assault and theft. The majority of public-order offenses were prosecuted by the state, but these were concerned largely with drunkenness, vagrancy, and breaking the peace. Thus there was direction by the local elite, but that was simply one element of the prosecutorial system.

Other research confirms the continuation of this story. In late-eighteenth-century Halifax, criminal indictments were 32 times the rate of its mother country, and one of the most startling figures is that a high proportion involved the victimization of women. Many of the homicides were casual, many were not prosecuted, and where prosecuted the conviction rate was low. Of women committed for capital offenses, nearly half were convicted and most were sent to the gallows. The circumstances of these killings were situations in which men had little fear of the consequences. Sexual assaults had the highest recorded rate of any country in the era, with a conviction rate of just 26 percent.[21] Thus Halifax was a city that had a high level of violence through killings and sexual assaults. It stands in sharp contrast to London, where John Beattie's celebrated work, reviewed here by Jennine Hurl-Eamon, depicts the efficacy of police, public courts, and borough officials in administering criminal justice.

The policing problem has been the subject of several recent books, none too favorable of its subject, and none of which has broken new ground, as Rod Martin assesses in his review. Maurice Martin's book demonstrates how Canadian police have failed to adapt to urbanization, maintaining a personnel that is reactive instead of proactive to criminal acts and deeply engrained in a subculture that is too thoroughly entrenched for change. Philip Rawlings and Rob Mawby, in rewriting the history of the British police, present the stereotype of a fragmented system still obsessed with social control and using the media to attain legitimation for its actions. Sometimes police officers could be well informed, as David Philips argues in his biography of William Miles, a Sydney police commissioner in the nineteenth century, reviewed by Mary Clayton. Even his career, however, was caught between British, colonial, and city officials while fighting financial corruption and drunkenness.

What Canada, and perhaps the United States needed, was a more European style of policing as described in Clive Emsley's book, *Gendarmes and the State in Nineteenth-Century Europe.* The book is reviewed by Simon Devereaux, who characterizes it as a path-breaking study of the origins of modern policing. Law and order was maintained in the rural hinterlands of Europe through military-style gendarmeries. Growing from the Napoleonic Empire in 1791 across Europe, they rose from peacekeepers to rulers of law, from enforcing conscription and pursuing deserters to carrying out political surveillance, patrolling roads, and filing criminal reports. Their military ethos can be seen in policing today, both domestically and internationally.

Moving west, David Bright's chapter, "Sexual Assaults in Calgary, Alberta, between the Wars," is part of the growing body of literature on aspects of violence in Canadian frontier towns. He questions the traditional historiography that violence was the product of frontier conditions and argues that it existed in equal effect in older Canadian communities. He also believes that shifts in economic conditions were significant. Bright wades through the squalid world of sex crimes beneath the surface of society, finding in police and court records that 90 percent of the cases were unreported and of those reported there was a conviction rate of 30 percent. There was a notable increase in such crimes from the mid-1920s to the late 1930s, with most of the offenders in their twenties, and most of the victims 6 to 10 years of age. He depicts a seasonal pattern, with crime incidence prevalent in the spring. The role of police, whether federal or local, was insignificant in crime prevention. Some of the themes in the work of Marquis and Bright resonate with studies of prostitution, rape, sex, and the city in nineteenth- and early twentieth-century America.[22]

VIOLENT CRIME ON THE WESTERN FRONTIER

Robert Waite's chapter, "Violent Crime on the Western Frontier: The Experience of the Idaho Territory, 1863–90," tests the reputation of frontier violence by eastern newspapers and pulp crime novels and specialized local histories that have no common view. His data reveal a high incidence of murders and violent crime, with few culprits found, tried, or executed. Residents attributed this to dissolute and vicious "adventurers" and the "local wrong." It led to vigilance committees, shootings, and lynchings. Territorial courts, however, were quite careful in their handling of those prosecuted, carefully instructing juries and sometimes retrying cases. Whether caused by outsiders or locals, this high level of violent crime existed throughout the period and increased each decade. Executions served as no deterrent, and guns in the hands of the disaffected only contributed to the loss of life for often petty disagreements.

Waite's study stands in sharp contrast to the work of John Phillip Reid, whose pioneering history depicts an area of little violence, murder, or theft where crimes were handled with elaborate attention.[23] His more recent book, *Patterns of Vengeance—Crosscultural Homicide in the North American Fur Trade*, reviewed here by Jonathan Swainger, examines how fur trappers and mountain men adopted indigenous responses to violence and homicides, albeit in a flawed state. For domestic homicide, they extended the Aboriginal family right of revenge; for international homicide, they used diplomacy to avert war and the interruption of trade. Reid shows the way foreign legal notions were pressed into northwest North America and were misread by trappers, demonstrating the problem of language in cross-cultural habitats. The desire for vengeance became part of the American imagination in the nineteenth century.[24]

Swainger's chapter, "Creating the Peace: Crimes and Community Identity in Northeastern British Columbia, 1930–50," challenges the "country life" ideology of rural society in western Canada. The development of transportation and communication did not make the area more peaceful; it brought new forms of criminality. He illustrates David Garland's thesis that the line between acceptable levels of disorder is a cultural expression.[25] Thus from the Klondike gold rush of the 1890s through the era of World War II, lawlessness was rampant as the local press turned a blind eye. While lawlessness in the early period included the Native population, by the 1930s it was generated by White immigrants through murders, suicides, burglaries, robberies, arson, and domestic violence. Local opinion, however, attributed it to "outsiders." Indeed, by 1950, the crime rate per capita had risen sixfold over 1941. Inept policing contributed to this increase, as well as an incorrigible local population who thrived on bootlegging, prostitution, and theft of building materials for the construction of the Alaska highway by the U.S. Army.

That cultural style influenced the way a murder case was argued in court, tried, and interpreted in the press has been demonstrated by Daniel Cohen, for New England towns.[26] Moreover, Andie Tucher and Amy Srebnick have argued that newspaper reports of sensational crimes reveal more of a town's urban culture than of the crime committed.[27] Studies of crime in the American-

Canadian borderlands have shown that there were many nuanced similarities in their experiences.[28] In Canada, as in the United States, violent domestic crime against women pervades the court records, if not the press.[29] Likewise, the statistics reveal that minorities were prejudiced in interracial interactions.[30] Thus one could conclude with an earlier author that violent crime in western Canada was an enduring feature of life, as in the western States, but without the organized gangs and corporate violence that were part of the American experience.[31]

VIOLENCE AND PUNISHMENT

Alexander Pisciotta's "Making 'Docile Bodies': Prison Science and Prisoner Resistance at the Minnesota Reformatory, 1889–1920" explores the development and diffusion of the new penology of the late-nineteenth and early twentieth centuries, which sparked "a paradigmatic revolution" that transformed punishment, corrections, and social control in the United States. Previous studies of the medical model and prison science by Michel Foucault and David Rothman were unsystematic and unfocused[32] and eschewed complexities. Created as a response to perceived increases in violent crime and social disorder, the model was structured to manage the souls and minds of convicts and build docile bodies. The reformatory was for first-time offenders, 16 to 30 years of age, who were given kind treatment, academic and vocational education, Christian values, and military drill. According to Brockway, the Elmira Reformatory in New York (1876) "saved" 70 percent to 80 percent of its inmates, a claim that was repeated in Massachusetts, Michigan, and Pennsylvania. Using inmate case histories, interviews, and staff and parole records, Pisciotta sketches a wide disparity of defects in the model, administrative problems, insufficient resources, parole officer reluctance, prisoner resistance, escapes, and suicides that contributed to marginal results. Building on David Garland's work on prisoner resistance,[33] Pisciotta explores how community-based corrections strategies worked on the ground.[34] The result was that most of those who were released and assumed to be corrected, were not. The failure, he argues, was in attempting to make Christian character and docile bodies out of unreceptive lower-class offenders.

Failure also came to those who had little interest in reform, as Greg Marquis illustrates in his review of Peter Oliver's *Terror to Evil-Doers*, a chronicle of the social history of penitentiaries and jails in nineteenth-century Ontario. While Kingston penitentiary adopted the model of Auburn, New York, in 1835, most of the colony's/province's prisoners were in county jails, where conditions remained deplorable down to the late-twentieth century. Changes in regulations and conditions were in the hands of a bureaucratic elite and were not the result of economic change or class tensions. Representing a rural society, prison was seen as a deterrent, not a place for rehabilitation. Underfunding and underpaid officials led to the use of convict labor for cost recovery and not for reform. Most of the inmates were debtors, and most criminals were alcoholics and vagrants. The prison reforms of nineteenth-century Europe and the United States were shunned; Blacks and Roman Catholics were overrepresented and the most disadvantaged inmates were women, children, and the insane.

A plea for just, humanitarian sentencing and intermediate sanctions has been made by Michael Tonry.[35] Some of these reforms have been made in Minnesota, a site of the previously failed experiment, as well as in Victoria in Queensland, and in Sweden.[36] They have also been targeted in Canada, where physical pain in prisons, for example, was abolished by midcentury.[37] The problem in the United States is that mass imprisonment has been embraced as a deterrent to violent crime, and it has not worked, with the result that ethnic minorities make up three-fourths of U.S. prisoners.[38] As Mary Beth Emmerichs notes in her review of a book of essays on the work of Leon Radzinowicz and the "Whig" school of criminal justice history, David Garland concludes that the penal welfare model of rehabilitation was replaced by one that stigmatized prisoners and hardened the wall between them and society. Whether the answer lies in criminologists and government agents using morality proactively, and not just managerial and technical skills, in solving these problems, as proposed by Anthony Bottoms, Roger Hood, and Seàn McConville, only time will tell.

BIBLIOGRAPHY AND HISTORIOGRAPHY

That crime and the institutions for its control are deeply embedded in history was the inspiration behind Eric Monkkonen's collected writings, *Crime, Justice, History*.[39] This idea has been manifested by a number of major works on the history of homicide in recent years, some of which are in the Ohio State University Press monograph series on the history of crime and criminal justice.[40] In the United States Lawrence Friedman has provided a foundation for its further study.[41] Dennis Weichman has added to that corpus of literature with a timely select bibliography, "Capital Punishment and the Death Penalty in the United States," which is published in this volume. A work of great effort, it should stand the test of time for future researchers.

Nothing like this bibliographic work exists for Canada, apart from that of Jim Phillips and an important, seldom-cited work by Russell Smandych and his collaborators.[42] Official government statistics remain fraught with difficulties.[43] Some useful recent works cover parricide and intrafamilial violence[44] and violence against women[45] and children;[46] violence in the workplace,[47] prisons,[48] and sport;[49] violence against minorities and their overrepresentation in the criminal justice system;[50] sexual violence in Canada and the United States,[51] youth violence in Canada,[52] and in Canada and the United States;[53] and violence by the police in Canada and the United States.[54]

VIOLENCE: THE LARGER CONTEXT

Genocide as a crime of government through murder is the subject of an extensive review essay by Augustine Brannigan and Kelly Hardwick of eight books published from 1997 to 2002. They look at the revival of histories of the Holocaust through the lenses of the massacres in Rwanda and Bosnia—the slaughter of unarmed noncombatants by ordinary people, often neighbors. In today's world death outside of war is more likely committed by the state than by the individual. Thus we should revisit armed conflicts for the study of crime and criminology. The reviewers define genocide as the extermination of a group, in which the killing is an objective in itself rather than (as in war) a means to an end (military victory); it is an act of murder by a governing elite that is delegated to ordinary men who become mass murderers. An example is the "Rape of Nanking," in which there was no issue of race, religion, or minority groups. The origins can be found in the crusades and witch-hunts of the medieval and early modern eras.

The doyen of the history of the criminal law, Leon Radzinowicz, believed that the criminal law, like history, advanced with the course of time (see Emmerichs's book review) and that it evolved on the shoulders of reformers. The scholarly community, however, is coming to the view that the experiments of local officials, conservative politics, and war and peace, may have been larger contributing factors to an ebb and flow. The French military gendarmes, for example, may have had a larger influence in Great Britain, Ireland, and North America than would be expected (Emsley's book reviewed), and policing crime may have been influenced more by politics than by humanitarian concerns. Likewise, the United States may not have been the experimental laboratory of criminological science that Radzinowicz envisioned. As well, the criminal justice system has been influenced in recent decades by factors such as civil society adapting to the growth of crime, insecurity, and more recently the war on terror and to a new style of more restrictive, means-tested, public management. All of which changes the cultural coordinates of crime control to the harsh treatment of offenders and more certain, fixed punishments, as observed by David Garland.[55] It also makes us vitally aware of the general failure of crime control and of institutions of correction.

NOTES

1. The enormously influential work of Norbert Elias is reviewed in this volume by Brannigan and Hardwick.

2. See generally, Stanley Cohen, *Visions of Social Control: Crime, Punishment and Classification* (Cambridge, UK and New York, 1985).

3. Roger Lane, *Violent Death in the City: Suicide, Accident and Murder in Nineteenth-Century Philadelphia* (Cambridge, Mass., 1979).

4. John Pratt, *Governing the Dangerous* (Sydney, Australia, 1997).

5. See P. and P. Brantingham, *Patterns of Crime* (New York, 1984).

6. Richard Maxwell Brown, *No Duty to Retreat: Violence and Values in American History and Society* (New York, 1991).

7. Christopher Waldrep, *Roots of Disorder: Race and Criminal Justice in the American South, 1817–80* (Urbana, Ill., 1998).

8. John D. Bessler, *Death in the Dark: Midnight Executions in America* (Boston, 1997).

9. Austin Sarat, ed., *The Killing State: Capital Punishment in Law, Politics, and Culture* (New York, 1999).

10. Scott Christianson, *With Liberty for Some: 500 Years of Imprisonment in America* (Boston, 1998), p. xi.

11. Jeffrey Ian Ross, ed., *Violence in Canada: Sociopolitical Perspectives* (Don Mills, 1995), which is re-emphasized in his new introduction to the 2nd ed. (2004), "Violence in Canada: Ten Years After." I wish to thank Jeffrey for providing me with a prepublication copy of his essay.

12. Lesley Erickson, "The Unsettling West: Gender, Crime, and Culture on the Canadian Prairies, 1886–1940" (Ph.D. diss., University of Calgary, 2003).

13. Laura F. Edwards, "Sexual Violence, Gender, Reconstruction, and the Extension of Patrimony in Granville County, North Carolina," *North Carolina Historical Review* 67 (1991): 250; and Carolyn Strange, "Patriarchy Modified: The Criminal Prosecution of Rape in York County, Ontario, 1880–1930," in *Crime and Criminal Justice: Essays in the History of Canadian Law*, ed. Jim Phillips, Tina Loo, and Susan Lewthwaite (Toronto, 1994), 210–12.

14. Helen Boritch, "Crime and Punishment in Middlesex County, Ontario, 1871–1920," in *Crime and Criminal Justice*, Phillips et al., 387–438.

15. Rosemary Gartner and B. McCarthy, "The Social Distribution of Femicide in Urban Canada, 1921–1988," *Law and Society Review* 25 (1991): 287–311.

16. Tina Loo, "The Road from Bute Inlet, Crime and Colonial Identity in British Columbia," in *Crime and Criminal Justice*, Phillips et al., 112–42.

17. See the timely special issue "Aboriginality and Normativity," *Canadian Journal of Law and Society* 17:2 (summer 2002).

18. David Long, "On Violence and Healing: Aboriginal Experience, 1960–1993," in *Violence in Canada*, Ross, 40–77.

19. David E. Wilkins, *American Indian Sovereignty and the U.S. Supreme Court: The Masking of Justice* (Austin, 1997).

20. Allen Steinberg, *The Transformation of Criminal Justice. Philadelphia, 1800–1880* (Chapel Hill, N.C., and London, 1989).

21. Jim Phillips, "Women, Crime, and Criminal Justice in Early Halifax, 1750–1800," in his *Crime and Criminal Justice*, 186–93.

22. Timothy J. Gilfoyle, *City of Eros: New York City, Prostitution, and the Commercialization of Sex, 1790–1920* (New York, 1992); and Mary E. Odem, *Delinquent Daughters: Protecting and Policing Adolescent Female Sexuality in the United States, 1885–1920* (Chapel Hill, N.C., 1995).

23. John Phillip Reid, *Policing the Elephant: Crime, Punishment, and Social Behavior on the Overland Trail* (San Marino, Calif., 1997).

24. Karen Halttunen, *Murder Most Foul: The Killer and the American Gothic Imagination* (Cambridge, Mass., 1998). See also the recent study by David Peterson del Mar, *Beaten Down: A History of Interpersonal Violence in the West* (Seattle, 2002).

25. David Garland, *Punishment and Modern Society: A Study in Social Theory* (Oxford, 1990), 198.

26. Daniel A. Cohen, *Pillars of Salt, Monuments of Grace: New England Crime Literature and the Origins of American Popular Culture, 1674–1860* (New York, 1993).

27. Andie Tucher, *Froth and Scum: Truth, Beauty, Goodness and the Ax Murder in America's First Mass Medium* (Chapel Hill, N.C., 1994); and Amy Gilman Srebnick, *The Mysterious Death of Mary Rogers: Sex and Culture in Nineteenth-Century New York* (New York and Oxford, 1995).

28. *Law for the Elephant, Law for the Beaver: Essays in the Legal History of the North American West*, ed. John McLaren, Hamar Foster, and Chet Orloff (Regina and Pasadena, 1992).

29. David Peterson del Mar, *What Trouble I Have Seen: A History of Violence Against Wives* (Cambridge, Mass., 1996).

30. Clare V. McKanna, *Homicide, Race, and Justice in the American West, 1880–1920* (Phoenix, Ariz., 1997).

31. Louis A. Knafla, "Violence on the Western Canadian Frontier: A Historical Perspective," in *Violence in Canada*, Ross, 10–39.

32. Michel Foucault, *Discipline and Punish: The Birth of the Prison* (New York, 1977); and David J. Rothman, *Conscience and Convenience: The Asylum and Its Alternatives in Progressive America* (Boston, 1980).

33. David Garland, *Punishment and Welfare: A History of Penal Strategies* (Brookfield, Vt., 1985).

34. See also Jonathan Simon, *Poor Discipline: Parole and the Social Control of the Underclass, 1890–1990* (Chicago, 1993).

35. Michael Tonry, *Sentencing Matters* (New York, 1996).

36. C.M.V. Clarkson and R. Morgan, ed., *The Politics of Sentencing Reform* (Oxford, 1995).

37. Carolyn Strange, "The Undercurrents of Penal Culture: Punishment of the Body in Mid-Twentieth-Century Canada," *Law & Society Review* 19:2 (summer 2001): 343–85.

38. The Oxford History of the Prison: The Practice of Imprisonment in Western Society, 2nd ed., (Oxford and New York, 1998).

39. Eric Monkkonen, *Crime, Justice, History* (Columbus Ohio, 2002).

40. David R. Johnson and Jeffrey S. Adler, general eds, "The History of Crime and Criminal Justice Series": especially Roger Lane, *Murder in America: A History* (1997), Martha A. Myers, *Race, Labor, and Punishment in the New South* (1998), and Gilles Vandal, *Rethinking Southern Violence: Homicides in Post-Civil War Louisiana, 1866–1884* (2000).

41. Lawrence M. Friedman, *Crime and Punishment in American History* (New York, 1993).

42. Jim Phillips, "Crime and Punishment in the Dominion of the North: Canada from New France to the Present," in *Crime Histories and Histories of Crime. Studies in the Historiography of Crime and Criminal Justice*, ed. Clive Emsley and Louis A. Knafla (Westport, 1996), 163–99; and Russell C. Smandych, Catherine J. Matthews, and Sandra J. Cox, *Canadian Criminal Justice History. An Annotated Bibliography* (Toronto, 1987).

43. T. Gabor, K Hung, S. Mihorean, and C. St.-Onge, "Canadian Homicide Rates: A Comparison of Two Data Sources," *Canadian Journal of Criminology* 44 (2002): 351–63; and C. Stark-Adamec, ed., *Violence: A Collective Responsibility* (Ottawa, 1996).

44. Jacques D. Marleau and Thierry Webanck, "Parricide and Violent Crimes: A Canadian Study," *Adolescence* 32:126 (1997): 357–59.

45. Douglas A. Brownbridge and Shiva S. Halli, *Explaining Violence Against Women in Canada* (Toronto, 2001); Joan Sangster, *Regulating Girls and Women: Sexuality, Family and the Law in Ontario, 1920–1960* (Toronto, 2001); Holly Johnson, *Dangerous Domains: Violence Against Women in Canada* (Toronto, 1996); and Holly Johnson and Vincent F. Sacco, "Researching Violence Against Women: Statistics Canada's National Survey," *Canadian Journal of Criminology* (July 1995): 281–302; Walter DeKeseredy, "Measuring Sexual Abuse in Canadian University/College Dating Relationships," in *Researching Sexual Violence Against Women: Methodological and Personal Perspectives*, ed. Martin D. Schwartz (Thousand Oaks Calif., 1997), 43–53; and Walter DeKeseredy and Brian MacLean, "But Women do it too: The contexts and nature of female-to-male violence in Canadian heterosexual dating relationships," in *Battered Women: Law, State and Contemporary Research in Canada*, ed. K. Bonney-castle and G. Rigakos (Vancouver, 1997).

46. Katherine Covell and R. Brian Howe, *The Challenge of Children's Rights for Canada* (Waterloo, ON, 2001).

47. Judy Fudge and Eric Tucker, *Labour Before the Law—The Regulation of Worker's Collective Action in Canada, 1900–1948* (Oxford, 2001); and Neil Boyd, "Violence in the Workplace in British Columbia: A Preliminary Investigation," *Canadian Journal of Criminology* (October 1995): 491–519.

48. Reyhan Yazar, "The Violence Prevention Program: Intensive Correctional Treatment," *Corrections Today* 63:2 (April 2001): 102.

49. Laura Robinson, *Crossing the Line: Violence and Sexual Assault in Canada's National Sport* (Toronto, 1998).

50. *Regulating Lives: Historical Essays on the State, Society, the Individual, and the Law*, ed. John McLaren, Robert Menzies, and Dorothy E. Chunn (Vancouver, 2002); and the special issue "Law, Race and Space," *Canadian Journal of Law and Society* 15:2 (summer 2000).

51. *Sexual Violence: Policies, Practices, and Challenges in the United States and Canada*, ed. James F. Hodgson and Debra S. Kelley (Westport Conn., 2002); and Elaine Grandin and Eugen Lupri, "Intimate Violence in Canada and the United States: A Cross-National Comparison," *Journal of Domestic Violence* 12:4 (1997): 417–43.

52. Anthony N. Doob and Jane Sprott, "Is the Quality of Youth Violence Becoming More Serious?" *Canadian Journal of Criminology* 40:2 (1998): 185 fl.; and Thomas Gabor, "Commentary: Trends in Youth Crime: Some evidence pointing to increases in the severity and volume of violence on the part of young people," *Canadian Journal of Criminology* 41 (1999): 385–92.

53. Lana D. Harrison, Patricia G. Erickson, Edward Adlaf, and Charles Freeman, "The Drugs-Violence Nexus Among American and Canadian Youth," *Substance Use and Misuse* 36:14 (2001): 2065–101.

54. James F. Hodgson, "Police Violence in Canada and the USA: Analysis and Management," *Policing: An International Journal of Police Strategies and Management* 24:4 (2001): 520–49; and Jeffrey Ian Ross, *Making News of Police Violence: A Comparative Study of Toronto and New York City* (Westport Conn., 2000).

55. David Garland, "Ideology and Crime," in *Ideology, Crime, and Criminal Justice* (2002), 1–19, reviewed in this volume.

CHAPTER 1

State, Community, and Petty Justice in Halifax, Nova Scotia, 1815–67

Greg Marquis

> The law is a useful and necessary profession, and therefore deserves to be honored and kept from disgrace, but the gambling spirit that leads weak people to go to law for trifling differences to obtain what they fancy is their right, although it may involve them in immense expense and loss of time, should be discouraged by all well wishers of society.[1]

Criminal justice literature emphasizes the imposition of law on society by the state, by economic and social elite, and by legal institutions. Historians often adopt the same perspective. Law is something that is done to people, and the results for the lower classes, women, and minorities generally are not equitable. Law, at best, is interpreted as a subtle legitimation of class interests, a process that secures the hegemony of society's dominant interests. At worst, it is the firm arm of a vigilant state and intolerant society.[2]

The ruling classes of colonial British North America habitually reflected the attitude that law's aim was not ensuring justice or protecting individual rights, but rather inculcating respect, discipline, and responsibility.[3] For the colonial legal elite of Nova Scotia, murder, breaking and entering, and burglary at night were particularly heinous. In 1817 Alexander Russell was indicted for having incited two apprentices to rob their master, allegedly explaining that "it was no sin to rob the rich." The Supreme Court justice who pronounced sentence on Russell declared that the crime was "pregnant with every species of villainy."[4]

This study suggests a modification of the law-as-imposition approach. Although petty justice in early nineteenth-century Halifax was marked by class, racial, and gender biases, it also functioned, in part, as a commodity pursued by litigants. All classes of Haligonians were determined to "have the law." This chapter's use of "community" does not imply harmony or equality, and I do not suggest that petty justice in Halifax was fair or that all disputants turned to magisterial authority. We should not ignore laws, police policies, and magistrates' rulings that reflected the growth of class-based state power. The punishment of vagrancy, rioting, and disturbing the peace—status and public-order crimes—indicates a growing emphasis by midcentury on respectable behavior. The police, by the 1860s, were a more intrusive force. And class or social status no doubt had a bearing on the decision to arrest, the chance of bail, and the disposition of a given prosecution, as they do today. But personal offenses—assault, threatening, abusive language, and many property crimes such as larceny—were prosecuted by Haligonians of all classes. In fact assault may have been an overwhelmingly lower-class prosecution.[5] If the criminal justice system, like the political apparatus, was staffed by the propertied middle class and elite, the lower orders were aware of that system's dispute-resolution functions. The working face of legal order was not the prosecution of felonies, but the response to petty crime. On these occasions the law, at least for the victorious party, was a welcome imposition. As Allan Steinberg concludes of contemporary Philadelphia, before the 1850s criminal prosecution was "shaped less by the need to combat crime than by community needs for third-party dispute resolution."[6]

If the criminal law was harsh, the early nineteenth-century Nova Scotia "state" was weak. Law and order were the preserve of the community, led by part-time amateurs. At its upper levels, the magistracy, this leadership was socially exclusive.[7] In 1815 Halifax instituted a police office under the jurisdiction of the county magistracy with a permanent magistrate. Constables who worked under the justices of the peace were supplemented from time to time by a night watch that at first was little more than a nocturnal militia under the direction of gentlemen magistrates. In 1841, following several years of dissatisfaction with town administration by magistrates, Halifax was incorporated. Ward constables nominated by elected aldermen and a police court conducted by the mayor and aldermanic assistants now delivered civic justice. In 1864 the day constables and night watch were amalgamated and placed under the direction of the city marshal, who reported to the mayor and council. The last important structural change in petty justice administration occurred in 1867 when an appointed stipendiary magistrate took over the police court.[8]

EIGHTEENTH-CENTURY ORIGINS

Halifax was founded as a fortified naval base, and although a military ethos permeated the colony's early decades, civil judicial officers were appointed quickly. In 1749 Governor Cornwallis named four justices of the peace for the new township and instructed each company of settlers to elect a constable.

The Lords of Trade had instructed him to increase the police of the town as it grew in population and area. The eighteenth-century term "police" connoted not uniformed officers on patrol, but "broad social regulation, especially of those ancient concerns governments had about cities: supplying them with food, controlling nuisances and preventing popular disorders."[9] A year later the town was divided into eight wards, each appointing two constables. In addition to a county jail for felons and persons awaiting trial, by 1758 the settlement had a bridewell, a small structure for the confinement and punishment of "disorderly and idle persons."[10] The bridewell, or house of correction, became an important part of the police of the town, functioning as a prison for persons guilty of nonindictable offenses. During the year 1790, for example, 42 individuals—26 men, 16 women, and 7 Blacks—were confined from 1 to more than 50 days. A majority were committed (and released) by Magistrate Gautier, which suggests that by this period one or two justices of the peace were handling most of the town's petty criminal business.[11]

As there was no police force, magistrates appointed from the elite mercantile and official class were expected to keep order and punish malefactors. The Sessions of the Peace, in addition to trying indictable offenses and appointing constables and a series of part-time regulatory officers for the county, functioned as a law-making body by passing ordinances. In keeping with the older notion of police, it also determined the assize of bread. In 1792 the assembly, perhaps in response to elite fears of rising crime and disorder, enacted a law that formalized regular sittings by three magistrates, a "rotation court," which anticipated the police court of the nineteenth century.[12] Specialized courts for determining minor criminal and civil matters were a trend in the larger Anglo-American world in the 1790s. The Middlesex Justices Act of 1792 set up seven police offices around London, each with a stipendiary magistrate and six constables. Six years later New York's common council created a police office to oversee the city's "police" and examine and try criminal offenders. New York's police justices helped supervise the night watch and often personally intervened to quell public disturbances. In both London and New York the police offices combined judicial with police functions, which as Philip Girard notes is "shocking to the modern eye" but reflects the duality of the office of magistrate circa 1800.[13]

With the exception of the magistrates of the rotation court, Halifax by the War of 1812 was administered much as it had been in the 1760s, by justices of the peace meeting in quarter sessions and special sessions and by the county grand jury. As David Sutherland explains, local elite preferred an ad hoc approach to town government, and suggestions for municipal incorporation in 1765, 1785, and 1790 received little sympathy from the governor, his council, or the assembly.[14] In 1812 the grand jury and a committee of magistrates examined "the State of Town Establishments" and noted the rapid increase in Halifax's "burdens" proportionate to its resources. The community had in excess of ten thousand inhabitants, not to mention, as the War of 1812 escalated, thousands of soldiers and sailors. War also brought refugees, such as two thousand Chesapeake Blacks brought to Nova Scotia by the Royal Navy. The impoverished "Refugees," fresh from slavery in Maryland and Virginia, became a target for magisterial surveillance and White animosity. Grand juries discussed municipal incorporation again in 1813 and 1814, but instead of an elected civic authority they advocated "an Efficient Police founded upon the principle of Equity and Justice." Haligonians were "attached to old habits," yet the jurors supported "a systematic reform in the Police of the Town." The problem of maintaining order was attributed not to the law itself, but to its enforcement: "The magistracy of this Country is confined to Gentlemen of much respectability but whose personal avocation preclude that attendance to the Duties of their stations which the increasing state of the population requires."[15] The issue of town governance prompted the publication of an anonymous draft charter of incorporation, a conservative plan that avoided "the unpleasant duty of electing" town officers. The draft charter proposed "trustee magistrates" to serve on a quarter sessions for the town and an appointed grand jury, drawing on "the whole of the leading members of the community" to serve as common council.[16]

THE POLICE OFFICE

The political class, reflecting the concerns of the merchant elite who dominated the assembly, the quarter sessions, and the grand jury, thought incorporation premature. Instead, a joint committee of the executive council and the assembly consulted with the magistracy and advised a more permanent police establishment. Magistrates, it recommended, should sit in rotation, daily, to try misdemeanors in "a public office." Rather than by fees, they should be remunerated on a per diem basis. Secondly, the police office should be attended by a "peace officer" or constable. Last, to punish misdemeanants properly, the county should manage the bridewell. Thus the elite, although concerned with the cleanliness of the streets, the regulation of public markets, and other police matters, linked reform of the courts to the punishment of petty offenders. The grand jury, echoing earlier commentators, had complained that the county poorhouse had become inundated with paupers and criminals ruined by drink.[17]

The legislature, despite the aroused suspicions of country members of the assembly, responded with permissive legislation for a bridewell, or house of correction, for Halifax County and a police office for the town. The aims of what became known as the "Police Act" seemed to be the punishment and disciplining of the deviant poor rather than the encouragement of criminal litigation. The court also invoked the authority of the vagrancy statutes of 1758, 1759, and 1774, reflecting the lingering importance of "degrees of freedom" governing slaves, servants, apprentices, children, and paupers. The stated purpose of the interrelated institutions was "the suppression of vice and the correction of disorderly persons." Three justices of the peace (or "police justices") appointed by the Sessions of the Peace would supervise the police office, assisted by a legally trained police clerk (a coveted patronage position for the Tory elite). The law also authorized three regular constables to attend the court, serve warrants, and otherwise assist the magistrates. The police office would be supported by rents, revenues, and fines of the town market houses, as well as other fines. The magistrates were authorized to commit a variety of "disorderly and idle persons" to the bridewell, including beggars, gamblers, fortune tellers, vagabonds, runaways, and "stubborn servants, apprentices and children." The police justices were empowered to perform all duties necessary for "the apprehension, committal, conviction and punishment of criminal offenders and for carrying into effect the Laws now in force for the preservation of peace and good order."[18]

In practice, the police office was conducted by the senior magistrate. For a decade or more the salaried "police magistrate," also referred to as the superintendent or chief of police,[19] was John George Pyke, one of Halifax's original settlers. A merchant and veteran MLA, Pyke had years of practical legal experience as justice of the peace, leading member of the Sessions of the Peace, and *custos rotulorum* (records keeper). His social connections are suggested by his other institutional offices: fire ward, militia officer, poorhouse commissioner, president of the Charitable Irish Society, warden of St. Paul's, and a prominent freemason. By the standards of the late nineteenth century, the new establishment was not imposing. It depended on part-time constables, other magistrates, and the night watch to bring in disturbers of the peace and on citizens to make complaints. One chronicler remembered how "Colonel" Pyke sat in the small police office "in drab knee breeches with gray yarn stockings and snuff coloured coat." The magistrate was assisted by three constables, including an African American dressed in a cast-off military uniform, who escorted prisoners to the gaol and bridewell and inflicted court-ordered floggings.[20]

Of the day-to-day operations of the early police office we know very little. With the exception of a record of jail and bridewell commitments for 1834–41 and some yearly expense totals, none of its records appear to have survived (see table 1.1).[21] The press, particularly before the 1840s, appears to have devoted little attention to police court reporting, preferring the more sensational trials of the Supreme Court. Even quarter sessions trials involving grand and petty juries were not described in much detail, although further research may modify those observations. By most accounts, the police office in the brick court building on the Grand Parade was small; this and the traditions of magisterial justice and the quarter sessions meant that there were few, if any, spectators. Hence, unlike the later periods when the police court was open to both press and public, its deliberations in the 1810s, 1820s, and 1830s probably were somewhat secretive. Victorian historian Thomas B. Akins recalled the earlier era: "Criminal charges of a delicate nature, or when personal character was likely to be affected, were usually investigated with closed doors, and no information made public until found to be necessary for the ends of justice."[22]

Table 1.1 shows police magistrate cases in the immediate preincorporation period; not all the cases before the police magistrate are included, only defendants who were convicted and sentenced to the bridewell or jail, or who were examined and committed for trial before a higher court. As table 1.2 suggests, the Supreme Court and quarter sessions also sent prisoners to the county's custodial institutions, as did the military. The surviving police court committal book covers 82 months ending in early August 1841. These relatively low numbers suggest that crime was not a primary social concern in early nineteenth-century Halifax. In this period the police office committed more than fourteen hundred individuals to bridewell or jail. On the basis of what can be discerned about later police courts in Halifax and elsewhere, persons who were committed, rather than discharged or fined, typically ranged from between 10 percent to 50 percent of the total brought before the magistrates in a given year. So the Halifax Police Court probably processed between three thousand and fifteen thousand cases from 1834 to municipal incorporation in 1841. But the only trustworthy statistics available for the pre-1841 period are the 1,462 individuals sent to jail or bridewell. Of these, 43 percent were committed as a result of citizen-initiated prosecutions, not public order charges laid by the police or watch. The former included, in order of importance, larceny, assault, master–servant disputes, threats and abusive language, possession of stolen goods, and bastardy. This finding is important, because it seems to echo Steinberg's findings on Philadelphia that private prosecution was "a part of both the popular life and political culture of the city."[23]

The local state provided legislation, a police office, constables, and custodial institutions, but the two out of five prisoners committed, and the greater if unknown number who were discharged or fined, were prosecuted not by agents of the state, but by private citizens acting in their own interests. They did not lose sleep over the fact that defendants unable to pay fines went to jail or the bridewell.[24]

THE NIGHT WATCH

When it was operating, the night watch was an important source of public-order arrests. Eighteenth-century colonial towns, such as New York, usually provided volunteer or paid watches during specific seasons or periods of warfare. New York's 1731 charter had authorized a citizen watch that was transformed into a paid organization by 1762. Beginning in 1776 the community was safeguarded by British military patrols. By the early nineteenth century New York was patrolled by 400 politically appointed, paid watchmen.[25] Halifax, whose first settlers feared Indian and French attack, was safeguarded by militia companies in the 1750s and placed under martial law during the Rev-

Table 1.1
Police Court Committals to Bridewell and Jail, July 29, 1834–August 1841

	1834	1835	1836	1837	1838	1839	1840	1841
Assault	15	14	11	41	29	30	43	3
Threats-								
Abusive language	2	1	3	12	12	18	24	6
Larceny	24	49	31	36	34	39	26	11
Vagrancy	55	82	66	47	43	82	124	35
Disturbing								
the Peace*	15	39	61	11	20	5	15	6
Drunkenness	15	12	10	2	2	5	7	8
Master/Servant**	14	19	11	10	12	4	20	10
Rec. Stolen Goods	1	3	-	3	5	-	-	1
Bastardy	1	3	3	3	-	1	1	1
Other	3	7	2	8	6	13	13	3
TOTAL	145	229	198	173	163	197	273	84

Source: Provincial Archives of Nova Scotia (PANS), RG34–312, (J.4A), Halifax Sessions of the Peace, Police Return of Commitments, 1834–41.

*Includes breach of peace, drunk and disorderly, and riotous conduct.

**Includes deserting ship, runaway apprentice.

Table 1.2
Quarterly Returns: Bridewell Prisoners, by Committal

	Supreme Court	Quarter Sessions	Military	Police and Vagrancy Acts		Total
				Male	Female	
Sept. 1820	11	5	-	8	10	34
Sept. 1825	4	4	3	5	3	19
June 1826	-	10	-	5	4	19
Jan. 1827	-	11	-	5	3	19
March 1827	-	6	-	7	5	17
Sept. 1827	-	9	-	7	2	18
March 1828	3	8	2	7	6	26
Sept. 1829	11	5	7	6	9	38
Sept. 1830	8	12	1	5	7	33
Sept. 1831	7	10	-	7	8	32
Dec. 1831	3	13	-	10	10	36

Source: Provincial Archives of Nova Soctia (PANS), RG 34–312 (J.4), Returns of Bridewell and County Gaol Commitments.

olutionary crisis in 1775. In subsequent years when the need arose, as in 1799 and 1802, the militia and civilian volunteers turned out at night to guard against fires and to watch for suspicious persons. Security concerns were heightened during the War of 1812, in part by the presence of naval and military personnel and prisoners of war. In March 1814, for example, the governor called out the volunteer watch or "patrol" under militia officers.[26]

The years immediately following the War of 1812 revealed a number of strains in Halifax society. Economic uncertainties were coupled with anxiety concerning an influx of poor British immigrants, rising crime rates, and a series of destructive fires. As it had in 1815 with the police court issue, the "merchantocracy" refused to consider municipal incorporation as a solution to these ills. In 1817 the quarter sessions appointed a committee to frame regulations for a citizen patrol. The magistrates laid out several patrol divisions, arranged for a rendezvous location for the watch, and requested that military guardhouses agree to hold civilian prisoners delivered by special constables who supervised the patrols. The final recommendation suggests that the volunteer watch had encountered opposition on its rounds: "That the Watch and the Constabulary shall be armed with clubs and bludgeons." A year later the *custos* (police magistrate Pyke) convened a special session of the magistracy to discuss the failings of the volunteer system. The sessions ultimately framed a bill establishing a conscript night watch and sent it to the House of Assembly, which complied with the request.[27]

The resulting law was permissive; the governor and council could order out the watch, much like the militia, when so requested by the county magistracy. The wording of the statute was revealing in that it suggested that the night watch was to protect not lives or the public peace, but "the property of the Inhabitants of the Town." The patrol would be supervised by the magistrates, and watchmen were accorded the power and authority of constables to safeguard them from "insults, opposition or resistance." Although the Halifax watch legislation would be renewed annually, the patrols, judging by later criticism, were not instituted on a regular basis.[28] That the magistracy could oppose municipal institutions, yet legislate the involuntary service of adult males in the watch, reflects what one historian has referred to as the "authoritarian" character of early Halifax society, or at the very least of its ruling class.[29]

The rules and regulations of the new watch system were printed immediately in pamphlet form and posted for public viewing. Each of the five patrol divisions was assigned a committee, appointed by the sessions, to make an alphabetical list of all adult males. The legislation specifically exempted Blacks, household servants, day laborers, and clergymen and provided a substitute option for the sick, the infirm, the aged, and physicians (although the fact that persons who secured a substitute had to pay a fine of one dollar excluded most of the working class). Eighteen men would serve each night, based out of three guardrooms. Overall nightly supervision was the province of magistrates serving in rotation. Each guardroom was to have a "high con-stable," appointed from the ranks of the "discreet householders," to check the duty roster, note absenteeism, and report to the police office in the morning. Each guardroom also was to appoint a number one watchman, who carried a constable's staff, and a number two watchman who carried a rattle with which to summon assistance. The patrols were to receive civilian prisoners taken into custody by the military guard and to report any licensed premises open past midnight. The watch ended with the firing of the morning signal gun.[30] A series of articles, "Reminiscences of the Night Watch," which appeared in the *Nova Scotian* years later, recalled fondly the era of the "patroles" (most likely the pre-1818 watch) and stressed not internal tensions but external threats. "The war was over," the author explained, "but no one could trust the French or the Americans." The patrol was depicted not as a paternalistic imposition but a communal activity with a certain amount of camaraderie, pranks, and high spirits. Although the men carried cudgels and darkened lan-terns, apparently they encountered little physical danger. The volunteers in-cluded merchants, lawyers, mechanics, and tradesmen, who appeared to share a fondness for "old Jamaica spirits," story-telling, and extended midnight suppers.[31]

At least one contemporary registered a class critique of the 1818 watch legislation and regulations. "Solon," a married man with no property, com-plained that the law was an infringement on the rights of the town's humbler classes and "a stretch of magisterial power." He objected to being forced to abandon his family and losing a night's sleep for no pay to safeguard the property of others. Watchmen also risked being assaulted or even killed. Mag-istrates and friends of magistrates, specifically the "committeemen" who com-piled the patrol lists, he charged, were exempt from the nocturnal patrols. The committees arbitrarily selected conscripts for the watch and sent a mes-senger to their dwelling place. Those who refused to serve were summoned to the police office and fined—a further infringement of "constitutional rights," according to Solon. He questioned the wisdom of encouraging young men to band together and walk the streets at night, even if it was for the public good. The watchmen were being led into all manner of "licentious indulgences," particularly grog houses and brothels by which they were "launched into the gulphs of debauchery." Solon's most damning criticism was that the "patroles" were too light on the ground and too poorly directed to do any good.[32]

POLICING BEFORE THE POLICE

In subsequent years the watch seems periodically to have fallen into dis-organization. In 1829 the Sessions of the Peace discussed the possibility of legislation to provide gaslights for Halifax, a measure that would undercut the need for a watch. Four years later the sessions, the grand jury, and the assembly conferred on the watch question. Conditions seemed to merit the formation of a paid organization, but the county authorities lacked a sufficient budget.[33] The new civic administration of the early 1840s also resisted the creation of a permanent, salaried night patrol. According to the *Nova Scotian*, in 1844 Halifax was too peaceful to justify a watch or an augmented constabulary. In the wake of a number of fires in late 1845 the mayor called a public meeting to examine the problem of nocturnal security. The involuntary watch had few supporters in this more liberal age. As the city council, like the Sessions of the Peace before it, was not prepared to hire additional constables for night duty, the mayor favored the voluntary system. A roster of 500 volunteers, he explained, could provide protection by 20 different men a night. A number of speakers, such as Beamish Murdoch, thought that the day of the volunteer patrol had passed and that only a paid, professional force could properly safeguard the streets. A local journalist agreed that the "voluntaries," who did little more than disturb sleepers with their loud cries of "All is well," were not as effective as the "regular Charlie." The *Morning Post* also favored a paid watch under a superintendent, arguing that the volunteer system was a burden on the more numerous working and middle classes that benefited persons of property. The *Post* also viewed the volunteer watch as inefficient and prone to carousing while on duty. The meeting ended with the appointment of ward committees to find volunteers and raise funds for a citizen patrol.[34]

Halifax's patchwork police system by the late 1810s included not only the watch, three police office constables, and a town crier, but also two or three dozen part-time constables for the town and additional constables for other divisions of the county such as Dartmouth, Hammond's Plains, and Spryfield. The county authorities appointed 44 town constables in 1817, 34 in 1820, 38 in 1837, and only 13 in 1840. Most of them were artisans, tradesmen, or shopkeepers. In January 1828 two of the township constables were Blacks, appointed to deal with "persons of colour." In addition to attending the quarter sessions these officials were expected to assist magistrates in conserving the peace and to serve warrants and writs from the criminal and civil courts. As Robert Storch notes, amateur "fee-for-service" constables, tied by "kinship, friendship and economic relationships to those they lived among," probably reflected "popular or folk conceptions of crime," vigorously pursuing murders, violent assailants, robbers, and thieves but easing up on gamblers, illegal drinkers, and other petty offenders.[35]

When journalists and judges, lawyers, prosecutors, and defendants in court referred to "police" before 1841, they were not speaking of salaried police office employees alone. The *Acadian Recorder* commented on the appointment of constables in 1816 following disorders at a fire. On this occasion constables had failed to attend justices of the peace, with their staffs of office, to prevent looting. Constables were selected from both too low and too high a station in life, the result being that "the respectable part of them will not associate with the other, and often run the risk of fine and censure by avoiding them altogether." Constables who encountered opposition in the performance of their duties did not always press the issue. James King, for example, decided that discretion was the better part of valor when he refused to assist a sheriff's deputy in serving an execution on a sword-wielding Robert Angus in 1818. The constable, by law, was an important and powerful office, but "our practice makes them merely fetch and carry and that because they are usually too ignorant to be trusted with the authority which the laws and very ancient custom give them." According to the *Recorder*, Halifax's constables required supervision by a salaried high constable; without such direction they would remain "very apprehensive of acting wrong." The timidity of most constables meant that magistrates in Halifax, rather than elderly squires who commanded respect by their mere presence, had to be "men of active habits and in the middle period of life." At a public meeting at the Exchange Coffee House in 1834 held to protest a recent judicial appointment and patronage matters in general, the subject of constables also came up. One speaker claimed that the office in Halifax was not shared by all classes of tradesman but monopolized by grocers.[36]

From 1815 to 1841 the criminal justice system was marked by an informality that would be alien to late Victorian Haligonians. The community, at least for serious crimes, was self-policing. The senior magistrate and his assistants usually were not legal professionals, but laypersons more familiar with accounts and exchange rates than statutes and precedent. Magistrates acted as investigatory officers, citizens acted as police officers, and constables sometimes did not act at all. Police magistrate John Liddell, in the course of an arson investigation in 1834, collected evidence at the scene of the crime and accompanied the plaintiff, who suspected a neighbor with a grudge, to the suspect's house to gather further evidence.[37] On other occasions, when it secured written confessions for capital and other serious crimes or appeared to overstep its authority, the police office engendered criticism. A week-long examination of a suspect and witnesses in an 1825 murder case, for example, "almost assumed the shape of a trial," causing "a great deal of animadversion" against the police office. The victim of a burglary in 1819 sent his boarders in pursuit of the suspected culprit. Other offenders were taken to the police office by magistrates, employers, fellow workers, tavern keepers, and bystanders.[38] Larceny victims executed search warrants in the company of constables. Constables were assisted by victims of crime, their families, and neighbors. The relative weakness of the formal police establishment is underscored by the fact that coroners' investigations and Supreme Court murder cases often involved no testimony by police office or town constables.[39]

The best-known public critique of the police office was Joseph Howe's 1835 attack on the Halifax magistracy and the provincial executive council that resulted in his trial and acquittal for criminal libel. In his January 1, 1835, public letter he had argued that the magistracy and police had, "by one stratagem or another, taken from the pockets of the people, in over exactions, fines, etc., a sum that would exceed in the gross amount £30,000." One town magistrate, he charged, was raking in three thousand pounds per year. In his six-hour defense speech, which was interrupted frequently by "expressions of popular feeling," he also charged the police office with failing to keep the peace. Despite the allegedly epic qualities of Howe's battle against the local oligarchy, most of his criticisms of municipal administration and criminal justice matters merely echoed those of earlier grand jurors, provincial politicians, journalists, and newspaper correspondents. In 1818 several members of the assembly spoke out against the police establishment, which they considered to be poorly run and extravagant in its expenditures. One representative decried the police office for its "shameful management" of the town and its paltry revenues. Country members feared that the "police" of the capital, including the bridewell, would become a burden of the provincial treasury.[40] Almost immediately Sabbatarians and temperance advocates were chastising Pyke and his assistants for not improving the morals of the community. Sabbath observance, the liquor license laws, and measures against disorderly houses, according to these critics, were enforced sporadically, if at all. Grand juries were vocal on these and other issues. In 1818 the jurors focused on the matter of public accounts, suggesting that the police office, which in addition to collecting fines and fees depended on market rents and a share of the license fees, should publicize its revenues.[41]

The most controversial indictment of the police office before 1835 was William Wilkie's pamphlet *A Letter to the People of Halifax; Containing Strictures Upon the Conduct of Magistrates*, which was published in 1819 under a pseudonym. Encouraged perhaps by recent letters to the press that had complained about taxation and the lack of public scrutiny of town revenues, Wilkie, who came from a modest background, assailed not just the magistracy but the Halifax elite in general. The police office was depicted as "a scene and sink of inequity, infamy, corruption and pollution," and petty justice was cruel and vindictive. Yet the author did not criticize the constables or the general role of the police office, only its lack of accountability. The police clerk, he argued, was compensated excessively while the hard-working constables were underpaid. The magistrates in charge of the town held the people in "ignominious thraldom" through their control of the markets, liquor, and truckmen's licenses, the collection of poor and road rates, and the police office. The latter indulged in illegal incarceration or imprisonment because of an inability to pay fines for trivial offenses. As a result citizens had ended up in the bridewell with "notorious thieves and vagabonds." The magistrates of the sessions, the pamphlet implied, were guilty of selling "the public justice" by pocketing fines and fees. These revenues were consumed "in eating, in drinking and revelling, in scenes of riot and dissipation." Wilkie, having pilloried the police office and county magistracy, turned his guns on the Supreme Court and the governor's council, the fount of corrupt place seekers. For his pains the author was indicted for criminally libeling the magistracy and sentenced to two years hard labor in the bridewell, the institution he so despised.[42]

Policing matters remained linked, for reformers, with the issue of town self-government. In 1823, as part of what Sutherland has described as the revolt of the shopkeepers against the merchant elite, the Society of Tradesmen, representing middle-class rate payers, petitioned for municipal incorporation. Two years later the *Acadian Recorder* (which had approved of the prosecution of Wilkie) decided that incorporation was a prerequisite for improving the efficiency of the police. A system of elected municipal officials under public scrutiny would afford all "qualified citizens an opportunity to be useful."[43] A bill to secure the incorporation of Halifax was introduced into the assembly in 1830 but went nowhere. In 1831 the quarter sessions examined the question of fees charged by the police office and ruled that the magistrates and clerk should demand only those fees allowed by law. Another controversy flared in 1832, this time at the county level, when barrister William Sawyers accused the Sessions of the Peace, Halifax magistrates included, of acting with "tyranny and injustice" in criminal trials. The grand jury's December 1834 presentment reflected growing dissatisfaction with the police office's lack of public accountability.[44]

Before 1841 the county authorities did little to augment the police presence in the town, despite population growth and the occasional riot—as in 1829 when a partisan crowd facilitated the escape of an individual from the custody of the assembly's sergeant of arms, or when incensed soldiers and sailors raided and destroyed several brothels in the upper streets in 1838. In 1831 the three police office constables, citing their arduous duties, petitioned for and received, a raise in pay to 20 shillings a week. A number of public order bylaws were passed, such as a draconian ordinance against sliding and coasting, which allowed citizens to seize sleds from boys, constables to detain the boys overnight in jail, and the police office to fine their parents or masters 20 shillings. In the absence of a day patrol or a night police, magistrates were expected to remain vigilant. According to one legislative councilor in 1840, Halifax justices of the peace were "expected to discharge the duties of common constable" by breaking up fights and collaring miscreants.[45]

Howe's acquittal and the humbling of the magistracy in 1835 helped clear the logjam on municipal and police reform, but only gradually. More attention was paid to public accounts. The grand jury viewed the books and accounts opened to record police office business. It was revealed that the office charged three shillings and six pence for every warrant issued (upon conviction), three shillings for each bond to keep the peace, and two shillings for each summons, fees that probably discouraged criminal litigation by the poor. In September the grand jury, citing the fact that Halifax was an imperial station and metropolis for the entire colony, argued that it had to maintain a larger police establishment than the population warranted. This, in the jurors' opinion, justified assistance from the provincial treasury.[46] In November the grand jury sent a memorial to Governor Sir Colin Campbell explaining the community's "general dissatisfaction" with its outdated system of local administration and continued lack of ratepayer accountability. Municipal institutions, it was alleged, would afford economy and efficiency and combat elite place seeking. A month later the jurors recommended that the work of the commissioners court for the collection of small debts (established in 1817) should not overlap with that of the police office.[47]

Small reforms continued to be introduced in the area of police administration. In 1839 the grand jury had complained that regular constables were spending too much time in court, serving legal documents and performing other duties not strictly related to keeping the peace and maintaining regularity on the streets, sidewalks, and wharves. The police office, it recommended, should be under a chief magistrate who also was president of the Sessions of the Peace. One justice of the peace, the clerk, and two constables should attend the court to hear complaints and conduct examinations from 10:00 A.M. until 4:00 P.M., six days a week. One constable should man the station overnight while the other constables, it was suggested, should hang lanterns outside their places of abode.[48] In 1840 the county authorities decided that police office constables had to be on call from 9:00 A.M. until 9:00 P.M., seven days a week, attend the police magistrate in rotation, and refrain from holding any other job or office. In return their salary was raised to £80 per year. The order suggests that police constables were expected to perform some patrol duty.[49] The *Morning Post* concluded that the city needed not 3 permanent constables, but at least 15, uniformed and organized along the lines of constabularies in London, Quebec City, and Montreal. The police system had to be rationalized, for local magistrates and constables were responsible for "a variety of duties the extent of which few are aware of."[50]

MUNICIPAL INCORPORATION

As support for municipal incorporation mounted among the middle class, so did criticisms of the police office. In 1837 and 1838 the grand jury pointed to the office's excessive budgets and the large earnings of its magistrates and clerk. The jurors objected to court officials charging fees for the enforcement of liquor-license regulations and suggested that the positions of clerk and senior magistrate could be amalgamated to cut down on expenses. In one of its presentments the body advised that the police office should be open longer hours and that it should vigorously enforce laws against Sabbath desecration and child vagrancy. The grand jury also recommended an expansion of summary justice to streamline the quarter sessions and Supreme Court. It proposed giving the police court exclusive jurisdiction over cases of assault and battery, petty larceny, and other minor crimes for which the fine did not exceed five pounds. By this point middle-class representatives were openly pushing for incorporation. At a public meeting on the subject in 1837 reformers portrayed civic self-rule as the logical culmination of British constitutional history. A committee prepared a draft bill that included a mayor elected at large, aldermen and assistants sitting on a common council, and a fairly liberal property franchise for candidates and voters. The *Nova Scotian* argued that municipal incorporation would improve the police and courts, but crime and disorder do not seem to have been important to the overall charter debate. An incorporation bill introduced in the assembly in 1838 passed the second reading stage but got no further. Although more than five hundred citizens had petitioned for the measure, one hundred and fifty-odd influential property holders—the merchantocracy—petitioned against it.[51]

During the 1840 provincial election Joseph Howe blamed the failure of the Halifax incorporation bill on obstructionist Tory members of the assembly, merchants, and magistrates and promised that a Liberal victory would convince the government to grant a charter. In 1841 a bill was sent down by Governor Falkland's executive council. The *Nova Scotian* credited "the whole weight of the Government, exerted through the various channels of official and social life" with the bill's passing in April of 1841. The bill was very much a compromise; as the attorney general explained, "the possessors of property should be conciliated." The measure had met violent opposition in the legislative council for being too democratic and in the assembly for being too restrictive. Thomas Forrester, a critic of the Tory old regime, supported a broader suffrage and argued that the "extreme quiet character of the town" was proof that the people could be trusted to govern themselves. In the legislative council Martin Wilkins argued that municipal institutions countered community apathy and served as a school for future administrators and politicians. Liberal opponents of the bill objected especially to the generous pension provisions for the outgoing police magistrate and clerk. The result of what the solicitor general called the "Charter from the Crown" was that civic administration, including the police and police court, would be responsible not to the executive branch, but a large minority of Halifax ratepayers.[52]

The new municipal government would be more accountable than the Sessions of the Peace, but it was not excessively democratic. The mayor had to possess at least £1,000 worth of property; for aldermen the amount was £500 or £50 rental value. Aldermen would also hold the office of justice of peace, allowing them to assist the mayor in judicial duties.

Electors had to possess property that rented for at least £20 annually, which limited the number of voters to roughly one hundred men per ward. The mayor, or chief magistrate, was elected not by the qualified ratepayers but the common council. The first mayor was a representative of the Tory-Anglican compact that considered Halifax its own, Stephen Binney.[53] Within three years the Liberals would control the corporation, and by midcentury charter amendments would broaden the suffrage and democratize the selection of mayor. But incorporation, according to Girard, did not challenge immediately the "Tory" or conservative model of justice, in which the judge was viewed as the bulwark of the community.[54]

Incorporation meant both change and continuity for the police and courts. Mayor Binney reappointed the three police office constables. The common council appointed a city marshal, a new officer created by the charter, as well as six ward constables (who had to reside in their respective wards) to serve full-time under the direction of their respective aldermen. As T. W. Acheson suggests of early-Victorian Saint John, the ward was an important administrative and social unit. Aldermen were expected to continue many of the broader community functions of the prereform justices of the peace.[55] Six reserve constables were to be employed on a per diem basis when needed. The police office (or station) would be open all night, with two constables on duty to handle citizen reports and complaints. Disturbers of the peace and other prisoners were lodged in the police lockup until they could be taken to the police court. The court, which sat from 10:00 A.M. until 4:00 P.M., was presided over by the mayor and assisting aldermen. A recorder, a trained barrister, would provide legal advice to the mayor and his assistants. The mayor was authorized to try, summarily, "all petty thefts, assault, batteries, riots, petty breaches of the peace, riot and disturbances at Elections" and other minor offenses. The court could sentence offenders to the bridewell or jail for up to 30 days and fine them up to five pounds.[56]

With the introduction of a more accessible and visible police establishment, the Halifax press began the tradition of detailed police court reporting, accounts that reflected the class, race, and gender biases of Victorian society. Critics referred to the tribunal as the "huckleberry" or "sheepskin" court because of the pettiness of most of the cases. The plebeian atmosphere of the police court prompted the *Acadian Recorder* to describe it as a "receptacle of ignorance, stupidity and villainy." The *Nova Scotian* was overoptimistic in its assessment of the first few weeks of "urban justice":

The Police appear active without over officiousness. Disgusting scenes of drunkenness no longer disgrace our streets. The population of the town appear nearly all reformed from pernicious vice and if a stranger sins against public propriety, he is soon removed out of sight, and placed in a new Lock-up house, under the Town Hall Building.[57]

The mayor published the police and court regulations in the fall. The city marshal, in addition to his various court duties, supervised the city constables. Each night one city constable and one ward constable manned the police station until relieved by two constables in the morning. The ward constable, staff in hand, was to patrol his beat twice daily, taking note of all nuisances; encumbrances of the streets; and breaches of license laws, the Lord's Day Act, truckmen's regulations, and other city ordinances respecting traffic, sanitation, and commerce. Constables were expected to seize stray pigs and cows and supervise town pumps and wells as well as quell riots or disturbances. Each ward constable, who displayed his number and ward outside his home, was on call 24 hours a day for citizens seeking the arrest of disturbers of the peace, beggars, drunkards, "disorderly and lewd characters," and other offenders. The ward constables were ordered to refrain from engaging in other occupations. As if to emphasize their community orientation, constables, although salaried, were not uniformed.[58]

The Halifax Police Court in the 1841–67 period continued the earlier tradition of allowing the common people to "go to law." Its business included "matters that ranged from the trivial to absurd to legitimate."[59] As Fingard notes, the institution, in addition to punishing criminals, became deeply involved in "family and neighbourhood arbitration."[60] The court kept fairly detailed minutes of examinations for assault, which allow the historian the opportunity to reconstruct litigants' attitudes toward and expectations of "having the law." Assault and larceny cases, in both the police court and quarter sessions, were prosecuted in the name of the Queen, but in practice there was no Crown prosecutor as in the Supreme Court. In assault and disturbing the peace cases in which no prosecutor or witness appeared, the prisoner was released. The fine for an assault at 10 or 20 shillings was minor, but a conviction was a public vindication of the plaintiff, "a source of individual power with state backing," which explains why lower-class individuals would prosecute for being called "a bloody old whore."[61] The injuries sustained in most assaults were minor or imaginary; in others they included life-threatening wounds and broken limbs. Weapons included fists, boots, sticks, chairs, stones, boiling water, knives, axes, and guns. Violent altercations were caused by disputes over money and property and by jealousy, wounded honor, and revenge. The violence often was random.

Persons of all classes and races lodged assault complaints with the police. In one instance justice was sought by a victim of racial discrimination. Mary Fallon, an African Nova Scotian, charged the captain of the harbor ferry with assault after he removed her forcibly from the ladies' cabin, where she had taken shelter during a rain squall. Fallon vowed that she would "make him pay dearly for shoving" and using abusive language. The police magistrate thought otherwise, sided with the defendant (and racial segregation), and dismissed the case. In March 1846 Margaret Crowley was "taken" by the watch after leaving a tavern; rather than face a vagrancy charge at the police station she preferred assault charges against Julia Dollard and Mary Ann Mellick, two other women of the town." Crowley told the magistrate that she and a friend were being treated to drinks by a man at the tavern when Mellick attempted to "cut in." A fight erupted, with hair pulling, finger biting, punches, and vulgar language. The magistrate, in exasperation, dismissed the charges. Only days earlier Dollard had charged two members of the garrison, John Parton and George Wood, with assaulting her in another public house.[62]

In the samples from 1846 and 1864 shown in table 1.3, citizen-initiated charges were 28.2 percent and 33.3 percent of the total, respectively, a not insignificant minority. Roughly one-quarter of the cases brought to court came under the heading municipal ordinances, bylaws relating to liquor sales, dog licenses, chimneys, and other regulatory matters. Although persons charged with theft came overwhelmingly from the lower classes, so did many of their victims. Larceny ranged from small amounts of money and personal property stolen from residents of limited means to well-planned thefts from wealthy merchants. Often the plaintiff suspected the defendant or caught the defendant attempting to sell the stolen items. Most of the master–servant disputes in this seaport town involved deserting sailors or apprentices disobeying their masters. Typically a master prosecuted his apprentice for running away, but a number of cases involved apprentices seeking to have the terms of indenture honored. A large proportion of assault and abusive language charges were aimed at social equals; personal dispute resolution of this variety was class blind.[63]

The court and the police also clearly pursued a public-order mandate that became more explicit over time. Of the 191 cases in the 1846 sample, 44.5 percent were police-initiated charges, mostly for drunkenness and disturbing the peace. The percentage from the 1864 sample was 52.2. A number of these

Table 1.3
Police Court Charges

CITIZEN-INITIATED CHARGES:	Jan.-Apr. 1846	May 19-Sept. 10 1864
Assault	35	100
Larceny	10	35
Abusive Language	-	28
Stolen Goods	4	1
Master-Servant Disputes	6	24
SUBTOTAL:	54	188
POLICE-INITIATED PUBLIC ORDER CHARGES:		
Vagrancy	8	39
Drunkenness	29	144
Breach of Peace	33	95
Interfering with Police or Watch	15	17
SUBTOTAL:	85	295
MUNICIPAL ORDINANCES AND 'OTHER':	50	82
TOTAL:	191	565

Source: PANS, RG42 (D) Vol. 1, Halifax Police Court Minutes, January–August 1846, vol. 19, May 19–September 10, 1864.

individuals had resisted or even attacked the night watch. These and vagrancy charges, it can be argued, were "produced" by the police and watch on proactive patrols consciously looking for deviant behavior. Yet the watch plucked dozens of helpless drunks off the streets in winter and gave shelter for persons with no place to go. Individuals were given in charge by other citizens for fighting, disturbing the peace, and being common drunkards. Jim Phillips shows that for the three decades after 1860, Halifax vagrants were poor. But they also shared other important characteristics. Many of them were "outsiders": nonresidents, Irish Catholics, and African Nova Scotians.[64] The amended charter of 1851 allowed the mayor and aldermen to confine individuals to the bridewell "whether for their own benefit or that of others," wording that allowed a broad interpretation of vagrancy or disturbing the peace.[65]

The mayor and aldermen, like the appointed magistrates before 1841, were expected to do more than simply run the police court and hire and pay the police. The town fathers, despite the fact that they had appointed a city marshal, were still obliged to perform police duties. The chief magistrate was expected to conserve the peace; in 1850 the mayor personally intervened to quell a near riot involving military personnel threatening one of their periodic attacks on a brothel. In 1853 it was reported that Alderman Scott, in the company of the marshal, regularly toured disorderly houses at midnight, removing young boys. The mayor also could appoint special constables in time of emergency, as in 1853 when a Royal Navy sailor was found dead outside the Waterloo Tavern on Barrack Street. "Entertaining just apprehension of riot and disturbance," the civic authorities swore in 70 "specials."[66] Custom and regulations (see the 1851 revised city charter) encouraged constables and watchmen to seek advice and direction from civic officials before acting; a number of citizens complained that when they approached police officers on the street for assistance, they were informed that they could not act unless they were so ordered by the mayor or aldermen. In the 1850s the police clerk, James Stewart Clarke, appeared to exercise similar powers in the police establishment, accompanying the marshal to inspect licensed premises and ordering constables to arrest suspects in serious crimes.[67]

Public-order offenses became more important statistically after 1841, reflecting the growth of respectability that also produced local philanthropic efforts directed toward the poor, drunkards, and "fallen women." In 1852 a local journal remarked that the city, despite the presence of almost four thousand servicemen, was fairly peaceful, owing in part to the activities of several permanent constables and the police court's swift justice. The one exception was public intoxication: drink was "the fruitful source of nearly all commitments." From October 1848 to October 1851 more than twelve hundred convictions had been secured for drunkenness or being drunk and disorderly.[68] Most public-order offenders continued to be taken by the night watch, which by the early 1850s was placed on a more permanent footing. In 1851 Watch

Captain G. P. Behan supervised six men in the summer months and an additional five during the winter. Despite this enhanced presence complaints continued to arise of "Charlies" sleeping in doorways or porches and otherwise neglecting their duty. The police station was open all night by midcentury, but the two constables on duty, according to one observer, did little more than "smoke their pipes and chat away over a snug fire." Citizens who had been assaulted or robbed had to wake the mayor or an alderman to secure an arrest warrant, a delay that allowed fugitives to escape or stolen property to be spirited out of town.[69]

RESPECTABILITY, REFORM, AND WATCHFULNESS

Criminal justice reform became an important issue by 1860. The city authorities had closed the decrepit bridewell and built a state-of-the-art city prison at Rockhead Farm to the north of the city, a symbol of a less passive approach to social order. Owing to the increased efficiency of the police and watch, the mayor reported in 1858, the inmate population often approached one hundred. By the early 1860s a new county jail and poorhouse also would open. Evangelical reform and temperance sentiment had led to several experiments in institutional philanthropy. These efforts produced an exposé of the underside" of the city, the 1862 pamphlet *Halifax: Its Sins and Sorrows*. Using the reports of the Protestant city missionary and other sources, the author claimed that Halifax was a "rum cursed" Sodom and Gomorrah, where unlicensed groggeries and several hundred prostitutes flouted all moral conventions and ordinary Haligonians flouted the Sabbath. The city had granted more than one hundred and thirty liquor licenses in 1858, but many houses sold spirits without a license. The author suggested that the police were failing to keep "Polly Malony and Billy Bluenose" in line and that unlicensed taverns were protected by the police court's excessive legalism.[70] Yet by 1862 the police court was convicting hundreds annually for public intoxication. One-third of the prisoners committed to the city prison in the early 1850s were vagrants (see table 1.4).[71]

By the late 1850s the city council was contemplating the amalgamation of the day police, which numbered 12, and the night watch. The city marshal, the *Morning Sun* reported, was saddled with too many court and administrative duties to direct the police effectively. The two patrol forces were still operating under different heads. Watch Captain Donald Fraser, in his 1861–62 report, noted that the annual summer visit of the Royal Navy had caused "much disorder and riot throughout the city" and that his men, whose numbers had been augmented, had made most of the public-order arrests. Yet despite its important role, the watch did not have uniforms, a situation that according to Fraser led to insults, resistance, and assaults. By 1863 the night patrol wore uniforms. In 1862–63 the watch, in addition to putting down the most recent military/naval riot with the assistance of special constables and the military police, was responsible for more than nine hundred arrests (although they were encumbered by large leather hats and dark lanterns suspended from their belts). Clearly, in public-order terms the watch was as or more important than the regular constabulary.[72]

The 1864 colonial legislation that amended the city charter not only rationalized police administration, it also enhanced the powers of the police court. The police force by law had to consist of at least 33 officers. The marshal was assisted by a deputy and 6 sergeants; one benefit of the rationalization was a reserve detail, which was kept on duty at the station. Marshall Garrett Cotter asked for uniforms for the old day police and satellite lockups for the north and south ends of the city. Another sign of professionalism was the existence of a "detective service," a fund for securing information on stolen goods and wanted persons and otherwise assisting the department's first detective, Sergeant Lew Hutt. The use of firearms by the police was still quite controversial, and none appear to have been issued to patrolmen. New police regulations reflected three goals: civility, restraint, and watchfulness. Patrolmen were to engage in no "unnecessary conversation" with citizens and were to be polite and businesslike. They also were discouraged from intervening in doubtful situations; magisterial advice was still prized. At the same time they were instructed to concentrate on surveillance: learning the names and addresses of people on their beat, strictly watching bad characters and others "whose behaviour at the time is such to excite just suspicion," and keeping notebooks of their activities and observations.[73]

Mayor P. C. Hill, an advocate of police reform, argued that the newly unified police department should offer higher wages and other inducements to attract high-quality candidates. In reality, constables continued to be "elected" annually by the city council and hired through political influence. This at times hampered discipline and efficiency. In 1863, for example, one of the aldermen presiding at the police court had fired the watchman, John Scully, for incompetence; the watch captain reported that although Scully was "a little stupid and hard of hearing," he was at least sober. The city council, probably just to assert its corporate authority, rehired him.[74]

Another trend in urban justice was the appointment of permanent stipendiary magistrates who, unlike the Halifax police justices during the 1815–41 period, were trained barristers. Saint John, where in the 1840s sectarian and anti-immigrant feeling had compromised the administration of justice, had been given a provincially appointed stipendiary magistrate in 1854. In time most Canadian cities with police courts under elected officials appointed stipendiaries.[75] The reform in Halifax, which was effected in 1867, was not a response to popular opinion. The bill that created the office of stipendiary magistrate was not requested by the civic authorities but imposed by the province. Conservative opinion was troubled by the supposedly democratic nature of city politics and administration that encouraged weak policing and partial justice. A temperance advocate, writing about the city council's opposition to a stipendiary in 1863, noted that the appointment of magistrates was in the hands of the people, a concession to the popular voice carried to excess in the republican United States. The result was a vicious circle, with the city issuing three hundred liquor licenses (the actual number was far lower) and encouraging the tavern as a nursery of misery and crime. The political power of the tavern owners in the wards was noticeable, the correspondent claimed, at election time. The police and courts had allowed the streets to become much more rowdy than they had been at midcentury. Arguing that a truckman was more likely than an upper-class claimant to curry favor in the courts, he concluded by calling for the city to be ruled by the owners of property.[76] A similar missive appearing in the *Morning Chronicle* demanded a more restrictive franchise to curb disorder and crime. The magistrates (mayor and aldermen) were elected; even the police constables were appointed indirectly by public opinion: "they owe their tenure of office as much to the people they are called upon to keep in decent order as the Alderman or Mayor."[77]

The 1864 stipendiary magistrate bill encountered strong opposition in the assembly because the city fathers had not been consulted. It was also thought to award powers that were too extreme or abstract and an overly generous salary (from civic coffers). The requirement that the prospective magistrate had to be a trained, experienced lawyer was particularly irksome; court duties, one commentator wrote, had been performed well for years by nonlawyer mayors and aldermen. The legislation, he suggested, was got up to favor a class, lawyers, or even an individual. Despite such reservations there was support for increasing the authority of the court to deal with recidivism. The *Morning Chronicle* noted in 1863 that the magistrates could not sentence offenders to more than 90 days, which did little to reform or punish hardened offenders. The court had become polluted with individuals "in every conceivable state of drunkenness, prostration, filth, disease, utter destitution and absence of shame." Short sentences prohibited officials from putting inmates to profitable labor. The police court had become a revolving door of petty recidivists; perhaps they would be deterred by stiffer sentences to Rockhead (and increased summary jurisdiction for magistrates).[78]

The new stipendiary magistrate, appointed in 1867, was Henry Pryor, a Tory Anglican barrister who had served as both alderman and mayor. He soon was busy dispensing petty justice six days a week, treating offenders "with an unpredictable mixture" of harshness and mercy. Mayor Hill supported the change as it relieved the mayor and aldermen of "arduous duties in the City and Police Courts." Supposedly it also had a salutary effect on the city's morals, as "old offenders" were now more wary of appearing in court "knowing the record of their previous transgressions is always at hand to confront them."[79] The permanent salaried magistrate, thought to be above politics, represented the third and final stage of urban justice in the nineteenth century. After a century or more, distinct magisterial and police functions had been formalized. Yet, as Weaver suggests for post-Confederation Hamilton, the police court remained "an unpretentious and open forum of justice."[80]

Petty justice in Halifax from 1815 to 1867, administered by magistrates, constables, watchmen, and police, was not simply an imposition by the state or middle class on the poor. A growing emphasis on public-order and vagrancy arrests and convictions (see table 1.4) appears to conform to the class-control model, but not in every case. Statistics of penitentiary, jail, and prison committals alone do not reveal the true complexity of "primary justice." Importantly, a minority of police court charges were instituted by the community, not agents of the state, a trend that continued under the stipendiary magistrate. In the 1864–90 period, for example, 1 out of every 10 women sent to Rockhead Prison was committed for personal crimes, almost as many as were sent for prostitution. As many or more were acquitted or fined as a result of criminal litigation initiated by citizens.[81] Over the years, as in Philadelphia and other North American urban centers, criminal justice in Halifax became more bureaucratic and centralized; yet as late as 1867 the community upheld the tradition of a lay magistracy.

Police reform in Halifax was a gradual process; policing "before the police" probably was quite effective in the case of serious offenses. From 1815 until 1841 the city had only three full-time police constables, and many of their duties were court related. There was never any sense of a policing crisis or that crime was an insurmountable social problem. Justice, increasingly, was less of a community process and more a task delegated to salaried officials. Municipal incorporation increased the number of permanent constables, but police administration remained decentralized in that aldermen-JPs played a supervisory role in the wards. By amalgamating and coordinating the day constables and watch in 1864 and providing them with uniforms and more detailed instructions and regulations, the civic authorities were attempting to

TABLE 1.4
Halifax Police Court Charges, 1857/58–1865/66

	ASSAULT	LARCENY	DRUNKENNESS	OTHER	TOTAL
1857/58	35.7%	8.4%	35.7%	37.5%	1283
1861/62	13.4%	8.0%	62.3%	16.2%	2058
1862/63	14.7%	7.7%	61.6%	16.0%	2161
1863/64	17.6%	7.8%	51.9%	12.6%	1820
1864/65	5.9%	7.8%	59.6%	26.7%	2120
1865/66	9.9%	7.0%	51.1%	32.0%	2103

Source: Annual Reports of the Several Departments of the City Government of Halifax, Nova Scotia, for the Municipal Year 1857/58–1865/66.

enhance the surveillance and disciplinary power of the local state. Police centralization and reform had pushed law enforcement beyond "upholding minimal standards of social intercourse."[82] Yet this was not the sole function of primary justice. Haligonians continued to take each other to court and continued to expect "informal, personal and accessible law enforcement."[83]

NOTES

This is a revised edition of a paper delivered to the 1995 Atlantic Law and History Workshop held at the Dalhousie University Law School. I wish to thank John Phyne and Mike Boudreau for their comments and suggestions.

1. *Acadian Recorder,* 29 October 1825.

2. Allan Greer, "The Birth of the Police in Canada," in *Colonial Leviathan: State Formation in Mid-Nineteenth-Century Canada,* ed. Allan Greer and Ian Radforth (Toronto: University of Toronto Press, 1992), 17–49, views the urban police in Lower Canada as an attempt at social engineering. See also Jim Phillips, "Poverty, Unemployment and the Administration of the Criminal Law: Vagrancy Laws in Halifax, 1864–1890," in *Essays in the History of Canadian Law: III Nova Scotia,* ed. Jim Phillips and Philip Girard (Toronto: Osgoode Society, 1993), 128–62. For recent historiography, see Jim Phillips, "Crime and Punishment in the Dominion of the North: Canada from New France to the Present," in *Crime Histories and Histories of Crime,* ed. Louis Knafla and Clive Emsley (Westport: Greenwood Press, 1996), 163–99; Margaret McCallum, "Canadian Legal History in the Late 1990s: A Field in Search of Fences?" *Acadiensis* 27:2 (spring 1998): 151–66.

3. Jim Phillips, "'Securing Obedience to Necessary Laws': The Criminal Law in Eighteenth-Century Halifax," *Nova Scotia Historical Review* 12:2 (1992): 87–124.

4. *Acadian Recorder,* 31 January 1817.

5. *Morning Post,* 24 July 1841. Aggrieved parties also had the option, until 1841, of prosecuting assault and battery before the Inferior Court of Common Pleas, a civil tribunal.

6. G. Marquis, "The Police as a Social Service in Early Twentieth-Century Toronto," *Histoire sociale/Social History* 25:50 (November 1992): 335–58. See also Judith Fingard, "Jailbirds in Mid-Victorian Halifax," in *Lawful Authority: Readings on the History of Criminal Justice in Canada,* ed. R. C. Macleod (Toronto: Copp, Clark, Pitmann, 1988), 78–79. According to Allan Steinberg, *The Transformation of Criminal Justice: Philadelphia, 1800–1880* (Chapel Hill: University of North Carolina Press, 1989), police professionalization undermined but never eradicated this function of "primary justice." See also Donald Fyson, "Women and Complainants Before the Justice of the Peace in the District of Montreal, 1779–1830" (Université Laval). For more of Fyson's important research findings, see http://www.hst.ulaval.ca/profs/dfyson/.

7. John Weaver, *Crimes, Courts and Constables: Transgression and Order in a Canadian City, 1816–1970* (Montreal: McGill-Queen's University Press, 1994), 37–40.

8. Philip Girard, "The Rise and Fall of Urban Justice in Halifax, 1815–1886," *Nova Scotia Historical Review* 8:2 (1988): 57–71; Judith Fingard, *The Dark Side of Life in Victorian Halifax* (Porters Lake: Pottersfield Press, 1989). For nineteenth-century Canadian police and police court reform, see Greg Marquis, "'A Machine of Oppression

Under the Guise of the Law': The Saint John Police Establishment, 1860–1890,"
Acadiensis 16:1 (autumn 1986): 58–77; "The Contours of Canadian Urban Justice,
1830–1875," *Urban History Review* 15:3 (February 1987): 269–73; "Enforcing the Law:
The Charlottetown Police Force," in *Gaslights, Epidemics and Vagabond Cows: Char-
lottetown in the Victorian Era*, ed. Douglas Baldwin and Thomas Spira (Charlottetown:
Ragweed Press, 1988), 86–102; Weaver, *Crimes, Courts and Constables*.

   9. Douglas Hay and Francis Snyder, "Using Criminal Law, 1750–1850," in *Policing
and Prosecution in Britain, 1750–1850*, ed. Hay and Snyder (Oxford: Clarendon Press,
1989), 5.

   10. Thomas B. Akins, *Selections from the Public Documents of the Public Archives of
Nova Scotia* (Halifax: C. Annand, 1869); *History of the City of Halifax* (Halifax: Morning
Herald, 1895); D. Owen Carrigan, *Crime and Punishment in Canada: A History* (To-
ronto: McClellan and Stewart, 1991), 305–6.

   11. PANS, RG34–312 (J.4) Return of Bridewell and County Gaol Commitments.

   12. Statutes of Nova Scotia, 1792, c. 14; Girard, "Rise and Fall of Urban Justice,"
58–59. No records seem to have survived of the magistrates' courts of the 1790s.

   13. Richard Vogler, *Reading the Riot Act: The Magistracy, the Police and the Army in
Civil Disorder* (Philadelphia: Temple University Press, 1991), chap. 2; Paul A. Gilje,
The Road to Mobocracy: Popular Disorder in New York City, 1763–1834 (Chapel Hill:
University of North Carolina Press, 1987), 280–81; Girard, "Rise and Fall of Urban
Justice," 59. The Middlesex Justices Act was a limited intervention by the central
government in local administration following the defeat of the 1785 London Police
Bill.

   14. David Sutherland, "The Revolt of the Shopkeepers: Municipal Reform in Halifax Through the 1830s" (unpublished paper); PANS, MG100, Vol. 235, No. 22. Halifax was not alone in terms of local administration. By the 1820s the only incorporated
British North American community was Saint John, N.B., which received its charter
in 1785. Boston was not incorporated until 1822. See Roger Lane, *Policing the City:
Boston, 1822–1885* (Cambridge: Harvard University Press, 1967).

   15. *Acadian Recorder*, 4 July 1815; RG34–312 (P.8), Halifax Grand Jury Minutes, 9
December 1812, 10 March 1814.

   16. *The Draft of a Charter for the Incorporation of the Town of Halifax in the Province
of Nova Scotia* (Halifax: John Howe and Son, 1814).

   17. Report of the Committee of the Council and House of Assembly Appointed to
Confer on the Subject of the Police of the Town of Halifax, May 1815, RG 2 vol. 305,
no. 21. For drink and the poor, see comments of the correspondent who witnessed
the proceedings of the Supreme Court in 1787 in Allan Everett Marble, *Surgeons,
Smallpox and the Poor: A History of Medicine and Social Conditions in Nova Scotia,
1749–1799* (Montreal: McGill-Queen's University Press, 1993), 149.

   18. S.N.S. 1815, c. 9. The bridewell returns for 1820–31 indicate that sentences for
vagrants and other misdemeanants were "not limited," suggesting that magistrates
released prisoners at their own discretion. For more on the bridewell, see Rainer
Bahre, "From Bridewell to Federal Penitentiary: Prisoners and Punishment in Nova
Scotia Before 1880," in *Essays in the History of Canadian Law*, Phillips and Girard,
167–69.

   19. *Halifax Morning Post*, 5 November 1840.

   20. Akins, *History of the City of Halifax*, 94, 206; *Acadian Recorder*, 6 September 1828.
Pyke was also a benefactor of the Black community. When he died in 1828 he left five

hundred acres of land at Hammond's Plains for "coloured people." See PANS, RG1 vol. 259, doc. 91.

21. From 1815 to 1820 the police court, together with individual magistrates, convicted 658 petty offenders. See Bahre, "From Bridewell to Penitentiary," 173.

22. Akins, *History of the City of Halifax*, 94.

23. *Journal*, 20 April 1835; Steinberg, *Transformation of Criminal Justice*, 3. In April of 1835 the bridewell keeper reported that the institution housed the unusually high number of 44 prisoners.

24. Weaver, *Crimes, Constables and Courts*, chap. 2, discusses private dispute resolution by magistrates.

25. James F. Richardson, *The New York Police: Colonial Times to 1901* (New York: Oxford University Press, 1970), chap. 1.

26. Stanley Palmer, *Police and Protest in England and Ireland, 1780–1850* (New York: Cambridge University Press, 1988), 76–77; Akins, *History of the City of Halifax*, 23, 94, 135; V. W. Mitchell, "History of the Halifax Police Department," *Royal Canadian Mounted Police Quarterly* 30 (April 1965): 3–8; PANS, RG34–312 (P.6), Sessions of the Peace Minutes, 19 March 1814.

27. David Sutherland, "The Merchants of Halifax, 1815–1850: A Commercial Class in Pursuit of Metropolitan Status" (Ph.D. diss.: University of Toronto, 1975), chap. 1; RG34–312 (P.6), Sessions of the Peace Minutes, 31 October 1817, 10 July 1818; *Halifax Free Press*, 21 January, 28 October, 16 December 1817. Even volunteer patrols incurred various expenses: see RG34–312 (P.8), Grand Jury Minutes, 27 October, 16 December 1817.

28. S.N.S. 1818, c.12.

29. Jim Phillips, "Women, Crime and Criminal Justice in Early Halifax, 1750–1800," in *Crime and Criminal Justice*, ed. Jim Phillips, Tina Loo, and Susan Lewthwaite (Toronto: The Osgoode Society, 1994), 174–75.

30. *Rules and Regulations For the Establishment of a Watch and Patrol in the Town of Halifax* (Halifax: Edmund Ward, 1818). The rules were reprinted in 1829, with minor alterations.

31. *Nova Scotian*, 22, 23, 29 December 1845.

32. *Acadian Recorder*, 25 July 1818.

33. RG34–312 (P.10), Quarter Sessions Minutes, 23, 25 March 1829, 15 March 1833. In 1833 a number of English communities organized local police under the Watching and Lighting Act.

34. *Nova Scotian*, 18 November 1844, 15 December 1845; *Morning Post*, 30 November, 7 December 1845, 10 February 1846.

35. RG34–312, Quarter Sessions Minutes, 1813–41; Halifax *Morning Herald*, 17 June 1843; Robert D. Storch, "Policing Rural England Before the Police: Opinion and Practice, 1830–1856," in *Policing and Prosecution*, Hay and Snyder, 224–25. In the early 1840s one of the "coloured" constables was Septimus Clarke, who became a leader of the local African Nova Scotian community.

36. *Acadian Recorder*, 27 June 1818, 29 December 1834.

37. *Acadian Recorder*, 30 April 1834.

38. *Acadian Recorder*, 30 January 1819, 1, 8 January, 19 February 1825, 20 November 1830.

39. *Acadian Recorder*, 4 July 1818; 23 January 1850; 12 October 1850; *Nova Scotian*, 25 December 1844; *Journal*, 22 November 1830.

40. *Nova Scotian*, 1 January, 12 March 1835; For a detailed account of Howe's trial, see J. Murray Beck, *Joseph Howe: Volume I* (Montreal: McGill-Queen's University Press, 1982), chap. 9; *Acadian Recorder*, 21 March 1818. In 1818, when new bridewell facilities were opened, the grand jury recommended that it be removed from police jurisdiction and placed under provincial control: see RG34–312 (P.8), Grand Jury Minutes, 19, 20 January 1818.

41. RG34–312 (P.8), Grand Jury Minutes, 26 January 1818; *Acadian Recorder*, 12 September 1818, 12, 31 August, 14 September 1822, 11 October, 22 November, 6 December 1828. In the 1820s the grand jury was more concerned with bridewell discipline and criminal recidivists than with policing. See Minutes, 23 December 1823; 28 January, 13 March 1824.

42. "A Nova Scotian," in *A Letter to the People: Containing Strictures Upon the Conduct of the Magistrates* (Halifax 1819); *Acadian Recorder*, 22 April 1820; "A Forerunner to Joseph Howe," *Canadian Historical Review* 8:3 (1927): 224–32.

43. Sutherland, "Merchants of Halifax," chap. 4; *Acadian Recorder*, 12 November 1825.

44. RG34–312 (P.10), Sessions of the Peace Minutes, 29 November 1830, 3 August, 27 October 1831, 5, 17 January 1832; *Acadian Recorder*, 2 May 1829; *Nova Scotian*, 10 December 1834.

45. RG34–312 (P.8), Sessions of the Peace Minutes, 24 March, 13 April 1831; 10 March 1836; 19 September 1838; *Halifax Morning Post*, 2 January 1841.

46. RG34–312 (P.13–14), Grand Jury Minutes, 8 June, 12 December 1835.

47. Ibid., 12 February, 14 November, 12 December 1835; *Nova Scotian*, 25 June 1835.

48. RG34–312 (P.14), Grand Jury Minutes, 3 January, 19 March 1839.

49. RG34–312 (P.16), Sessions of the Peace Minutes, 20 March 1840.

50. *Morning Post*, 27 October 1840. For police in Lower Canada see Greer, "Birth of the Police"; Michael McCulloch, "Most Assuredly Perpetual Motion: Police and Policing in Quebec City, 1838–1858," *Urban History Review* 19 (October 1990): 100–112.

51. RG34–312 (P.14), Grand Jury Minutes, 17 December 1837; March, December 1838; *Halifax Times*, 29 January 1839; *Nova Scotian*, 10 January 1839; *Halifax Morning Herald*, 27 July 1840; Sutherland, "Revolt of the Shopkeepers," 32–35.

52. Sutherland, "Revolt of the Shopkeepers," 38–40; *Nova Scotian*, 5 November 1840, 11, 18 March, 29 April 1841; *Acadian Recorder*, 13, 27 March 1841; *Morning Post*, 30 March 1841.

53. S.N.S. 1841, c. 55.

54. S.N.S. 1848, c. 39; 1850, c. 4; Girard, "Rise and Fall," 64.

55. T. W. Acheson, *Saint John: The Making of an Urban Colonial Community, 1815–1850* (Toronto: University of Toronto Press, 1985), chap. 11; S.N.S. 1841, c. 55, s. 53.

56. S.N.S. 1841, c. 55, s. 53.

57. *Morning Post*, 19, 22 June, 8 July 1841; *Acadian Recorder*, 3 December 1853, 21 January 1854; 15 July 1855; *Nova Scotian*, 15 July 1841. The charter also established a city or mayor's court for the recovery of small debts. The city marshal assisted in the execution of writs from this court. From June to December of 1841 the court handled over six hundred plaintiffs. See RG42 Series B, Vol. 1.

58. *Morning Herald*, 9 November 1841.

59. Steinberg, *Transformation of Criminal Justice*, 25.

60. Fingard, "Jailbirds in Mid-Victorian Halifax," 79. See also Marquis, "A Machine of Oppression," 73–77, Joan Sangster, "'Pardon Tales' from Magistrate's Court: Women, Crime and the Court in Peterborough County, 1920–50," *Canadian Historical Review* 79:2 (1993): 161–97.

61. Steinberg, *Transformation of Criminal Justice*, 54. In four months of 1846, 12.5 percent of the charges ended with an admonition and release or a discharge because of lack of prosecution witnesses. About 10 percent of the charges resulted in custodial commitments; an additional number of commitments came from people unable to pay fines.

62. RG42 (D) Vol. 1, Halifax Police Court Minutes, January–April 1846; Vol. 19, 19 May–10 September 1864. For African Americans and the courts, see G. S. Rowe, "Black Offenders and Criminal Courts in Philadelphia in the Late Eighteenth Century," *Journal of Social History* 22 (summer 1989): 685–712.

63. RG42 (D) Vols. 1, 19; Rowe, "Black Offenders." Theodore Ferdinand, in *Boston's Lower Courts, 1814–50* (Toronto: Associated University Press, 1992), 114–19, concluded that "neither Irish nor lower-class defenders received routinely harsher punishments than their counterparts" in antebellum Boston.

64. Ferdinand, *Boston's Courts;* Fingard, "Jailbirds in Mid Victorian Halifax"; Phillips, "Poverty, Unemployment and the Administration of the Criminal Law," 146–47. Interpretations that stress the class, not deviancy, aspects of vagrancy arrests tend to ignore the attitudes of the local working class toward these individuals.

65. Beamish Murdoch, *The Charter and Ordinances of the City of Halifax in the Province of Nova Scotia* (Halifax: William Gossip, 1851), 42.

66. *Halifax Morning Sun*, 5 July 1850; *Acadian Recorder,* 30 September 1853; Murdoch, *Charter of the City of Halifax*, 42.

67. *Acadian Recorder,* 28 December 1850; *Morning Post*, 17 April 1846; *Nova Scotian*, 26 April 1854.

68. *Morning Sun*, 6 January 1852. For social and moral reform in this period, see Fingard, *Dark Side of Life in Victorian Halifax*, 117–95. The construction of a provincial penitentiary beginning in 1843 was another manifestation of these efforts.

69. *Morning Sun*, 8 January 1852; *Acadian Recorder,* 13 September 1851, 1 July, 18 November 1854; *Halifax Morning Chronicle*, 1 December 1863.

70. *Annual Reports of the Several Departments of the City Government of Halifax, Nova Scotia for the Municipal Year 1857–58* (hereafter *Annual Reports*) (Halifax: James Bowes and Sons, 1858); *Halifax: Its Sins and Sorrows* (Halifax: Conference Job Printing Office, 1862); *Halifax Evening Examiner*, 6 June 1862.

71. Phillips, "Poverty, Crime and Unemployment," 132–33.

72. *Morning Sun*, 21 October 1861; *Annual Reports*, 1857–58, 1861–62, 1862–63. Police and night watch amalgamation took place in New York in 1845 and in Boston and Philadelphia in 1854.

73. *Annual Reports*, 1863–64, 1865–66, 1866–67; S.N.S. 1864, c. 81; *Rules and Regulations of the Mayor and Aldermen for the Government of the Halifax Police Department* (Halifax: James Bowes and Son, 1864). In 1865 the court was authorized to sentence juvenile offenders to up to three years confinement in a reformatory.

74. *Annual Reports*, 1863–64; PANS Micro 12412, RG35–102, Series I, Halifax City Council Minutes, 2 June 1863. Most city council minutes for 1841–1867, unfortunately, are missing but its meetings were covered by the press.

75. Marquis, "Contours of Canadian Urban Justice."

76. *Nova Scotian*, 21 December 1863.

77. *Morning Chronicle*, 1 December 1863.

78. *Morning Chronicle*, 12 November 1863. Judith Fingard, Jim Phillips, and B. Janet Price have all pointed to the importance of recidivists in inflating Halifax arrest and imprisonment statistics from the 1860s onward. See Price, "'Raised In Rockhead. Died in Poor House': Female Petty Crime in Halifax, 1864–1890," in *Essays in the History of Canadian Law*, Girard and Phillips, 200–31. For police magistrates and indictable offences, see Nancy Parker, "Swift Justice: The Decline of the Criminal Trial Jury: The Dynamics of Law and Authority in Victoria, 1858–1905," in *Essays in the History of Canadian Law VI: British Columbia and the Yukon*, ed. Hamar Foster and John McLaren (Toronto: Osgoode Society, 1995), 172.

79. Philip Girard, "Henry Pryor," *Dictionary of Canadian Biography*, vol. 7, *1891–1900*, 870–71; S.N.S., 1867, c. 82; *Annual Reports*, 1866–67.

80. Weaver, *Crimes, Courts and Constables*, 72.

81. Price, "Raised in Rockhead," 209.

82. Ferdinand, *Boston's Lower Criminal Courts*, 38, 43–44.

83. Steinberg, *Transformation of Criminal Justice*, 232.

CHAPTER 2

Making "Docile Bodies": Prison Science and Prisoner Resistance at the Minnesota Reformatory, 1889–1920

Alexander W. Pisciotta

The development and diffusion of the "new penology" in the late-nineteenth and early twentieth centuries sparked a paradigmatic revolution that transformed American punishment, corrections, and social control. The spread of the "medical model" and "prison science" introduced a new conception of crime and criminals and a number of new treatment strategies which, in theory, were aimed at reforming offenders.[1] Criminal justice historians have examined the medical model and prison science. However, most studies of the new penology have provided general discussions that are unsystematic and unfocused (e.g., David Rothman's *Conscience and Convenience*) or are theoretically grounded (e.g., Michel Foucault's *Discipline and Punish*) and deal with the abstract dimensions of the new penology as a form of social control.[2]

The implementation and impact of the medical model at specific correctional institutions and the inmate response to prison science (prisoner resistance) have received little attention.[3] The study addresses this gap in the literature by examining the aims, form, and impact of prison science at the Minnesota Reformatory—the nation's fifth reformatory prison for males—from its opening in 1889 through the close of the Progressive Era.

A complex portrait emerges. The Minnesota Reformatory, like many other correctional institutions, opened in response to perceived increases in crime and social disorder. Minnesota designed its version of the new penology—as Foucault concisely expresses it—to manage the minds and souls of offenders and build "docile bodies." The institution's parole system focused on "normalizing" the behavior of former inmates and fitting them into their proper places in the social, economic, and political order.[4]

However, primary and secondary sources—inmate case histories, inmate

interviews, misconduct and punishment records, inmate and staff correspondence, parole records—reveal a wide disparity between the idealized aims and
achieved results of prison science. Prisoner resistance (escapes, violence, disobedience, smuggling, arson, homosexuality, suicide) disrupted the institution's operation and challenged the authority of the keepers. Administrative
difficulties (underfunding and overcrowding), the inherent defects of the
medical model, and the reluctance of some institutional employees—especially parole officers—to repress their charges undercut the state's effort to
manage the souls of men. Minnesota's attempt to use prison science to tame,
train, and discipline criminal elements of the working class achieved, at best,
marginal results.

ORIGIN: ROOTS OF THE MINNESOTA
REFORMATORY

In the late 1870s and early 1880s Minnesota citizens became increasingly
concerned with crime, delinquency, and social disorder. The rise of cities,
increasing migration from the East, and the arrival of a new wave of "inferior
immigrants" were perceived to be the catalysts for the state's moral and social
decline. Eroding faith in the state's penal system—particularly the Minnesota
Reformatory for juvenile offenders at Red Wing and the Minnesota State
Prison at Stillwater—magnified the concerns of prominent citizens, prompting politicians and penologists to search for new approaches to crime control.[5]

Minnesota reformers turned to New York for the solution to their crisis in
crime, corrections, and social disorder, in particular, to the Elmira Reformatory.[6] The reformatory—which opened in Elmira, New York, in 1876—was
hailed widely as the most important penal institution in the United States, if
not the world. Elmira was the nation's first reformatory prison for males. But
more important, it was the first institution to introduce prison science and
implement the recommendations of the acclaimed declaration of principles.[7]

Under the direction of Superintendent Zebulon Brockway, the world's fore-
most prison warden, male first-time offenders between the ages of 16 and 30
were subjected to a unique regimen of reform that was based, in theory, on
kindly treatment and benevolent reform. Academic and vocational education,
a carefully designed mark and classification system, indeterminate sentencing
and parole, and military drill were designed to instill offenders with the habits
of order, respect, discipline and, as Brockway concisely expressed it, to build
"Christian gentlemen."[8]

Brockway's claim that 70 percent to 80 percent of his charges miraculously
were "saved" attracted national and international attention, sparking a paradigmatic revolution that transformed the American criminal justice system.
Adult prison and juvenile reformatory keepers across the country, on hearing
of Elmira's remarkable success, embraced the rehabilitative ideal, incorporat-
ing key elements of the Elmira system and prison science into their own

regimens. Elmira's success contributed to the discovery of a new class of criminal offender (the dangerous youthful offender), the rise of "scientific criminology," the professionalization of penology, and the diffusion of indeterminate sentencing and parole laws.[9]

Elmira's claims of success also laid the foundation for the birth of America's "third penal system": the reformatory prison movement.[10] New adult reformatory prisons opened in Michigan (1877), Massachusetts (1884), and Pennsylvania (1889). The keepers of these institutions wasted little time in reporting that they, much like Brockway, were achieving remarkable success. Gardiner Tufts, superintendent of the Massachusetts Reformatory, proclaimed in 1887 that "ninety-five percent of the men who have gone out from the Reformatory, have gone out desiring and intending to do right." In 1889 the managers of the Pennsylvania Industrial Reformatory declared that their institution would "fully answer the expectation of its founders and friends and prove to be a blessing to thousands who shall be consigned to its care, as well as a source of great pride to the people and our noble Commonwealth."[11]

Minnesota's reformers were convinced that the keepers of the Elmira, New York; Michigan; Massachusetts; and Pennsylvania reformatories had discovered the cure for crime, deviance, and social disorder. The passage of "An Act to Secure the Location of a Second State Prison" by the state legislature on March 9, 1885, marked the beginning of Minnesota's experiment with the new penology and its scientific battle against youthful elements of the criminal class.[12]

MANAGING THE SOULS OF MEN: TAMING AND TRAINING MINNESOTA'S "DANGEROUS CLASSES"

The opening of the doors of the Minnesota Reformatory at St. Cloud on October 15, 1889, to 75 inmates transferred from the Minnesota State Prison marked the birth of the nation's fifth adult reformatory for males. O. J. C., a 21-year-old mason, had the dubious distinction of being the institution's first commitment.[13] O. J. C. received a seven-year sentence for assault and robbery. The superintendent noted that he was intemperate, illiterate, and exhibited a number of bad habits. O. J. C. was, quite simply, a product of Minnesota's "dangerous class"—the root of crime, deviance, and social disorder.

However, O. J. C. and his counterparts were not transferred to the Minnesota Reformatory to receive the benefits of the new penology. By October 1889 the institution's first cell house, administration building, hospital, school, chapel, kitchen, laundry, and superintendent's residence were complete. But a number of other important buildings—including workshops—were not even started: O. J. C. and his peers were transferred to complete the construction of the Minnesota Reformatory. The institution was, in essence, a work camp. The Minnesota State Prison inmates were not enthusiastic or cooperative workers. Disobedience, escape attempts, and other forms of inmate resistance delayed construction and occupied the attention of Superintendent D. E. Myers and his staff. In fact, 11 of the institution's first 75 inmate workers became so disruptive that the board of managers transferred them back to the state prison at Stillwater.[14]

Superintendent Myers and the managers confronted other distractions that also delayed the introduction of prison science. The legislature's appropriation was penurious. "I have had to economize to such an extent as to seriously retard our business," complained the superintendent.[15] The unexpected commitment of a female offender in November 1889 created a serious logistics problem.[16] By the end of 1890 the institution had 139 inmates but only 128 cells, forcing inmates to sleep on cots in the corridors. "I am at a loss to know what to do," said the superintendent in desperation.[17] Despite these difficulties, Superintendent Myers was confident that his institution—much like the adult reformatories opened in New York, Michigan, Massachusetts, and Pennsylvania—would be an unqualified success, a "moral sanitarium."[18] In 1889 the managers declared that "the grand experiment of reformation, which is now in its infancy . . . promises such glorious results."[19]

The central aim of the Minnesota Reformatory was clear. Following the example of Elmira, it was designed to instill criminal elements of the working class with respectable values and to fit them into their "proper place" in the economic, social, and political order. Superintendent Myers explained that "It is a well recognized fact among penologists that in the lower strata of humanity, the appetite and passions largely govern the man."[20] The Minnesota Reformatory would teach its charges the habits of "punctuality, regularity, truthfulness, self control, justice, kindness and industry."[21]

The gradual release of the Minnesota State Prison inmate workers and the completion of the institution's infrastructure allowed the keepers of the Minnesota Reformatory to turn their attention from the construction of buildings to the reform of men.[22] A three-stage regimen of reform, adapted from the Elmira system, was introduced to remold the diseased character of Minnesota's youthful offenders.[23] First, a diagnostic interview exposed the "root cause" of each offender's deviance. Second, in-house treatments reshaped the minds and morals of inmates, building "docile bodies." Finally, parole supervision made certain that the lessons of conformity were carried into the community.[24]

Each incoming inmate was required to meet with Superintendent Myers or one of his successors—William Lee (1894–96), William Houlton (1896–1900), Frank Randall (1900–16), H. K. W. Scott (1916–20)—for a personal interview. These interviews replicated scientific diagnostic procedures used by Brockway at Elmira, grounded on the new penology's notion of multifactor positivism: each offender was a unique individual whose behavior was the product of a variety of dynamic and dialectically interacting social, psychological, economic, and biological factors. An individualized diagnosis and treatment plan was needed, then, to redirect each pathological personality.

Interviews conducted by Superintendent Lee in 1895 reflect the hetero-geneous character of Minnesota's dangerous class, as well as inherent prob-lems in applying the medical model and predicting future dangerousness. Some inmates had promising prospects for reform. Twenty-eight-year-old John P., who "kicked the front of a saloon in," smoked, drank, and exhibited a checkered work history. However, the superintendent concluded, "I think we will have no trouble with this man, unless it comes from a lack of industry. Don't think he has ever worked very hard or applied himself constantly for any length of time." The superintendent was also optimistic about Robert B., a 19-year-old robber: "This is a very bright young fellow & if he tells the truth is not a very bad boy. I am favorably impressed with him and think he will give us no trouble."[25]

But other inmates appeared less malleable. William H., a 19-year-old pick-pocket, was a "cigarette fiend" and "all around vagabond" with "rat cunning." The superintendent predicted: "He will give us trouble by getting into petty mischief & will violate the rules in small things. Will lie & steal. Will be easily subdued & will promise anything to escape punishment." Twenty-year-old Jacob C., convicted of "running a confidence game and swindling people," would also resist scientific reform: "This is a bright fellow but has the wrong idea of life. He has been tramping all over the country, running foot races, 'skin games' & generally dead beating it on every body. I believe his makeup is that of a 'crook' & it will be difficult to get him to work. If we are obliged to punish him he will be a stubborn fellow to deal with."[26]

The second stage in Minnesota's regimen of reform—long-term, in-house treatments—centered on labor. The Minnesota Reformatory was built on a 22-acre granite quarry with the "sole intention to employ convict labor in quarrying stone."[27] But an 1892 law limiting 33 percent of the inmates to quarry work forced the keepers to expand the institution's farm, which in-creased to one thousand acres by the close of the nineteenth century. Quarry and farm work shared a common end: instilling offenders with the habits of order, discipline, self-control, and cheerful submission to authority. "There is something peculiarly elevating about labor, it comes nearer being a panacea for crime than any other one thing," explained Superintendent Myers.[28]

Academic education also was stressed. The school department, which was organized in January 1890, met three nights each week. Teachers, who were also guards, taught basic reading, writing, and arithmetic, as well as more advanced subjects such as geography, map drawing, history, and shorthand. By 1900 the manual training class offered instruction in a variety of trades and positions: blacksmith, carpenter, mason, electrician, plumber, pipe fitter, cook, shoemaker, waiter, clerk, florist, truck gardener, teamster, printer, and farmer.[29] Franklin Miner, the school director, concluded that "the results ob-tained are equal to those of a good common school for the same period of attendance."[30]

Religious instruction attempted to instill respectable values. Inmates could attend the religious service of their choice on Sundays. Ministers, priests, and rabbis exhorted their flocks to work hard, respect their keepers, obey the rules, renounce their bad habits—drinking, smoking, swearing, fornication—embrace God, and become good workers and citizens.

A military drill system, copied from Elmira, tried to make certain that inmates learned the habits of discipline and self-control. Minnesota Reformatory inmates were dressed in uniforms, assigned ranks, divided into companies, and provided wooden guns. They drilled at least one hour every day under Upton's army tactics, the same system used by West Point cadets and Elmira Reformatory inmates. Inmate soldiers learned how to salute, march, execute orders, and even make bayonet charges (sans bayonets). The inculcation of "military habits" in theory, would transform shiftless, immoral, and amoral offenders into law-abiding citizens.[31]

Indeterminate sentencing was the key to building disciplined moral workers. Indeterminate sentencing—in contrast with traditional fixed sentencing—was designed to force inmates to take responsibility for their actions and work toward reform. The guiding principle of the new penology—"let the punishment fit the offender"—prompted Minnesota legislators to prescribe maximum and minimum penalties for each offense: for example, first-degree grand larceny, not less than 1 year or more than 10; first-degree robbery, 5 to 20 years; first-degree assault, 5 to 10 years; first-degree manslaughter, 5 to 20 years; rape, 5 to 30 years.[32]

An elaborate mark and classification system was used to encourage compliance and "scientifically" measure each inmate's progress toward salvation. Each inmate was in one of three grades. First-grade inmates wore dark gray uniforms, could have visitors once a month, could write letters every Sunday, and received 12.5¢ for each day of work. Second-grade inmates wore blue uniforms, could have visitors every other month, could write letters every second Sunday, and received 9¢ for each day of work. Third—or punishment—grade inmates wore red uniforms and did not receive visitors, write letters, participate in holiday celebrations, or receive pay for their labor.

Following the initial diagnostic interview with the superintendent, new inmates were placed in the second grade and informed that they would be required to earn their release by working their way through the mark system. Each inmate received grades on a monthly basis in three categories: school work, general deportment, and labor. Inmates who earned a score of 75 percent or higher on a monthly examination received 50 credits. Inmates with no disciplinary demerits received 50 credits for general behavior. Inmates who fulfilled the expectations of their work supervisors received 50 credits for labor. An inmate who earned 750 credits within five consecutive months or 880 within six consecutive months became eligible for promotion to the first grade. An offender became eligible for parole when he reached the first grade and served the minimum indeterminate sentence.

Parole was the third and final element in the reformatory regimen. The six members of the board of managers met monthly and made release decisions by considering cases on an individualized, scientific basis.[33] They reviewed each inmate's file and consulted the superintendent and other key personnel. They considered correspondence from interested parties—parents, spouse, relatives, victim, prosecutor, defense attorney, presiding judge, prospective employer—and examined the parole officer's recommendation. Finally, they interviewed the prospective parolee. Release criteria were clear: cooperative, docile inmates who accepted responsibility for their actions and acted like Christian gentlemen received parole; troublesome inmates were denied release and afforded an extended dose of prison science.[34]

Community supervision was designed to make certain that parolees became good workers and respectable citizens. Parole agents had the responsibility of reintegrating offenders back into the community. They assisted inmates in securing employment, investigated complaints, tracked down rule violators, and made prerelease background checks and recommendations to the board. Each inmate submitted a monthly report, signed by his employer, testifying to work habits, expenditures, savings, and general behavior. Unannounced visits were made to make certain that parolees were "keeping away from saloons and bad company."[35]

The keepers of the Minnesota Reformatory instituted a number of changes before 1920. They introduced the Bertillon system to track recidivists.[36] Professional teachers replaced guard-teachers in the schools. Academic programs and industrial trade—as well as recreational, musical, and entertainment programs—expanded. Mental testing began in 1909 to identify mentally defective offenders. A farm colony for 50 men was begun in 1917.[37]

However, the regimen of the Minnesota Reformatory remained remarkably stable from the institution's opening in 1889 through the close of the Progressive Era.[38] The keepers of the Minnesota Reformatory remained confident that their experiment in prison science was, indeed, building solid citizen-workers and making an important contribution in the state's battle against crime and social disorder. In 1892 Superintendent Myers announced that "the results of our efforts for the reformation of the prisoners of this institution are of the most encouraging nature." The managers were equally optimistic: "Most of our discharged inmates return to society and become respectable and respected citizens."[39]

PRISONER RESISTANCE: COPING WITH THE "PAINS OF IMPRISONMENT"

Michel Foucault's seminal study of corrections and social control, *Discipline and Punish*, demonstrates that nineteenth-century penal institutions—England's Panopticon Prison, the French juvenile reformatory at Mettray, New York's Auburn Prison—attempted to manage the minds, bodies, and souls of their charges and build "obedient individuals." The opening of prisons and the discovery of the new penology and prison science introduced a form of power relations and social control designed to build "machine-men, but also . . . proletarians."[40]

The keepers of the Minnesota Reformatory also attempted to transform their charges into "docile workers." Minnesota's three-stage adaptation of the Elmira system was designed to regulate each offender's dress, posture, speech, thought, and action. This "collective coercion of bodies" aimed at transforming criminal elements of Minnesota's working class into "meticulously subordinated cogs of a machine."[41] However, as David Garland has pointed out, Foucault and other criminal justice historians have failed to consider adequately the question of "prisoner resistance."[42] How did Minnesota's youthful offenders respond to the new penology? Did they willingly submit to the state's attempt to transform them into "docile workers"?

The historical record reveals that the power, authority, and control of the keepers of the Minnesota Reformatory were far from complete. Many inmates resisted prison science and the state's attempt to fit them into their proper place in the economic, social, and political order. The works of Gresham Sykes and Erving Goffman provide a foundation for understanding the nature of inmate resistance and rebellion. Inmates pursuing, as Goffman concisely expresses it, "primary adjustment," obeyed the rules and worked hard to become law-abiding Christian gentlemen.[43] However, many inmates incarcerated at the Minnesota Reformatory responded to the "pains of imprisonment"— deprivation of liberty, deprivation of autonomy, loss of material goods and services, loss of heterosexual contacts, and threats to personal security—by resorting to innovative forms of resistance.[44] Inmates pursuing the course of "secondary adjustment" rejected prison science and the authority of their keepers and followed a path aimed at "getting around the organization's assumptions as to what he should do and get and hence what he should be."[45]

Ben B., a 29-year-old "colored" offender, was an exemplary case of "primary adjustment." Convicted of assault with a deadly weapon, Ben was committed to the Minnesota Reformatory on July 12, 1912. Superintendent Randall noted that he "does not seem to be such a very bad fellow" and he "might make a good porter, janitor or waiter." Letters from former employers and relatives provided glowing accounts of his personal habits, character, and work record. Ben fulfilled the superintendent's expectations: he did not receive a single disciplinary demerit during his 2 years of incarceration and completed 15 months of parole without incident.[46]

But other inmates followed the path of "secondary adjustment," resisting prison science and battling their keepers. John S. was particularly troublesome. John, at 16, was committed to the Minnesota Reformatory on February 10, 1890, on a 5- to 10-year indeterminate sentence for first-degree grand larceny. During his 30-month stay, he received 35 misconduct violations, including fighting, disobedience of orders, shirking work, insolence to officers,

abusive language, smoking, malicious mischief, crookedness, begging for to-
bacco, and throwing stones at fellow inmates. John was placed in solitary
confinement 11 times (over 1,100 hours) on bread and water. He was transferred finally to the Minnesota State Prison in August 1893 for incorrigibility.[47]

Charles P. was equally disruptive. Charles, also 16, was committed to the
reformatory on February 16, 1891, on a 5-year indeterminate sentence for
second-degree grand larceny. Over the next 37 months he received 40 misconduct reports, including insolence to officer, disobedience of orders, not
enough work, inattention in shop, shirking, singing, laughing, whistling, failure in school, mutilating a geography map, and having a live gopher in his
cell. Charles was placed in solitary confinement on bread and water on nine
separate occasions (470 hours). A pardon by the governor issued in March
1893 no doubt saved Charles from further punishment.[48]

The Minnesota Reformatory inmates were collectively troublesome. Although few inmates matched the resistance records of John S. and Charles P.,
Minnesota's youthful offenders received thousands of misconduct reports each
year resulting, in the most extreme cases, in transfer to the state prison or
solitary confinement in the "dungeon."[49] For example, 192 inmates were incarcerated in July 1903. Between August 1, 1902, and July 31, 1904, inmates
were placed in solitary confinement on 75 occasions; 16 were transferred to
state prison for serious offenses or general incorrigibility.[50]

This resistance is not surprising in light of the fact that many of Minnesota's
"first time youthful offenders" were, in fact, hardened recidivists. A survey
conducted in 1902 revealed that 118 (61.4 percent) of 192 inmates in the
institution confessed to previous incarceration in adult prisons, jails, houses
of correction, juvenile reformatories, and adult reformatories. Twenty-eight
(14.6 percent) admitted that they committed offenses but were not caught.
Superintendent Randall was confident that these statistics underestimated the
recidivism rate of his charges: "It must be remembered that some among the
one hundred ninety two refused to disclose their identity." And other inmates,
he noted, were simply "tramps."[51]

The hardened nature of many offenders, coupled with the pains of incarceration, made escapes a nagging concern. A 16-foot-high "tight board fence"
surrounded the reformatory, but parts of the wall "frequently [blew] down."[52]
Although guards were armed with rifles and ordered to shoot to kill, dozens
of inmates attempted to "elope"—including five successful escapes in 1897,
five in 1902, nine in 1909, and eight in 1915. The state legislature appropri-
ated funds to build a 22-foot-high stone wall but this was still under construction in 1920. Security remained a pressing concern for the administration
through the close of the Progressive Era.

Other inmates responded to the pains of incarceration by resorting to violence. Inmates at the Minnesota Reformatory—much like their counterparts
in adult prisons, juvenile reformatories, and reformatory-prisons—demon-

strated considerable innovation in fashioning homemade knives and in transforming pipes, boards, rocks, and shop supplies such as hammers, into
dangerous weapons. Between August 1, 1902, and July 31, 1906, for example,
33 inmates went to solitary confinement for violent acts. Twenty-six cases
involved attacks on other inmates, and seven involved attacks on staff
members.[53]

Arson was a serious threat at the Minnesota Reformatory. Fearing the possibility of conflagration, keepers strictly prohibited smoking and the possession of matches. However, some inmates did manage to steal or smuggle
matches, with serious consequences. A fire of "unknown origin" destroyed
the upper floor and roof of the main administration building in December
1899. The blacksmith shop was destroyed in 1902 and again in 1911.[54]

The keepers were constantly on alert to prevent "crimes against God and
nature": homosexuality. Notes taken by a guard who was eavesdropping on a
conversation between three inmates—Bell, Thomas, and Bulman—while they
were locked in solitary confinement, reveal that concerns were well-founded:

Bell: Say, kid, come over here and I'll kiss you . . .

Thomas: I can't.

Bell: Would you if you could?

Thomas: Sure.

Bell: Say, kid, did you ever suck a fellow off?

Thomas: No. How does it taste?

Bell: Just like sugar and milk. Kid, don't you wish you were over here with me?

Bulman: Sure . . . Gee, I wish I had a little girl 8 or 6 years old in here.

Bell: Can't you stick your a__ out and work your way to me? . . . Say, kid, I wish I had
you in here.

Bulman: What for? Oh, I know. . . . No, I can't. . . . Did you ever f____ a kid, or a
cow, or a calf? . . . I f_____ a calf once when I was a kid, and the old lady caught
me at it. . . . [55]

Inmates who could not cope with the pains of incarceration sometimes
resorted to the ultimate form of escape: suicide. Louis P., an 18-year-old convicted of grand larceny, was not a promising prospect for reform. The superintendent noted that he was "a vagrant drunkard of low spirit and evil
experience. He is not a hopeful case because he doesn't amount to much in
the way of a man, for any purpose." Louis was placed in solitary confinement
on November 15, 1903, for assaulting an officer. The next day, he was found
hanging in his cell.[56] In 1897, Charles L., a 19-year-old burglar, was found
"having hanged himself by the neck with a rope made from his bed sheets."
Superintendent Houlton noted that "the coroner's inquest showed no cause;
that there had been no sign of melancholy, ill-health, or mental unsoundness,
and that he had no trouble here, having never been reported."[57]

The historical record suggests that Minnesota's attempt to introduce prison science and implement the new penology was not received well by many of the state's youthful offenders. Ben B. followed the path of primary adjustment and appeared to live the life of a Christian gentleman. But John S., Charles P., and many other inmates did not bend to the will of their keepers and become "obedient subjects" and "docile workers." Prisoner resistance and secondary deviance undermined the state's attempt to civilize and socialize Minnesota's dangerous classes.

DISCIPLINARY PAROLE: COMMUNITY SURVEILLANCE AND SOCIAL CONTROL, 1889–1920

David Garland's penetrating historical study *Punishment and Welfare* maintains that parole and other forms of community-based corrections were key components of the new penology, which were introduced to "straighten out characters and to reform the personality of their clients in accordance with the requirements of 'good citizenship.'" However, the state's attempt to "normalize" the behavior of parolees in natural settings—the home, workplace, neighborhood—also represented an extension of the "shallow end of penality."[58]

Jonathan Simon's extensive study of parole, *Poor Discipline*, demonstrates that late-nineteenth- and early twentieth-century community corrections were structured around the notion of "disciplinary parole." Disciplinary parole aimed at establishing the boundaries of acceptable behavior (for example, no drinking or gambling), but above all else, supervision was designed to make certain that parolees participated in the labor force. "The reports throughout this period continue to reference the idea that parole was reformative and linked to a scientific knowledge of offenders," concludes Simon, "but overall they suggest that, for all practical purposes, the work of parole was work."[59]

However, the state's effort at surveillance of parolees was, by design, limited. Correctional officials in California—the focus of Simon's study—as well as in other states, did not establish large parole offices in the late-nineteenth and early twentieth centuries. "Parole didn't need to mount a credible supervision effort because it claimed to be releasing men who were not essentially criminal," explains Simon.[60] Interested parties in the community—employers, parents, spouses, neighbors—served as the eyes and ears of the parole staff to make certain that parolees did, indeed, behave and become "good men."[61]

The observations of Garland and Simon provide a context to understand the aims and operation of parole in Minnesota. Legislators, it seems, accepted the claim that inmates being released from the state's correctional institutions, essentially, were reformed. As a result, the legislature called for the appointment of just one agent to supervise all parolees released from the Minnesota Reformatory and from the Minnesota State Prison.

The parole officer F. A. Whittier had a difficult task. In 1900 he was responsible for monitoring over two hundred inmates, scattered across eighty-four thousand square miles and several states. Complicating matters, his office was located in St. Paul, over twenty miles from the prison at Stillwater and nearly seventy miles from the reformatory at St. Cloud. Parolees in some parts of the state were more than three hundred miles from the agent's office and were, in effect, nearly impossible to reach. Complicating the task of communication and supervision, the parole officer did not have a telephone until 1904 or a car until 1914.

The keepers of the Minnesota Reformatory were not, however, pleased with their limited supervisory and surveillance function. Parole agent Whittier, in frustration, charged that parole supervision was "nothing more than an experiment."[62] Superintendent Randall concurred with Whittier's assessment. In 1906 he described parole supervision as "the weakest feature in our whole system."[63] Whittier's successor, J. Z. Barncard, was also frustrated and overwhelmed by the extraordinary demands placed on him. The appointment of an assistant parole agent in 1908 did not improve the situation. Barncard admitted that "there is much more work than two men can do."[64] In 1910 Randall warned that "Young men on parole from the reformatory have never had proper attention, I believe, and do not have it now. They are not supervised as they should be. Because of this some of the men relapse."[65]

The quality of supervision did not improve as the parole staff increased between 1910 and 1920. In 1912 three officers supervised over six hundred reformatory and prison parolees. In 1915 and 1916 parole agent D. H. Knickerbacker and his assistant, H. B. Whittier, traveled over 33,000 miles by rail and 9,000 by car to make 543 visits. In 1917 and 1918 they traveled over 31,000 miles by rail and over 8,000 by car to make 317 visits.[66] The agents' daily reports highlight the arduousness of their work. Knickerbacker and Whittier were on duty six days each week. Workdays started before 9:00 A.M., often extending far into the evening. On December 26, 1919, for example, Whittier made 14 visits and was on duty until midnight. On December 30, 1919, he worked in the office until 1:00 P.M., made four visits in the afternoon, then sat in a parole violator stakeout until 4:00 A.M.[67]

Despite the ineffectiveness of supervision, it is clear that inmate work participation was the central focus of the parole system. Parolees were placed in low-status, low-pay jobs and treated as economic commodities.[68] In 1915, for example, 121 inmates were paroled from the reformatory. Thirty worked as farm laborers (24.8 percent), 9 as general laborers (7.4 percent), 9 in "railroad car shops" (7.4 percent), 7 as clerks (5.8 percent), 7 as teamsters (5.8 percent), and 6 as factory workers (4.9 percent). The others filled a variety of low-skill positions such as janitor, cook, porter, or coal-dock man.[69]

Parole agent Barncard realized that many employers were not motivated by altruism and the Christian spirit. "I find many employers only interested in getting as much work out of the paroled men as possible, and usually for smaller wages than he pays other help." Economic exploitation, Barncard noted, complicated his task and contributed to parole violations. "This condition tends to discourage, and offers an excuse to the men on parole, who view their being held as an injustice and they are then ready to throw off the yoke and run away. There seems to be no remedy for this condition except to be more careful in the future in placing the paroled men."[70]

Letters from prospective employers confirm Barncard's suspicion that inmates were wanted as a cheap source of labor. Minnesota employers were desperate for workers, including convicts. S. McGuire's letter to the parole agent was typical: "I would like to get one teamster & one choreman." The choreman "must be a good milker age or nationality is not object but I would prefer young men old ones sometimes get cranky [sic]."[71] Other letters requested dishwashers, waiters, shoeshine boys, porters, laborers, quarry workers, and factory workers. Employers generally were not particular. W. L. Chandler noted that he "would take a white or colored boy" to shine shoes. Pat Dooley, a farmer, wanted a "man that can talk English and that I can depend on." O. R. Ondler wanted "a man with two hands." O. A. Lindberg summarized the sentiments of many employers: "Would not care to have a murderous desperado or one who would steal me blind but aside from these generalities would not care so much."[72]

However, Minnesota's parole officers were not willing participants in the economic exploitation and repression of their charges. Agent Barncard attempted to find parolees good jobs and protect them from unscrupulous employers. Agent Knickerbacker screened inmates before he placed them on farms: "[W]e cannot expect to find more than five out of every forty-five men that are suitable for farm work." Knickerbacker did not view his primary role as policing parolees. When the superintendent of the Minneapolis police requested a list of parolees, Knickerbacker balked: "I do not approve of furnishing the Police Department with a list of our paroled men as we have had some very unpleasant experiences in the past."[73] The closing to a 1900 report from Whittier to Superintendent Randall on six parolees summarized the spirit of Minnesota's agents: "I write this only as a matter of information to you, having no wish or thought of doing them any injury in any way."[74]

This sensitivity to the plight of their charges was also evident in the handling of parole violations. Agents made an effort to strike a balance between their policing and helping functions. Parolees who committed new criminal offenses were summarily returned, but offenders who committed technical violations often received a warning and a second chance.[75] Parole officer Knickerbacker, for example, learned that L. E. was violating the conditions of parole by frequenting pool halls. He received a warning and "promised to be more careful in the future." W. B. lied in his monthly reports about the amount of money he contributed to his mother's support. He was reprimanded and "promised to be more careful."[76]

Inmate reactions to indeterminate sentencing and parole were mixed. Many inmates became delighted to learn that they had earned parole and would not serve their 10-, 20-, or 30-year sentences. But others realized that the maximum sentences imposed by the court were primarily a symbolic, psychological deterrent—only the most incorrigible offenders would actually ever serve long sentences.[77] Some inmates were even astute enough to realize that they were, despite the kind intentions of their parole officers, the victims of economic exploitation. One succinctly expressed this view in his appearance before the parole board: "I believe this is not reformation for the time I have been here. I do not believe in parole because when a man goes out on parole he has to work for ten dollars a month and is ground down to nothing, and I do not believe in it. . . . I have been a floating laborer since I came to this country."[78]

The impact of Minnesota's disciplinary parole system was, then, questionable. The parole system served the economic needs of the state—especially rural farmers—by providing a steady supply of low-priced labor.[79] However, parole officers were overwhelmed by their task and could not guarantee that parolees would, indeed, become reliable "docile workers." Minnesota's attempt to extend the "multiplication of the judicial gaze" into the community was largely symbolic.[80] Parole did little to assist inmates, protect the public, or effectively extend the "shallow end of penality" into the community.[81]

CONCLUSION

Minnesota's legislators and penal reformers had good reason to believe that the opening of the Minnesota Reformatory and the implementation of the medical model and new penology would save offenders, reduce crime, and contribute to the state's battle against social disorder. The keepers of the Minnesota Reformatory were confident that their "moral sanitarium"—much like Brockway's "reformatory hospital"—would transform dangerous youthful offenders into productive citizens.

The records of the Minnesota Reformatory reveal, however, a complex and often conflicting portrait of institutional social control. There was, in the final analysis, a wide disparity between the promise and practice of prison science at the Minnesota Reformatory. In theory, Minnesota's experiment was intended to "treat" and "reform" youthful offenders. However, the Minnesota Reformatory—like the Elmira Reformatory and the prisons and juvenile reformatories analyzed by Foucault—was structured to instill lower-class offenders with Christian character and build "docile bodies."

The state's effort to tame, train, and discipline criminal elements of the working class was, however, marginally successful. A variety of internal and external forces disrupted the rehabilitative/disciplinary aims of the keepers of the Minnesota Reformatory. Inmates were not passive and malleable recipients of prison science. They responded to the pains of imprisonment by resorting to prisoner resistance and a wide range of secondary adjustments:

escapes, violence, disobedience, smuggling, arson, homosexuality, and suicide. Administrative difficulties (e.g., underfunding, legislative interference, over-crowding) disrupted the operation of the institution and the implementation of prison science. The inherent defects of the medical model and the unwill-ingness of parole officers to repress and economically exploit their charges also undermined the state's effort to "normalize" the behavior of parolees and build "obedient subjects."

The introduction of the new penology in the late-nineteenth and early twentieth centuries, indeed, did transform America's approach to thinking about crime and treating criminals. However, the new prison science did not alter the essential aims and impact of social control. But in the final analysis, the keepers of the Minnesota Reformatory—like their counterparts at the Elmira Reformatory in New York—were unable to manage the minds, bodies, and souls of the dangerous class.

NOTES

1. The term "new penology" has taken on a variety of meanings in the fields of criminal justice and criminology. I am referring to the movement toward rehabilitation that emerged in the United States in the late-nineteenth and early twentieth centuries. This movement had its roots in the 1870 meeting of the National Congress on Pen-itentiary and Reformatory Discipline, held in Cincinnati, Ohio, in 1870. The terms "medical model" and "prison science" are products of the new penology and refer to strategies aimed at identifying the "root cause(s)" of deviance and prescribing treat-ments. Finally, "scientific criminology" refers to the emergence of experts on crime and crime control and the discourses and debates that surrounded the introduction of the new penology.

2. David J. Rothman, *Conscience and Convenience: The Asylum and Its Alternatives in Progressive America* (Boston: 1980); Michel Foucault, *Discipline and Punish: The Birth of the Prison* (New York: 1977).

3. For an exception, see Alexander W. Pisciotta, *Benevolent Repression: Social Control and the American Reformatory-Prison Movement* (New York: 1994).

4. Foucault, *Discipline and Punish*, 135–69. Foucault analyzes the rise and transfor-mation of French prisons; however, his analysis also examines American prisons and juvenile reformatories. His themes on power and social control are, then, directly applicable to correctional institutions in the United States.

5. On Minnesota's development and search for order, see Lowry Nelson, *The Min-nesota Community: Country and Town in Transition* (Minneapolis: 1960); Theodore C. Blegen, *Minnesota: A History of the State* (Minneapolis: 1963); William W. Folwell, *A History of Minnesota*, vols. 3 and 4 (St. Paul, Minn.: 1969); William E. Lass, *Minnesota: A Bicentennial History* (New York: 1977); June Holmquist, *They Chose Minnesota: A Survey of the State's Ethnic Groups*, ed. J. D. Holmquist (St. Paul, Minn.: 1981).

6. Minnesota's reform effort was led by Hastings H. Hart, secretary of the Min-nesota Board of Corrections and Charities. Hart was particularly impressed with Brockway's system: Folwell, *History of Minnesota*, 3:179–81, 4:407–13.

7. The Declaration of Principles can be found in Enoch C. Wines, ed., *Transactions*

of the National Congress on Penitentiary and Reformatory Discipline (Albany: 1870), 541–47.

8. Zebulon R. Brockway, "The Ideal of a True Prison System for a State," in *Transactions of the National Congress*, 63, 65. Brockway's *Fifty Years of Prison Service: An Autobiography* (Montclair N.J.: 1969 [orig. ed. 1912]) provides a detailed account of his views on the causes and treatment of crime.

9. Pisciotta's *Benevolent Repression* provides the fullest account of Brockway, Elmira, and the adult reformatory movement. The importance of Brockway and Elmira is also discussed in Torsten Eriksson, *The Reformers: An Historical Survey of Pioneer Experiments in the Treatment of Criminals* (New York: 1976), 98–106; Blake McKelvey, *American Prisons: A History of Good Intentions* (Montclair, N.J.: 1977), 168–69; David Garland, *Punishment and Welfare: A History of Penal Strategies* (Brookfield, Vt.: 1985), 98; Beverly A. Smith, "Military Training at New York's Elmira Reformatory, 1888–1920," *Federal Probation* 52:1 (1988): 33–40; Nicole H. Rafter, *Partial Justice: Women, Prisons, and Social Control*, 2nd ed. (New Brunswick, N.J.: 1990), 24–29, 43, 48; Robert G. Waite, "From Penitentiary to Reformatory: Alexander Machonochie, Walter Crofton, Zebulon Brockway, and the Road to Prison Reform—New South Wales, Ireland, and Elmira, New York, 1840–1870," in *Criminal Justice History* 12 (Westport, Conn.: 1993): 85–105.

10. Historians have described the adult prison movement, which is often traced to the Walnut Street Prison (1790), as the nation's first penal system, and the juvenile reformatory movement, which is traced to the New York House of Refuge (1825), as the second penal system. The opening of the Elmira Reformatory in 1876 introduced the third penal system, the reformatory-prison (or adult reformatory) movement.

11. Massachusetts Reformatory, *Third Annual Report* (Boston: 1888), 32; Pennsylvania Industrial Reformatory, *Biennial Report, 1889–1890* (Harrisburg: 1891), 13.

12. Minnesota State Reformatory, *Laws, By-Laws, Rules and Regulations for the Government and Discipline of the Minnesota State Reformatory* (St. Cloud, Minn.: 1898), 3–4. The 1885 act authorized a committee to find a location for "a second state prison." After hearing about Elmira, legislators and reformers changed the institution's purpose and decided to open an adult reformatory.

13. Minnesota State Reformatory, "Convict Register, 1889–1897," Case History #1, 1: Records of the St. Cloud State Reformatory, State Archives, Minnesota State Historical Society, St. Paul.

14. Ibid., Case History #1–75, 1–11.

15. Minnesota State Reformatory, *First Annual Report, 1889* (Minneapolis: 1890), 9.

16. Superintendent Myers warned that the institution did not have facilities for females. However, judges continued to commit females—generally several each year. They were given domestic chores and placed in the superintendent's house, or they were transferred to a county jail or county penitentiary. On the treatment of females and other minorities in reformatory-prisons, see Rafter, *Partial Justice*, and Pisciotta, *Benevolent Repression*, 143–48.

17. Minnesota State Reformatory, *Second Annual Report, 1890* (Minneapolis: 1891), 6. Overcrowding remained a chronic problem: 18 men were on cots in the corridors in 1893, 30 were on cots in 1904, and 160 were without cells in 1916: Minnesota State Reformatory, *Sixth Annual Report, 1893* (Minneapolis: 1894), 3; *Fourth Biennial Report, 1903–1904* (St. Cloud, Minn.: 1905), 6; *Tenth Biennial Report, 1915–1916* (n.p., 1916), 5–6.

18. Reformatory keepers frequently used medical and educational terminology in describing their institutions. Brockway referred to Elmira as a "reformatory hospital" and the "college on the hill": *Fifty Years of Prison Service*, 163, 212, 232.

19. Minnesota State Reformatory, *First Annual Report, 1889*, 11, 5.

20. Minnesota State Reformatory, *Fifth Annual Report, 1892* (Minneapolis: 1892), 9. It should be noted that the printer erred: The report covering 1892 is the institution's fourth annual report, not the fifth. Between 1889 and 1920 there were 4,960 inmates committed to the Minnesota Reformatory. The managers did not, as in some institutions, keep a demographic profile of the entire prison population. But an overview of the 1895 inmate population provides a profile of Minnesota's youthful offender during the institution's early years. Fifty-five (47.0 percent) of the 117 inmates sentenced in 1895 were between the ages of 16 and 20; there were 43 (36.7 percent) between 21 and 25, and 19 (16.3 percent) between 26 and 30. Seventy-one (60.7 percent) were convicted of first- or second-degree grand larceny; others were convicted of a range of offenses, including assault, burglary, attempted rape, forgery, indecent assault, manslaughter, robbery, and counterfeiting. Ninety-nine (84.6 percent) had less than 7 years of education, 57 (49.5 percent) worked as laborers or farm hands, 59 (50.4 percent) were recorded as having "no religion," and 47 (40.1 percent) were intemperate. Twenty-eight (23.9 percent) were foreign born; the fathers of 66 (56.4 percent) of the inmates were born in foreign countries. See the Minnesota State Reformatory, *Eighth and Ninth Annual Reports, 1895–1896* (St. Paul, Minn.: 1897), 18–22.

21. Minnesota State Reformatory, *Fifth Annual Report, 1892*, 16.

22. The Minnesota Reformatory was relatively small. The institution held 127 inmates in May 1895, in May 1910 it held 363, and in May 1920 it held 417. *Eighth and Ninth Annual Reports, 1895–1896*, 18; *Seventh Biennial Report, 1908–1910* (n.p., n.d.), 19; *Twelfth Biennial Report, 1919–1920* (Stillwater, Minn.: 1920), 6.

23. Minnesota legislators copied Elmira's commitment criteria regarding age and prior record. The institution accepted offenders between the ages of 16 and 30 who never received a reformatory or prison sentence.

24. The Elmira system is described in detail in Pisciotta, *Benevolent Repression*, 17–22.

25. Minnesota State Reformatory, "Record of Interviews with Inmates and Contact with References, 1895–1897," 37–38, 58–59, and "Inmate History and Record, 1896–1899," Case History #604 and #618: Records of the St. Cloud State Reformatory, State Archives, Minnesota State Historical Society, St. Paul.

26. "Record of Interviews with Inmates and Contact with References, 1895–1897," 40–42, 75–76, and "Inmate History and Record, 1896–1899," Case History #605 and #625.

27. Minnesota State Reformatory, *Laws, By-Laws, Rules and Regulations for the Government and Discipline of the Minnesota State Reformatory*, 4.

28. Minnesota State Reformatory, *Fifth Annual Report, 1892*, 8.

29. Minnesota State Reformatory, *Eighth and Ninth Annual Reports, 1895–1896*, 34; *First Biennial Report, 1897–1898* (St. Cloud, Minn.: 1898), 5–6.

30. Minnesota State Reformatory, *First Biennial Report, 1897–1898*, 12. Samples of "Inmate Schoolwork, 1917": Records of the St. Cloud State Reformatory, State Archives, Minnesota State Historical Society, St. Paul.

31. Minnesota State Reformatory, *Sixth Annual Report, 1893*, 5.

32. Traditional fixed sentencing systems were based on Beccarian classical theory

and the notion that criminals were free, rational, and hedonistic actors who deserved punishment. This perspective, which guided determinate sentencing in adult prisons before the rise of the new penology, was based on the theme "let the punishment fit the crime." In contrast, indeterminate sentencing was based on the medical model and the theme "let the punishment fit the offender."

33. The governor appointed manager/parole board members to successive one-year terms. To avoid partisan politics, appointments required senate approval and only three members could be from the same party. Following the national trend, a state parole board was instituted in 1911. This board had three members: the longest serving member of the Board of Control of State Institutions, the warden of the state prison, and one citizen appointed by the governor. However, the procedures and release criteria of both boards were quite similar.

34. F. A. Whittier, "The Prisoner on Parole," in *National Prison Association, Proceedings* (1906), 305–10; Frank L. Randall, "The Indeterminate Sentence," in *American Prison Association, Proceedings* (1917), 53–56; Henry C. Swearingen, "The Indeterminate Sentence and Parole from the Viewpoint of a Parole Commissioner," in *American Prison Association, Proceedings* (1922), 311–19. Unfortunately, the parole board did not keep records of its meetings. It is, then, difficult to determine how release decisions were actually made.

35. Minnesota State Reformatory, *Laws, By-Laws, and Regulations for the Government and Discipline of the Minnesota State Reformatory*, 46.

36. Alphonse Bertillon developed a system to track recidivists in the 1880s, which was based on anthropometrics. A series of physical measurements was taken on each inmate and used to identify repeat offenders. This system was widespread before the introduction of fingerprinting in the 1890s.

37. Minnesota State Reformatory, *Second Biennial Report, 1899–1900* (St. Cloud, Minn.: 1900), 9; *Seventh Biennial Report, 1908–1910*, 10; *Eleventh Biennial Report, 1917–1918* (Stillwater, Minn.: 1918), 3–4; *Twelfth Biennial Report, 1919–1920*, 2, 35.

38. Ironically, during the Progressive Era, the keepers of the Minnesota Reformatory made fewer changes in the Elmira system than their New York counterparts. Elmira's managers were greatly influenced by psychological and eugenic theories and, accordingly, introduced a new—but less optimistic—version of prison science, which was based on psychoeugenics: Pisciotta, *Benevolent Repression*, 104–26.

39. Minnesota State Reformatory, *Fifth Annual Report, 1892*, 6; *Second Biennial Report, 1899–1900*, 5.

40. Foucault, *Discipline and Punish*, 129, 242. My purpose is to apply Foucault's key themes, not provide a detailed critique of his work. David Garland, *Punishment and Modern Society: A Study in Social Theory* (Chicago: 1990) provides a thorough analysis of the strengths and shortcomings of Foucault's work, especially chap. 6 and 7.

41. Foucault, *Discipline and Punish*, 169.

42. Garland, *Punishment and Modern Society*, 170–75.

43. Erving Goffman, *Asylums: Essays on the Social Situation of Mental Patients and Other Inmates* (Garden City, N.Y.: 1961), 189.

44. Gresham Sykes, *The Society of Captives: A Study of a Maximum Security Prison* (Princeton, N.J.: 1958), 63–83. Sykes's study describes the inmate social world and inmate subculture at the Trenton State Prison in the 1950s, but the "pains of imprisonment" can be found in other adult prisons, juvenile reformatories, and adult reformatories.

45. Goffman, *Asylums*, 189.

46. "Inmate History and Record, 1912–1913," Case History #3023, 134.

47. Minnesota State Reformatory, "Misconduct Record, 1889–1897," 7–8: Records of the St. Cloud State Reformatory, State Archives, Minnesota State Historical Society, St. Paul; "Convict Register, 1896–1897," Case History #112, 16.

48. "Misconduct Record, 1889–1897," 29; "Convict Register, 1889–1897," Case History #191, 28.

49. Minnesota State Reformatory, "Solitary Register, 1907–1912": Records of the St. Cloud State Reformatory, State Archives, Minnesota State Historical Society, St. Paul.

50. Minnesota State Reformatory, *Fourth Biennial Report, 1903–1904*, 13–15.

51. Minnesota State Reformatory, *Third Biennial Report, 1901–1902* (St. Cloud, Minn.: 1902), 2. Systems for tracking recidivists were primitive in the late-nineteenth and early twentieth centuries. Reformatory keepers relied on court records, reports from the community, and interviews with inmates to determine recidivism. But it was difficult—if not impossible—to determine whether an inmate had served time in another state; and, as might be expected, inmates sometimes used aliases and lied about previous incarcerations. The "first time offender" commitment clause was, then, difficult to enforce.

52. Minnesota State Reformatory, *First Annual Report, 1889*, 3; *Fourth Biennial Report, 1903–1904*, 4.

53. Minnesota State Reformatory, *Fourth Biennial Report, 1903–1904*, 13–14; *Fifth Biennial Report, 1905–1906* (St. Cloud, Minn.: 1906), 15–16, 35.

54. Minnesota State Reformatory, *Second Biennial Report, 1899–1900*, 8; *Third Biennial Report, 1901–1902*, 1; *Eighth Biennial Report, 1910–1912* (n.p., n.d.), 32.

55. "Inmate History and Record, 1912–1913," Case History #2931, 42–43.

56. "Inmate History and Record, 1902–1904," Case History #1522, 122; Minnesota State Reformatory, *Fourth Biennial Report, 1903–1904*, 22.

57. "Convict Register, 1889–1897," Case History #606, 87; Minnesota State Reformatory, *Eighth and Ninth Annual Reports, 1895–1896*, 31.

58. Garland, *Punishment and Welfare*, 238.

59. Simon, *Poor Discipline: Parole and the Social Control of the Underclass, 1890–1990* (Chicago: 1993), 52. The social control dimensions of parole and other forms of community based corrections have also been analyzed by Andrew T. Scull, *Decarceration: Community Treatment and the Deviant—A Radical View*, 2nd ed. (New Brunswick, N.J.: 1984) and Stanley Cohen, *Visions of Social Control: Crime, Punishment and Classification* (Cambridge, U.K.: 1985). Rothman's *Conscience and Convenience*, 159–201, provides an excellent analysis of the promise and practice of parole.

60. Simon, *Poor Discipline*, 45.

61. Simon, *Poor Discipline*, 17–38, traces the roots of the "disciplinary parole" system—which dominated American corrections from the 1880s through the 1950s—to medieval England and the system of "suretyship." Under the system of suretyship a private citizen would vouch for the good character and behavior of another person. This was an early form of community supervision in which citizens assumed the primary responsibility for detecting crime (i.e., "surveillance") and promoting "good behavior." Unfortunately, it is difficult to determine from the records of the Minnesota Reformatory whether citizens played an active role in the supervision of parolees. The parole board solicited four or five prerelease recommendations from former employ-

ers, clergymen, neighbors, judges, attorneys, and police officials who knew the inmate. But, it was not clear that they played a central role in supervision.

62. Whittier, "The Prisoner on Parole," 305.

63. Minnesota State Reformatory, *Fifth Biennial Report, 1905–1906*, 9.

64. Minnesota State Reformatory, *Seventh Biennial Report, 1908–1910*, 66.

65. Ibid., 9.

66. Minnesota State Reformatory, *Tenth Biennial Report, 1915–1916*, 47; *Eleventh Biennial Report, 1917–1918*, 45.

67. Minnesota State Reformatory, Board of Parole Correspondence, "Monthly Report of H. B. Whittier—December 1919," and "Monthly Report of D. H. Knickerbacker—August 1919." The parole officers also spent a great deal of time answering parole-related questions for the superintendent and managers; "Superintendent's Correspondence, General, 1889–1922," and "Minutes of the Board of Managers and Board of Control, 1892–1902," *passim* Records of the St. Cloud State Reformatory, State Archives, Minnesota Historical Society, St. Paul.

68. Children released on parole from juvenile institutions were also treated as economic commodities: Beverly Smith, "Female Admissions and Paroles of the Western House of Refuge in the 1880s: An Historical Example of Community Corrections," *Journal of Research in Crime and Delinquency* 26:1 (1989): 36–66; and Alexander W. Pisciotta, "Child Saving or Child Brokerage? The Theory and Practice of Indenture and Parole at the New York House of Refuge, 1825–1935," in *History of Juvenile Delinquency*, vol. 2, ed. Albert G. Hess and Priscilla F. Clement (Aalen, Germany: 1993), 533–55.

69. Minnesota State Reformatory, *Tenth Biennial Report, 1915–1916*, 46.

70. Minnesota State Reformatory, *Seventh Biennial Report, 1908–1910*, 66. Agent Barncard's concern about the economic exploitation of parolees was shared by James Comfort, the parole officer at the Indiana State Reformatory: "Many employers of labor are glad to engage these men, for the rules that paroled men 'shall obey the law, avoid evil associations, abstain from intoxicating liquor or going places where it is sold,' and report once a month to the Management, insure steady, painstaking and punctual work on the part of men sent out from the Institution": Indiana Reformatory, *Second Biennial Report, 1899–1900* (Jeffersonville, Ind.: n.d.), 22.

71. Minnesota State Reformatory, "Paroled Men, Offering Employment," letter from S. McGuire—14 March 1916: Records of the St. Cloud State Reformatory, State Archives, Minnesota State Historical Society, St. Paul.

72. Ibid., letter from W. L. Chandler—30 August 1916, letter from Pat Dooley—24 August 1916, letter from O. R. Ondler—13 March 1918, and letter from O. A. Lindberg—4 March 1918.

73. Minnesota State Reformatory, "Board of Parole Correspondence," letter from D. H. Knickerbacker to H. K. W. Scott—12 March 1918, and letter from D. H. Knickerbacker to H. K. W. Scott—20 February 1919.

74. Minnesota State Reformatory, Board of Control: "The Agent's Correspondence, 1909–1910," letter from F. A. Whittier to Frank L. Randall—15 June 1900. Despite their antipolicing orientation, the parole officers made a concerted effort to return parole violators. They circulated wanted posters and offered rewards of $25 and $50: "Escapee Record, 1913," and "Superintendent's Correspondence Regarding Fugitives, 1900": Records of the St. Cloud State Reformatory, State Archives, Minnesota Historical Society, St. Paul.

75. The institution kept summary parole statistics for 1890–1900. Between 1890 and 1900, there were 1,163 inmates committed to the institution, 781 (67.1 percent) were paroled, and 136 inmates (17.4 percent) violated their parole by committing a new criminal offense, drinking, or leaving their place of employment. Twenty-nine (21.3 percent) inmates received a second parole, and 13 (44.8 percent) broke it; 9 (69.2 percent) inmates received a third parole, and 3 (33.3 percent) broke that: *Second Biennial Report, 1899–1900*, 2. Note: The pages in this report are, for some reason, repeated. This is page 2 under "Statistics of Inmates."

76. Minnesota State Reformatory, "Board of Parole Correspondence," letter from D. H. Knickerbacker to H. K. W. Scott—16 May 1919.

77. Modern criminologists—especially conservatives—often characterize indeterminate sentencing and parole as liberal reforms that shorten sentences. In fact, indeterminate sentencing was introduced to lengthen sentences. Henry Swearingen, a member of Minnesota's parole board, assured critics that indeterminate sentences were "twice as long as that served by those who were under the old [fixed-sentencing] plan": "The Indeterminate Sentence and Parole from the Viewpoint of Parole Commissioner," 316.

78. Minnesota State Reformatory, "Board of Parole Correspondence," Summary of Inmate Testimony Before the Parole Board—15 February 1916.

79. This observation supports the contention of radical-Marxist historians—for example, Georg Rusche and Otto Kirchheimer, *Punishment and Social Structure* (New York: 1939)—that penal systems reflect labor conditions and serve the economic needs of the state. However, this notion must be tempered. The fate of Minnesota's economy, to be sure, was not affected significantly by the labor of several hundred parolees.

80. Garland, *Punishment and Welfare*, 239.

81. Ibid., 238.

CHAPTER 3

Violent Crime on the Western Frontier: The Experience of the Idaho Territory, 1863–90

Robert G. Waite

Few topics in American history have attracted as much attention as violence and crime on the western frontier. Beginning in the mid-nineteenth century, as the frontier pushed steadily westward, correspondents provided eastern newspapers with a steady stream of accounts of shoot-outs and vigilante actions. The number of pulp novels dealing with bandits, outlaws, and desperados soared as the reading public hungered for accounts of crime and violence in the other parts of the country.[1] The image of the western frontier as a violent place where young men (and women) would pull a gun and shoot it out over the slightest provocation has endured in both print and film. These were years when, as Richard Maxwell Brown wrote recently, "the violence of the region was not only heavy but destined to become an enduring aspect of the national mythology."[2] Frontier violence is very much a part of the country's history.

Since the 1960s historians have devoted considerable attention to violence and crime in America, and the view of the western frontier has been clarified. A number of local studies have revealed that this was a region in which acts of violence and brutal crimes were common in a large number of communities but were absent in others. Scholars studying crime and violence face the continuing problem of sources. In frontier areas, where law enforcement and any form of centralized government were just forming or largely absent, accurate figures are lacking. The reliability of criminal data remains an issue of debate even to the present date in the most populated and extensively policed urban centers. With the lack of data for the western frontier in the nineteenth century, how can the crime rate best be gauged? How can the factors that contributed to the image of a violent and lawless area be identified, and how reliable are they? This chapter offers a look at violent crime in the Idaho Territory, and it examines the crime problem largely through the view of the regional press.

THE IDAHO FRONTIER

Throughout the years of territorial rule in Idaho, residents viewed violent and serious crime as a major problem and a threat to the future of the territory. As miners flocked to the gold and silver fields of Idaho in the 1860s, fortunes were made and lost quickly, often illegally. The precious minerals were packed out by stagecoach or on horseback, making the new wealth vulnerable to thieves and the miners targets of violence. In addition, most men carried firearms and they did not shy from using them. Lawlessness and acts of violence became distressingly frequent. *The Idaho Tri-Weekly Statesman*, a leading territorial newspaper, described the conditions of the mining camps and wrote that "lured by the scent of gold and the hope of plunder, idle, dissolute and vicious adventurers from many other quarters and from various distances" came to the Idaho Territory. "To these are joined the resident wrong, bad element with which every community is to some extent affected." Furthermore, the establishment of an effective law enforcement system came only gradually to the Idaho Territory.[3] Acts of lawlessness were recorded most often in the territorial newspapers, which regularly carried accounts of shootings, robberies, assaults, murders, and trials. The newspapers strived to keep the reading public of the Idaho Territory informed about crime, a topic that also helped sell newspapers.[4]

Local newspapers frequently are reliable in gauging crime, particularly violent crime, and the public's reaction to what one newspaperman in the Idaho Territory called "this era of violence and crime."[5] While journalists did not record or document every criminal deed, they did keep track of the more serious and violent offenses. Although reports are sketchy for the 1860s, numerous accounts of shootings, assaults, robberies, and murders can be found in the newspapers published during the 1870s and 1880s, as society and the criminal justice system in the Idaho Territory became more established and better organized. Overall the figures were not particularly high—at least thirty reported killings during each of the decades. More important than the actual figures were the concern and anguish caused by these acts of violence, and these sentiments were widespread and genuine.[6]

In the absence of extensive police and court records for the western frontier, newspaper accounts provide the most extensive and reliable information on patterns and incidents of violent crime.[7] They offer a reasonably accurate measurement of the frequency of serious offenses, although the number of murders cited is sometimes exaggerated. Furthermore, reporters and editors of local newspapers reflected, or even shaped, popular attitudes toward law enforcement and crime. It is clear that the concern of the general public with the crime problem was mounting steadily. As the social and legal systems matured, so too did attitudes toward crime. Demands for the control of serious offenses grew more common and vociferous, as citizens and even political leaders called for greater protection in their new communities.[8]

MOUNTING CONCERNS ABOUT CRIME

During territorial rule in Idaho there were good reasons for citizens to be worried about crime and for newspapers to speak out against the prevailing lawlessness. Already in 1870 *The Idaho Tri-Weekly Statesman* reported: "Something like two hundred [men] have been hurried into eternity during the last eight years at the hands of violence—a large proportion being downright murders." Of those involved in these crimes, only five killers were apprehended, found guilty of first-degree murder, and hanged.[9] Another assessment of the problem appeared in the *Coeur d'Alene Weekly Eagle*, which commented in 1884 that "two or three hundred bad men have escaped the hangman's noose and the mobs since the organization of the territory, who richly deserved death" [sic].[10]

While the figure of several hundred bad men was an exaggeration, one reporter offered an opinion on why more offenders had not been prosecuted fully. He suggested that many of the criminals had, in fact, left the Idaho Territory and "got killed or hung" somewhere else in the West. Most newspaper editors were, however, not so confident. In 1870, for example, *The Idaho Tri-Weekly Statesman* blamed the legal system for the violent crime problem, stating that "one or two [murderers], we believe, by some mismanagement, are in prison but will no doubt be released at the term of court now held at Idaho. When to punish for murder is the exception and not the rule, and frequency of the crime ceases to excite astonishment."[11] The high incidence of murder made violence a part of everyday life in the Idaho Territory.

Although the territorial newspapers of the 1860s often reported on acts of violence, the details of the specific crimes were frequently sparse. The *Boise News*, for example, ran an article in the fall of 1863 about a murder that had occurred on the Middle Boise River, somewhere between Moore's Creek and the North Boise River. A traveler who passed the "grave with a bloody axe" three weeks after the killing gave the information to the newspaper. He told the newspaper that at the head of the makeshift grave was a note reading simply "Howard, murdered 7th of September." No further identification of the victim or the murderer was available, and no report of an arrest ever appeared.[12]

THE MURDER OF A PROMINENT CITIZEN

The November 1863 murder of Lloyd Magruder, "a gentleman well known and universally esteemed," attracted much attention throughout the territory.

The senseless killing outraged the public, and the *Boise News* reported: "Often we have heard and read of fiendish murder, unprovoked except by sordid greed of gold and wanton and depraved hearts, but never has anything come home to us with such terrible distinctness as this." Those accused, described as "a band of hell-deserving miscreants," had robbed Magruder of $50,000 and then killed him.[13]

The Magruder murder sparked an extensive manhunt, with the sheriff beginning pursuit immediately. He picked up the trail and tracked the suspects all the way to Portland, where he made the arrest. The suspects were returned to Idaho, and the trial began in early 1864. The *Boise News* carried regular accounts. It was a speedy trial, and on February 21, the court returned its verdict. On the first ballot the jury found the defendants guilty of first-degree murder and sentenced them to death by hanging on March 4 at Lewiston. The *Boise News* continued its reporting on the events leading up to the execution. Immediately following the trial, the three men were separated from each other, and they "exhibited an inclination to be communicative upon the subject of the murder." For the two weeks preceding the hanging, they were permitted to be together and, as the newspaper reported, "all former signs of penitence, for the awful crime of which they stood convicted, disappeared, and instead the most ribald jests and sacrilegious allusions followed."[14]

Despite the apparent contempt of the condemned prisoners, local citizens did have a Catholic priest "minister to their spiritual wants," and he remained with them until the end, the *Boise News* reported. The night before the execution the prisoners each received morphine to help them sleep. At 11:00 the next morning, "the Infantry from Fort Lapwai entered town and the vehicle that was to convey the prisoners and their guard to the gallows, approached." At 12:15 the troops lined up behind the wagon, and the handcuffed prisoners were escorted out of the jail. They were led to the wagon, each placed between two guards. At the gallows the soldiers got out of the wagon and stood guard while the condemned were led to the scaffold.[15]

A newspaper reporter also described the execution: Each man was first escorted to the gallows and climbed the steps. While one of the condemned, the reporter wrote, "mounted the steps in a quick, tripping manner," another "followed with a slow, steady and firm step, with the appearance of as little concern as though treading the public thoroughfare an unsuspected man." The last of the condemned "followed up with an unsteady step like one laboring under an insupportable burden of mental agony." Once all three were on the gallows, the men sat in chairs, listening "attentively to the exhortations of the Minister and the short prayer customary on such occasions."[16]

When the prayer was completed each of the condemned was given the opportunity to address the crowd. According to accounts, one of the convicted took hold "of the rope that was soon to pass over his head. He held it up and remarked that it would soon end his career, and that it would strangle an innocent man." The next to speak looked at his two partners and told them that "he could in five minutes clear both the others." But to do so, he "would have to implicate seven other men, one of whom was dearer to him than life." The last of the condemned "attempted to speak, which was a difficult matter, as he was laboring under a paroxysm, evidently of fear of or anger." He then shouted out that he was an innocent man.[17]

As soon as the formalities had been completed, the sheriff and his deputy moved from one to the other, adjusting the ropes around the necks of the condemned killers who offered "various suggestions." One even stepped forward to make sure "that it was all arranged right." With the ropes set, the sheriff asked the condemned if they were ready. When the affirmative reply came, "the crank was moved, the fatal drop was heard, and the three bodies at the same instant were suspended through the platform." They were left hanging for 30 minutes, and then "they were pronounced dead by Dr. M. A. Kelly, cut down and placed in their coffins."[18]

Despite the press coverage given to this execution and the fatal ending of some killers, violent crime in the Idaho Territory continued unabated; executions appeared to have little deterrent effect. And it was not long before territorial newspapers reported the killing of yet another prominent citizen. Late in January 1864 the *Boise News* described how one of its community's "most quiet and peaceful citizens" had been killed "under circumstances that betrayed on the part of his murderer a degree of malignity of heart and a recklessness of human life seldom equaled and never excelled, even in the most uncivilized communities." The newspaper concluded that "it is time a stop should be put to such lawlessness." And it suggested that tough "punishment will be meted out to offenders against the peace and good order of society as they severally deserve, and particularly should an example be made of those who set so light a value on the lives of others." Such sentiments of outrage were common in territorial newspapers.[19]

Over the next couple of weeks the *Boise News* carried accounts of two additional murders. One was committed by a woman who shot a neighbor for "remarks she considered insulting." In another case a "well known and respected citizen" was gunned down. These crimes and several other shootings led a reporter to conclude that "The climate must have the effect to set men shooting that never shot before, on the same principle that men, women and children are said to be seized with an uncontrollable inclination to steal horses after inhaling the atmosphere of the Dales for a few months however honest they may have previously been."[20]

VIGILANCE COMMITTEES

The frequency of violent crime and the criminal justice system's seeming inability to curb it led some Bannock City residents to talk about organizing a "vigilance committee" in the fall of 1863. Alarmed by the shooting of a miner, they wanted "to try the case outside the forms of law, better counsels prevailed, however, and it was considered best to let the law take its course and abide by the result," the *Idaho World* reported. Occasionally, mobs did storm jails, seizing the suspected killer and taking him to a nearby site to be lynched. By 1884, according to the *Coeur d'Alene Weekly Eagle*, "seven illegal executions" had occurred in the Idaho Territory.[21]

When feelings in a community ran high against a suspected criminal, the authorities sometimes would move him to another town. For example, after the funeral of John Coray, a popular Idaho City resident gunned down in September 1864, the deputy sheriff suspected that a mob might attempt to take Thomas Fitz Gibbons, the accused, forcibly from the county jail. A group of several hundred assembled "for the purpose of executing summarily with lynch law punishment." The deputy, as a "precautionary move," had placed a large posse in the jail yard, and he persuaded the crowd to disperse.[22]

The *Boise News* reported that the shooting of two residents in late 1863 prompted citizens in Placerville to talk about forming a vigilance committee, "hoping by breaking the laws themselves to induce others to respect them." One of the killings had taken place on Christmas Day when Hugh Donohue, "furiously drunk," went into a saloon with his pistol drawn and called on "someone to fight him." Friends tried to disarm him, but he refused and barricaded himself in a corner. He then began firing, killing one person before escaping.[23]

Public outrage over such random acts of violence remained strong in the Idaho Territory. Three murders along the Placerville Road on June 4, 1865, for example, attracted a great deal of local attention during the trial of the alleged killers. According to the local newspaper, a "large crowd" had watched the court proceedings, and throughout the community "strong feeling against the prisoners" prevailed. The sheriff ordered that the suspects be taken to another jail to provide some additional protection from a feared vigilante action.[24]

Another murder in Boise during April 1866 led to the arrest of a soldier, who was held in confinement at the military post "until the matter should undergo a judicial examination." With public sentiment running high, a group of "fifteen to twenty five" men overpowered the guards, "threatening death if they resisted." The vigilantes took the suspect away, assaulted him, and broke several of his bones before lynching him. A note posted near the body declared this act to be simply "the Commencement." Other such acts would follow.[25]

The lynching of the soldier, taken by a mob from the fort's stockade, spurred strong feelings of indignation among the troops. Threats "of burning down the town" were made, and the local vigilance committee posted "a constant guard" each night "on all the street corners for protection." The local newspaper strongly condemned the action taken by the vigilance committee. By lynching a suspected killer and "by assuming this responsibility, the Vigilantes placed themselves in the same category with their victim. If he was guilty, so were they. If he placed himself beyond the law and beyond mercy, so have they. His guilt is their guilt. The crime of one is no greater than the crime of the other." Furthermore, "once the barriers of law and public security are thrown down, there is no protection for anyone, guilty or innocent."[26]

Another newspaper, the *Idaho World*, commented, "Who wants this state of things in Idaho Territory? Who wants a gang of irresponsible outlaws to control the Territory—to murder its people, a gang to make their individual hates and resentments and interests the governing power of society?" The newspaper feared that such acts would cause more violence and described the "evil war" and "the destruction of every personal security which must grow out of a persistence of these acts." The courts and the territorial laws, it asserted, ought to handle these matters.[27] The territorial governor, however, was more optimistic, and he told the legislature in 1866 that "Everywhere in our Territory, the increased promptness and stability of our courts is looked upon as a just source of increased confidence on the part of the people."[28]

During the mid-1860s, the activities of vigilance committees in the Idaho Territory increased, and more newspapers began to speak out against their actions. An April 1866 incident in Boise City prompted the *Idaho World* to write "Matters are being carried with a high hand," and "Lawless recklessness has found a vent, and broken out in the shape of murder, committed by the shadowy, veiled form of a Vigilance Committee." The editor likened the group's activities to that of "an assassin stealing in the darkness to its crimes."[29]

There were other reasons for public concern about violence by criminals as well as by the vigilance committees. Some residents of the Idaho Territory, for example, feared the high rate of violent crime would frighten prospective settlers. As a journalist wrote in March 1864, "We do not offer an asylum for the outcasts of other countries where they can, with impunity, begin anew their outrages against law and good government, but we will offer quiet, peaceable homes to those lovers of good order who see fit to cast their lot with us."[30] Already in the early years of the territory, there existed a real desire for law and order that would ensure a bright future.

TERRITORIAL COURTS

Despite such noble ideas, there was still a great deal for law enforcement officials to do. During the first two months of 1864 the grand jury in Boise County handled 47 cases, the bulk of which dealt with murder or assault with the intent to commit murder. A dozen of these cases involved first- or second-degree murder, while there were only 2 cases each of robbery and grand larceny and 4 cases of exhibiting a deadly weapon. In April 1864 the district court handed down several indictments, but most of the serious cases were continued over into the next session. The authorities nevertheless stayed busy; an additional 10 shootings were reported in the newspapers during the rest of the year.[31]

Judging from newspaper accounts, Idaho territorial courts appear to have exercised care in prosecuting capital cases. Before retiring to deliberate in the case of Ferdinand Patterson in November 1865, the members of the jury received lengthy instructions from the judge. While congratulating them for their patience and attentiveness during the trial, Judge McBride reminded them of their responsibility. Their decision, he told them, should be reached after careful thought, discussion, and a weighing of the evidence. The members of the jury should "discard all feeling, all passion, all prejudice, and in the face of God, and regardless of the wrath of man, examine and determine what are the facts of the bloody tragedy, to the story of which you have listened."[32]

Patterson's trial had been impassioned, with persuasive arguments coming from both the prosecution and the defense. In his statement to the jury, printed in the *Idaho World* newspaper, Judge McBride cautioned against "the appeals to your passions made by the counsel of either side of this case." The judge explained further that "the object of the employment of professional gentlemen in these trials is to aid in educing the truth and to assist the jury in coming to a just conclusion." While recognizing the "indispensable importance of that aid, we should not let its influence to extend beyond its legitimate bounds."[33]

Judge McBride had additional instructions for the jury in which he provided directions for evaluating the testimony and circumstances of the fatal shooting. He described to the members of the jury a crucial factor in determining the degree of guilt of the defendant: "When the fact of a homicide is found, and that the accused is guilty of killing it becomes necessary to enquire whether it was malicious and premeditated, and if those facts are established, the case for the prosecution is made out."[34]

Since the evidence had already established that Ferdinand Patterson killed Sumner Pinkham, it was now up to the jury to determine the issue of "malice aforethought." Judge McBride advised that it might be proved by "the manner and circumstances of the homicide." For, "if a person is slain by another and the weapon used is a deadly one,—which would only be used in a case where life was actually sought,—the law presumes from the manner of the killing and the weapon used that it was done of malice purpose and aforethought." Once this precondition was established, the accused "can only escape from punishment by over throwing the presumptions of law and showing that it is either a lower grade of the offense, or that is excusable or justifiable." The judge added lengthy comments, summarizing each possible decision that could be reached by the jury and its meaning under the law.[35]

Judge McBride concluded his instructions by reminding the members of the jury that "no outside pressure should be permitted to influence your verdict." Nor should they yield to "any morbid feeling that it is time somebody was punished in this community for crime." Rather, he continued, "You should take the facts, weigh them patiently and on your oath as honest men return them into Court, and whatever may be the consequence to others, you will have the satisfaction of having done your duty. I now commit the case to your charge."[36]

In those capital cases in which the jury returned a guilty verdict to the charge of first-degree murder, the territorial supreme court often reviewed the case. Occasionally, it called for a retrial. The conviction of Michael Dunn on first-degree murder was returned on May 2, 1866. The court sentenced him to death by hanging, and the execution was scheduled for July 6. On review, however, a second trial was ordered, and the result was a conviction on a lesser charge, second-degree murder.[37]

During the rest of the decade a number of murders and other crimes of violence were reported, though none attracted as much attention as the Patterson case. One individual convicted of manslaughter in the fall of 1866 was released on bond, but arrested after he failed to appear for his hearing. He told the judge that he had simply forgotten which day he was supposed to be in court. In another case a young man murdered his father, "chopping his head open with an axe." The *Idaho World* reported the man's lack of remorse, writing "he seemed entirely unconscious of the deed." Also in 1866 four prisoners were sent to the territorial prison after convictions for murder.[38]

Several other murders reported in the newspapers stemmed from arguments or disagreements, which commonly resulted in shootings. In March 1867 a "desperado" was shot dead at a "dancing party," and the killing was judged by the local newspaper as justified; the victim and "another rough, came uninvited to the party," apparently looking for trouble. In another case, disagreements between two business partners led to the shooting death of one at a railroad stage station on February 8, 1869. In the following summer, on July 4, the foreman of a mine near Idaho City was shot and killed by a drunken miner.[39] Also in 1869 Simeon Walter was tried for murder. Commenting on the case, the Silver City newspaper stated that "if guilty of the crime with which he is charged, [he] has developed a degree of human depravity seldom equalled." Walter was, in fact, convicted and sentenced to death.[40]

The trial of two Chinese men for the murder of Ah Son, a Chinese worker, in June 1869 attracted much attention. According to the local newspaper, the "novelty of swearing witnesses" for this case, which involved hacked off rooster's heads, broken saucers, and oaths written on paper and then burned, actually followed Chinese custom. The defendants were found guilty of first-degree murder and sentenced to death by hanging. One of the convicted, Ah Chop, committed suicide on November 24, 1869, thereby beating his own scheduled execution.[41]

In 1870 newspapermen in the Idaho Territory continued to be alarmed by the extent of violent crime. Under a headline reading "But Few Left," a reporter for the *Idaho Tri-Weekly Statesman* wrote that "of the crowd of reckless spirits who congregated at Boise City in 1864, there are none left in Idaho, and but few any where else." Their fates were mixed; "we can enumerate 10 or 12 of them who have been killed in bar room and street fights, others have been hung, and some who have not [but] ought to be." A number had found their final resting places in "graves unmarked," "planted about in different spots on the mountains and valleys."[42]

Even though only a few of the notorious troublemakers remained alive, the incidence of shootings and killings continued at about the same rate as in the 1860s. Early in 1870, for example, a reporter identified "four more men" who in the last two weeks had been shot to death. "And something like two hundred have been harried into eternity during the last eight years at the hands of violence—a large proportion of them being downright murders." During the same period, he added, "five murderers only have been hung." Although the newspaper reporter exaggerated the extent of the killings, the territorial governor was concerned. In his annual address to the legislature in 1870, Acting Governor E. J. Curtis urged the legislature to pass "some stringent law to suppress the practice of carrying concealed weapons." He also condemned "the deep and damning results of such a barbarous practice upon the moral status of the community."[43] But the carrying of concealed weapons persisted.

SOURCES OF VIOLENCE

Searching for additional causes of violent crime, a reporter blamed the territorial courts for the high incidence: "When to punish for murder is the exception and not the rule, the frequency of the crime ceases to excite astonishment. The ratio of bloody crime is increasing and will increase until the law is more rigorously enforced. This is a conclusion 'jumped at' from a long array of incontrovertible facts."[44]

Despite the mounting crime rate, citizens occasionally petitioned the territorial governor to reconsider a guilty verdict and to issue a pardon to a capital offender. Petitioning was common practice in less serious offenses, and it was not unusual for members of the jury that convicted the individual to add letters supporting a pardon. The success of these requests for reducing the sentences of convicted killers was mixed.[45]

Throughout the fall of 1870 territorial newspapers reported yet another increase in the number of murders. One case in September involved a well-known Mexican packer who was found dead, killed by an unknown assailant. The *Statesman* expressed its outrage, writing "The crime is bad enough when a man kills another in public brawl or private quarrel; but when an old man is murdered in a lonely spot in the darkness of night for the possession of a little money with no clue to the perpetrator of deed, it is attended with unusual horror." The crime remained "a painful mystery," and was "still shrouded in an impenetrable darkness that baffles the eye of justice." In a later article a reporter commented on the "growing impatience" of the public for a solution to this heinous crime, and the "nervous-thought [that only a] few dollars needed to repeat the crime."[46]

Although several other murders were committed during the fall months, only a handful gained more than passing notice in the newspapers. In one such case, the trial of Abbot in October 1870, a journalist commented that it was "remarkable in having excited a general public interest, even in this era of violence and crime, which is accounted for to some extent by the fact of Abbot having committed a double homicide—one of the victims being his own brother." During the two-week trial, the first jury was dismissed after it failed to reach a verdict, and a second jury voted for acquittal.[47]

The shooting stemmed from a long-standing dispute between Abbot and a local teacher, whom he had accused of having "attempted improper liberties with his little daughter." Threats followed, and a chance meeting on June 26, 1870, escalated from an argument to a gunfight. The teacher was killed. At the trial much conflicting evidence was presented as to who had shot Abbot's brother, another casualty. The proceedings "excited intense interest," for the teacher "left many warm friends, who felt his death should be avenged by the punishment of his slayer." But Abbot had many friends too, and his "most ardent friends, and the devotion and ability of them and his counsel have been fortunate in procuring his acquittal in the face of a vigorous prosecution and strong public sentiment."[48]

Reflecting on the trial, the *Statesman* considered it to have been "fairly and impartially conducted." The editor, concerned about the frequency of violent crime in the territory, added "The people themselves must reform. They must reform their ways of thinking and acting. They must cultivate more forbearance and less intemperate revenge toward one another for fancied or real wrongs." To support his position, the editor pointed out that even at this date, the public still occasionally took the law into its own hands. Mike Goldman was arrested shortly after he killed a man in White Pine. But "within half an hour" a vigilance committee pulled him out of jail and hanged him.[49]

VIOLENT CRIME PERSISTS

During the decade of the 1870s the territorial newspapers carried reports of more than two dozen homicides. In fact, killings became so common that headlines in the *Statesman* during the fall of 1870 simply read "And Still Another Murder" and "Simply Another Man Killed."[50] In discussing an incident from mid-September 1870, the *Statesman* wrote: "The last outrage on the public peace, which will probably result in the death of another citizen by violence, furnishes impressive comment on the pernicious practice of carrying concealed and deadly weapons." Barely a week later, another reporter commented, "The frequency with which the crime of murder is committed is rendering it monotonous." A November headline read simply "Another Terrible Tragedy."[51] After years of warning about the adverse impact of violence on potential settlers and well-being in the territory, newspaper editors had grown pessimistic and discouraged that violence would abate.

The circumstances of most of the killings were strikingly similar—a misunderstanding or quarrel escalated into a fight, and knives or a revolver were used with lethal consequences. For example, a dispute over debts owed to the other miners on Loon Creek led to the death of George Mayer in January 1871. According to reports he had fled the area, "leaving creditors holding the bag." But two men followed, caught up with him, and in the ensuing fight Mayer was shot dead. In another case later in the year a "drunken row" at Rocky Bar resulted in a miner fatally shooting his partner. The feeling against this killer was "intense and universal, and a fund was immediately subscribed by the citizens to defray the expense of prosecution."[52]

This pattern of violence persisted, as disputes over trivial issues continued to escalate to violence and death. In late 1874, for example, a "drinking spree" led to a fight and the shooting death of one man and the stabbing of another who was "not expected to survive." Later, in June 1876, an altercation in an Idaho City gambling house frequented by Chinese residents cost one man his life. According to the newspaper account, two Chinese held the victim while a third stabbed him in the heart. Another dispute over pay led to the shooting death of a man near the Cold Spring Station. The accused was acquitted a short time later.[53]

Territorial newspapers, concerned by the high murder rate, criticized the courts for spending more time on assault cases than on murders. One assault trial began on November 11, 1870, and it appeared that "great furor [is being] kicked up about a very small affair." The reporter added that "taking the past as evidence it would be far better for a man to use his weapon after drawing than it would to simply threaten," which is what the defendant in this case had done. In addition, the reporter wrote, "Those men who draw and kill generally get away with it, and that ends the matter—and they do not have to answer for drawing a deadly weapon afterwards. The rigor with which the above little case has been prosecuted leads us to suggest that hereafter the killing part be ignored altogether and the authorities go after the crime of simply drawing a weapon."[54]

The newspapers were also quick to report unusual cases, such as that of James Picket, a White miner arrested in September 1872 for the killing of an Indian. Picket had, according to a local newspaper, committed "a cruel cold blooded murder" of "Jack's squaw" near Pierce City. As a result of his crime, Picket was arraigned before the grand jury on the charge of first-degree murder. The trial began later in the year and continued into the spring. Finally, on June 3, 1873, the jury handed down a guilty verdict, and the defendant was sentenced to death. The *Statesman* maintained that Picket was the "first white man ever legally tried and executed for the murder of an Indian." The scheduled execution did not take place, however, and Picket was sent to the penitentiary.[55]

Territorial newspapers devoted a considerable amount of attention to the case of Tambiago, an Indian accused of killing a White man, which had a different outcome. According to reports, Tambiago shot "the first white man seen" after the November 1878 arrest of his brother on manslaughter charges. The *Statesman* commented that, "As it was an out and out cold blooded murder this Indian will be likely to stretch hemp." Tambiago came to trial in May, and he pleaded not guilty. The district court in Malad convicted him of first-degree murder and sentenced him to be "hanged by the neck until he is dead" on June 28, 1878.[56]

After his conviction and sentencing Tambiago was sent to the territorial prison in Boise. In mid-June construction of the scaffold for his hanging began, and Tambiago "seemed entirely unconcerned at the preparations that have been made for his death." The *Statesman* provided an account of his execution, which was open to the public. And "notwithstanding the heavy rain which poured down almost continuously yesterday, about 250 persons visited the Territorial prison and witnessed the execution of Tambiago." The newspaper further reported that the condemned had "walked composedly to the scaffold, mounted the steps with a firm tread and met his fate with the proverbial stoicism of his race."[57]

Judging from newspaper accounts, the patterns of violence for the 1880s, the last decade of territorial rule, remained much the same as the previous decades, although there was a steady increase in the number of killings. In early 1880 a list of prisoners in the penitentiary identified eight who were serving sentences of 10 to 20 years for second-degree murder convictions. The number of these prisoners grew, in part because of the improvement of the criminal justice system. This decade also witnessed several executions of murderers, which did little to deter crime.[58]

A number of murders stemmed from quarrels over minor issues. The *Statesman* reported a March 1880 shooting of two men, one of whom was killed; the "difficulty arose over four logs" with a "value of $2.00." This incident led the newspaper to comment: "The best way in the world for a man to get himself shot is to carry a pistol to shoot someone else, and have the habit of clasping his hand on his howitzer pocket at every little passion."[59] The carrying of a concealed weapon continued to be a serious problem.

The high incidence of violent crime did not always upset the editors of the territorial newspapers, who did not shy from passing moral judgment. The opinion of the *Wood River Times* on the shooting death of Bill Noyce in early August 1881 is apparent in the headlines: "A Good Riddance Of Bad Rubbish." According to this account two men rode to the saloon owned by Noyce at Campaign Station, about fifty miles east of Hailey. They asked for Noyce at the saloon and found him in a nearby cabin. The men then unloaded two shotgun blasts into Noyce and fled the scene. Noyce had been in the territory only for the past couple of years, "but has always been looked upon as a natural thief and a check guerilla." The killing was never solved.[60]

Two murders in the fall of 1882 attracted considerable attention. In November Samuel Ridgway was convicted of first-degree murder and sentenced to hang. But the governor reviewed the case and commuted the sentence; he announced simply that "I am satisfied that the ends of justice and the interests of society will be best subserved by the infliction of a lesser penalty." Ridgway received a sentence of life imprisonment at hard labor and was sent to the penitentiary. In another case, a capital offender, Ah Foo, was sentenced to death and scheduled to hang on February 2, 1883. Here there was no bid for clemency.[61]

Later in the year Michael Mooney, on trial for the October 27, 1881, murder of Joel Hinckley in Franklin, was convicted and sentenced to death. The execution was scheduled for January 20, 1882. The territorial supreme court rejected his appeal, and the execution was carried out on December 29, 1882. According to a newspaper account, "This morning . . . a peculiar stillness has prevailed and the expression of everyone you meet revealed that fact that he was aware that the day for the execution of Michael Mooney had arrived and that his life was only measured by hours." The scaffold had been constructed only that morning "a few feet from the jail door."[62]

During the mid-1880s three other executions took place in the territory. In the summer of 1883 George Pierson was sentenced to death for the killing of Johnny Hall, better known as Johnny-behind-the-rocks. While waiting to have his case heard by the territorial supreme court, Pierson escaped from the jail in Hailey, but he was captured a few days later. By the summer of 1884 his appeals were exhausted, and an effort to gain commutation from the governor also had failed. The *Statesman* commented that while these efforts were "no doubt commendable and we regret as much as any one to know that the life of a poor human being must be sacrificed on the scaffold," but, it continued, "as long as a man will deliberately take the life of a fellow being, so long must he pay the penalty of the law."[63]

A TERRITORIAL GOVERNOR SPEAKS OUT

The territorial governor responded to Pierson's clemency petitions with a statement that read in part, "I deeply regret that I have been unable to find in them sufficient reasons to warrant executive interference with the sentence pronounced upon the ill fated man by the Court; and most devoutly hope he may find mercy in Heaven." Pierson was executed in Hailey on August 1, 1884. An estimated eight hundred to one thousand spectators witnessed his death.[64]

The repeated acts of violence prompted the territorial governor in his 1884 address to the legislature to urge them to take action to curb this problem. "I direct your attention to the importance of expeditious and stringent legislation for the better preservation of law and order," he stated. "While in the main there is, perhaps, as much security for life and property now in Idaho as in other Territories, it cannot be gainsaid that we are far from having perfect order and complete security." In light of this the governor termed those who "avenge the slightest provocations with a 'gun' shot," a "source of public jeopardy [that] is great and threatening in proportion to the freedom of the government and the consequent limited restraint of the law." Furthermore, the public reaction had been one of outrage, for "no good citizen hears of any violation of law without being filled with fear, aversion or disgust." The governor concluded by reminding the legislatures that "the great majority of the people of this Territory possess the virtue of industry, frugality, moderation combined with energy, physical and moral courage, justice, benevolence, enterprise and good faith, and they should be, must be, protected against the vices and undisciplined passions of the few."[65]

The problem of violence persisted, and the brutal slaying of a Blackfoot man by Dr. E. J. O'Callahan on May 4, 1885, almost led to his lynching. According to reports O'Callahan got drunk after being fined for contempt of court. He asked another man to buy whiskey for him. When he returned, O'Callahan shot him five times. An early June trial resulted in his conviction on the charge of murder in the first degree; O'Callahan was sentenced to be executed in Blackfoot on June 17, 1885.[66]

The last two executions of the territorial years took place at sites other than the penitentiary. On September 19, 1885, "the earthly existence of the Chinese Kock Wah Choi, convicted of murder at Hailey, was abbreviated by means of rope and the sheriff," the *Statesman* reported. About two hundred persons witnessed the hanging. The final execution of the decade took place on June 9, 1886, in Mount Idaho. There, Theodore Warlick, a miner who had killed his partner, was hanged, and "the condemned man died with scarcely a struggle." This was also "the first execution of legal process by capital punishment ever witnessed in Idaho county."[67]

These executions did little, however, to curb the incidence of violent crime in the Idaho Territory, for during the 1880s more than thirty-five individuals were reported murdered. In April 1883 Walt Coffin was murdered while trying to arrest a suspect, and his death, the *Wood River News-Miner* commented, was the "only instance of an officer being killed in attempting an arrest that ever happened in the Territory." The newspaper went on to call the incident "an act of fiendishness unparalled in the annals of crime."[68] While that murder was exceptional, most killings followed the established pattern: killings resulted from arguments or drunken brawls, and most took place during the spring, summer, or fall months. For example, in early July 1883, Mark Johnson told a Mexican sitting in front of Boise's Overland Hotel that "It has been about a year since I shot a greaser." William Sues took offense, pulled his gun, and shot Johnson dead. Later that fall, two more shootings were reported in the *Statesman*.[69]

Other cases included the shooting death of James Daisy in April 1884. Authorities arrested Denis McCarty on charges of first-degree murder stemming from a disputed card game. The trial began in August and concluded later that month when the jury returned a verdict of guilty of murder in the second degree. On August 27 McCarty began serving a life sentence in the territorial penitentiary.[70] Later in the summer another murder attracted considerable attention. The body of a prominent Wood River Valley businessman, Aaron Morris, was found about a mile south of Ketchum—he had been robbed and shot in the head. Governor Bunn quickly offered a $1,000 reward for the arrest and conviction of the guilty party, and the reward was later raised to $5,000. Less than a week later the *Statesman* reported that three suspects had been arraigned on the charge of murder and held over for the October grand jury session.[71]

While accounts of further crimes of violence were not common in late 1884, the next spring recorded a number of homicides. In mid-February the *Statesman* reported on a "shooting scrape" that led to the conviction of a Silver City man for second-degree murder. In another case a young boy in Soda Springs shot and killed the owner of a local hotel. According to accounts, the shooting took place at a bar owned by the youngster's father. The reports on the child's age varied from 9 to 15 years old. Details on the shooting also varied. One report maintained that the victim, "better known as 'J. S. Bad Man,'" had walked into the saloon and begun "abusing the proprietor." The boy took offense and shot him through the heart. Another report claimed that the father and the victim had been drinking, while a different newspaper wrote that they had been wrestling "all in the best of humor" before the shooting. After the incident the boy and his father went to the authorities in Blackfoot. The youngster was placed on trial, convicted, and sentenced to eight years in the penitentiary.[72]

In mid-August the *Statesman* reported "Another Homicide," the account of a shooting death near Emmettsville that had resulted from a long-standing feud. In the fall a "cold blooded murder" took place at Soda Springs when a drunken cowboy forced another to "dance a jig for amusement," and his gun went off, killing the man. Other shootings were also reported.[73]

During the rest of the decade, several additional murders were reported. In July 1886, for example, James Jones was convicted for the murder of his wife, and he received a 15-year sentence for second-degree murder. In August widespread attention was given to the case of a sheepherder murdered near Arco. After Frank Armstrong was arrested for the shooting, he told authorities that other sheepherders had given him $25 for the job. The trial in Hailey continued through the fall, and on November 15 he was found guilty of first-degree murder and sentenced to "hang by the neck till you are dead, dead, dead."[74]

In 1886 two capital cases from Bingham County came before the territorial supreme court. One involved a double homicide at a mining camp, and the other the murder of a Pocatello woman by her husband. The newspaper, showing impatience with the number of appeals, commented that "It seems that all murder cases have to go through the supreme court in Idaho." The territory's high court upheld the second-degree murder conviction of Charles Evans in early 1888 and sentenced him to life imprisonment.[75]

With the decade and territorial rule coming to an end, only a few additional capital cases were reported. The killings continued, however, and displayed familiar patterns. A dispute over a mining claim precipitated the shotgun killing of a Rocky Bar miner. In Star a family quarrel led to the murder of an Ada County man in March 1889, and the killer's subsequent trial and conviction of second-degree murder attracted considerable interest in the local press.[76] In other cases a deputy sheriff was killed, and a shooting incident involving cavalry soldiers and "three notorious toughs" resulted in additional deaths.[77]

CONCLUSION

In the 1860s, 1870s, and 1880s local newspapers recorded most of the acts of violence committed in the Idaho Territory. And the newspapers revealed not only the frequency of murder on the frontier, but also the widespread concern that violence would discourage settlement. The newspapers of the Idaho Territory generally reflected, as well as shaped, public opinion toward crime, and the anxieties caused by the widespread violence were readily apparent. Already in the 1860s such concerns were voiced. Journalists rejected not only the shootings and killings, but also the vigilantes, the attempts of some citizens to administer their own justice.

Although common through the years of territorial rule, violence was by no means a daily occurrence, and the residents of the Idaho Territory struggled to control it. Concern among journalists about the incidence of violent crime remained strong during this time, and a number of them offered their views on its causes. Frequently, a misunderstanding or slight escalated into a fight and, with many well armed, a shooting was not an unlikely outcome. By the 1870s newspaper writers began voicing their opinions that the high incidence of violence stemmed from the fact that too many individuals carried weapons and, with the lack of an effective law enforcement system, they did not shy from using them.[78]

Increasingly, the rate of violent crime sparked resentment and outrage. Some residents attempted to act in place of a legal system, but the vigilante movement received only scorn from the territorial newspapers. Most settlers were eager to have a stable society emerge in the northern Rockies, and they wanted the Idaho Territory to grow, prosper, and become a safe home. For that to occur, centralized government and a law enforcement system that reached throughout the territory were essential. As the population increased, more settlers arrived, and the forces of order grew in strength. The public demanded changes, and a growing climate of respect for the law gradually replaced the violent frontier. Although weapons remained widespread, people became less willing to use them to settle an argument or dispute. Violence gradually declined, but it has remained a factor in Idaho's history.

NOTES

The views expressed in this article are solely those of the author and do not necessarily reflect those of the Department of Justice.

1. See, for example, Thos. J. Dimsdale, *The Vigilantes of Montana or Popular Justice in the Rocky Mountains* (Norman, Okla., 1953), which first appeared as a series of articles in the *Post* and was published as a book in 1866; and General D. J. Cook's *Hands Up; Or, Twenty Years of Detective Life in the Mountains and on the Plains* (Norman, Okla., 1958), which was published in 1882 and sold on trains. This genre of literature has been discussed by John G. Cawelti, *The Six-Gun Mystique*, 2nd rev. ed. (Bowling Green, Ohio, 1984); Christine Bold, *Selling the Wild West: Popular Western Fiction, 1860 to 1960* (Bloomington, Ind., 1987); Michael Denning, *Mechanic Accents: Dime Novels and Working-Class Culture in America* (London, 1987); and Cynthia S. Hamilton, *Western and Hard-Boiled Detective Fiction in America: From High Noon to Midnight* (Iowa City, 1987).

2. Richard Maxwell Brown, "Violence," in *The Oxford History of the American West*, ed. Clyde A. Milner II et al. (New York, 1994), 393.

3. "The Signs of the Times," *Idaho Tri-Weekly Statesman* (hereafter *ITS*), 17 April 1876. On the problems of establishing an effective court system in the Idaho Territory, see "The District Attorneyship," *ITS*, 13 October 1870; "Our Jury System," *ITS*, 31 December 1870; "House C.R. No. 9," *ITS*, 4 March 1871; "An Act Concerning the Practice in Territorial Courts," *ITS*, 25 April 1974. See also W. J. McConnell, *Early History of Idaho* (Caldwell, Idaho, 1913), 59–68, 100, 269–74; "Council Bill No. 73, An Act Entitled 'An Act to Amend An Act Entitled An Act Concerning Crimes and Punishments,'" Approved 4 February 1864, National Archives, Record Group 48, Interior Department Territorial Papers, Idaho, 1864–1890, microfilm 445, frame 229; Stuart H. Traub, "Reward, Bounty Hunters, and Criminal Justice in the West: 1865–1900," *Western Historical Quarterly* 9 (1988): 287–301; and R. E. Mather and F. E. Boswell, *Gold Camps Desperadoes: Violence, Crime, and Punishment on the Mining Frontier* (Norman, Okla., 1990), 81–106.

4. The crimes of violence referred to in this chapter include murder and manslaughter as defined in the penal code. See "Title VII: Of Crimes Against the Person," *Revised Statutes of Idaho* (Boise, 1887), 726–27. On the evolution of the legal definition of homicide in Idaho, see *Idaho Digest 1866 To Date*, vol. 5 (St. Paul, Minn., 1937), sections "I. The Homicide," "II. Murder," "III. Manslaughter," "IV. Assault With Intent To Kill," "V. Excusable or Justifiable Homicide," "VI. Indictment and Information," "VII. Evidence," "VIII. Trial," "IX. New Trial."

5. "The Trial of Abbot," *ITS*, 29 October 1870. On the trends in reporting violent crime, see Dane Archer and Rosemary Gartner, *Violence and Crime in Cross-National Perspective* (New Haven, 1984), 34–35.

6. In the absence of criminal statistics, historians have used newspapers to study crime on the western frontier. See, for example, Roger D. McGrath, *Gunfighters, Highwaymen & Vigilantes: Violence on the Frontier* (Berkeley, 1984), and George Thomson,

"The History of Penal Institutions in the Rocky Mountain West, 1846–1900" (Ph.D. diss., University of Colorado, 1965), 116–32. For a discussion of the development of criminal justice systems, see Ted Robert Gurr, "Development and Decay: Their Impact on Public Order in Western History," in *History and Crime: Implications for Criminal Justice Policy* (Beverly Hills, Calif., 1980), 31–52. The estimated number of killings in each decade of territorial rule comes from accounts in the various newspapers.

7. For an overview of the literature on crime in the Northwest, see Roland L. De Lorme, "Crime and Punishment in the Pacific Northwest Territories: A Bibliographic Essay," *Pacific Northwest Quarterly* 76 (1985): 42–51.

8. An October 1870 newspaper article suggested that "something like two hundred" men had been killed in the territory, a figure surely too high: "Four More," *ITS*, 6 October 1870; McConnell, *Early History of Idaho*, 254–55; *Biennial Message of William M. Gunn, Governor of Idaho, to the Thirteenth Session of the Legislative Assembly of Idaho Territory* (Boise City, 1884), 10–11. See also David R. Johnson, *American Law Enforcement: A History* (Arlington Heights. Ill., 1981), 89–104.

9. "Four More," *ITS*, 6 October 1870.

10. "Legal Executions in Idaho," *Coeur d'Alene Weekly Eagle*, 18 July 1884.

11. "Four More" and "And Still Another Murder," *ITS*, 24 September 1870. In those frontier areas where an effective police system existed crimes of violence were not serious problems; see William R. Morrison, "The North-West Mounted Police and the Klondike Gold Rush," in *Police Forces in History* (Beverly Hills, Calif., 1975), 263–76.

12. "Murder," *Boise News* (hereafter *BN*), 6 October 1863.

13. "Another Good Man Murdered," *BN*, 10 November 1863; "Lloyd Magruder," *BN*, 21 November 1863; "Trial and Sentence of David Howard, James P. Romain and Christopher Lover Before His Honor, Judge Parks, at Lewiston," *BN*, 13 February 1864; McConnell, *Early History of Idaho*, 142–51.

14. "Execution of the Magruder Murderers," *BN*, 26 March 1864; McConnell, *Early History of Idaho*, 152–60.

15. "Execution of the Magruder Murders."

16. Ibid.

17. Ibid.

18. Ibid.

19. "Murder Most Foul," *BN*, 9 January 1864; "Wells the Murderer," *BN*, 9 January 1864; McConnell, *Early History of Idaho*, 234–39, 275–80.

20. "Man Killed by a Woman" and "Examination of Holbrook," *BN*, 30 January 1864. See also "Singular Attack," *BN*, 12 March 1864, and "Death of Sim Oldham," *BN*, 19 March 1864.

21. "Legal executions in Idaho." See also "Judge McBride's Charge to the Jury in the Patterson Case," *Idaho World—Supplement*, 11 November 1865. On vigilantes see Ruth and Mike Dakis, "Guilty or Not Guilty? Vigilantes on Trial," *Idaho Yesterdays* 12 (1968): 1–5; Dimsdale, *Vigilantes of Montana*; and Helen Fitzgerald Sanders, ed., *X. Beidler: Vigilante* (Norman, Okla., 1957).

22. "Death of John Coray" and "Mob Matters," *BN*, 3 September 1864.

23. "Shooting at Placerville," *BN*, 2 January 1864.

24. "Three Murders on the Highway," *Idaho World* (hereafter *IW*), 10 June 1865; "Examination of Prisoners," *IW*, 17 June 1865; "Dead Body Found," *IW*, 17 February 1866.

25. "Vigilance Committees," *ITS*, 1 April 1866.

26. Ibid.

27. Ibid.

28. *First Annual Message of Governor Ballard, to the Legislature of Idaho Territory, Delivered December 5, 1866* (Boise City, 1866), 5–6.

29. "Vigilance Committees," *IW*, 14 April 1866; "The Vigilance Organization," *IW*, 11 August 1866. See also "Wife Murder & Suicide," *BN*, 5 December 1863.

30. "Grand Jury Report," *BN*, 19 March 1864.

31. Ibid. "District Court," *BN*, 2 April 1864; "District Court," *ITS*, 2 April 1864; "Met Bledsoe," *ITS*, 23 April 1864; "Killed" and "Another Fatal Shooting Affray," *BN*, 14 May 1864; "The Killing of Wash Smith," *BN*, 16 July 1864; "More Cutting and Shooting" and "Sheriff Pinkham," *BN*, 23 July 1864; "Shooting," *BN*, 13 August 1864; "Fatal Shooting," *BN*, 5 October 1864; "Another Murder," *BN*, 22 October 1864.

32. "Judge McBride's Charge to the Jury in the Patterson Case," *Idaho World—Supplement*, 11 November 1865.

33. Ibid.

34. Ibid. For detailed instructions to the jury by a territorial judge, see "Insanity. How Far It Constitutes A Defense For Murder," *Wood River Times* (hereafter *WRT*), The Hailey Case, 8 November 1882.

35. "Judge McBride's Charge to the Jury."

36. Ibid.

37. "Sentence of Michael Dunn" and "District Court Proceedings," *IW*, 23 February 1867.

38. "Re-Arrested," *IW*, 3 November 1866; "A Horrible Murder," *IW*, 9 February 1867. On the four murderers, see *First Biennial Report of the Territorial Prison Commissioner* (Boise City, 1868), 3–4.

39. "Killing at Rocky Bar," *IW*, 30 March 1867; "Homicide on Raft River," *ITS*, 9 February 1869; "The Murder at Idaho City," *Semi Weekly Tidal Wave* (hereafter *SWTW*), 13 July 1869; "Insane Man," *SWTW*, 18 May 1869; "Chinaman Killed," *SWTW*, 4 June 1869.

40. "Sim Walters," *SWTW*, 15 December 1868; "Trial and Sentence of Simeon Walters," *SWTW*, 30 March 1869.

41. "Trial of Ah Chop and Ah Sam," *SWTW*, 25 June 1869; "Hung Himself," *SWTW*, 25 November 1869.

42. "But Few Left," *ITS*, 18 October 1870.

43. "Four More"; *The Biennial Message of E. J. Curtis, Acting Governor of Idaho, to the Sixth Session of the Legislature of Idaho Territory* (Boise City, 1870), 10.

44. "Four More."

45. "Firmness in Duty," *ITS*, 25 August 1870.

46. "And Still Another Murder. The Crime Grows Monotonous," *ITS*, 24 September 1870; "Sota the Packer," *ITS*, 27 September 1870; "Still a Mystery," *ITS*, 1 October 1870.

47. "Bring Them to Justice," *ITS*, 13 September 1870; "Another Murder, Probably," *ITS*, 13 September 1870; "En Route," *ITS*, 10 November 1870. "The Trial of Abbot."

48. "The Trial of Abbot."

49. Ibid. "Aid the Debt," *ITS*, 24 December 1870.

50. "And Still Another Murder" and "Simply Another Man Killed," *ITS*, 10 November 1870.

51. "The Last Outrage," *ITS*, 15 September 1870; "And Still Another Murder" and "Another Terrible Tragedy," *ITS*, 3 November 1870.

52. "The Killing of George Mayer," *ITS*, 28 January 1871; "Homicide at Rocky Bar," *ITS*, 5 September 1871.

53. "One Man Shot," *ITS*, 22 December 1874; "Chinaman Killed," *ITS*, 29 June 1876; "Shooting Affray—Man Killed," *ITS*, 22 August 1876; "Examination and Acquittal of Daniel McGinnis," *ITS*, 26 August 1876. See also "A Fatal Affray," *ITS*, 25 February 1879, and "Homicide," *ITS*, 14 June 1879.

54. "A Man Arrested Last Summer," *ITS*, 12 November 1870; "Case Not Settled Yet," *ITS*, 15 November 1870. On the courts, see "The Trial of Wethered," *ITS*, 19 November 1870, 22 November 1870, and 24 November 1870.

55. "The Homicide," *ITS*, 18 September 1872; "A White Man To Be Hung for Killing An Indian," *ITS*, 26 August 1873; "Convicts in Penitentiary," *ITS*, 5 June 1875.

56. "An Indian Murderer Caught," *ITS*, 19 January 1878; "In District Court, Third Judicial District of the Idaho Territory," AR 42/6, vol. #13, in "Tambiago file," Old Idaho Penitentiary, Boise, Idaho.

57. "Willing to Die, But Unwilling to Talk Much," *ITS*, 27 June 1878; "The Hanging of Tambiago," *ITS*, 29 June 1878.

58. "List of Prisoners in the Idaho Penitentiary," *ITS*, 5 February 1880; "United States Prisoners," *ITS*, 7 February 1880.

59. "Shooting Affray," *ITS*, 13 March 1880; "Murder At Blackfoot," *ITS*, 27 July 1880.

60. "Bill Noyce Dead. He Is Shot In Bed With His Wife. A Double Barreled Charge Poured Into Him. A Good Riddance Of Bad Rubbish," *WRT*, 3 August 1881.

61. "Ridgway's Sentence," *WRT*, 22 November 1882; "Proceedings of the District Court," *ITS*, 12 December 1882.

62. "The Gallows," *The Register*, 6 January 1883.

63. "George Pierson," *Wood River News-Miner* (hereafter *WRNM*), 17 August 1883; "Pierson," *WRNM*, 30 August 1883; "Pierson Captured," *WRNM*, 9 September 1883; "Pierson's Fate," *ITS*, 5 August 1884.

64. "Governor Bunn's Action in the Pierson Case," *ITS*, 31 July 1884; "Wood River Correspondence," *ITS*, 5 August 1884; Executive Department, "Requests-Commute-George Pierson," 30 July 1884, NA, RG 48, microfilm 191, roll 1.

65. *Biennial Message of William M. Buny, Governor of Idaho, to the Thirteenth Session of the Legislative Assembly of Idaho Territory* (Boise City, 1884), 10–11.

66. "A Brace of Murders," *ITS*, 5 May 1885; "Dr. O'Callaghan," *ITS*, 2 June 1885. "Dr. E. J. O'Callaghan," *ITS*, 14 July 1885.

67. "Warlick Hung," *ITS*, 15 June 1886; "The Recent Execution," *ITS*, 26 June 1886.

68. "Murder of Walt Coffin," *WRNM*, 26 April 1883; "The Coffin Murder," *WRNM*, 2 May 1883.

69. "Shooting at Boise City," *WRNM*, 8 July 1883; "Shooting at Shoshone," *WRNM*, 7 November 1883; "Shooting at Atlanta," *WRNM*, 8 November 1883.

70. "Homicide," *ITS*, 1 April 1884; "District Court Proceeding at Idaho City," *ITS*, 21 August 1884; "District Court Proceedings at Idaho City," *ITS*, 28 August 1884.

71. "The Wood River Murder," *ITS*, 21 August 1884; "The Morris Murder," *ITS*, 26 August 1884.

72. "Shooting Scrape," *ITS*, 14 February 1885; "Wm. H. Dewey," *ITS*, 19 February

1885; "A Shooting Affair," *ITS*, 28 April 1885; "A Shooting Affair," *ITS*, 30 April 1885; "A Nine Year Old Boy Shoots and Kills a 'Bad Man,'" *ITS*, 5 May 1885; "Published Accounts of the Shooting," *ITS*, 8 May 1885; "A Shocking Affair," *IW*, 8 May 1885; "Baker Boy," *ITS*, 2 June 1885.

73. "Another Homicide," *ITS*, 18 August 1885; "The Emmettsville Affray," *ITS*, 20 August 1885; "News From Payette," *ITS*, 22 August 1885; "Cold Blooded Murder," *ITS*, 13 October 1885; "Shooting Scrape" and "Charles Tennet," *ITS*, 15 October 1885.

74. "Case of James C. Jones," *ITS*, 20 July 1886; "Paul Klubert," *ITS*, 31 August 1886; "Sheriff Delivers," *ITS*, 2 September 1886; "In the First Degree," *ITS*, 16 November 1886; "Motion New Trial," *ITS*, 9 December 1886.

75. "Two Cases," *ITS*, 25 January 1888; "Supreme Court," *ITS*, 28 February 1888.

76. "Shooting at Rocky Bar," *WRNM*, 23 June 1888; "Murder in Ada County," *WRNM*, 23 March 1889; "Chasing the Murderer," ITS, 19 March 1889; "The Bedell Trial," ITS, 13 September 1889; "Bedell Sentenced," ITS, 22 September 1889.

77. "$1,000 Reward," *WRNM*, 14 July 1889; "Fifty-Eight Shots," *ITS*, 10 September 1889.

78. For other views, see Brown's essay "Violence."

CHAPTER 4

The Wendigo Killings: The Legal Penetration of Canadian Law into the Spirit World of the Ojibwa and Cree Indians

Sidney Harring

A series of wendigo killings brought to the attention of Canadian law around the turn of the twentieth century represent symbolically the complete extension of Canadian law over Native people. These killings, however, also represent the extent to which traditional society defied or ignored that law. Only one of these killings, *Regina v Machekequonabe*, led to a reported opinion. That opinion is one of the best-known Native law cases in the common law world, often cited for the proposition that the common law holds jurisdiction even when the Native people involved had never been exposed to Western law and were completely ignorant of it.[1] This was a foundational principle of British colonial law, extended around the world to diverse Native peoples who had no comprehension of its principles.[2] Machekequonabe, an Ojibwa, was found guilty of manslaughter in an 1896 trial for killing a "wendigo," an evil spirit clothed in human flesh.[3] At least six other wendigo killings were processed by Canadian law in the dozen or so years following *Machekequonabe*, and others had come to the attention of Canadian authorities before.[4] Furthermore, in additional cases it seems that Native people carefully distorted the facts of homicide cases to conceal that they were wendigo killings to protect their religious and cultural beliefs from Canadian law.[5]

THE WENDIGO IN OJIBWA AND CREE SOCIETY

There is an extensive anthropological literature on the wendigo[6] and on wendigo killings in Native Canada.[7] The wendigo lived in the cultural worlds of the Algonkian-speaking Indians of the Northeast, most commonly the Ojibwa and Cree tribes. They were cannibal spirits that could inhabit the bodies of living people, causing them to kill even members of their family.[8] In appearance:

[T]he windigo [*sic*] is a particularly abhorrent creature. He has a frightening and menacing mouth, wholly devoid of lips. He has tremendous, jagged teeth through which his breath flows with a sinister hissing, making a loud and eerie noise, audible for miles. His eyes are protuberant, something like those of an owl except that they are much bigger and roll in blood. His feet are almost a yard in length, with long, pointed heels and only one toe, the great toe. His hands are hideous with claw like fingers and fingernails. . . . His strength is prodigious. With one mighty stroke of his hand, he can disembowel a man or a dog. He rips off the surface of the earth as he wanders about, snapping off the tops of trees. . . . He seeks out victims, trailing them hauntingly and relentlessly, waiting until darkness before seizing and eating them. Whenever a hunter disappears, failing to return from the forest, the Indians invariably account for this misfortune by explaining that a windigo has devoured him. [He has] a heart of ice, [and] a body swelled to the size of a pine tree and as hard as stone, impenetrable by a bullet or arrow and insensitive to cold.[9]

The wendigo legends are graphic and detailed, threatening the daily lives of the Ojibwa and Cree hunters who had to go, alone or in small bands, into the forests every day for their livelihood. The wendigo, with such powers, was a real threat, not only on his own terms as a large, dangerous figure in the woods, but also because he could inhabit living Indians, turning a loved one into a killer and cannibal. This was perhaps especially dangerous given the dispersion of these Indians into small hunting and fishing bands for so much of the year, bands isolated from each other and at the mercy of the elements.[10] Since wendigos could not easily be killed, their existence also encouraged the development of a powerful tradition of sorcery in these bands.

This sorcery tradition merged with the customary law of the Ojibwa. Diamond Jenness describes the place of the wendigo in Ojibwa law at the Parry Sound Reserve. Although disputes between families or clans might be settled by the heads of household or clan leaders in council, many crimes, especially homicides, occurred in secret. In this situation, individuals might fear to inform or take action lest they be subject to sorcery later. Fear of sorcery was always present in the minds of the Indians. If a man discovered or suspected that another hunter was trespassing on his hunting grounds, he would not visit the trespasser's camp and demand redress because the wrongdoer might take offense and through witchcraft cause him to break through the ice or meet with some other misfortune. Instead, he would himself employ the witchcraft against his adversary or engage a medicine man for the same purpose.

Murder by violence was probably rare, but these Ojibwa attributed many, if not most, deaths to sorcery, which was murder in another form; and murder called for a compensating life unless the deed were compounded with goods or hunting territory. A convicted sorcerer might be killed at sight by the relatives of his victim, although the executioner still ran the risk of possible vengeance. The chief and council here assumed responsibility for the killing, legitimating it under customary law. They investigated serious cases of theft and alleged murder, summoned the accused man before them, and sanctioned the death penalty or a fixed amount of indemnity. If the culprit belonged to another band, they conducted the negotiations with the envoys that came to settle the issue.[11]

Wendigo mythology was central to Ojibwa law with a well-established traditional legal order, inseparable from religion, existing to resolve disputes and punish killers. Jenness gives one account of a wendigo killing, although he does not identify it as such. A man had camped in the forest with his wife and baby while on a long and unsuccessful hunt. While he was away, his wife killed their baby by putting it in a pot of boiling water. She then went to rejoin her people, trying to cover her trail. Her husband followed her, finding her in the wigwam of her people, sitting with the women on one side while the men sat on the other. "Here is the murderer," he cried, "she has killed our baby." Her eldest brother exclaimed, "Has she killed the baby?" Upon affirming it was true, he seized his war club and struck his sister dead. He then ordered a younger sister to go live with the man in her sister's place.[12]

The brother's action, carried out in the open in front of the men of the clan, was legal for it was an official sanction, an execution within the clan. He was not subject to retaliation for the only source of retaliation would have been the aggrieved relatives of his sister, and all of them had been present at the killing. This closed the matter. If she had been of another clan, a much more complex process would have occurred, with envoys of one clan negotiating with the other, attempting to get their sanction for the killing. If this was not done, they ran the risk of beginning a cycle of revenge as her relatives sought to avenge her death. Since most wendigo killings were carried out in secret, it was not easy to identify and punish the offenders.[13]

This execution contains much more detail, but is not very different from the wendigo execution described by George Nelson among the Cree in 1823. There, the members of a hunting band observed a member of their band become a wendigo. He himself recognized some of the signs and asked them to kill him on their first recognition of wendigo symptoms. They left his brother behind to kill him, but hid nearby to provide backup and support because it was so difficult to kill a wendigo. Although his brother shot him in the heart, there was no blood. The others attacked him and bound him, burning his body on a large pile of dry wood.[14] The final decision to kill the wendigo was left to the members of the hunting band, who designated a person, usually a close relative, to carry out the execution. Reliance on a relative for the execution legitimated it, eliminating the danger of retaliation and revenge.

The wendigo "legend" fascinated Whites in the North, and wendigo accounts entered dozens of journals and logbooks. Teicher meticulously (but surely not exhaustively) lists 70 accounts, including 36 in the nineteenth century and 10 in the twentieth: 30 among the Ojibwa, 15 among the Saulteaux (a western branch of the Ojibwa), and 9 among the Cree.[15] These White observers, traders, missionaries, ethnographers, officials, and travelers lacked their own cultural references for understanding the place of the wendigo in Native society. The wendigo "stories" were recorded as intriguing windows into Indian life.

This understanding is Eurocentric in that it views these "stories" as myth. Wendigos were just as real to Native hunters as "traitors" were real to European kings. Although there were many dangers in the great north woods, the danger of a hunter being killed by a wendigo was particularly frightening. Not only was it a horrible death, but Indian people lived in a rich spirit world. The dead spirit of an Indian killed by a wendigo was not at rest, nor was it happy in the afterlife. It was a killer spirit, roaming the evil world of the wendigo. Whites dismissed this as superstition. Teicher, using a culturally biased psychological framework, termed it a "psychosis."[16] No one questions that for Native people, the wendigo was seen as a real threat to human life.

The earliest wendigo cases came to the attention of Canadians through the Hudson's Bay Company traders. By the mid-nineteenth century a number of these cases were known, and they were beginning to be described in a common language that showed some degree of knowledge of Native tradition. While the Hudson's Bay Company had political and legal sovereignty over its lands as delegated by letters patent from Parliament, it did not extend such authority to crimes among Indians.[17] The Cree religious leader Abishabis, Small Eyes, led a messianic revival in northern Manitoba in the early 1840s. This was a mixture of Christianity and Cree religions. It was so strong that some of its adherents ceased to hunt for either furs or food, which led to starvation.[18] Using what influence they had with the Cree, Hudson's Bay traders opposed the movement because it cut into their business.

By 1843 the movement was in decline when Abishabis murdered an Indian family at York Factory while returning to Fort Severn. John Cromartie, the local Hudson's Bay Company trader, put him in irons on the complaints of local Indians that Abishabis was threatening them and they were afraid to go out hunting while he was near. He was allowed to escape in the hope that he would leave the area, but he did not, and he was put back in chains on August 28. Two days later three Cree "resolved to mete out their own justice." They dragged him out of confinement, killed him with an ax, and burned his body "to secure themselves against being haunted by a wendigo."[19] It is likely that Cromartie was in collusion with the Indians who killed Abishabis; Indians did not routinely break into Hudson's Bay premises and release prisoners held in irons.

MACHEKEQUONABE'S CASE

Machekequonabe's case arose at Sabascon Lake, northeast of Lake of the Woods in the wilderness of northwestern Ontario, among Ojibwa who had little previous contact with Canadian society. We know more about this case than most others because it is one of two wendigo cases that left a full transcript. Machekequonabe also draws the distinction of being the only wendigo killer represented by counsel, affording him the opportunity to mount a legal defense in common law terms.[20]

The trial was held at Rat Portage (now Kenora) on December 3, 1896. The entire case was based on the testimony of one man, Wasawpscopinesse, and judging from the length of the transcript, took not more than a few hours.[21] The killing occurred on a small reserve on the night of June 11 or 12, 1896. A wendigo had been seen around the camp for months, driving the people there to an increasing state of alarm. Prosecutor H. Langford examined Wasawpscopinesse on the meaning of the wendigo and on the impact of his appearance in the community. Wasawpscopinesse's testimony is through an interpreter, but still reflects his reluctance to describe much about the wendigo:

Langford: Do they believe there is more than one [wendigo]?

Wasawpscopinesse: I do not know. . . .

Q: What form has it?

A: I do not know, I never saw one. It is in the form of a man. . . .

Q: You never saw a wendigo?

A: No.

Q: Did you know anybody who did?

A: Our forefathers have seen them. . . .

Q: How can you tell a wendigo from a man?

A: I could not tell, because I have never seen any.

Q: How could you tell if you had seen one?

A: Sometimes it is a man that goes to work and eats other men.

Wasawpscopinesse's testimony then went on to establish that the community was very alarmed by the appearance of the wendigo:

Last spring it was seen around there [the camp] quite a few times. We hid everything, took the canoes up and hid them. Quite a while afterwards he was seen again. He was around the camp quite a long while; we were having a dance one night, and we saw him coming towards the school-house. One man followed and fired at him with shot. He shot at him twice. There was some blood on the left side of his track, in the leaves. We went the next morning and seen the blood. They followed the trail quite a piece.

About half a day; they would lose it for about three steps, and then find it again. [The footsteps] were two spans long of the fingers. It was in bare feet.[22]

This testimony covers the events preceding the killing. It establishes that the community was under the belief that it was imminently threatened by a wendigo. Beyond this, more can be gleaned from this testimony. First, it seems that Wasawpscopinesse was a reluctant witness, saying as little as possible about the community's belief in wendigos. His descriptions are sparse, even evasive. This is true even if we recognize that all of this occurs through an interpreter. Second, a part of his testimony was to the shooting in the left side of a wendigo the night before Machekequonabe shot anyone. The next morning members of the band had followed the well-described wendigo tracks. It is impossible to say how this occurred, but it was honestly believed by Wasawpscopinesse and everybody else in the community.

Responding to this threat, the community took action. That night Machekequonabe was one of eight Indians placed on sentry duty around the village. These sentries, including Wasawpscopinesse and Peskawakeepuic, who was killed, spaced themselves "quite a piece" apart, at regular intervals around the community. The man who was shot, "a tall Indian with a blanket over him" "started to run" with both Machekequonabe and Wasawpscopinesse chasing after him. Machekequonabe called out to him three times, but he did not respond. Wasawpscopinesse continued: "I saw a flash of the gun . . . He gave a war whoop, the one who was shot . . . He did not fall right away, but made a circle going around back." Machekequonabe cried on learning that he had shot his foster father, Peskawakeepuic.[23]

The Indian Department, sensitive to the underlying legal issues in the case, had retained a lawyer, A. S. Wink of Port Arthur, for Machekequonabe. Wink mounted a dull, unimaginative common law defense. Wink's first questions of Wasawpscopinesse were aimed at determining whether he was a pagan or a Christian. When Langford objected that the religion of the witness did not make any difference, Wink argued that he intended to show that "this is a form of insanity to which the whole tribe is subjected." The judge intervened, saying "this is not insanity at all, it is superstitious belief."[24] Wink then proceeded on his apparent belief that two shots, not one, had been fired, confusing the events of the night before with the killing at hand. Finally, he established that Machekequonabe was a pagan, a "good Indian," and remorseful about the killing—all facts that were legally irrelevant.[25] After Wink ceased questioning, the trial judge asked whether the tribe was large, receiving an affirmative answer.[26] Obviously, a small band could not post eight sentries around its community.

We know more about Wink's defense because of documents in the case file. Two pages of handwritten notes refer to cases establishing the common law defenses of mistake of fact and justification. Since these defenses would only benefit Machekequonabe, it appears likely that the handwriting is Wink's. The notes also accompany correspondence between Wink and the Indian Department concerning his bill and probably were submitted to show the amount of work he did in preparation for the defense. Neither of these defenses was raised at the trial, although they were good defenses under the common law. In a letter to Oliver Mowat, minister of justice, Wink states that following the presentation of evidence and before the case was submitted to the jury, he raised a kind of insanity argument with Judge Rose, but it was not accepted.[27] Wink's failure to raise the other issues cannot be accounted for, although with an unsympathetic judge it might well not have mattered.[28] Wink billed the Indian Department $201.25 for his services at trial with a two-page itemized bill. This was reduced to $75 by the department.

The trial court rejected the defendant's defenses and convicted him of manslaughter, sparing him, at least, the death penalty for intentional murder.[29] Judge Rose, in a common practice of the day, led the members of the jury through their verdict by asking them a series of rhetorical questions that led them to the only legal conclusion, that the defendant was guilty. This one-sided colloquy was directed by the judge, beginning with his assertion that "I think we may take it for granted that the prisoner did kill the Indian" and extending through "His appearance in the box indicates not only sanity, but intelligence." Rose concluded: "I think I must direct you, as a matter of law, that there is no justification here for the killing, and culpable homicide without justification is manslaughter . . ."[30] Rose balanced the harshness of his judgment with a lenient sentence for manslaughter, six months in jail.[31]

The Indian Department financed an appeal, a recognition that the case had important implications in Indian administration.[32] In divisional court Machekequonabe's lawyer, J. K. Kerr, argued the common law defense of reasonable mistake of fact.[33] The divisional court refused to look beyond the narrow question of whether there was adequate evidence to support the jury verdict, ignoring the question of law posed by the defense, an issue that the judge withheld from the jury in his instructions. The verdict was upheld in a seven-line opinion.[34] This is among the shortest of any opinion in an Ontario criminal appeal of that time, indicating that the court did not address the important issues raised, either at the level of Indian policy or at the level of Canadian criminal law. Many Whites, while defending Canadian jurisdiction over the criminal activity of Indians, were troubled by the case's failure to take any cognizance of the subjective fear held by an Ojibwa band of the wendigo. The transcript paints a vivid picture of a community of Indians in real danger, as posting eight sentries illustrates. The intricate and very real cultural world of the Ojibwa found no recognition in Ontario courts. A string of wendigo cases followed over the next 15 years in central Canada, leading to parallel results, although none ever again went up on appeal.[35]

What were the goals of Canadian justice in such cases? There is direct evidence of this in the case of *Rex v Tushwegeh*, another Ojibwa murder case from northwestern Ontario.[36] Tushwegeh, for unknown reasons but with facts quite indicative of a wendigo killing, strangled Geeshingoose, his brother-in-law, in their camp at Cat Lake. When the story of the crime became known, a police constable was sent to Cat Lake to gather evidence. This constable died before his evidence could be given, raising the issue of whether another officer should be sent to the north in another attempt to try Tushwegeh. Ontario Department of Justice officials were reluctant to proceed with "such a doubtful case," now two years old. The Indian Department, however, took a different view and through the Canadian Department of Justice, prevailed on Ontario officials. It was "important that this Indian be put on trial even though prospects of seeing conviction are extremely weak, as it is necessary that the Indians should understand they are within reach of the strong arm of the law."[37] Tushwegeh was brought out of the wilderness in November 1905, too late in the year to bring out the witnesses so that a trial could be held. He was held in jail all winter and tried at Kenora in the summer of 1906. He was acquitted, for the evidence was inadequate. Nevertheless, the criminal law had served its purpose: Tushwegeh, although acquitted, had served as much time in jail as Machekequonabe after his conviction. It had extended the power of the Canadian state to the farthest reaches of the country.[38] The law could effectively be used to control and socialize Native people, a powerful instrument to force assimilation. Therefore, the symbolic reach of the law was the object, showing Native people that they must defer to Canadian power, and that was more important than convictions and prison sentences.[39]

CHARLEBOIS, DRESSY MAN, AND BRIGHT EYES

An earlier wendigo trial, the first in Canada, had occurred in the fall of 1885 at Battleford, Northwest Territories, lost in the context of dozens of trials of Native warriors involved in the Northwest Uprising. Among the over two hundred defendants charged with various violations of Canadian criminal law were Charlebois, Dressy Man, and Bright Eyes, charged with the murder of She Wills, an old woman. The scene near Frog Lake two weeks after the killings of nine Whites in an uprising over the general denial of treaty rights and poor treatment of Native people by White officials must have been tense as warriors debated their next actions and waited for the arrival of Canadian troops. On April 13 She Wills announced that she would turn into a wendigo unless someone killed her.[40]

Terrified members of Big Bear's Cree band selected three warriors to carry out the killing, a disagreeable task that no one wanted to perform, but one necessary for the survival of the group. Prisoners carried the woman well away from the camp. As she sat cross-legged on the ground, her head wrapped in a shawl, Charlebois struck her in the head with a club. Bright Eyes shot her three times as Dressy Man cut off her head with a saber and threw it off into the brush. The men ran away from the body because of the power of her spirits. Later, to prevent the body and head from being reunited, the body was buried. The killing had to occur in a certain ritualistic way to prevent the wendigo from using her body to do injury to the tribe.[41]

The three men were tried on November 27, well into the series of trials of warriors before Judge Charles Rouleau. These trials were show trials, with juries quickly returning convictions of warriors charged with various offenses occurring during the uprising. After perfunctory deliberation, the jury convicted Bright Eyes of manslaughter, and Charlebois and Dressy Man of murder. Judge Rouleau sentenced Bright Eyes to 20 years and the other two to death by hanging. The two death sentences were later commuted to life.[42]

Only the presence of White prisoners among the Cree permitted the trial of this case. Because of the power of the wendigo, the Cree had used prisoners to carry the woman out of their camp, allowing them to witness the execution. They were then available to testify against the Cree warriors who had carried out an execution sanctioned under tribal law. In the context of many other rebellion cases that involved offenses against Whites, this case was not as notable as Machekequonabe's case 10 years later.

PAYOO AND NAPAYSOOSEE

Queen v Payoo and Napaysoosee was tried twice, once at Fort Saskatchewan and again at Edmonton, apparently about 1900. Although the case went unreported, one of the lawyers thought it of ethnographic interest and preserved a record.[43] A band of 32 Cree was camped near Little Slave Lake in northern Alberta in the winter of 1898–99. Moostoos, one of the adult men in the band, convinced the others that he was about to become a wendigo and would first kill his children and then "clean out" everybody else in the band unless his friends killed him first.

Eliza, the first witness called, testified that Napaysoosee, Chuckachuck, and she had held one leg while praying. Mayasksaysis held the other leg, while Payoo struck Moostoos with an ax, all the while Moostoos saying, "You will all die tonight if you don't kill me first." Eliza, incredibly, remembered nothing else—nothing that was said, nor whether Moostoos cried out when he was struck.[44] Her account is not likely complete. She must have withheld most of the details of the event.

Most of the band was called to testify, providing some view of the group process behind the killing, although a view that was clearly distorted by the band to protect some of their people. Entominahoo, a powerful medicine man and the leader of the band,[45] testified that Chuckachuck killed Moostoos and that Napaysoosee gave him a second blow, followed by Payoo after a little time, not immediately. Then, because wendigos often rise up after death, they staked his body down with trap chains and moved their camp far out of the area.[46] Marie added that Chuckachuck struck Moostoos with an ax as well, although he was already dead.[47] Napaysoosee testified that Moostoos had that day refused to eat and had acted like he never had before. He got worse all day long, threatening people and biting them. Napaysoosee claimed to have struck him in the side with an ax, although not hard, and only after "his brother in law" had hit him in the head.[48] He put the band's actions in a self-defense context: "The reason we struck him was because he had threatened to kill us all. It was to save our lives. We were all foolish with fear." Later, he cut off Moostoos's head so that he could not come back. Napaysoosee also differed in his account of the actual killing, saying that Chuckachuck had been handed the ax by Eliza, but that he did not see which of them actually struck Moostoos in the head.[49]

Payoo confirmed Napaysoosee's account, denying that he had struck Moostoos with an ax and accusing the others of lying: "They are lying when they say I struck the first blow. They are all related to one another, and I am alone among them. When I went in he was dead, and no one was holding him." Payoo further claimed he recognized the ax as Eliza's and the knife as Napaysoosee's. He also claimed that Napaysoosee, Chuckachuck, Entominahoo, and Mihkooshtikwahnis were all medicine men and that "the medicine men always help one another. It is a rule of their order."[50] Kunuksoos, father-in-law of Moostoos, testified that "Chuckachuck struck first. Napaysoosee second. Payoo third blow. The first blow killed him, but he was moving until after the third."[51]

Napaysoosee was recalled, and repeated his claim that Chuckachuck had given Moostoos the first blow and that Moostoos had "never moved" after that blow. Then, according to Napasoosee, Chuckachuck taunted him: "You are a coward if you do not strike him, we will all be killed." Chuckachuck gave him a knife and somebody else gave him an ax. Napasoosee then hit Moostoos with the ax and drove the knife into his bowels.[52] Payoo, also recalled, claimed that he was outside the house while the first two blows were struck and had no idea who struck them. When he entered the house he was handed weapons and told to strike Moostoos. "I took an ax and struck. I thought on the body but it seems it was on the head. I felt afraid. I was thinking about my children."[53]

After four hours of deliberation, the jury convicted Napasoosee of manslaughter but acquitted Payoo.[54] The case is important because it is one of the rare cases involving Indians in which there was a substantial difference in the testimony, indicating that different people in the band constructed mutually exclusive versions of the facts, which necessarily meant that some people lied. Most of the evidence pointed to Chuckachuck as the killer, for he seems to have struck Moostoos in the head with an ax before any of the others, leaving him unconscious, perhaps even dead. For reasons that cannot be determined, Chuckachuck was not even charged. Entominahoo, a powerful medicine man, was present throughout the killing and was probably in control of the actions of Chuckachuck and Napaysoosee but again, he was not charged. The jury sorted out the contradictory testimony of nine people and, for reasons that are not clear, decided that the testimonies of Payoo and Chuckachuck were more credible than that of Napaysoosee. Yet, there was no difference in testimony that the central motivation behind the crime was self-defense. However, it was not a reasonable exercise of self-defense under Canadian law because the cultural world of the Cree was not legally recognized. Judge Charles Rouleau, deciding that some punishment was necessary, sentenced Napaysoosee to two months imprisonment. Fifteen years before, this same judge had brought in death sentences at Battleford for the same offense, but in the context of the Northwest Rebellion.[55]

Napaysoosee's punishment seems symbolic and unfair. The killing of Moostoos was done by the entire band, probably decided on by Entominahoo and carried out with Chuckachuck, Napaysoosee, and Payoo each striking blows with an ax while at least four others held Moostoos, a strong man, down. It seems likely that the band had manufactured a story that, while partially accurate in describing the wendigo killing, protected the core of the band leadership, deflecting responsibility to Payoo and Napaysoosee. The contradictions in testimony follow from keeping so many people in agreement on the details of a false story, as well as the ultimate reluctance of Napaysoosee and Payoo to volunteer themselves for imprisonment. Most often these schemes probably worked because, as can be seen here, Canadian law frequently was satisfied with any reasonable explanation that satisfied the symbolic functions of the law—providing some punishment and advancing Canadian hegemony over tribal customary law.[56]

JACK AND JOSEPH FIDDLER

The remaining transcript of a wendigo killing is of the most detailed trial, that of Joseph Fiddler, a leader of the Sucker clan of the Saulteaux Ojibwa on the Upper Bay River in northeastern Manitoba. Fiddler was tried at Norway House in 1906, convicted of murder, and sentenced to death for the killing of Wasakapeequay, an old woman who had been delirious for days, to prevent her from becoming a wendigo.[57] The case received considerable attention at the time and ended in a popular letter-writing campaign to spare Fiddler's life.[58] His sentence was commuted to life, and he died in Stony Mountain Prison after 18 months there.[59] Tragically, his death occurred just as the government had decided to pardon him and send him home.[60]

Fiddler's case came to the attention of the Royal Canadian Mounted Police (RCMP) in much the same way as other wendigo killings. The killings were important events in tribal life, and people talked about them. William Campbell, a Hudson's Bay Company trader at Island Lake, stopped in at Norway House on the way back to his post from a visit to Winnipeg. He engaged in a story session with Sergeant Daisy Smith of the RCMP and revealed that he had heard of killings among the Sucker band seven years before. Probably beyond the intention of Campbell, Smith reported the talk to his superiors:

. . . at Sandy Lake, about three days travel from Island Lake, there is a band of pagan Indians and it is generally believed that these people are in the habit of killing one another whenever one gets delirious through fever or other causes. They are very superstitious . . . they kill through superstitious belief not through malice. But from the information I have obtained, I cannot get but one case that there is proof of, and that Mr. Campbell gave me, but it transpired seven years ago.[61]

Headquarters ordered Smith to "have a patrol made to Sandy Lake . . . and fully investigate the rumor as to the alleged homicides amongst the Indians."[62]

The life of the Sucker clan at the turn of the century was a life of poverty and starvation. Fur prices had dropped, overtrapping and trapping out of season had made furs scarce, and the market economy had transformed traditional hunting and fishing patterns to the point at which the clan could no longer subsist. Hard winters and a scarcity of game had led to starvation in northeastern Manitoba. Although the Sucker clan had survived without starvation, it was a time of hardship. RCMP Constable O'Neil, after a stay at Island Lake, moved on to Narrows Lake, where he found Robert and Adam Fiddler, sons of Jack. They agreed that the band would come by canoe to hold a council with the RCMP officer as soon as the ice melted, making canoe travel possible.[63] The Sucker clan was delayed, but members of the Crane clan arrived. They were questioned by O'Neil, and one of them, Norman Rae, informed the Mounties that Jack and Joseph Fiddler had killed a wendigo the previous fall. Although some of the Sucker band came in the next day, Jack and Joseph were not among them, inducing the Mounties to follow the band members back to their camp on Caribou Lake. There they found Jack Fiddler and others building birch bark canoes. They camped there for two days until Joseph arrived, then called both men into the RCMP camp, "explained to them the crime they had committed, and that they must come . . . to Norway House." They also, quite meaninglessly, cautioned them not to speak to anyone about the murder.[64] After the band members had discussed their option to kill the Mounties, they agreed to let Jack and Joseph go with them to Norway House. The group, which left later that day,[65] included Angus Rae, son-in-law of Jack Fiddler, who the Mounties somehow discovered had been a witness to the killing.

The group proceeded back to Sandy Lake to hold the now long-delayed council. The RCMP used it to inform the bands gathered there that they must follow Canadian law. Sucker band men cried openly when they were told that Jack and Joseph Fiddler were being taken to Norway House for trial for the wendigo killing. However, the Mounties' goals were much broader: Robert Fiddler was told that he would have to get rid of two of his three wives. The Indians raised a question about being forced to trade with the Hudson's Bay Company, but stopped talking when the Mounties demanded the names of the traders who had threatened them. Finally, the tribe raised a concern about getting a treaty, which the RCMP promised they would report to Ottawa.[66] The Mounties then left for Norway House with two Fiddlers and two Raes in custody.

There, after a brief preliminary examination based on the testimony of Angus Rae, the two were held over for trial on murder charges.[67] Yet, this decision was troubling because it was clear that the band had no exposure to Canadian law whatsoever. The summer passed without any action on the part of Canadian authorities to arrange the trial. This may have been due to confusion on how to proceed, for on September 15, Superintendent C. E. Saunders wrote to the assistant commissioner in Regina urging that the charges be dropped and the Fiddlers be sent home. Saunders based this assessment on his judgment that there was a "lack of evidence," an improbable excuse since Rae's eyewitness testimony was sufficient, and it appears that Saunders' action was based more on humanitarian or policy grounds. A more practical concern was that unless the men were released by mid-September they would be unable to return home because of winter.[68] Still, there was no decision from Regina, and on September 30 Jack Fiddler fled into the woods. He was found a few hours later, having hanged himself.[69]

The trial of Joseph Fiddler began a week later on October 7. Following a custom perhaps unique to Canadian justice, the entire court traveled to Norway House to conduct the trial. This practice was designed to impress the Natives of the hinterlands with the majesty of Canadian law, an advantage thought to be lost by the more efficient option of taking the defendant far away from his country to a sitting court. Yet, the trial process was incestuous. Commissioner Aylesworth Bowen Perry of the RCMP, the man who had made all of the policy decisions leading to the arrest and indictment, served as judge, a stipendiary magistrate of the Northwest Territories. The Crown prosecutor, D. W. McKerchar, was a Liberal lawyer. He faced no opposing counsel because Canadian law did not provide for defense counsel, even for an Indian who did not speak English facing a capital charge. The Indian Department sent an "observer," C. Crompton Calverley, when it might better have sent Joseph Fiddler a lawyer. Other Mounties served as court functionaries, and a jury of six White men was found in the vicinity of Norway House, probably mostly employees of the trading post since few other Whites lived there.[70]

The first witness, RCMP constable William J. Cashman, testified to the circumstances of the arrest, but was then asked if any White people lived among the Sucker band to instruct them in the law. Cashman responded that, although none lived in the immediate area, two Whites, a trader and a mission schoolteacher, lived at Island Lake, two hundred miles away by river travel.[71]

Norman Rae, also known as Pesequan, provided the main part of the government's case. The woman killed was Wahsakapeequay, the daughter-in-law of Joseph Fiddler and the wife of his son Thomas. Wahsakapeequay was delirious and, at some point, was laid out on a cotton cloth, held down by John and Norman Rae, and strangled with a cord by Jack and Joseph.[72] Prosecutor

McKerchar asked Rae whether this execution carried out a law of the band, and Rae answered that it did.[73]

Angus Rae followed Norman to the stand. After he gave essentially the same version of the killing, McKerchar's questions ventured further into tribal culture. Angus was asked whether he had objected to the killing. When he responded in the negative, he was asked whether a member of the band was bound to obey the "ogema," or medicine man, Jack Fiddler. "Yes," responded Angus, "If the ogema tells me to do a thing I must do it." When pressed whether something would happen to him if he refused, Angus was clear that harm would come to him, although he did not know from what source or what kind of harm.[74] Angus also provided the motivation for the killing and testified that people who died while delirious came back as wendigos, who would kill and eat people, and that they had to be killed to prevent this transformation.[75]

Then, perhaps by surprise, but more likely by prearrangement, Angus Rae opened up the history of wendigo killings in the Sucker band: there had been others. David Meekis had been killed and his body burned by Joseph Fiddler, James Meekis, Joseph Meekis, and Elias Rae. David Meekis had been delirious as well.[76] Years before, Angus had seen Askamekeseecowiniew burned as well, killed by James Meekis, Lucas Meekis, Joseph Meekis, and John Rae.[77] When asked whether the ogema, Jack Fiddler, had given any reason for killing these people, Angus Rae responded, incredibly, that "When they are sick and so long in misery they put them out of their misery."[78]

As if this motive was so trivial as to be unbelievable even to the government, McKerchar continued to follow this line of questioning, but he could not shake Angus Rae on this point. Finally, he asked directly, "Did you ever hear the ogema say that anyone who died out of his mind turned into a cannibal?" Rae responded, "Yes, that is what the ogema says."[79] Rae was reluctant to state that the tribe was afraid that the woman would come back as a cannibal and kill people and only did so after prompting by the Crown attorney.

At the very end of his testimony the Crown attorney asked Angus Rae if others were sick at this time. Incredibly, Rae testified that a man, Menewaseum, had been sick shortly after the woman. As Angus Rae walked past a wigwam he was handed a piece of string and told to pull it. "Only then I knew that I had strangled a man." Jack Fiddler was holding the other end of the string, but Angus did not know that until Joseph Fiddler told him.[80] It has to be obvious that Angus Rae's testimony cannot be true. The physical act of strangulation takes a number of minutes, requires great force, and provokes a strong response from the victim. The walls of a wigwam are not thick or sound proof and you cannot be ignorant of the struggle of a strangling man inside a wigwam, nor of the identity of another man holding another end of a rope only a few feet away. Even Crown prosecutor McKerchar was skeptical, asking "Why, when you were asked before did you not tell us about this other man being killed this way?" Angus Rae responded, again incredibly, that he was "leaving this till last because they were Crane tribes."[81]

The digression of Angus Rae raises a number of important issues, perhaps the least of them legal ones. The other killings had nothing to do with Fiddler's trial and were prejudicial to his case. Beyond this, they raise important ethnographic questions about the motivation of Angus Rae and Indian witnesses generally in such cases. It is impossible now to reconstruct Rae's motivations for testifying against Fiddler. He may have been afraid; however, he may also have perceived that he had something to gain in terms of band politics. He faced potential murder charges, and the promise that he would be sent home if he cooperated may explain his testimony. While parts of his testimony were probably true, other parts were false. As in the other wendigo cases, his testimony reveals that many people in the band were involved in the killings. One common pattern in Native testimony points toward an effort to protect the chiefs and medicine men, which was clearly not the case here, but Rae was from the Crane band and may have been protecting another set of headmen.

The trial consumed all of one day, ending with the testimony of an Ojibwa missionary, Reverend Paul Paupanakiss, who testified that he knew nothing about the wendigo phenomenon, testimony that must also have been false. Paupanakiss's testimony, since he was not a witness to any of the events at issue, can only have had one function in the government's case: the Crown was attempting to deny the whole existence of the wendigo phenomenon in an effort to undermine Fiddler's defense, leaving the jury with no option but intentional homicide. Following Machekequonabe, while killing a wendigo was not legitimate self-defense, the mistaken belief did lower the mens rea from murder to manslaughter. The Crown in the Fiddler case wanted a murder conviction, rather than the manslaughter conviction it was otherwise certain to get, evidently even at the price of perjury.[82]

At six the court adjourned for dinner, and then at seven Joseph Fiddler was asked whether he wanted to take the stand. He declined, but asked that Crompton Calverley speak for him. Calverley gave a short speech defending Fiddler's actions on the grounds that they followed tribal custom. Prosecutor McKerchar spoke briefly to the jury, asking for a conviction.[83]

Commissioner Perry next addressed the jury. He instructed that if they believed the evidence in the case that Mrs. Thomas Fiddler was killed by the accused, then they must find Joseph Fiddler guilty of murder. Once this was established, it was up to the jury to have the crime lessened to justifiable homicide or manslaughter. Like Judge Rose, Commissioner Perry interjected his own views into the charge:

Was he justified in killing her because she might have turned into a cannibal? This might possibly be urged as a defense. The tribe was ignorant of the law of the land. We questioned both witnesses as to that and the impression left on my mind is that they do know what the law forbids . . . As to the question of pagan belief, if you find that the accused is justified in killing because of his pagan belief where will it land us if we accept such a belief. What the law forbids no pagan belief can justify. The law says: "Thou shalt not kill."[84]

Perhaps more disturbingly, Perry, in his charge to the jury denied that Joseph Fiddler had been acting according to tribal customary law, a critical issue in the case. "To my mind the evidence is not clear on the customs of the Sucker tribe."[85] Berry cited the testimony of Reverend Edward Paupan-akiss, an Ojibwa missionary, who stated that he had no knowledge of the custom of killing wendigos, as well as Angus Rae's testimony that he knew only what Jack Fiddler had told him about wendigos.[86] If this evidence was deficient, it was because Fiddler did not offer a defense, something he could only have done with a lawyer or with some basic education in Canadian law. The effort of the Crown to deny that any customary law existed relative to wendigos was part of the Crown's purpose to get a death sentence for Fiddler by denying the existence of any mitigating factors. This reflected a policy decision to retreat from the leniency in sentencing shown Machekequonabe because the wendigo killings had persisted. Their continued existence, into the twentieth century, was an embarrassment to the Indian Department.

The jury was understandably confused and returned asking for two legal definitions: guilt of manslaughter and death from the result of self-defense. Self-defense was defined as resulting from an immediate danger, manslaughter from a loss of self-control. The jury, obviously not having accepted the pros-ecution's improbable story, also wanted to ask some more questions of the Raes concerning how the woman got into the wigwam, but the judge denied this request. The jury reported it was deadlocked, but it was ordered to retire to reconsider its verdict. It returned a verdict of guilty of murder, with a recommendation for mercy.[87] Under existing Canadian law, the death penalty was the punishment for murder, and Berry sentenced Fiddler to death.[88]

This result can be analyzed in narrow legal terms, as well as in broader political ones. From a narrow legal standpoint, as long as the burden fell to the defendant to prove some mitigation or defense after the Crown had proven an intentional killing, Fiddler's failure to offer a defense was necessarily fatal. Berry's statement of the law in this respect was correct, although given that he knew the defendant did not have a lawyer, he had more of a duty to charge the jury on manslaughter, self-defense, and common law justification. His charges were inadequate in the context and determined the outcome of the jury's deliberations. Similarly, since the Crown had tried wendigo cases before and had acted with full instructions from Ottawa (also knowledgeable about wendigo cases), it was improper and misleading for Berry to instruct the jury that doubt existed as to whether wendigos existed in Ojibwa custom-ary law: It was absolutely clear, and Berry knew it. As a judge, he had a responsibility to secure a fair trial for Fiddler, a responsibility redoubled by the absence of a defense lawyer.

During this period the Canadian government maintained a "get tough" policy aimed at Indians who violated Canadian law based on tribal custom. The Indian Department was embarrassed by the Indians' continued adherence to their traditional customs into the twentieth century and was rethinking its policy of "lenience," which had produced very short sentences for earlier cases of this type. The government of Canada wanted to make an example of Joseph Fiddler.[89]

However, it did not want to hang him. Commissioner Perry, two weeks after obtaining Fiddler's conviction, wrote to the minister of justice in Ottawa urging a commutation of his sentence. It is instructive that Perry gave Ottawa the opposite view of tribal customary law from that which he gave in his jury instruction:

He believed, however, that insane persons were dangerous to the well being of his tribe and that unless they were strangled they would turn into cannibals . . . It is clear that it has been the custom of the tribe from time immemorial to put to death members of their band, and other bands, who were thought by them to be insane or incurable.[90]

Joseph was transferred to the infirmary of the Stony Mountain Prison in January 1908. RCMP inspector Pelletier and Constable Cashman took Angus Rae back to the Sucker band, arriving at Narrows Lake in February. Pelletier used the occasion to lecture the band, with a Hudson's Bay trader as an interpreter. He spoke for about two hours, explaining the law. He characterized them as "the worst band in the district, murderers, liars, and very crooked."[91] He threatened to appoint a new chief if the band did not change its ways. He reminded the band members that just because they live in isolation, it does not mean that the government does not hear what goes on.[92] Angus Rae had spent eight months imprisoned with the Fiddlers and lived in fear, digging a cellar under his lodging so that he could escape if the police ever came after him again.[93]

There followed a considerable popular effort to free Fiddler, led by Hudson's Bay traders and others at Norway House, including three of the six jurors.[94] The government was divided on the issue, with the Indian Department urging Fiddler's release. However, the Ministry of Justice, while favoring eventual release, took the position that he needed to serve more time. Commissioner Perry, probably concerned that if Indians were released too quickly from prison, they would return home to their tribes without imparting sufficient fear of Canadian law among them, was particularly adamant that Fiddler not be released too soon.[95]

Fiddler pleaded for his own life with a petition to the minister of justice:

I desire to ask you not to look upon me as a common murderer. I was the Chief of my tribe, we had much sickness, and the sick ones were getting bad spirits and their friends were afraid of them . . . If you let me go back to my place I will teach my family and people the white man's law. I am sick now and can't walk, but I think I will live if you let me go home. I will tell them how the white man lives. I wish you to consider that I am a poor Indian and don't know anything.[96]

Fiddler, a chief, was reduced through his imprisonment to depression and begging for his freedom. The government's lack of decision on the issue led to a tragic conclusion. Again, the season for travel was ending, and the government was aware that Fiddler was very sick. On September 4 the governor general ordered his immediate release from Stony Mountain, but Fiddler had died three days before, on September 1.[97]

OTHER WENDIGO KILLINGS: PAUL SABOURN AND SWIFT RUNNER

While the three cases discussed above are the only ones for which substantial trial records remain, there were other cases. Given the number of ethnographic accounts and the remote character of many Native communities in the nineteenth century, there were an unknown number of wendigo killings. As in the Tushwegeh case, it appears that tribes often did not talk honestly to the Mounties about the killings. When they did, various levels of distortion permeated their stories. The case of Paul Sabourin, a Slave Indian from the Northwest Territories, appears to involve a tribe completely unwilling to discuss the case, producing a record that is obviously a cover-up.

The facts are deceptively simple, belying the cultural complexity of these cases. In the spring 1899 encampment of a hunting band of seven men and seven women, four men and four women were in a tent when Joseph Sabourin told Charles Martel to go out and shoot a sick dog. Martel answered that he would do it but needed to find his shoes first. Paul Sabourin then said, "I will shoot the dog myself if you don't do it." He went outside, and the others heard a shot. Paul came back into the tent, took a blanket, and lay down. The others went outside and found Josephine Laudry shot in the back of the head. According to the testimony of Michel Lefoin, another Slave Indian in the camp, Sabourin never spoke to anyone in the band about the killing, and no one had any idea why he did it.[98]

The testimony of Lefoin, followed by that of Charles Martel, provides a great deal of detail about the event, however, no direct testimony on the reasons for the killing. Both testified that Paul Sabourin was given to "preaching" the word of God, but only occasionally and in generalities. The victim had stopped sleeping in either of the two tents and, incredibly, was sleeping outside—impossible in March and April in the Northwest Territories, again, with no reason given. Previously she had been sleeping in a second tent with her husband and two other couples but then had moved outside. Her husband and another man were away hunting when she was killed.[99]

Sabourin had a lawyer, H. C. Taylor, appointed by the court to defend him. Taylor cross-examined both witnesses, but appears to have lacked any theory for a defense. The jury returned a verdict of murder after a short deliberation. Sabourin, when asked if he had anything to say before sentence was passed, admitted to the killing but claimed he "had not my mind to myself."[100] He was sentenced to death by Judge Charles Rouleau, the same judge who had presided at the Battleford trials and the trials of the killers of Moostoos. Both Judge Rouleau and the Crown prosecutor, N. D. Beck, urged that the sentence be commuted to life because of the mental condition of the prisoner.[101] Others petitioned for commutation as well, and Sabourin's sentence was commuted to life.[102] He died of consumption in Stony Mountain Prison on November 20, 1902.[103]

The Indian Department interceded with the Department of Justice on Sabourin's behalf and arranged the commutation according to explicit policy grounds. Rarely, do we have such a detailed statement of policy underlying a criminal case. James Smart, deputy superintendent of Indian Affairs, wrote the minister of justice:

I have the honour to draw attention to the fact that the accused was from Great Slave Lake, a section of the country inhabited by Indians with whom no Treaty has as yet been made and which is not yet in touch with civilization, and that he can therefore hardly be regarded otherwise than as an untutored savage . . .

I submit for your consideration the impossibility of judging only by the white man's methods, the conduct of a savage governed by superstitions and whose habits are entirely opposed to those of civilization . . . the enforcement of the extreme penalty might create an impression, amongst the Indians with whom the accused is connected, that contacted with civilization imperiled their existence. Such an impression would defeat the object, recognized by the Indian Act and the provision made by Parliament from time to time for the Indians, namely gradually to inculcate in them habits of thought similar to those of the white population in this country. As a first step in this direction it may be necessary in the most remote future to negotiate a Treaty with the Indians of Great Slave Lake; and it would be unfortunate if these people were found then to hold the view that the white man's justice was without mercy and without consideration of their ignorance and general condition . . .

. . . I have the honour to ask your consideration of the question whether the interests of justice would not be best served by treatment of an Indian unacquainted with civilization in a manner no more severe than would be accorded a child below the age of fourteen years, concerning whom there is a prima facie presumption that he does not understand the nature and consequences of his act. Even the most highly educated Indian until enfranchised is subject to civil disabilities though capable of crime. Whatever his actual age he is still an infant in the eyes of the law; and in view of the wide distinction between him and an Indian of the class of the accused it appears to be a matter fairly open to question whether the latter should be considered more responsible for his actions than a child of the age mentioned.[104]

Smart's policy statement is remarkable for two reasons. First, desirous of negotiating Treaty 8, it was necessary to convey an impression of the humanity of Canadian justice. Second, the direct assertion that an Indian was a child and should be punished as such, while it underlay much of Canadian Indian policy, was never explicitly stated. Indians, in fact, were not punished as children.

The testimony of the two witnesses in this case is unbelievable, and it is obvious that they were covering up a series of events that had occurred in the band. It is impossible that no one in the band had "any idea" why Sabourin shot Josephine Laudry. Obviously, it could have been for a number of reasons, including some kind of sexual jealousy, as well as insanity. However, super-imposed on this case are facts that look like a wendigo killing that was delib-erately covered up. Josephine was isolated from the rest of the group, sleeping outside near the campfire, instead of in either of two tents. There is no com-pelling reason to go out and shoot a "sick dog," but there was clearly an urgency here. The original order to shoot the sick dog came not from Paul Sabourin, but from his brother Joseph. The sick dog then disappears from the testimony. Finally, the complete denial of any knowledge of any reason for the crime reveals a cover-up. A fight, or sexual jealousy, would have been easy to testify to, had either occurred. Paul Sabourin would not defend himself beyond the statement that "he was not in his own mind" when he did it. A more reasonable theory is that the group decided to kill the woman as a wendigo and, for whatever reason, Paul was selected, or had agreed, to take responsibility for it to protect others, including Joseph.

The Swift Runner case is also a wendigo case, but it differs from all of the above in that it does not involve a killing occurring within and protected by a Native community. Swift Runner, it seems, became a wendigo. He was a Cree trapper, living 80 miles north of Edmonton. By reputation he was re-peatedly seeing spirits, including the wendigo, urging him to become a can-nibal. One fall he took his wife and children, moved to new trapping grounds, and had a successful trapping season. Suspicion fell on him, however, when he returned to his former home without his family. When he could not give a satisfactory account of their disappearance, his wife's family reported the matter to the Mounted Police. The police mounted a patrol to his former camp and came back with ample evidence of cannibalism.[105]

He was tried for murder before Magistrate Richardson in Edmonton on August 8, 1879. Swift Runner confessed to the killings, and the jury was pre-sented with a horrible story. "How did it start?" asked the judge. Swift Runner replied that he went on a moose hunt, and all that he could hear when he returned to camp were young moose, nothing but moose. While Swift Runner might have benefited from an insanity defense, he was suicidal, believing that he had to be hanged. In the best British hanging tradition, he made a speech from the gallows, acknowledging his guilt and thanking those who had taken care of him in prison and scolding the guard for keeping him waiting in the cold for his hanging.[106]

Under customary law Swift Runner's tribe would have killed him for this action, not to punish him but to prevent future cannibalism. His wife's people would have been justified in doing so under tribal law. The fact that his wife's family turned to the RCMP for justice shows that traditional justice in the Fort Edmonton area was not in a position in which it could carry out an execution, either because tribal norms of criminal justice had been eroded or because White legal hegemony in the area around Fort Edmonton was well established. It is clear that the immediate area of trading posts was under White law, initially the law of the Hudson's Bay Company, and later, Canadian law.[107] The tribes had come to accept this as a necessary condition for stability in the fur trade and did not view it as an affront to tribal sovereignty. In return, the traders did not interfere in tribal law beyond the outer reaches of the trading area.

CONCLUSION

On one level the wendigo trials can be understood as an exercise in legal imperialism, showing the limits that Canadian authorities would go to impose their law on Native communities. These trials occurred at the very margin of Canadian political and legal authority, just ahead of the assertion of Canadian legal authority over Indian tribes. All of these tribes, however, had been in a trading relationship with Hudson's Bay Company traders for over a hundred years, but the company had not interfered in matters of tribal law. The death penalty imposed on Fiddler is not unrelated to the negotiations for adherence to Treaty 5 and the incorporation of northern Manitoba into the province. The power of Canadian authorities could not be expressed more strongly than with the death penalty. Only Swift Runner was executed, however, because Canada rarely executed Indians for intra-Indian killings.[108]

However, that analysis alone is unsatisfactory. The wendigo trials also provide a window into the legal world of Cree and Ojibwa communities beyond the frontier at the turn of the century. Traditional law, like traditional sorcery, was still intact as a force in Native communities. They were interlinked closely in the world view of the Indians of the north woods. Death was common, and the distinction between a murder and a death by "natural causes" was not obvious in Ojibwa and Cree culture. The traditional legal orders of these Native societies provided legal mechanisms designed to let small hunting bands make difficult legal decisions involving life and death.

The fact that the wendigo killings were legal in Ojibwa society undoubtedly made it easier for the RCMP to "solve" the crimes: they simply arrested the band members who were responsible for carrying out traditional law in the execution of wendigos. While, as in the case of the Fiddlers, this might involve actual bandleaders, more often it appears to have involved the young hunters selected by band leadership to carry out the killings. The killings came to the attention of authorities because everybody talked about them, and word passed from band to band, until it reached Whites probably, as in the Fiddler case, through traders. Once the Mounties went to remote communities, always accompanied by interpreters, to ask about those killings, they often found forthright witnesses. It also appears that the Mounties carried an enormous coercive power with them, including the power to remove even the witnesses from the band to faraway guardhouses for months at a time.

The coercive power of the Mounties, however, had its limits. It seems likely that most of the witnesses' stories were at least partially manufactured with a definite goal in mind. Some of these stories may have been completely false. Often they seem to be protecting some people at the expense of others, perhaps reflecting family loyalties or band hierarchy. Often it is also a protection of the wendigo tradition and tribal culture. Traditional healers, or medicine men, were deeply involved in these events, and this involvement did not often emerge at trial.

The protection of that culture took the full energy of traditionalists because there are few areas of tribal custom more inherently at odds with Canadian law than the wendigo killings. Not only were these killings beyond the reach of Canadian law, but the traditional religious motivation for them defied the moral sense of White Canadians. A world of strange spirits in the forest that would kill you if you did not kill them first made complete sense to Ojibwa and Cree Indians. A traditional law that provided for that defense was fundamental to those societies.

Canadian law might have accommodated the tribes by attempting to incorporate the honestly held beliefs of Native people into the traditional common law defenses. However, this was beyond the jurisprudence of Victorian and Edwardian society.[109] This also raised policy issues that Canadian authorities did not want raised. It might have been argued that to recognize a wendigo killing as the reasonable exercise of self-defense would have encouraged the continuation of the practice, rather than have permitted justice in individual cases. Nothing in Canadian Indian law was concerned with justice in individual cases; greater policy goals colored every issue. The royal prerogative of the pardon or commutation was not unaffected by the scope of this policy but was more removed from it. By the late nineteenth century most convicted murderers had their sentences commuted, and there was no clear reason why Indians should be any different. There were important cultural differences, however, in the meaning of imprisonment. There was no parallel in Native society for being transported to Stony Mountain Prison and being caged in a small cell. Many Indians died in prison, even during short sentences. Few lived long lives after release. Even a short prison sentence often became a death sentence.

NOTES

1. Robert Seidman, "Witch Murder and Mens Rea," *Modern Law Review* 28 (1965): 46–61; "Mens Rea and the Reasonable African," *International and Comparative Law Quarterly* 15 (1966): 1135–64.

2. Sidney L. Harring, "Please Send Six Copies of the Penal Code: British Colonial Law in Selangor, 1874–1880," *International Journal of the Sociology of Law* 19 (1991): 193, provides an introduction to this literature, although there are hundreds of individual studies of the process of the imposition of British law in the colonies in the 19th and early 20th centuries. See also S. B. Burman and B. E. Harrell-Bond, *The Imposition of Law* (London, 1979); and M. B. Hooker, *Legal Pluralism: An Introduction to Colonial and Neo-colonial Laws* (Oxford, 1975).

3. *Regina v Machekequonabe* 28 O.R. 309 (1896). George Nelson, a fur trader, provides a classic account of the wendigo in Ojibwa life. Nelson served in the Ojibwa country from 1802 to 1804; 1804 to 1816; 1818 to 1823; the last time, keeping very extensive ethnographic notes on the Cree at Lac La Ronge, now in northeastern Saskatchewan. See Jennifer S. H. Brown and Robert Brightman, *The Orders of the Dreamed: George Nelson On Cree and Northern Ojibwa Religion and Myth, 1823* (Winnipeg, 1988). A wendigo execution under tribal law is described at 92–93.

4. These cases are discussed below at pp. 83–92.

5. These cases are discussed below at pp. 92–95.

6. Wendigo is spelled in a variety of ways by different anthropologists. Throughout, I use the spelling "wendigo" chosen by the judges in Machekequonabe. It is also spelled windigo, wintego, wihtigo, wetigo, windego, wendigo, wendago, windago, wintigo, wintsigo, wehtigoo, windagoo, windikouk, weendigo, wentiko, wiitiko, whittico, weendegoag, weendago, and weetigo. Morton I. Teicher, "Windigo Psychosis: A Study of a Relationship between Belief and Behavior among the Indians of Northeastern Canada," *Proceedings of the Annual Meeting of the American Ethnological Society* (1960), 2.

7. Teicher, "Windigo Psychosis" is the most complete analysis of the meaning of the wendigo phenomenon in Native society and is accompanied by a complete bibliography. See also Robert Brightman, "The Windigo in the Material World," *Ethnohistory* 357–79; Lou Marano, "Windigo Psychosis: The Anatomy of an Emic-Etic Confusion," *Current Anthropology* 23:4 (August 1982): 385–412; Leo G. Waisberg, "Boreal Forest Subsistence and the Windigo: Fluctuation of Animal Populations," *Anthropologica* 17 (1975): 169–85; Thomas H. Hay, "The Windigo Psychosis: Psychodynamic, Cultural, and Social Factors in Aberrant Behavior," *American Anthropologist* 73 (1971): 1–22; Regina Flannery et al, "Witiko Accounts from the James Bay Cree," *Arctic Anthropology* 18:1 (1971): 57–77; Jennifer Brown, "The Cure and Feeding of Windigos: A Critique," *American Anthropologist* 73 (1971): 20–22; Thomas H. Hay, "The Windigo Psychosis: Psychodynamic, Cultural, and Social Factors in Aberrant Behavior," *American Anthropologist* (1971): 1–19; D. H. Turner, "Windigo Mythology and the Analysis of Cree Social Structure," *Anthropologica:* 19:1 (1977): 63–73; Diamond Jenness, "The Ojibwa Indians of Parry Island, Their Social and Religious Life," *National Museum of Canada, Bulletin* 78 (1935). The repeated references to psychoanalytical categories in analyzing the wendigo phenomenon stems from several sources, most commonly the frequency with which Indians became afflicted with the belief that they were becoming wendigos, often taking some form of mental illness. While this is related to the spiritual belief that wendigos are dangerous creatures that live in the forest, it is not the same thing. For example, Machekequonabe killed in an ordinary case of self-defense and was not afflicted with any form of mental disturbance. Mental disturbance takes many forms and obviously takes distinct forms in different cultural contexts, but the comparative study of mental disorder is not within the scope of this study.

8. Teicher, "Windigo Psychosis," 2.

9. Ibid., 3.

10. Ibid., 7–16.

11. Jenness, "Ojibwa Indians of Parry Island," 3.

12. Ibid., 3. The killing has all of the earmarks of a wendigo killing: it was sudden, with no apparent reason, and with hints of cannibalism.

13. Ibid., 3.

14. Brown and Brightman, *Orders of the Dreamed,* 92–93.

15. Teicher's methodology, which can be deduced from his bibliography, was to read existing ethnographic accounts of Native people. He cites about 150 of these in his bibliography and presumably did not cite many more in which he failed to find evidence of the wendigo phenomenon. These works are cited at 123–29. Teicher also cites *Machekequonabe* by its case citation, showing that he used legal records.

16. Teicher, "Windigo Psychosis," 5–6.

17. Hamar Foster, "Long Distance Justice: The Criminal Jurisdiction of Canadian Courts West of the Canadas, 1763–1859," *The American Journal of Legal History* 34(1990): 1–48; "Sins Against the Great Spirit: The Law, the Hudson's Bay Company, and the Mackenzie's River Murders, 1835–1839," *Criminal Justice History: An International Annual* 10 (1989): 23–76; and "Killing Mr. John: Law and Jurisdiction at Fort Stikine, 1842–1846," in *Law for the Elephant. Law for the Beaver: Essays in the Legal History of the North American West,* ed. John McLaren et al (Regina, 1992).

18. Abishabis, in *Dictionary of Canadian Biography* 7 (1988): 3–4.

19. Ibid., 4.

20. Here it is important to point out that in the late twentieth century legal scholars benefit from the fact that both sides of a dispute are represented and have the opportunity to present their respective arguments to the court. For Indians before the middle of the twentieth century this was a rare phenomenon, thus most "Indian law" is based on a one-sided analysis of every case. This is not to suggest that the resulting state of Indian law would necessarily be different if only the Indian position had had legal representation, because obviously considerations of politics and economics may well have determined the outcome of Indian cases, but clearly we would have different understandings of many of the legal issues, as well as more development of the underlying facts of all the cases in Indian law.

21. *Queen v Machweekequonabe* (*sic*), Canadian National Archives, RG 13-C1, vol. 2089. This file contains both a 12-page official transcript and legal documents.

22. Transcript, 2–3. Langford's questions are omitted.

23. *Regina v Machekequonabe* 28 O.R. 309 (1896).

24. Transcript, 7.

25. Transcript, 8.

26. Transcript, 8.

27. Letter, Wink to Oliver Mowat, 9 December 1896, in the original case file, *Queen v Machweekequonabe* (*sic*).

28. "The prisoner should not be found guilty of manslaughter, contending that the shooting was due to misadventure, or that the act of shooting was done by the prisoner when laboring under such a disease of the mind and to such an extent as to render him incapable of appreciating the nature and quality of the act and of knowing that such act was wrong, or that he was laboring under a specific delusion, but in other

respects sane, which caused him to believe in the existence of a state of things which, if it existed, would justify or excuse his act": Ibid, 3.

29. Ibid., 310.

30. Transcript, 10, 11.

31. Transcript, 12.

32. There is no record of any Indian Department policy on the financing of criminal appeals of Indians, either for policy reasons, or because they were wards of the state. Indeed, the paucity of Indian criminal appeals necessarily proves that the Indian Department financed very few of them: every criminal appeal leaves a record. This conviction could not have been appealed because of the sentence—six-month sentences for Indians were common. The decision to file an appeal must have had policy significance. None of this is apparent in the correspondence in the case file, but it appears likely that the Justice Department wanted a judicial ruling against customary law defenses. This would have occurred at a time when both Plains Indians and Northwest Coast Indians were mounting customary law defenses.

33. This defense essentially removes the mens rea of intending a criminal act. See Keedy, "Ignorance and Mistake in the Criminal Law," *Harvard Law Review* 22 (1908): 75; Rollin Perkins, "Ignorance and Mistake in the Criminal Law," *University of Pennsylvania Law Review* 88 (1939): 35.

34. Correspondence relating to the appeal and a handwritten outline of the appellate argument is held in the Canadian National Archives, RG 13, vol. 2089. Attorney J. K. Kerr of Toronto argued the appeal, billing the Indian Department $120.08 for his services.

35. *Rex v Tuswegeh* (unreported), Ontario Provincial Archives, RG 3, file 181 (1906); *Queen v Payoo & Napaysoosee* (North-West Territories), *Ontario Sessional Papers* 36:5 (1904): 128–45; *Jack & Joseph Fiddler,* National Archives of Canada, RG 13, vol. 1452, file 386; and Paul Saborin, *Queen v Paul Saborin,* National Archives of Canada, RG 13, vol. 1439, file 315.

36. This case is unreported. The case file is held in Ontario Provincial Archives, RG 3, file 181 (1906).

37. Ibid. "Letter, Deputy Minister of Justice to Deputy Attorney General of Ontario," 15 March 1906.

38. Exactly 10 years later Canadian law reached the farthest corner of the country when a RCMP patrol reached the Arctic Ocean at the mouth of the Copper River to arrest Sinnisiak and Uluksuk, two Copper Inuit accused of the murder of two Roman Catholic priests. R. G. Moyles, *British Law and Arctic Men: The Celebrated 1917 Murder Trials of Sinnisiak and Uluksuk, the First Inuit Tried Under White Man's Law* (Saskatoon, 1979).

39. On the symbolic purposes of early Canadian law in the Arctic, see Teicher, "Windigo Psychosis," 63; on the Northwest Coast, see Douglas Cole and Ira Chaikin, *An Iron Hand Upon the People* (Seattle, 1990).

40. Bob Beal and Rod Macleod, *Prairie Fire: The 1885 North-West Rebellion* (Edmonton, 1984), 212–13; W. B. Cameron, *Blood Red the Sun* (Edmonton, 1987; orig. ed. 1924).

41. Cameron, *Blood Red the Sun.*

42. "Epitome of Parliamentary Documents in Connection with the North West Rebellion, 1885" (Ottawa, 1886).

43. See *Queen v Payoo and Napaysoosee*, an unreported Northwest Territories case of 1899, printed in "The Killing of Moostoos the Wehtigoo," in *Archaelogical Report* (1903), Appendix to the Report of the Minister of Education, Ontario, 1903, *Ontario Sessional Papers*, vol. 36, pt. 5 (1904): 128–41.

44. "Killing of Moostoos the Wehtigoo," 129.

45. The report confuses the nature of the leadership of a Cree hunting band, claiming that while Entominahoo was not a "chief" he was looked up to as a Medicine Man of considerable authority. A hunting band, composed of members of an extended family (as these people were) would not have a chief. Rather, leadership would be informal, following the prestige and experience of the men. The evidence is clear that Entominahoo performed this role.

46. "Killing of Moostoos the Wehtigoo," 130.

47. Ibid., 131.

48. Chuckachuck and Apishchikisaynis were both Moostoos's brothers-in-law.

49. "Killing of Moostoos the Wehtigoo," 131–33.

50. Ibid., 133–34. During the day and a half over which these events took place there was a recurrent resort to sorcery to cure Moostoos, but it was to no avail.

51. Ibid., 135.

52. Ibid., 138–39.

53. Ibid., 140.

54. Ibid., 140.

55. Ibid., 141.

56. It might be pointed out that, in terms of modern criminal law, this is still most often true. If any member of a criminal plot takes responsibility for the event with an explanation that exculpates the others, that is ordinarily the end of the case. The law is satisfied if some culprit is punished, even if few people really believe his story that limits the culpability of the others.

57. A full transcript of this case is printed in the *Annual Archaeological Report* to the Minister of Education, Ontario (1908), 91–120. This transcript is the core of a book, augmented with oral histories and other government documents, Robert R. Stevens and Chief Thomas Fiddler, *Killing the Shaman* (Winnipeg, 1986). There is also an extensive RCMP file on the case held in the Canadian National Archives, fonds RG.

58. Stevens and Fiddler, *Killing the Shaman*, 111–15. This book essentially parallels the archival account and represents a much more accessible account of the arrest and trial of the Fiddlers.

59. Ibid., 109.

60. Ibid., 116.

61. Letter, Sergeant Daisy Smith to commanding officer, RCMP, Regina, 1 October 1906. These various reports are the basis of the account given in *Killing the Shaman*. Sergeant Smith's story seems too naive to be real. For example, the idea that these killings followed from fever or delirium, which must have been common given the state of public health of the day, must have been false, but his story exaggerates the frequency and cause of the killings. Similarly, Smith must have been aware of the wendigo killing phenomenon since the RCMP in that region had been involved in earlier cases.

62. Commissioner Aylesworth Bowen, RCMP, to Sergeant Smith, 28 December 1906.

63. Constable O'Neil, Report.

64. Ibid.

65. Ibid.

66. The Indians of Northern Manitoba signed adhesions to Treaty 5 during 1908, 1909, and 1910. Frank Tough, "Economic Aspects of Aboriginal Title in Northern Manitoba: Treaty 5 Adhesions and Métis Scrip," *Manitoba History* 15 (1988): 3–16.

67. RCMP Inspector E. A. Pelletier to Commissioner A. Bowen Perry, June 1906.

68. Letter, C. E. Saunders to Assistant Commissioner, RCMP, 20 August 1906.

69. Constable Daisy Smith, Report.

70. It is not easy to determine the employment of Whites living at Norway House in October 1906. It seems that neither Mounties nor missionaries, Whites who did live at Norway House, served on the jury. In addition to a number of employees of the fur trading post, there would have been schoolteachers, government clerks, and other government functionaries around the post as well.

71. Stevens and Fiddler, *Killing the Shaman*, 88.

72. Ibid., 89–90.

73. Ibid., 90.

74. Ibid., 92–93.

75. Ibid., 95.

76. Ibid., 97–98.

77. Ibid., 99.

78. Ibid., 99.

79. Ibid., 100.

80. Ibid., 101.

81. Ibid., 103. McKerchar may also be disingenuous here in the way this killing was raised in court. His final question is incongruous as a final question: why would he ask if any other people were sick at the end of his direct examination unless this was intended to prompt Rae to raise this very killing? It seems that Rae had, in fact, told the Mounties everything, so they knew of this killing all along. McKerchar's sense of ethics required him to raise this killing, but he wanted to do so only on his own terms, and after he had safely presented his case.

82. This concededly harsh conclusion assumes simply that it is impossible that an adult Ojibwa had never heard of the wendigo myth. Obviously Native missionaries functioned in constrained environments, and Paupanakiss honestly believed that Ojibwa religion and myth interfered with the Christianization and advancement of his people. At the same time, his testimony had the effect of eliminating the only defense that could save Fiddler from hanging. It is not clear, however, that Paupanakiss was aware of this, although the Crown certainly was.

83. Stevens and Fiddler, *Killing the Shaman*, 105–6.

84. Ibid., 106–7.

85. Ibid., 106.

86. Ibid., 106. This obviously accounts for Paupanakiss's strange testimony, and the fact that the Crown Attorney called Paupanakiss to the stand only to testify that he had never heard of any of this, or had never visited the Sucker band in over 16 years. Thus, Paupanakiss's complete lack of knowledge about the case became powerful evidence against Fiddler, used to deny his main defense that he was acting according to tribal custom. Paupanakiss apparently allowed his testimony to be used in this way. He could, for example, simply have told the court about the place of wendigo killings in Ojibwa society, information that he, as an Ojibwa, obviously knew.

87. Ibid., 107–8.

88. Ibid., 108.

89. See Chaikin, *Iron Hand Upon the People.*

90. Commissioner Perry to Minister of Justice, 30 October 1907. Since this letter was sent two weeks after the trial, it seems impossible to conclude anything other than that Perry had deliberately misinstructed the jury on the issue of the role of Ojibwa customary law in this case. He could only have done so with the intention of eliminating any possibility that the jury would use this information as a basis to acquit Fiddler of the murder charge.

91. Stevens and Fiddler, *Killing the Shaman,* 110–11.

92. Ibid., 111.

93. Ibid., 112.

94. Ibid., 111–12.

95. Ibid., 113–14.

96. Ibid., 115.

97. Ibid., 116.

98. *Queen v Paul Sabourin*, RG 13, vol. 1439, file 315, Canadian National Archives, Ottawa. Transcript, 1–2.

99. Transcript, 1–6.

100. Transcript, 7.

101. *Queen v Paul Sabourin*, unpaginated memorandum in case file (no date). This is the same judge that presided in two other wendigo killings.

102. Telegram, governor general to Joseph Pope, undersecretary of state, 4 December 1899. Contained in case file, *Queen v Paul Sabourin.*

103. Telegram, A. G. Irvine to inspector of penitentiaries, Ottawa, 20 November 1902.

104. Public Archives of Canada, RG 10, BS, file 190, 194, Smart to minister of justice, 15 November 1899, quoted in Rene Fumoleau, *As Long As This Land Shall Last* (Toronto, 1976), 99.

105. Teicher, "Windigo Psychosis," 85–86.

106. Ibid., 86–87.

107. The literature on Hudson's Bay Company law is still meager. See Hamar Foster, "Killing Mr. John: Law and Jurisdiction at Fort Stikine, 1842–1846," in *Law for the Elephant*, McLaren, 147–93; John Phillip Reid, "Restraints of Vengeance: Retaliation in Kind and the Use of Indian Law in the Old Oregon Country," *Oregon Historical Quarterly* (1994): 48–91; "Certainty of Vengeance: The Hudson's Bay Company and Retaliation in Kind against Indian Offenders in New Caledonia," *Montana: The Magazine of Western History* 43 (winter 1993): 4–17; and "Principles of Vengeance: Fur Trappers, Indians, and Retaliation for Homicide in the Transboundary North American West," *Western Historical Quarterly* 24 (February 1993): 21–43.

108. Except for British Columbia and the Saskatchewan Uprising, only a handful of Indians were executed in Canada in the nineteenth century, although the exact number of hangings is not clear: Hamar Foster, "'The Queen's Law is Better than Yours': International Homicide in Early British Columbia," in *Essays in Canadian Legal History*, vol. 5, ed. Jim Phillips, Tina Loo, Susan Lewthwaite (Toronto, 1994), 41–111, and 84. Swift Runner's case may be distinguished in that, unlike the other apparent wendigo killings, his did not occur beyond the frontier, but near Edmonton, and the family of his victims sought out the RCMP to prosecute the case, essentially bringing

it within the orbit of ordinary Canadian law. In addition, Swift Runner, determined to die, did not raise any kind of wendigo defense, or indeed, any defense at all.

109. It seems that none of the common law jurisdictions recognized self-defense claims arising from a Native person's honestly held belief. Reasonable belief of an immanent threat to life, however, is at the core of the law of self-defense. The common law casts the reasonableness of such belief in culturally biased terms, reflecting a reasonable English male, the "man on the Clapham omnibus."

CHAPTER 5

Sexual Assaults in Calgary, Alberta, between the Wars

David Bright

More than a decade ago the historian Terry Chapman produced a ground-breaking study of sex crimes in western Canada during the frontier period. In particular, she identified the various problems that victims—mostly women—faced in bringing their attackers to justice. Difficulties in defining consent (or lack thereof), testimony uncorroborated by physical evidence, the reputation and moral character of the woman in question, and delays in reporting the attack: all these could lessen the likelihood of prosecution.[1] Chapman's study, focusing on the years 1880–1920, is part of a growing body of literature that examines various aspects of violence on the Canadian frontier at the turn of the century. As a result of this work the traditional historiographical view that western Canada enjoyed a "peaceful settlement" has come under critical scrutiny, with Louis Knafla recently concluding that "violence in the Canadian frontier west appear[s] to have been at least equal to that in the rest of North American society."[2]

There is no doubt that Chapman, Knafla, and others are right to note the extent that violence, in all its manifestations, existed on the western Canadian frontier in the late-nineteenth and early twentieth centuries. However, to claim that such violence was a product of specific frontier conditions is an assumption that surely requires further demonstration. After all, recent works by Judith Fingard, Karen Dubinsky, and John Weaver, among other historians, have shown that violence also prevailed in older, more settled communities in central and eastern Canada.[3] Similarly, by ending her analysis in 1920, Chapman does not explore whether sex crimes were also a feature of post-frontier western society. Tom Thorner and Neil Watson's earlier study of crime in Calgary in the years 1875–1939, for example, suggested that shifts in economic conditions were more significant than the frontier per se.[4] The causal association between Canada's western frontier and social violence thus deserves further consideration. One way of doing this is to examine the level of violence in the era, namely the years after World War I.

This chapter addresses the question of violence in postfrontier western Canada. Specifically, it extends Chapman's investigation of sex crimes into the interwar period, focusing on sexual assaults committed in Calgary between 1926 and 1939. With the exception of Chapman's work, historical study of criminal sexual activity in this city—as in western Canada more generally—for the most part has looked at the limited world of prostitution.[5] By its very nature, however, this time-honored transaction rarely had a direct effect on members of the public, notwithstanding their frequent and vociferous demands that local police should rid their town or city of this scourge. In contrast, virtually no attention has been paid to a range of sex offenses—rape, indecent assault, and indecent exposure—that had at the least the potential to touch any and every member of society.[6] In addition to extending Chapman's study of sex crimes in the frontier period, then, this chapter serves two additional purposes. First, it supplies some historical background to current assertions by politicians, media, and other commentators that the near-recent past (the "old days" of common parlance) was more innocent and less abased than present-day society, especially in the field of sexual assault and similar offenses. Second, despite the substantial advances made in western Canadian social history in the past two decades, past attitudes toward sex and sexual propriety (outside prostitution) remain largely unexplored. With its focus on sexual assaults in the interwar years, this study marks a tentative entry into this relatively unexplored field.

The 1920s and 1930s were a period of major social adjustment across the West, as the outburst of postwar labor unrest gradually gave way to acceptance of the new realities of modern industrial capitalism. A new mass consumer society, centered on the trinity of the motor car, movie theatre, and wireless set, bore little resemblance to its prewar predecessor.[7] In Calgary, as elsewhere in the West, the rapid population growth that had fueled the economic boom in the decade to 1913 gave way to more moderate increases. Between 1901 and 1911 the city grew from forty-four hundred to forty-four thousand, an average annual growth rate of more than 25 percent. By comparison, between 1921 and 1941 Calgary's population expanded from sixty-three thousand to eighty-nine thousand, or an average annual increase of little more than 1 percent. During the same time the ratio of men to women narrowed from its prewar high of 1.6:1 to almost parity by the outbreak of World War II. In short, interwar Calgary was a society that was—in demographic profile at least—achieving a measure of equilibrium after its hectic infancy and the class-based tensions of World War I. Beneath this veneer of social stability, however, lay the dark stain of sexual assault, a phenomenon unrecorded in existing histories of the city.[8]

Historians have often noted the difficulties involved in plumbing the record of past criminal activity. "We reconstruct the lives of others at our peril," warns Fingard, noting that "the experiences of the Victorian underclass are reflected through the prism of middle-class sources."[9] The same may be said, *mutatis mutandis* (the necessary changes having been made), of Calgary between the wars. Similarly, in his study of working-class incest in Victorian England, Anthony Wohl cautions that "the historian of the family must often be prepared to pick his [*sic*] path among the delicate sub-structure of his subject and delve into a twilight region of uncertainties where evidence is more latent than overt."[10]

Questions of evidence are particularly pertinent when reconstructing the incidence and pattern of sexual assault in Calgary. Two major problems may be identified. First, as in all studies of crime, there is the nature of the surviving evidence itself. Published crime statistics, such as those contained in the chief of police's annual report or in the police charge books, provide information on the number of cases that come to trial and the number of convictions secured. Such figures, of course, represent only a small proportion of all incidents that actually occurred, for they do not include those that went either unreported or undetected. This "dark figure" of offenses, those that never come to official notice, is beyond historical recovery and so the true "total" picture of sexual assaults can never be known. However, there is a source that provides a better idea of the extent of criminal sexual activity in Calgary. The occurrence books contain a daily record of all complaints and reports of crime brought to the attention of the police, regardless of whether they resulted in a prosecution or conviction. Even here it is clear that the entries represent only the tip of the iceberg of sexual assault, for frequently complaints were made only after a number of offenses were witnessed or experienced.[11] Again, the occurrence books can give no clue to those incidents that were never reported. Still, the relative completeness of this source—books are available for the periods 1926–30 and 1933–39—produces a revealing picture of criminal sexual activity in Calgary in the interwar years.

The second major problem is one of definition or nomenclature. The occurrence books categorize local sex crimes according to the Criminal Code of Canada, distinguishing sharply between rape (section 298), indecent assault (sections 292–93), acts of gross indecency (section 206), and indecent acts (section 205, and encompassing indecent exposure). Accepting these contemporary definitions would perhaps be the simplest approach to the subject. At least, it is the one recommended by Eric Monkkonen in his *Police in Urban America:* "For the historian to adopt any definition of crime other than the conventional one, crime as behavior violating the criminal law, would be pointless, for the conventional definition has remarkable clarity and historical specificity."[12] Yet this same "remarkable clarity" can be misleading, for it defines and compartmentalizes each offense from the point of view of the state.[13] Occasionally, such rigidity of definition could produce a minor farce. In 1921, for example, young James G. was arrested for indecent exposure in Midnapore, just south of Calgary, and fined $10 plus costs. As it turned out, the boy simply had been bathing in the nude and, as his defense counsel later remarked, "had no intention at all of doing any indecent act." Nevertheless, it still required the personal intervention of police magistrate Colonel Gilbert Sanders to get the original conviction and fine overturned.[14]

From the victim's point of view—surely the most important point of view—it is less than clear that the state's distinct categorizations of sexual assault were always relevant. For example, the dividing line between indecent exposure and indecent assault depended as much, if not more, on the perception of and impact on the individual in question as it did on the clinical wording of the criminal code. Certainly there is a wide chasm separating penetrative rape from verbal abuse, but they exist on a continuum of sexual assault rather than as discrete and unconnected phenomena. After all, at what point does exposing himself in public—a seemingly harmless, if distasteful offense—cease to provide sufficient gratification to the violator and so give way to more intrusive forms of sexual assault? Accordingly, while this study retains the terminology of the criminal code and focuses mainly on those offenses defined as rape, indecent assault, and indecent exposure, it is more concerned with the broader phenomenon of sexual assault than with its internal gradations.

No attempt is made here to explain or fathom the psychological motivations that led men to offend.[15] Yet by viewing the array of sexual assaults as a collective phenomenon rather than as a series of discrete events, what emerges is the common theme of power. As Dubinsky notes in her study of sexual assault in Ontario, "Criminal case files and newspaper commentary are surprisingly rich, revealing heart-rending details of the many ways sex became a matter of power and conflict between men and women, parents and children, communities and regions."[16] Rapists, pedophiles, and indecent exhibitionists all share the fact that, for a brief moment at least, it is they who control a given situation, while their victims find themselves cast in a passive role or at best a reactive one. This is especially true of young children, who number disproportionately among sexual assault victims in Calgary in the interwar period. As a result, in addition to suffering the act of abuse itself, many such children were at a loss to make sense of their experience, so total was their loss of control. The case of nine-year-old Olga W. in 1932 illustrates this point. In a breathless narrative that perfectly captured the tumbling sequence of events, she described for the court her encounter with one Ivan W. that summer:[17]

I went there Saturday at 9 o'clock in the morning and he said was going to shoot me and kill me and pulled me into the house on Saturday morning. . . . He took off my clothes everything and put me in bed. . . . Then he laid on me he unbuttoned his pants and his shirts. . . . I felt a bone right here then he kissed me 3 times he said he would like to do everything. I staid there till about 12 o'clock on Sunday. . . . I went over to play with the little Stevens children and he called me in. On Sunday he just done the same thing I stayed till about 1/2 past one he had me in the house on Sunday just once a pain in my head he hot me hard on my head he said he was going to shoot me and kill me he tickled me I went down Monday he came and got me he pulled all my clothes off and got into bed with me Louise came to the door and he dressed me then he opened the door and said goodbye. I did not know it was wrong for this man to do this to me nobody ever took my clothes off before.[18]

To the justice system this episode was simply a breach of the criminal code; to Olga W. it was an event that ended her world of innocence.

In the 12 years for which the police occurrence books provide details—1926–30 and 1933–39—there were 253 reports of sexual assault in Calgary. The greater number of these were recorded officially as indecent exposure, but as argued above, the line separating such acts from overt physical assaults should not be overdrawn. Accounting for less than 0.5 percent of all occurrences reported, the incidence of sexual assault appears to be statistically insignificant, even though it was in fact far more common than murders in the city, crimes that have received a fair amount of attention from historians.[19] The average number of 21 assaults per year is misleading, for annual totals ranged from just 3 in 1926 to 36 in 1939, with an earlier peak of 34 coming in 1929. As figure 5.1 shows, however, no clear pattern emerges from these raw annual data, even if the incidence of sexual assault is calculated on a per capita basis (see fig. 5.2).

Other general observations may be made with more certainty. First, there was a clear seasonal rhythm in the occurrence of assaults (see fig. 5.3). Not surprisingly, perhaps, given Calgary's long and often very cold winters, indecent exposure and other assaults were relatively rare in the months of October through January, these four months accounting for just 21 percent of the total. By contrast, the spring months of February to May accounted for 42.5 percent, possibly reflecting the coincidence of improved weather with a new school term. (As discussed below, schools were a popular site among sex offenders.) The remaining 37.5 percent of reported incidents took place during the four summer months of June to September, when the weather was good and the evenings long.

Second, although sexual assault is commonly associated with the hours of darkness, this was only partially true in the case of Calgary. More than half of all reported cases specify the time at which the assault occurred, from which it is possible to construct an approximate pattern of distribution. Dividing the day, somewhat arbitrarily, into morning (4:00 A.M. to 12 noon), afternoon (12 noon to 8:00 P.M.), and night (8:00 P.M. to 12 midnight), it turns out that less than 40 percent of incidents occurred after sundown. By contrast, almost 50 percent of assaults—mostly, but by no means exclusively, consisting of indecent exposure—took place in the afternoon or early evening. Perhaps most surprising is the fact that a full 20 percent of incidents were reported to have

Figure 5.1
Sexual Assaults, 1926–39

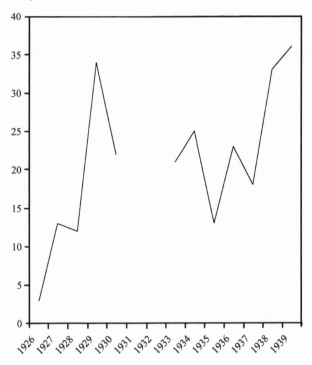

taken place in the hours before noon, In short, while parents sensibly may have warned their children—especially their daughters—to take care after dark, such precautions in themselves were no guarantee of safety when it came to sexual assault.

The third and most basic observation is that in every single case the assailant was a male. While the victims could be and were of either sex—and in one case a dog—their attackers were always either a man or a boy.[20] This may seem a rather obvious statement to make, but it serves to remind that the realm of sexual assault was one of the few in which gender differences were absolute and not relative.[21]

A fourth and final note should be made of the extent to which victims either knew or recognized their attackers. Dubinsky makes this observation in her study, arguing that "any degree of familiarity between a man and a woman raised the possibility of consent" and thus lessened the probability of a rape conviction.[22] While this is no doubt true, the extent to which the victim was able to identify her or his attacker to the police was a basic determinant of whether or not the case would come to court in the first place. As it happens,

Figure 5.2
Sexual Assaults per 100,000, 1926–39

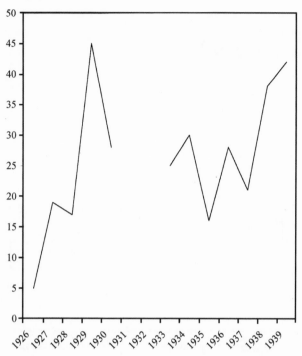

there was no pre-existing relationship between assailant and victim in the majority of assaults in Calgary, and descriptions given to investigators were frequently so vague as to be of little assistance. "No description, except that he was wearing a cap," reads an entry for October 1926 in the occurrence book.[23] In February 1930 a 13-year-old girl was on her way home from a skating rink when she was "chased by a man who wanted to have sexual intercourse with her," but upon questioning by the police "was unable to give any description of this man." Many other reports were no more enlightening.[24]

Those victims who were able to provide descriptions often gave the police the slimmest of clues to work on. "Fat Chubby Face, Speaks Broken English," "looked like a working man with something under his arm," "was wearing dark clothes and a dark overcoat, and was riding a yellow bicycle," and "sometimes dresses like a woman" were a start, but not much more. Even more questionable were those descriptions that revealed more about the Anglocentric biases of the witnesses themselves than the actual offenders.[25] Phrases such as "foreign looking," "looks like a foreigner," "looked like a Jew" were of marginal value to the police.[26]

Figure 5.3
Sexual Assaults by Month, 1926–39

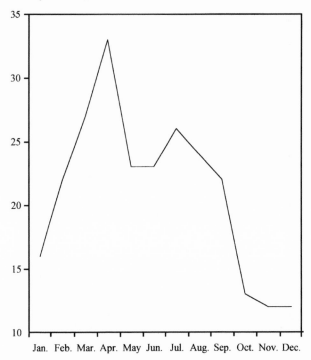

On other occasions, however, victims or members of their family were able to give the police a name or an address where the alleged culprit might be found. In April 1934, for example, Mrs. G. reported to the police that her daughter had been indecently assaulted in suite 15 of Crown Block. The police took the girl with them, she identified the occupant as her assailant, and the police charged him with the offense.[27] Yet even the possession of this sort of information could not guarantee a prosecution. A few months later in December 1939 the police received a complaint that a man had been exposing himself to schoolchildren at 4 o'clock each day from a window of his house on 17th Street East. When they arrived, however, the two male tenants denied all knowledge of the incident, and the officers left without arresting either of them.[28] This problem of obtaining sufficient evidence was evident in the singular case of incest reported in this period. In August 1939 Else G. went to the police and told them that her father had been having sexual relations with her since the fall of 1937. Police visited their house at 10th Avenue West and interviewed Victor G., but he too denied the accusation, and the matter ended there as far as the legal system was concerned. Whether the same is true for Else G. is unknown.[29]

Difficulties in securing sufficient evidence were a constant problem for the police when it came to prosecuting alleged sex offenders. As in the case above, all too often it was a question of one person's word against another's. Both Chapman and Dubinsky make this point, the latter stating that "Prejudice, mistrust and outright misogyny were the order of the day for women who brought their stories to the criminal court."[30] The question of personal credibility appears to have been a factor in Calgary. In June 1936, for example, a woman complained that someone had tried to indecently assault her while she was attending an afternoon show at the Variety Theatre. She gave the police the man's name, but on being questioned he stated in fact "that it was she who created the disturbance." The police declined to take the matter further.[31]

More serious was an incident in July 1930, when 16-year-old Doris L. reported to police that she had been raped by two youths on the previous evening. In her initial complaint and during the subsequent preliminary hearing, the young woman maintained that while she stood on 4th Avenue at 10:00 p.m., waiting for mother to arrive, 20-year-old Gordon O. and 19-year-old Frank W. drove up to the sidewalk and forced her into the car. With Doris jammed in between them, they then headed north to a deserted spot in the city where they took turns raping her. After three hours of this ordeal, the two men returned Doris to her house, whereupon she told her mother and other family members what had happened. Three times in court Doris was asked to describe in close detail the alleged assault, with defense counsel T. J. O'Connor clearly seeking to expose any inconsistencies in her account. Most of his questioning, however, was aimed at discrediting Doris's character. In the first place, he attacked the girl's ability to tell the truth under oath, a point he pursued relentlessly even to the exasperation of magistrate Sanders. The following is just part of the exchange:

Q: What difference does it make to you whether you tell the truth or not?

A: My conscience would bother me if I did not.

Q: What difference would it make to you if you just stood up and said, I will tell the truth or when you are sworn to tell the truth, what is the difference?

A: I would not want to lie, anyhow. I do not understand what you mean.

Q: Don't you know what an oath means to you.

A: Yes, to tell the truth.

Q: Yes, but what—would it make any difference to you anyway if you only said I will tell the truth?

A: Yes, I would tell the truth.

Q: What difference does taking that oath mean to you?

A: I just tell the truth. I would not think of lying if I was brought to court.

Q: Do you know what so help me God means?

A: No.

Q: Do you know what God means?

A: Yes.

Court: She is old enough to understand. She is not a child. She is 17 years of age.[32]

This form of questioning, a virtual attack on the victim's credibility, was by no means an uncommon practice in cases of sexual assault. As Dubinsky notes, in the face of such hostility and disbelief, assaulted women often found themselves victimized twice over, once by the perpetrator and again by the legal system.[33]

At this point it might be asked what standard of evidence was in fact required to secure a conviction of sexual assault. The answer to this question depends, in part, on the jurisdiction under which the case was being tried. In Calgary, sexual offenses—as defined by the criminal code—could be tried either in the local police magistrate's court or else in the District Court of Calgary (formed in 1907) and its successor the District Court of Southern Alberta (formed in 1933).[34] Little is known about the routine operation of the superior courts, with Louis Knafla and Richard Klumpenhouwer recently noting that "the history of the courts remains to be reconstructed, and the various judicial districts to which the judges were assigned has not yet been compiled"[35] Before such basic work has been completed, it is not possible to say with certainty how sexual assault cases fared in Alberta's district courts.

In the case of the Calgary police magistrate's court, more is known of the day-to-day administration of justice. Ruling from the bench for most of the interwar years was Colonel Gilbert E. Sanders, who served as magistrate from 1911 to 1932.[36] A former officer in the North-West Mounted Police, Sanders shared many of the biases and prejudices of Calgary's social elite of the day, and these inevitably influenced his dispensation of justice. As he explained in 1913, "it is my duty, I think, to take an ordinary common sense view of the law. I do not mean to get into subtle distinctions, but to view the law in a broad way."[37] Sanders's "ordinary common sense view" encompassed his racist and class prejudices, leading him to disparage Calgary's Jewish, Black, and Chinese populations, as well as any alleged labor radicals who came before him.

As for sexual assault cases tried in the magistrate's court, Chapman argues that Sanders was not disposed to accept the word of the complainant as sufficient to convict, especially if she was young or if doubts about her moral character and reputation could be raised. Instead, victims were expected to disclose evidence of physical resistance as proof that they had not been consenting partners. "It is readily apparent that the greatest display of physical resistance on the part of the female was the loss of her life," comments Chapman. "Indeed, this seemed to be the only sure way for a woman to quell any doubts about the issue of consent which may have arisen at the trial."[38] The evidence of the police occurrence books suggests that women continued to face such obstacles in the years after World War I. The reputation or character of the complainant, a lack of physical evidence, her willingness to initiate and pursue charges, and her maturity, continued to influence the way in which the criminal justice system handled cases of sexual assault.

The case of Doris L., described above, underlines the role that a woman's alleged reputation could play when it came to prosecuting sexual assaults. A woman's previous sexual history or even her alleged reputation as an "easy" woman was admissible as evidence and could even constitute grounds for the dismissal of a rape charge. In Doris's case, one of her alleged attackers, Gordon O., had testified at the hearing that she "appeared to be a flapper who ran around with nothing to do and if she was a good girl she did not act that way." He confessed to having had sex with her, but claimed it was consensual.[39] Switching from his emphasis on the immaturity (and hence unreliability) of Doris, O'Connor took his cue from Gordon's characterization of her and next began to suggest that she was sexually experienced beyond her young years, naming various men with whom she was alleged to have flirted before the assault. By this portrayal of Doris, O'Connor hoped to reinforce the idea that she had been a consenting partner to sex with Gordon and his friend Frank W., as they maintained, even though an examining doctor had already testified that "there had been force used to have the intercourse."[40]

The problem of finding evidence to support the otherwise unsubstantiated claims of sexual assault victims was apparent in many other instances. In June 1930 Mrs. Ambrose R. reported that a man had exposed himself to her from his house on a number of occasions. The police, however, noted that "Quite a time has elapsed between each occurrence and sufficient evidence could not be obtained to warrant prosecution" and as a result had to be satisfied with warning the man to be more careful in future. The outcome was the same in June 1935 after two men complained that 14-year-old Arthur H. had indecently assaulted their young daughters. Police acted on the complaint but could do little more than to caution the boy's mother "to keep a close check on him." Again and again this was the case, with police unable or unwilling to pursue prosecution of offenders for a lack of material evidence.[41]

Another difficulty faced by the police was the fact that many victims of sexual assault were reluctant to pursue the matter or formally press charges. Given the experience of Doris L., subjected to all manner of personal and intrusive questioning in front of her mother and other family members, this reluctance is understandable. In April 1930 Grace C. complained that a man had been exposing himself to her from the sidewalk opposite her home on President Avenue; police investigated and subsequently arrested Charles M., only to see Mrs. C. decline to prosecute. Similarly, when Fred B. reported that Carl N. had exposed himself to his wife as she crossed a field opposite the Pat Burns meatpacking plant, the police noted that the complainant "would like to have him checked up but his wife does not wish to give evidence." Without her testimony prosecution was impossible.[42] In other cases the decision not to press charges appears to have been a family decision. In March 1938, for example, although Joyce N. claimed to have been indecently assaulted by a man in a car, she "refused to furnish detailed particulars and the parents did not wish any further action to be taken."[43] In such cases parents weighed their desire to see justice done against the potential harm such action might have on their children, in terms of either psychological damage or tarnished reputation. Often this deliberation could take some time, as in September 1930 when Edmund C., whose 7-year-old daughter had been indecently assaulted by a 15-year-old youth, requested "that this matter be held in abeyance for a day or two while he considers laying a charge."[44]

A further problem that impeded successful prosecution of sexual assault cases was the young age of many victims. As Chapman notes in her study of sex crimes, although section 29 of the Criminal Evidence Act admitted the testimony of children in cases of actual or attempted carnal knowledge, conviction could not result from such testimony alone. On the other hand, Dubinsky argues in her study of rape in Ontario that assaults against children had a conviction rate of over 50 percent, markedly higher than in the cases involving adult women. In Calgary even reasonably mature teenagers such as Doris L. were subjected to intensive questioning by defense counsel, whose aim was to discredit the truth of the complainant's account. In many cases the victim was a good deal younger than this, which made securing reliable testimony—in the court's eyes, at least—even more problematic. The case of 9-year-old Olga W., already cited, demonstrates the difficulty such children had in making sense of the assault itself and then in constructing a coherent narrative of the incident. Complicating this matter further was the fact that, in Dubinsky's words, "Whether or not women were really innocent, sexual modesty was expected in court."[45] As a result, even as they sought to discover the "truth" of an assault, examiners were reluctant to accept that a young girl might already possess the knowledge or vocabulary with which to describe the incident. This could lead to long exercises in circumlocution in which it was left to the victim to cut to the chase. In 1932, for example, 10-year-old Edna H. was asked what she had told her mother after an alleged assault on her by Charles L. The following exchange took place:

A: I told Mamma that Mr. L—— had tried to do something to me.

Q: What do you mean when you said he tried to do something, do you know what he was trying to do?

A: Yes.

Q: Did your mother ask you what he was trying to do?

A: Yes.

Q: What did you say? Just tell Mr. Fowler and I what he said.

Mag. Fowler: Do not be frightened, little girl, just tell us.

Sgt. Purdy: What did you tell her he tried to do?

A: He tried to do it to me. She said "What" and I told her.

Q: Told her what, just tell us exactly what you told her.

A: I told her he tried to . . .

Q: Eh? Do not be afraid now. We all have little girls at home just about your age, so you can tell us exactly what happened. What did you tell her?

Mag. Fowler: Just tell us.

A: I told her that he was trying to fuck me.[46]

A final problem in securing convictions was raised when the victim in question fell under the legal category of "idiot or imbecile." Section 219 of the criminal code prohibited sexual intercourse with any such woman "under circumstances which do not amount to rape but which prove that the offender knew, at the time of the offense, that the woman or girl was an idiot, imbecile, or insane or deaf and dumb."[47] Proof of such knowledge was obviously open to contest, as was the degree to which the woman in question gave her active consent to the act. The case of Mary H. in 1923 illustrates the difficulties such cases could raise. This 18-year-old girl, described by her doctor as "mentally deficient" and possessing the mental age of an 8-year-old, visited Culver C. with her sister Kate several times during the spring that year. The man had asked their mother if they might wash his dishes for him, as he had recently cut his finger, and she agreed. Mary H. told the court what happened on one such visit there in March:

C—— did something to me. He screwed me. He screwed me in the [work]shop. He put me on the bed, pulled down my bloomers. He then took down his pants. He then screwed me. He then laid on top of me. He said he couldn't put a young girl in the family way. I did not say anything or struggle. . . . I told C—— I was not feeling good. I went home after he screwed me. . . . Kate was up with me two times and I was up twice without Kate. The last night Kate was up at the workshop with me he screwed Kate too. He screwed me too. Nobody called for assistance. . . . I was not willing to be screwed by C——. I did not do or say anything to show I was unwilling to be screwed by C——.[48]

Mary's 16-year-old sister, Kate, the only other person present, largely confirmed this version of events. She explained how C. had had sex with them both, but insisted that it was consensual. "We could have left anytime we wanted to," she told the court, adding that "he has always been a gentleman." Despite—or perhaps because of—these confessions, and even though Mary was pregnant as a result of the incident, charges against C. were dismissed, and the case never went to trial.[49]

Of the 250 or so reported assaults in Calgary in this period, at least 10 involved children 5 years or younger in age. In one particularly sordid instance, the victim was a baby of only 6 months, whose mother had left her in a carriage on the front lawn. Other cases included two men approaching two young girls, 3 and 5 years of age, as they played in a public park and "suggesting to them that they remove their pants," and the indecent assault of a 5-year-old boy by the CPR tracks in southwest Calgary. That the police sometimes had trouble in accepting such complaints at face value was evident in June 1930. A man reported that his 5-year-old daughter had come home crying that "a Big Boy had taken her to a lumber yard close by and had got on top of her and hurt her stomach." Despite the fact that another young boy, 7 years old, was prepared to testify to the assault, the police concluded that "There was no evidence to show that the child had been injured or penetrated."[50] That the police were inclined to place more weight on physical evidence—or the lack thereof—than on the testimony of young children led to many reported cases of assault being dismissed. On other occasions, while the police accepted the fact of an assault, they were unwilling to accept the complaint's unsupported identification of the offender. In February 1933, for example, Edith S. identified a man who she claimed had indecently assaulted her 6-year-old daughter. The police investigated the case, but concluded that while "The little girl was undoubted assaulted by someone . . . no evidence could be obtained to substantiate the story."[51]

Young children such as these featured prominently in reported instances of sexual assault in Calgary between the wars. The age of the victim is specified in 134 separate entries—that is, in more than half of the total occurrences— and of these, 77 were 10 years old or younger. A further 21 victims were between the ages of 11 and 15. In other words, almost three-quarters of all reported sexual assaults involved young children. Of the remaining cases, 17 (or 13 percent) were between the ages of 16 and 20, while just 19 (14 percent) were legally adults (see fig. 5.4).

In addition to being young, the majority of victims were also female, accounting for more than 90 percent of all reported cases. The abuse of young boys, however, and even some young men, was by no means uncommon in Calgary. In April 1927 police arrested a man for the repeated indecent assault of boys from 10 to 12 years of age, an offense for which he was later sentenced to 2 years of hard labor and 15 lashes. In the same month 14-year-old Fred W. reported that a man had caught hold of him at Nose Creek Hill "and endeavored to take out his Privates."[52] Such assaults were typical in that they involved an older man abusing a younger boy, but in a few cases the victim was also an adult male. On the night of June 9, 1934, for example, unemployed Carl S. was sleeping at the Salvation Army Hostel when "a man offered him a job and took him to a house at 8th Avenue and 6th Street East where they went to bed." The former later complained to police that at some point during the night, the man, about 50 years of age, attempted to sodomize him. At the other end of the age spectrum, in September of the same year John H. reported that "recently a number of young boys between 7 and 10 years of age . . . have been practicing the act of sodomy."[53]

Figure 5.4
Age of Victims

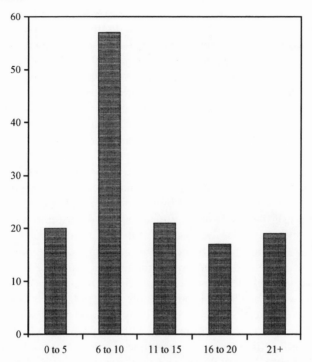

Almost all the incidents mentioned so far relate to assaults that took place out of doors. This raises the question whether such attacks were randomly distributed across the city or whether there were certain "high risk" areas.[54] From the information available in the police occurrence books it seems that the latter was more likely, for a number of locations appear repeatedly as the scene of sexual assault. Calgary's public parks were a prime site, accounting for more than 10 percent of all reported cases, as their open space was an obvious magnet for young children, while bushes and other foliage offered the perpetrator cover for his act. Riley Park, Mewata Park, Victoria Park, and Elbow Park all appear frequently in the police record. In May 1929, for example, a 12-year-old boy took 5-year-old Bernice H. into the public toilets in Riley Park and removed her underwear. The same park was later the venue for the indecent assault of an 8-year-old boy by an elderly man. On a summer's evening in 1929 a woman reported seeing a man in Mewata Park "chasing three young girls, at the same time working with his hands at the front of his pants."[55] The presence of lakes or swimming pools in Calgary's parks further enhanced their appeal to sex offenders, with complaints being made of men exposing themselves to seminaked children playing in the water.[56] A number of incidents took place on the two islands standing on the Bow River, which ran through the center of Calgary. In August 1933 a man enticed two young boys on to Prince's Island, where he indecently assaulted them; the island was the site of a similar assault in May 1938. That same year, a spate of indecent exposures took place on nearby St. George's Island, home to the city's zoo.[57]

More generally, the banks and bushes along the river itself were the scene of several assaults. In March 1929 Henry T. reported that a man had attacked four young girls, including Henry's two daughters, as they played on the north bank. The man allegedly took one of the girls into a nearby cave and attempted to have sexual intercourse with her. A similar assault took place in June 1936, while reports of indecent exposure were frequently made by residents in the area.[58] The pattern of assaults extended into the district of Sunnyside, a heavily bushed area just north of the river. In September 1928, for example, a local woman reported a naked man "acting in a peculiar manner" at the foot of a path that was used by schoolchildren, but unfortunately was unable to furnish the police with a more detailed description. Other assaults were later reported in the same area, while Sunnyside Boulevard, a major thoroughfare running through the district, appears to have been especially popular among men wishing to expose themselves in public.[59]

Two other general locations merit attention. First, and perhaps most obvious of all, were the city's various schools. The police received numerous complaints of suspicious-looking men hanging around school property, as pupils made their way to or from school or as they played in the yard during lunch-hour recess. To give just one example, a series of incidents occurred at schools in the city's Rideau district during the spring of 1937. One afternoon in early April, 8-year-old Pamela H. reported that, as she was walking home from school, a young man exposed himself to her from some bushes at the corner of Rideau Park School. Less than two weeks later, a girl at Rideau Junior High School claimed that a different man—at least, she gave his age as between 45and 50—had exposed himself twice, once at noon and again at 4:00 P.M. The police were called in but failed to arrest anyone. A month passed without incident, but then in the middle of May a parent of a 13-year-old pupil at Rideau High reported that an elderly man—possibly the same one as before—had exposed himself to her from bushes near the school as she was on her way back from lunch.[60] In themselves, such incidents might be dismissed as being relatively innocuous, but coming as they did in the wake of several more serious attacks in the city they should be viewed as part of a broader pattern of sexual assaults that spring.

Calgary's street railway stations were the final location that featured prominently in reported assaults. Established in the years before World War I, the streetcar system had soon become popular among Calgary's working-class population, enabling people to move out of those districts immediately adjacent to the city's factories, warehouses, and industrial plants.[61] The downside of this arrangement, of course, was that it meant a lengthy commute for many workers. In the decade after World War I a growing proportion of this work-force consisted of young women who found employment in the expanding service and clerical sectors of the economy. They, too, made frequent use of the street railway, especially at night when it offered the cheapest and most convenient form of transport. However, one unforeseen result of this devel-opment was that a woman disembarking at her station could be particularly vulnerable to attack. In May 1927, for example, a young woman was walking home from her streetcar stop when a man drove up in a car, got out, exposed himself, and then attempted to rape her. Fortunately, Rainer screamed and struggled sufficiently to scare the man away.[62] Two years later, in March 1929, it was a dog that came to the rescue of 19-year-old Edith G. It was just after midnight as she left the streetcar on 14th Street Northwest, when a man grabbed her and began to indecently assault her. Just then, however, a nearby hound was woken by the noise and began to bark loudly, which in turn led to the man fleeing the scene. There was also at least one occasion when an indecent assault took place on a streetcar itself, underlining the fragile security available even in the most public of locations.[63]

Indeed, while there were certain areas that were particularly prone to in-cidents of sexual assault, the simple measure of avoiding such locations did not guarantee an individual's safety. In July 1937, for example, a woman was shopping in a confectionery store on 4th Avenue when suddenly a man "caught hold of her arm and suggested that she have intercourse with him."[64] On a few reported occasions, the danger of assault from a stranger even found its way into the victim's own home. On an evening in February 1930, a woman was at home when a man called at the door. He was, she later told the police, "selling pencils and pieces of cotton as he was in destitute circumstances," but as she looked down at his wares she saw that he was also exhibiting his penis to her. A few months later in May that year a man claiming to be the medical representative of the Prudential Assurance Company visited a number of houses in west Calgary. On each occasion he would talk his way into the house, saying he had been sent to examine the occupant, and then proceed to inde-cently assault the woman at home.[65] While none of these occurrences involved physical violence, this was not always the case. In July 1929 Mrs. Simone W. answered her door at 9.30 P.M. to a man who asked her if he "could have a good time." On being told to go away, he seized the women's hair, struck her several blows in the face, and kicked her severely in the stomach.[66] Beyond the question of physical harm, there is also the mental or psychological impact of such assaults to consider. At midnight on 14 May 1938, for example, a 50-year-old man exposed himself to two girls who were alone in a house in east Calgary. The man then loitered around the house for two hours, and as the police report notes, "the girls were too frightened to call for help."[67]

From the police occurrence books, then, it is possible to discover a fair amount of information regarding the incidence, victims, and location of sexual assault in Calgary. What do they reveal about the men who committed these offenses? As seen already, a problem in answering this question lies in the frequently vague descriptions provided to the police, sometimes offering no detail at all. Still, certain observations may be made.

In 135 of the 253 reported incidents, either the victim or some other witness gave the police an estimate of the offender's apparent age. While errors of judgment were no doubt made, the common practice of giving a range of years—45 to 50—to some extent counteracts this fact. As figure 5.5 shows, in 29 cases, or 21 percent of the known total, the attacker was between the ages of 10 and 19; in 44 instances, or 33 percent, he was between 20 and 29. This means that fewer than half of all assaults, 46 percent, were committed by men 30 years of age or older. A separate source, the police charge books, confirms this picture. Obviously dealing with a far smaller sample of offenders, namely those caught and convicted, the charge books show that nearly 50 percent of those prosecuted for various sexual assaults between 1926 and 1939 were under 30. The typical sex offender in Calgary, then, was as likely to be a young male—and in some cases very young—as he was to be the dirty old man of popular imagination.[68]

Figure 5.5
Age of Offenders

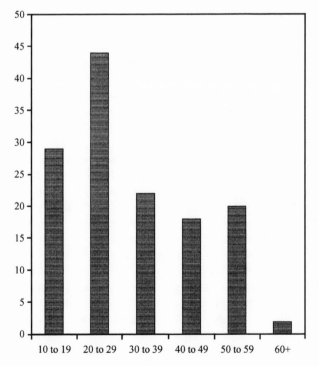

In terms of the offender's background or occupation, it is more difficult to make any general observation. While many complaints recorded the assailant's disheveled appearance or apparent poverty, in others the victim might note the man's well-trimmed beard or the quality of his suit. At the very least, then, any attempt to link sex offenders as a whole with either the working class or the urban poor should be resisted. This is important, for the picture of convicted sex offenders according to the police charge books is one in which unskilled workers are the dominant feature. "Labourer," "Farm hand," or "nil" is entered under the heading of occupation in 20 of the 36 entries, while various crafts or trades—baker, butcher, painter, cook—account for more than half a dozen of the rest.

Whether or not sexual assault was more prevalent in Calgary during the interwar years than in previous decades is difficult to say, as we do not have comparable sources for the earlier period.[69] Chapman's study, for example, gives no sense of the magnitude of the problem in the period 1890–1920. However, one development in the 1920s and 1930s suggests that it was at least becoming easier to commit such offenses. The rise of the privately owned automobile, made possible by the new processes of mass production pioneered by Henry Ford, transformed the streets of Calgary in the years after World War I. As early as 1923, for example, there were more than six thousand such cars in the city. Some of these, as the occurrence books show, belonged to men prepared to sexually assault women, and the new mobility that a car gave them may well have been the factor that tipped the balance in their case. In any event, cars were a feature in at least 19 of the reported assaults in the interwar period. We have already seen the role of Gordon O. and Francis W.'s car in the rape of Doris L. On another occasion in February 1929, a young man picked up 15-year-old Daisy B., drove to an area north of the city, and raped her. In an echo of the Doris L. case, two men forced Jessica T. into their car in July 1934 and took her out to the country where they took turns raping her. A year earlier a young man had driven around the city in a Chevrolet coupe with a revolver lying on the seat next to him, threatening women so that they would get into the car with him. Perhaps it was coincidence, but in August 1934—18 months later—the same model of car was used in the indecent assault of 14-year-old Phyllis F.[70]

Young children were particularly vulnerable to this new mode of abduction, perhaps enticed by the apparently innocent offer of a ride around town. In November 1938 a "big, fat man" picked up three children between the ages of five and six "and tried to get them to commit indecent acts." They refused and on this occasion were returned home without physical harm.[71] Other children were less fortunate. A few months after this incident, for example, someone abducted a 5-year-old girl and drove her out to the country where she was assaulted. In yet other cases the offender selected an isolated spot in the city to violate his victim. On an evening in August 1938, a young man driving a Ford sedan accosted Ronald J. and took him to a deserted baseball diamond whereupon he "opened his pants and asked [the boy] to rub his penis." In this case the young boy managed to escape and run home. One year later 8-year-old Cecil B. was playing in Victoria Park when a man in his forties grabbed him, drove out to nearby Lowrey Gardens, and assaulted the boy "by sucking his privates."[72]

A subset of such offenses involved taxi drivers, another aspect of the new car culture in Calgary. On a number of occasions in this period the police arrested cab drivers for assaulting—and in one case raping—female passengers.[73] While such incidents would have occurred, and indeed did occur, without the use of an automobile, the arrival of the affordable motor car in large numbers provided the sex offender not only with a new sense of mobility but also with a new cloak of anonymity.

Having waded through the squalid world of sexual assault that lay just beneath the surface of Calgary society, it would be a relief to end on the positive note that Calgary's criminal justice system was equal to the challenge. That is not possible. The charge book figure of 36 convictions between 1926 and 1939—compared with 253 reported occurrences—understates the success that the police had in prosecuting sex offenders, for the chief of police annual reports suggest a total closer to 80. But even this latter figure represents a conviction rate of barely 30 percent. In other words, 7 out of every 10 assaults that were reported went unpunished. The "dark figure" of unreported and undetected offenses is unknown and unknowable, but if a conservative estimate is accepted that only one-third of assaults were ever reported to the police, the conviction rate falls to just 10 percent.[74] More often, facing the lack of evidence other than the complainant's accusation, investigating officers would only caution or otherwise warn the alleged offender.[75]

How does the record of sexual assault in the interwar years compare with that of the preceding "frontier" period in Calgary's history? No direct answer to this question is possible, as comparable records do not exist for the years before World War I. Nevertheless, the prevalence of sexual assaults in the city, as recorded in the police occurrence books, suggests that to explain violence as a function of the frontier is a mistake. In his recent survey of the subject, Rod Macleod argues that "By creating the most powerful law enforcement agency it could devise, the [federal] government hoped to keep violence to a minimum, not by avoiding change but by implementing it as quickly and thoroughly as possible."[76] Maybe this is true on the larger scale, but in terms of combating intimate violence, especially that by men against women, the development of the Royal North-West Mounted Police and improvements in Calgary's city police were of little effect.[77]

Sex crimes are not a function of frontier society, but rather are an enduring feature of urban society. While Calgary witnessed no event so brutal as the gang rape of 2 women by 15 men in Toronto in 1858, related by Constance Backhouse in her study of nineteenth-century Canada, the comparison across time and space is useful. As works by Backhouse, Dubinsky, Fingard, Judith

Walkowitz, and others show, the common features of urban life—anonymity, mobility, vulnerability—increased the opportunities for sexual assault and lessened the likelihood of conviction.[78] The prejudices, assumptions, and biases of the criminal justice system compounded this situation. Calgary's record of sexual assault between the two world wars exhibits all of these features and suggests the need to rethink the traditional juxtaposition of a youthful, frontier society before World War I and the more orderly, mature, and urbane one that followed. The problems that Chapman identifies in the prosecution of sex crimes before 1920 continued to exist in the 1920s and 1930s.

Sexual assault in Calgary is neither a manifestation of frontier violence nor a recent phenomenon, a symbol of declining social morality. Instead, it is an enduring feature of the city's history and one that needs examination and explanation. "Rape," argues Dubinsky, "is . . . an act which contains a different meaning at different moments in history, shifting according to prevailing standards of sexual conduct, gender relations, and race and class contexts."[79] The reverse is also true: the way in which a society (and its criminal justice system) responds to rape and other sexual assaults tells us much about its broader values, beliefs, and biases. Delving into Calgary's world of sexual assault may not be pleasant, but it is an important contribution toward a fuller understanding of the social history of that city. More important, any denial of that world is an insult to those who suffered and survived the assaults in the first place.

NOTES

1. Terry Chapman, "Sex Crimes in the West, 1890–1920," *Alberta History* 35: 4 (fall 1987): 6–18. See also Chapman, "'Til Death do us Part': Wife Beating in Alberta, 1905–1920," *Alberta History* 36: 4 (autumn 1988): 13–22; and "'Inquiring Minds Want to Know': The Handling of Children in Sex Assault Cases in the Canadian West, 1880–1920," in *Dimensions of Childhood: Essays on the History of Children and Youth in Canada*, ed. Russell Smandych, Gordon Dodds, and Alvin Esau (Winnipeg, 1991), 183–204.

2. Louis A. Knafla, "Violence in Canada: An Introduction to its Sociopolitical Dynamics," in *Violence in Canada: Sociopolitical Perspectives*, ed. Jeffrey Ian Ross (Don Mills, Ontario, 1995), 28. See also R. C. Macleod, "Law and Order on the Western-Canadian Frontier," in *Law for the Elephant, Law for the Beaver: Essays in the Legal History of the North American West*, ed. John McLaren, Hamar Foster, and Cher Orloff (Pasadena, 1991), 90–105; Richard Maxwell Brown, "Western Violence: Structure, Values, Myth," *Western Historical Quarterly* 24:1 (February 1993): 5–20, and "Law and Order on the American Frontier: The Western Civil War of Incorporation," in *Law for the Elephant, Law for the Beaver,* ed. McLaren, Foster, and Orloff, 74–89. For a broader overview, see Kenneth McNaught, "Violence in Canadian History," in *Studies in Canadian Social History*, ed. Michiel Horn and Ronald Sabourin (Toronto, 1974), 376–91.

3. Judith Fingard, *The Dark Side of Life in Victorian Halifax* (Porters Lake, Nova

Scotia, 1989); Karen Dubinsky, *Improper Advances: Rape and Heterosexual Conflict in Ontario, 1880–1929* (Chicago & London, 1993); John C. Weaver, *Crimes, Constables, and Courts: Order and Transgression in a Canadian City, 1816–1970* (Montreal & Kingston, 1995).

4. T. Thorner and N. Watson, "Patterns of Prairie Crime: Calgary, 1875–1939," in *Crime and Criminal Justice in Europe and Canada*, ed. Louis A. Knafla (Waterloo, 1981), 219–56.

5. James H. Gray, *Red Lights on the Prairies* (Toronto: Mcmillan of Canada, 1973); S. W. Horrall, "The (Royal) North-West Mounted Police and Prostitution on the Canadian Prairies," *Prairie Forum* 10:1 (spring 1985): 105–27; Judy Bedford, "Prostitution in Calgary, 1905–1914," *Alberta History* 29:2 (spring 1981): 1–11; Thorner and Watson, "Patterns of Prairie Crime," 219–56; Margaret Gilkes, *Ladies of the Night: The Recollections of a Pioneer Canadian Policewoman* (Hanna, 1989).

6. In addition to works already cited, see Terry Chapman, "'An Oscar Wilde Type': 'The Abominable Crime of Buggery' in Western Canada, 1890–1920," *Criminal Justice History* 4 (1983): 97–118.

7. For example, see Suzanne Morton, *Ideal Surroundings: Domestic Life in a Working-Class Suburb in the 1920s* (Toronto, 1995).

8. Max Foran, *Calgary: An Illustrated History* (Toronto, 1978), 174–75. See also David Bright, *The Limits of Labour: Class Formation and the Labour Movement in Calgary, 1883–1929* (Vancouver, 1998), 120–44.

9. Fingard, *Dark Side of Life in Victorian Halifax*, 189.

10. Anthony S. Wohl, "Sex and the Single Room: Incest among the Victorian Working Class," in *The Victorian Family: Structure and Stresses*, ed. Anthony S. Wohl (London, 1978), 197.

11. For example, see Calgary Police Service Museum/Archives, Occurrence Books (hereafter OB), 7 January 1930 (#44), 23 May 1933 (#1873), 13 April 1934 (#1166), 28 March 1938 (#983). For a comparative use of this source, see John Weaver, "A Social History of Theft in Depression and Wartime; The Police Occurrence Books for Hamilton, Ontario, 1934–42," *Criminal Justice History* 12 (1991) 161–87.

12. Eric H. Monkkonen, *Police in Urban America, 1860–1920* (Cambridge, 1981), 17.

13. Dubinsky makes this point in *Improper Advances*, 6–7. For a changing perception of a specific form of assault, see Bruce A. MacFarlane, Q.C., "Historical Development of the Offence of Rape," in *100 Years of the Criminal Code in Canada*, ed. Mr. Justice Josiah Wood and Richard C. C. Peck, Q.C. (Ottawa, 1993), 111–88.

14. Glenbow Museum Archives (GMA), M6840, J. McKinley Cameron papers, box 25, file 329, *King v James G.*, J. M. Cameron to A. G. Browning KC, Deputy Attorney General, 12 November 1921, and Police Magistrate to Deputy Attorney General, n/d. For details of Sanders's career as police magistrate, see Thomas Thorner and Neil B. Watson, "Keeper of the King's Peace: Colonel G. E. Sanders and the Calgary Police Magistrate's Court, 1911–1932," *Urban History Review* 12:3 (February 1984): 45–55.

15. For an important debate on this issue, see Susan Brownmiller, *Against Our Will: Men, Women and Rape* (New York: Simon and Schuster, 1975); and Edward Shorter, "On Writing the History of Rape," *Signs* 3:2 (1977): 470–82. Roy Porter provides a valuable review of these works in his essay "Rape—Does it have a Historical Meaning?" in *Rape*, ed. Sylvana Tomaselli and Roy Porter (Oxford, 1986), 216–36. For further insights on this issue, see Sylvia Levine and Joseph Koenig, eds., *Why Men Rape: Interviews with Convicted Rapists* (Toronto, 1980); Rochelle Semmel Albin, "Psycholog-

ical Studies of Rape," *Signs* 3:2 (1977): 423–35; and Raymond A. Knight, Ruth Rosenberg, and Beth Schneider, "Classification of Sexual Offenders: Perspectives, Methods and Validation," in *Rape and Sexual Assault: A Research Handbook*, ed. Ann Wolbert Burgess (New York and London, 1985), 222–93.

16. Dubinsky, *Improper Advances*, 6, 126–42. See also Walter S. DeKeseredy and Desmond Ellis, "Intimate Male Violence against Women in Canada," in *Violence in Canada*, Ross, 97–125.

17. In all cases cited in this study, the victims and perpetrators of sexual assaults are identified by their given name and the first letter of their surname only. It should be noted that Olga W. and Ivan W. shared no familial relationship.

18. Cameron papers, box 56, file 656, *King v Ivan W.*, deposition of Olga W., 10 August 1932.

19. For example, Frank W. Anderson, *Western Canadian Desperadoes: Little Known Tales of the Old West* (Saskatoon, 1985) and *Oldtime Sheriffs and Outlaws* (Saskatoon, 1982).

20. Mr. Harrison, foreman at the CNR yards in Calgary, reported seeing a man committing an act of gross indecency on a dog in February 1936. OB, 3 February 1936 (#325).

21. This observation, of course, lies at the heart of Susan Brownmiller's *Against Our Will*.

22. Dubinsky, *Improper Advances*, 23, 37–43.

23. OB, 29 October 1926 (#2720).

24. OB, 5 February 1930. See also OB, 21 September 1928.

25. OB, 24 September 1928 (#3042), 21 July 1926 (#1580), 6 January 1928 (#58), 22 March 1929 (#862). For background on this issue, see Howard Palmer, *Patterns of Prejudice: A History of Nativism in Alberta* (Toronto, 1982).

26. OB, 6 June 1930 (#2142), 16 January 1935 (#139), 16 November 1936 (#4182).

27. OB, 30 April 1938 (#1329). Other cases in which specific identification was made, but cannot be repeated here, may be found in OB, 6 July 1930 (#2858), 13 September 1933 (#3401), 17 May 1934 (#1653), 12 July 1934 (#2442), 7 March 1938 (#718), 24 July 1939 (#2620), 3 December 1939 (#4384).

28. OB, 9 December 1939 (#4491).

29. OB, 11 August 1939 (#2841). In her study of wife beating in Alberta, Chapman discusses the domestic dangers faced by assault victims when pressing charges. See Chapman, "'Til Death do us Part' 20. See also Elizabeth Pleck, "Wife Beating in Nineteenth-Century America," *Victimology* 4:1 (1974): 60–74; and Nancy Tomes, "A 'Torrent of Abuse': Crimes of Violence between Working-Class Men and Women in London, 1840–1875," *Journal of Social History* 11:3 (spring 1978): 328–45.

30. Dubinsky, *Improper Advances*, 23. See also Chapman, "Sex Crimes in the West."

31. OB, 30 June 1936 (#2118).

32. OB, 8 July 1930 (#2690); J. McKinley Cameron papers, box 52, file 600, *King v Gordon O. and Francis W.* (1930), depositions, 9 and 10 July 1930.

33. Dubinsky, *Improper Advances*, 163–69.

34. See the Honourable Mr. Justice John N. Decore, "The District Court of Alberta," *Alberta Law Review*, 25th Anniversary (February 1980): 23–24; and the Honourable H. S. Patterson, "The District Court of Southern Alberta," *Alberta Law Review*, 25th Anniversary (February 1980): 25–29.

35. Louis Knafla and Richard Klumpenhouwer, *Lords of the Western Bench: A Biographical History of the Supreme District Courts of Alberta, 1876–1990* (Alberta, 1997), 10.

36. See Thorner and Watson, "Keeper of the King's Peace."

37. Quoted in Thorner and Watson, "Keeper of the King's Peace," 48.

38. Chapman, "Sex Crimes in the West," 11.

39. *King v Gordon O. and Francis W.*, deposition of Gordon O.

40. *King v Gordon O. and Francis W.*, depositions. On the question of a victim's character, see Dubinsky, *Improper Advances*, 24–29; Chapman, "Sex Crimes in the West," 12–13.

41. OB, 13 June 1930 (#2251), 24 June 1935 (#1968). See also Chapman, "Sex Crimes in the West," 12.

42. OB, 28 April 1930 (#1526), 17 July 1939 (#2516).

43. OB, 15 March 1938 (#822).

44. OB, 8 September 1930 (#3654). On delays in reporting assaults, see Chapman, "Sex Crimes in the West," 20.

45. Dubinsky, *Improper Advances*, 128.

46. Cameron papers, box 55, file 642, *King v Charles N. L.*, preliminary hearing.

47. *Criminal Code* (1922), section 189.

48. Cameron papers, box 33, file 403, *King v Culver C.* (1924), depositions, 12 June 1924.

49. *King v Culver C.*, depositions. The family later sought financial compensation from C. to provide for the baby. Cameron papers, box 26, file 433, *Mary Ellen H. and Kate H. and Frank H. v Culver C.* (1924–25). Dubinsky argues that "Women who became pregnant as a result of "illicit" sexual relations also decreased their chances of successful criminal prosecution." Dubinsky, *Improper Advances*, 26.

50. OB, 6 June 1930 (#2143).

51. OB, 10 February 1933 (#489).

52. OB, 12 April 1927 (#783), 25 April 1927 (#907).

53. OB, 11 June 1934 (#1971), 12 September 1934 (#3295).

54. Weaver also discusses the location of assaults in *Crimes, Constables, and Courts*, 238–39.

55. OB, 31 May 1929 (#1803), 7 March 1938 (#717), 26 July 1929 (#2795).

56. OB, 26 July 1933 (#2807), 20 August 1936 (#2881).

57. OB, 23 August 1933 (#3155), 10 May 1938 (#1518), 5 July 1938 (#2215).

58. OB, 23 March 1929 (#877), 9 August 1929 (#3001), 28 August 1934 (#3108), 17 June 1935 (#1846), 30 June 1936 (#2118), 20 February 1939 (#537).

59. OB, 29 October 1926 (#2720), 21 September 1928 (#3014), 13 June 1929 (#1995), 22 January 1934 (#215), 16 January 1935 (#139), 28 July 1936 (#2578).

60. OB, 10 April 1937 (#1154), 21 April 1937 (#1347, #1348), 19 May 1937 (#1672).

61. See Barbara Grinder, *Local Colour: A Commemoration of the 75th Anniversary of the Amalgamated Transit Union Local 583* (Calgary, 1990). More generally on this theme, see Sam Bass Warner Jr., *Streetcar Suburbs: The Process of Growth in Boston, 1870–1900* (New York, 1972).

62. OB, 26 May 1927 (#1165).

63. OB, 8 March 1929 (#664), 22 March 1929 (#861), 29 December 1930 (#5282), 26 June 1936 (#2040).

64. OB, 12 July 1937 (#2539).

65. OB, 6 February 1930 (#405), 25 July 1930 (#3010).

66. OB, 22 July 1929 (#2713).

67. OB, 16 May 1938 (#1590).

68. Calgary Police Service Museum/Archives, Police Charge Books, 1926–39.

69. However, see accounts contained in William M. Baker, ed., *Pioneer Policing in Southern Alberta: Deane of the Mounties, 1888–1914* (Calgary, 1993), 173–87.

70. OB, 18 February 1929 (#450), 12 July 1934 (#2452), 6 February 1933 (#456), 30 August 1934 (#3137).

71. OB, 17 November 1938 (#4260).

72. OB, 20 February 1939 (#539), 29 August 1938 (#2948), 18 August 1939 (#2954).

73. OB, 6 June 1928 (#1574), 10 April 1929 (#1090).

74. Roy Porter cites studies that claim as few as 8 percent of rapes and attempted rapes committed in London during the 1980s were reported to the police. Porter, "Rape—Does it have a Historical Meaning?" n 3, 271.

75. In addition to the instances already cited, see OB, 24 June 1939 (#2099).

76. Macleod, "Law and Order on the Western-Canadian Frontier," 102.

77. On the state of policing in Calgary at the end of the frontier period, see David Bright, "The Cop, the Chief, the Hooker and her Life," *Alberta History* 45:4 (autumn 1997): 16–26, and "The Murder of John Middleton," *Alberta History* 46:4 (autumn 1998): 2–12.

78. In addition to works already cited, see Judith Walkowitz, *Prostitution and Victorian Society: Women, Class, and the State* (Cambridge, 1980), and *City of Dreadful Delight: Narratives of Sexual Danger in Late-Victorian London* (Chicago, 1992); Lucia Zedner, *Women, Crime, and Custody in Victorian England* (Oxford, 1991); Graham Parker, "The Legal Regulation of Sexual Activity and the Protection of Females," *Osgoode Hall Law Journal* 21:2 (1983): 187–244.

79. Dubinsky, *Improper Advances*, 14.

CHAPTER 6

Creating the Peace: Crime and Community Identity in Northeastern British Columbia, 1930–50

Jonathan Swainger

At some point in 1936 Bert Sheffield and Henry Courvoisier decided to rob the Hudson's Bay Company (HBC) post at Fort Nelson in northern British Columbia. Motivated by the opportunity to steal a year's worth of fur before it was transported out of the region, Sheffield and Courvoisier effected a daring late night robbery on July 12, 1936, during which they tied up post bookkeeper Bob Gillard, Nels Natland, and Oliver McMartin. Making good their escape, Sheffield, Courvoisier, and unknown accomplices carried off 29 bales of fur valued at approximately $32,000.[1] Having planned and executed the robbery, however, they faced the considerable challenge of secretly removing the unwieldy bales from a region serviced only by rivers, forest trails, and small bush planes. Queried by the *Peace River Block News* as to the means necessary to pull off such a heist, a local trader offered the opinion that "a well organised" raid transferring the stolen fur to Alaska to be rebaled and shipped south to the lower states would be a "fairly simple undertaking."[2] Even if such a scheme were actually feasible, Sheffield and Courvoisier had in fact failed to get the stolen fur out of the region. Hidden three miles downriver from Fort Nelson, the fur remained there until August 8, 1937, when just as they were culling and repacking the bales, a local Aboriginal man named Netsena stumbled on the cache along with a tarpaulin bearing Sheffield's name.[3]

The discovery confirmed suspicions that had been swirling around Sheffield and Courvoisier since the robbery. Indeed, a mere week after the heist the two had been arrested at Fort Nelson and committed for trial at Prince George, some nine hundred kilometers south in the central interior of the province.[4] In the interim between being committed for trial and being flown down to Prince George, Sheffield and Courvoisier sold the fur that they possessed at the time of the arrest to HBC post manager Tommy Clark for approximately four thousand dollars. When Sheffield and Courvoisier attempted to cash the HBC bank draft in Prince George, payment was refused because the company now suspected that the furs sold to Clark were those that had been stolen from the HBC post at Fort St. John on June 13, 1934. In response to the stop payment, the two men instructed their lawyer, A. McB. Young, to file a civil suit against the company to enforce payment of the draft.[5] Although the trial on the Fort Nelson robbery was scheduled to go forward on October 7, 1936, the Crown sought and obtained a continuance until the spring assize, arguing that key witnesses were difficult to locate during the trapping season. As a result Sheffield and Courvoisier were released on their own recognizance with sureties of $1,000 each.[6]

Having returned to the Fort Nelson region, Sheffield and Courvoisier were then charged in the spring of 1937 with the Fort St. John fur robbery. The preliminary hearing before stipendiary magistrate Jack Abbott was held on April 13 in a packed hall above Bowes and Herron's garage in Fort St. John, where the two accused were committed for trial.[7] Tried six weeks later at the Prince George assize on May 26, Sheffield and Courvoisier were acquitted on charges stemming from the Fort St. John robbery.[8] Having avoided a conviction, they returned to the cached furs from the Fort Nelson robbery where, on August 8, 1937, they were almost caught by Netsena. Realizing that the discovery of the cache and Sheffield's tarpaulin ended their chances of escaping with the stolen fur, the two fled across country to Fort St. John, where they traded their horses for an old car and started for Edmonton, Alberta. From there they headed south and almost made good their escape before being apprehended by the RCMP, who were notified by a suspicious U.S. immigration official at Sweet Grass, Montana, in late September.[9] Returned to the Peace for their trial on October 18 in Pouce Coupé, Sheffield and Courvoisier were convicted of robbing the HBC at Fort Nelson and received five-year penitentiary sentences.[10]

The robbery captures our attention not only because of its flawed execution and the tangle of events that ensued, but also because of a comment it inspired in the *Peace River Block News*. In reporting the crime the *News* claimed that "it was said at one time that when the frontier was left behind, hold-ups such as characterised the centres of population were impossible owing to the difficulty of getting out of the country. It now appears evident that either the frontier has been pushed back beyond our realisation or else bandits are using more modern methods of making their get away."[11] Evidently, not only did one encounter a different type of crime after passing through the frontier and into the wilderness, but the settlement side of the frontier allegedly engendered specific forms of criminality as well. In the very least this latter possibility ran counter to then-prevalent notions that settled agricultural regions were relatively free of disorder and crime, because those who tilled the soil evinced a higher morality.[12] This so-called "country life ideology" depicted rural life as highly moralistic and essentially crime free and it represented those who gained their living from the land as the nation's moral backbone. In fact, their lives offered a salient example for the denizens of decadent and crime-filled cities. Here was the "image of a new and better society—the Promised Land, a garden of abundance in which all material wants would be provided and where moral and civic virtues would be perfected."[13] Perfection proved elusive, but the notion that crime and criminality were, by their very nature, foreign to the hard-working citizens of the Peace was to remain a central theme in their own self-perception well beyond the early settlement years and on into the 1950s. Indeed, the ideal of the crime-free Peace remained a predominant notion despite ample evidence that the region and its residents were not nearly as law-abiding as some may have wished.

In detailing the incidence, nature, and perception of crime in the British Columbia Peace, this chapter explores the relationships between the region's settlement history, the "metropolitan" influences felt from both the prairies and British Columbia, and the consequent emergence of a Peace country identity or localism that resisted incorporation into those broader cultures. In essence, this research aims at depicting northeastern British Columbia's criminal legal history as a "cultural artefact" arising from the region's particular evolution.[14] Notions of law and order and the line between acceptable levels of disorder and criminality are, as David Garland has suggested, cultural expressions and, therefore, the manner in which criminality was constructed reveals basic characteristics and predominant beliefs in a community. As such, the evolving "sense" of crime and criminality in the Peace during these years not only illuminates the development of that community, but casts into sharper relief the rationale that attracted settlers to the region and the extent to which they reshaped their perceptions of the surrounding world to remain true to those founding ideals.

POLICING THE PEACE

The 1896 discovery of gold on Rabbit Creek in the Yukon ignited a flurry of activity that was, in Canadian terms, unparalleled. And while many of the Klondikers opted for the ocean route to the north, some chose to depart from Edmonton in the Northwest Territories (NWT), pursuing an ill-defined all-Canadian route to gold field riches. In the midst of that path the aspirant miners traversed the Peace, and near Fort St. John they clashed with the Denne-za and Cree, the Aboriginal peoples of northeastern British Columbia. According to Reverend George Holmes, an Anglican missionary resident at Lesser Slave Lake, it was shameful the way that "these white heathen have treated these poor harmless Indians—stealing and shooting their horses; robbing their caches which until the white man came were always as safe as in the Bank." Indeed, "by their ungodliness and barbarian treatment of the

Indians they are endangering the lives of every white person in the country including missionaries."[15] Less than a week later Holmes had altered his tone somewhat in voicing concerns that the rumored arrival of "a contingent of ten Police which[,] of course[,] will be almost more dangerous than none. The sight of Redcoats would be accepted by the Beavers [Denne-za] as a challenge and to kill ten soldiers and a few 'big men' would swell their breasts with the proud impression that they had annihilated the British Army."[16] Such possibilities aside, reports from various sources stressed the deteriorating state of affairs in 1899 and advised that in anticipation of a treaty being signed, police were needed in the area "in the event of any friction between the White and Native elements."[17]

Informed of the situation, North-West Mounted Police (NWMP) comptroller, Frederick White, demurred and pointed out that Fort St. John and area were in British Columbia "and therefore beyond the ordinary jurisdiction of the Mounted Police."[18] Apprised of the situation and the jurisdictional difficulty, the minister of the interior, Clifford Sifton, advised White to inform British Columbia's attorney general of the reported unrest. To this directive White replied that past experience suggested "that the B.C. government would immediately disclaim responsibility on the ground that any trouble likely to arise would be in connection with the Indians, and that it is the duty of the Dominion Government not only to care for them, but also to keep them in order."[19] The matter rested there for a year until White was informed by J. A. Macrae, inspector of Indian Agencies at Lesser Slave Lake, NWT, that he had deputized Sergeant G. D. Butler of the NWMP, to act as a dominion constable in British Columbia.[20] White's reply made it clear that Macrae's actions were not only unauthorized but also constituted a direct reversal of the policy prohibiting the Mounted Police from going beyond the territorial boundary between the NWT and British Columbia. As such, White directed the immediate withdrawal of the authority erroneously bestowed on Butler.[21]

The enforcement vacuum existing in the Peace country was an early demonstration of how the region fell in a jurisdictional crack. British Columbia was uninterested in shouldering responsibility for the distant corner of the province, and the NWMP, while conscious of potential problems, was not authorized to act. Further, the Aboriginal resistance to the presence of the miners represented an example of Peace country localism wherein arms were raised and passage refused until treaty negotiations were effected. Indeed, it is all too clear that responding to Native concerns was the ostensible reason behind the completion of Treaty 8 in 1899 and 1900 while, in fact, securing the safe passage of those heading to the Yukon was of primary importance.[22]

In the aftermath of the gold rush, the decision to carve out a NWMP trail from the Peace to the Yukon in 1905 provided the means for the official arrival of the Mounted Police into the British Columbian Peace.[23] From the perspective of actual policing, however, the NWMP presence was rather insignificant. Inasmuch as the trail provided them with the opportunity to detail the terrain and the various Aboriginal peoples encountered in the Peace, monthly police reports noted consistently the almost complete absence of crime. As Inspector C. W. West recorded on March 31, 1905, "crime has been conspicuous by its absence since my arrival here [;] this district has never been as quiet and orderly . . . I attribute the orderly state of the district to the absence of intoxicants, which in former years deprived the half-breeds and whites to some extent of their cattle and any personal possessions which they could exchange for liquor . . . "[24] Once established at Fort St. John, the police continued to remark on the absence of any crime, other than those incidents constituting discipline offenses in the ranks.[25]

Assigned to patrol the trail, the NWMP remained headquartered at Fort St. John until Constable Thomas Jamieson of the British Columbia Provincial Police (BCPP) assumed his post at Fort St. John on November 1, 1909.[26] For the next 41 years policing in the region fell to the BCPP who, after occupying the former NWMP quarters at Fort St. John, eventually established a second post in the south Peace at Pouce Coupé in May of 1914.[27] During the following years the number of officers and men stationed in the Peace traced the region's slow population growth. By 1938 eight patrolmen and officers were resident in the Peace River subdistrict, and an NCO, two constables, and a corporal staffed the regional headquarters at Pouce Coupé.[28] At the end of World War II the strength had risen to 15, with 4 men stationed in Pouce Coupé, 6 in Dawson Creek, 2 in Fort St. John, and 1 each at Lower Post and Muskwa.[29] This overall total would be maintained until August 1950, when the RCMP absorbed the BCPP.[30]

Described by retiring Inspector G. J. Duncan, who as a young constable opened the Pouce Coupé station, police duties in the region constituted a wide variety of responsibilities including acting as game warden, deputy mining recorder, registrar of vital statistics, license issuer, notary public, coroner and, occasionally, physician.[31] Indeed, the provincial superintendent's annual report a decade later observed that "there appears to be no general appreciation of the varied duties police are called upon to carry out. Apart from their natural function—the prevention and suppression of crime—members of the British Columbia Police are both requested and expected to perform a multiplicity of labours only partially identified with the preservation of law and order."[32] The recollections of Constable L. W. Clay of the BCPP, who was stationed in Fort St. John from 1938 to 1943, confirm this diverse collection of official and informal duties, responsibilities, and expectations.[33] Although this peacekeeper, social worker, and government agent combination continued to characterize much of the police work, the 1930s also marked an important transition in the nature of the job and the public awareness of crime and criminal activity. For while it remained common currency to assert that the Peace was untroubled by crime, it became increasingly difficult to ignore that crime and lawlessness had become as much a part of the region's identity as were the desired attributes of life on the land. In effect, to maintain their self-perception as a law-abiding and orderly community, residents of the Peace were obligated to create an explanation for the region's increasing level of violence and reported crime during the 1930s.

THE 1930s

The rise in reported crime from 1930 to 1932 is attributable to a number of factors. According to the census of 1931 there were 7,013 residents in the Peace, a figure constituting almost a sevenfold increase in the 40 years since the 1891 census counted 940 inhabitants. Further, the change was not merely one of number; by 1931 the population of the Peace was decidedly non-Native whereas in 1891, most if not all of the inhabitants had been Aboriginal. Indeed, when F. C. Campbell, the first provincial government agent in the Peace, filed his inaugural report in late 1909, he identified a total of 18 resident non-Natives in the entire northeast.[34] By 1931 the Aboriginal population accounted for only 454 of the 7,013 residents noted by the census. Even accounting for a significant underrepresentation of the Native population in the data, the sevenfold increase between 1891 and 1931 reflected the displacement of the original Native inhabitants by White settlers. Consequently, the increase in reported crime occurring in the early 1930s was, as the court records bear out, almost wholly a product of non-Aboriginal behavior.

The Peace region also became more aware of crime in the early 1930s after the *Peace River Block News* initiated weekly publication. Founded at the crossroads community of Rolla, the newspaper eventually moved to Dawson Creek from where it provided news coverage and community service for much of the northeast. As was often the case in small-town newspapers, crime and disorderly behavior made good copy and thus, by merely covering any incidents of lawlessness, the *News* suggested that crime was on the rise. Not only was there a newspaper to report incidents of lawlessness to the reading public, but the actual number of criminal cases did increase in the first half of the decade. The extant court records document that during the 1920s there were never more than 5 felonies per year and, in most instances, there were 3 or less. On the other hand, throughout the 1930s there were usually at least 4 cases per year and, in 1935, there were 10 felonies tried in county court at Pouce Coupé.[35] Although these figures certainly were not staggering, they nonetheless reveal that if crime was not yet a problem in the Peace, it was becoming a larger concern than it had been in the past.

Finally, from 1930 to 1932, and after 1936, a number of prominent and violent cases occurred in the Peace. The murder of homesteaders John and Annie Babchuck in early September 1930 in their rough cabin near Cecil Lake, a small community east of Fort St. John, shocked the region and ignited a year-long investigation.[36] In the midst of the murder trial of Mike Sowry for killing the Babchucks, Dawson Creek experienced a crime wave in the form of a series of burglaries in the spring and summer of 1931.[37] And by the time that Sowry had been found guilty and sentenced to hang, residents of the north Peace were reading of "a desperate character" named Bryan who, in fleeing capture on May 25, exchanged gunfire with Constable A. J. Pomeroy of the BCPP beyond the Tompkins's farmstead northwest of Fort St. John.[38] Although a thorough search at the time of the gunfight failed to locate any trace of Bryan, his remains eventually were found in late October 1931.[39]

A month after the Pomeroy shoot-out with Bryan, the continuing burglaries in Dawson Creek assumed a prominent place in the *News* and fostered calls for improved police protection.[40] In fact, the third successful burglary of the local cooperative store compelled the newspaper to suggest that the provincial attorney general be contacted with the message, "Eighth burglary last night with gun play. If you cannot send us a policeman, for God's sake send the militia."[41] Six weeks later the police finally gained the upper hand with the arrest of Ira Gordon, Charles Castonguay, and Lloyd Harker for the burglaries. Applauding the police success in apprehending the gang, the *News* offered an instructive lesson for local residents; the investigation and prosecution would teach prospective criminals respect for the law and there would be "no wild-west tactics here."[42] This, after all, was the crime-free Peace.

Following the flurry of criminal cases and newspaper reporting in late 1930 and throughout 1931, coverage dropped off sharply during the three years after 1932. The decline, however, did not mirror an actual decrease in the number of cases brought before the county court. In fact, prosecutions for unlawful carnal knowledge, theft, assault, theft from the mails, horse theft, fraud, and receiving stolen goods among a variety of other offenses were recorded with increasing regularity during these years.[43] Ironically, one of the cases that did garner headlines, a charge of attempted murder laid against Ross Jeffrey for attacking his step-father, mother, and half-brother with an ax in the spring of 1934 near Fort St. John, is missing from extant local records since it was tried in Quesnel, a forestry community in the provincial interior. The newspaper reports in the Peace are uniformly vague as to the events surrounding the attempted murder, save to say that the evidence of the trial revealed "one of the most terrible stories of social and living conditions which could be placed before any court."[44] Less encumbered by local sensibilities where the incident had occurred, the *Cariboo Observer* explained that Jeffrey, a bachelor homesteader, had invited his family from Saskatchewan to stay with him while they settled into the Peace. Weeks turned into months. Confined as they were to a cabin measuring roughly 9 by 14 feet, conditions soon deteriorated for Jeffrey and his six guests. In later summarizing the situation, defense counsel E. D. Woodburn offered the view that this was simply a case of "too much family."[45] After deliberating for 45 minutes and despite the attack having been clearly proved, the jury "ignored all lesser matters," acquitted Jeffrey of the charges, and recommended that he undergo a mental examination.[46]

Coming as it did in summer and autumn of 1934, the Jeffrey case proved to be the exception to the lull in newspaper crime reporting in the Peace from 1932 to 1936. Although there were a few reported thefts, a suicide, and a variety of other infractions covered in the *News*, there was little in the newspaper to indicate that 1935 was to be the busiest year for the criminal courts in the Peace between 1920 and 1942.[47] This lacuna came to a dramatic end on January 3, 1936, when the murder of Albert Demean on December 20, 1935, west of Tupper Creek in the south Peace was reported.[48] Neither the subsequent arrest of George Miller and Chris Mueller, two of Demean's neighbors, or the preliminary hearing in March provided an explanation for, or indication of, circumstances leading to the homicide.[49] The trial revealed that the three men, along with a Carl Schall, were involved in a dispute over the right to cut hay on Crown land. Evidently Demean had claimed the exclusive right to the hay and was suspected of having burned a haystack belonging to Miller and Mueller. Plans to tar and feather Demean had been laid, but Mueller and Miller took matters into their own hands to administer a "licking" to Demean. This they accomplished with a bullwhip and a homemade sandbag. Demean later was found dead on the road beside his farm. After a jury trial lasting two days, Miller and Mueller were each found guilty of manslaughter and sentenced to 10 years in the penitentiary.[50] Much like the Jeffrey case, the events surrounding the Demean murder provided a sharp rebuttal to the *Peace River Block News*'s contention that so-called "wild west tactics" would not be tolerated in the Peace. Just as important, the two cases demonstrated that given the wrong mix of ingredients, even conditions in pioneer agricultural communities could give rise to violence and murder. Distance from urban settings was no guarantor that life would be untroubled by disorder and crime. Evidently the relationship between lawlessness and locale was not nearly as unproblematic as adherents to the country-life ideology might have claimed.

Indeed, events in the Peace seemed to be conspiring against the notion that rural and small-town life was relatively untroubled by crime. As the Fort Nelson fur case worked its way through the criminal justice system, local residents were shocked by the news of another outbreak of domestic violence. Yet unlike the Jeffrey case less than three years earlier, the reports from the Stephen Delorie farm near Fort St. John were more tragic and deadly; before committing suicide, Delorie had killed his wife, Nora, and their two children, Steven and Stella.[51] According to William Shea, the hired hand who discovered the grisly scene, Stephen Delorie had been attempting to obtain a gun all winter and when he finally succeeded in borrowing one, Nora Delorie secretly asked Shea to take the weapon away. Excepting Delorie's sustained efforts to obtain a firearm, however, there had been little to indicate that something was amiss on what was considered to be a farm in fair circumstances.[52] For much of the rest of 1937 the final act of the Fort Nelson fur robbery and trial captured the lion's share of local attention. However, almost as if to reinforce the message that crime and violence were becoming more prevalent, in the early morning of December 8, a badly beaten Morley Reid Kier was found on 2nd Avenue in Dawson Creek, clad only in his underwear and near death; he in fact died shortly after being delivered to St. Joseph's Hospital. His assailant, William Matthews, almost died as well from the injuries he sustained in the 20-minute brawl during which the two men, neither of whom had been drinking, thrashed each other with a two-foot-long iron bar.[53] Despite the extreme violence of the fracas, Matthews's open admission that he was involved, and his elusive explanation that the fight began when he had dropped into Kier's room to chat before leaving town, the Prince George jury remained unconvinced of guilt: Matthews was completely exonerated.[54] Strangely enough though, despite being acquitted, Matthews was held under house arrest on his mother's farm for some time after the trial.[55]

Although 1938 failed to add to the growing list of violent crimes during the decade, it nonetheless provided Peace country residents with an indication that all was not right with the world. Speaking at the Carlsonia Theatre in Dawson Creek on December 25, former Sing Sing inmate "Silent" Bill Biddle addressed a small gathering on the circumstances that led to his life of crime and violence.[56] Emphasizing the lack of a "proper" home environment and poor economic conditions, Biddle warned that without constant parental vigilance, even Peace country children could be swayed by undesirable influences. He also spoke in favor of a Borstal Home, where young offenders would be rehabilitated rather than being schooled for a life of crime. Almost as if to reinforce Biddle's message, six weeks later the *News* reprinted portions of provincial attorney general Gordon S. Wismer's speech extolling the virtues of the youthful offenders rehabilitation center opened over a year earlier outside Vancouver. Arguing that "there are no bad boys," Wismer claimed that the center had already graduated 60 youths and "most of them are employed and are making good. We have not had a single case of return [*sic*] to a life of crime."[57] Although most residents undoubtedly chose to believe that Biddle and Wismer's concerns were essentially "big city" problems, one suspects that even in late 1938 and early 1939 some were given reason to pause. And in the aftermath of what some would term the comic book murder 10 years later, it must have been unnerving to reflect on the speeches and the warnings they had proffered.

Of course no one knew what the future would bring, but in the spring of 1939 residents were reminded yet again that despite hopeful expectations, rural and small-town life were not untroubled by crime. Early in the morning on April 17, Mrs. Austin of Tupper Creek noticed smoke was rising from the large barn on the family ranch. She sent her neighbor, Mr. Leonard Healy, to investigate, and he discovered a number of farm buildings on fire along with the body of Al Hoover, the newly hired ranch manager, who had been shot in the back. It was later learned that the outgoing manager, Otto Schwartz, had been seen carrying a rifle and fleeing the scene. Shortly thereafter, a single shot was heard from southeast of the farm. According to the police commissioner's annual report, a thorough search of the area failed to locate Schwartz, and it was believed that after shooting Hoover and setting the farm buildings alight, the suspect committed suicide in the bush.[58]

The Hoover murder and Schwartz's apparent suicide brought to a close the succession of prominent criminal investigations and trials recasting the reality of crime in the region during the 1930s. For although the rhetoric of country life claimed a higher morality for those who lived on the land, these crimes provided occasionally brutal evidence that such assertions were suspect. Further, the *News*'s admission that settled areas would be necessarily exposed to a greater range of criminal activity added yet another ingredient to local constructions of the relationship between lawlessness and community identity. These revelations did not, however, prove fatal to the belief that the Peace was less troubled by crime than more urban areas. Rather, these events merely produced a refinement in the notion by asserting that despite the higher morality of agrarian life in northeastern British Columbia, there would always be some individuals in a growing population who, in response to varying motivations, would find themselves on the wrong side of the law. Identifying the existence of this criminal class provided the means to preserve the idea of the crime-free Peace while adjusting that perception to account for the unavoidable fact that crime was very much in evidence. As such, the "real" Peace remained a well-ordered and law-abiding society that as much as was possible, continued to provide a safe haven from the depredations of urban crime and disorder.[59] Through this trick of mind, the crime-free Peace was maintained despite the rising profile of disorder, violence, and crime during the decade.

THE 1940s

Although news of gathering war clouds in Europe pushed crime reporting from the front pages of the *Peace River Block News*, the outbreak of hostilities in September 1939 did not have an immediate effect on the Peace. Some residents enlisted for service while others committed themselves to the effort through increased agricultural production, war bonds, and belt tightening at home. However, the announcement in late February 1942 that an all-weather road would be built to Alaska from northeastern British Columbia pushed the Peace to the forefront of the domestic war news.[60] Rationalized by the context of war, the highway provided an opportunity for northeastern British Columbia to play a prominent role in the war and, as time would reveal, marked a critical turning point in the region's history.[61] Not only did the highway represent a link to the broader North American community but also, in the short term, the Peace was flooded with U.S. soldiers and the military's version of American culture. That such an influx potentially created an environment for disorder was recognized by the U.S. Army request, made shortly after the highway construction was unveiled, that more civilian police be assigned to duty in the northeast.[62] As the war years would reveal, the concern was warranted.

Although the figures are incomplete, there was an unmistakable increase in the number of police investigations during the war and postwar years.[63] As detailed in tables 6.1 and 6.2, investigations along with the number of complaints laid and convictions obtained during the decade also increased dramatically. Of particular note is the fact that by 1949, with the U.S. Army long since departed and the war having been over for four years, reported crime was still six times greater than prewar levels, despite the population having not quite doubled from 8,439 in 1941 to 14,349 in 1951.[64] Although these statistics indicate that the number of police investigations and the level of reported crime increased during the decade, they obscure the fact that by December 1943, the Canadian government had surrendered all criminal jurisdictions over both military and civilian personnel connected with the highway construction.[65] Therefore, with the exception of the occasional case wherein military authorities turned over an American citizen for trial before

Table 6.1
Number of Police Investigations: Peace River Subdivision

Year	1941	1943	1945	1946
Investigations	1,082	6,571	5,000	6,681

Table 6.2
Criminal Statistics Breakdown: Peace River Subdivision

Year	Cases	Convictions	Dismissals	Awaiting Trial
1938	92	67	25	-
1939	64	51	10	3
1940	79	72	7	-
1941	76	68	8	-
1942	179	167	11	1
1943	570	548	20	2
1944	515	492	21	2
1945	353	336	15	2
1946	321	307	10	4
1947	397	380	17	-
1948	335	307	24	4
1949	483	463	19	1

a Canadian court, Canadians were completely responsible for the dramatic rise in reported crime after 1942. That said, newspaper reporting and the incidence of a number of high-profile cases may well have driven local citizens to conclude that the Americans were responsible for a disproportionate amount of crime, regardless of how the cases were handled.

The first half of 1943 proved to be especially unsettling. In February of that year, W. Evans, an African American soldier stationed near Dawson Creek was accused of attempting to rape a Dawson Creek woman. Consistent with the policy set two months earlier, U.S. authorities refused to release Evans to Canadian officials but initiated a court-martial in which the accused was found guilty and sentenced to 15 years at hard labor. Dishonorably discharged, Evans was returned to the United States to serve his sentence.[66] Reflecting on the case in his year-end report, Commissioner T. W. S. Parsons of the BCPP offered the view that in the hands of American military officials, Evans was answerable to a considerably harsher penalty than that provided by Canadian law.[67] Two days after Evans was arrested, Dawson Creek was thrown into chaos. As it was later revealed, a subcontractor to the U.S. Army illegally stored 60 cases of dynamite and 20 boxes of blasting caps in a downtown livery stable. When the stable caught fire on February 13, the subsequent explosion and fire wrecked an entire downtown block, save for one building. Although the official death toll numbered only 5 individuals, Joseph Kosick, who in fighting the fire suffered a broken back and ruptured eardrums when he was blown off the roof of the livery stable, recalled that 17 people were killed and that he attended the first of 7 inquests on a stretcher.[68] Although the subcontractor was found liable for the explosion and subsequent damage to downtown Dawson Creek, the conviction and imposed $10,000 fine were reversed on appeal, and no one was ever held accountable.[69] Although locals disagree as to the degree that the explosion and fire soured relations with the Americans, at least one author has suggested that "for many in Dawson Creek, nothing was ever quite the same—including their feelings about the 'Yankee boys'".[70]

By the summer of 1943 conditions in Dawson Creek had deteriorated enough to warrant a confidential meeting between Canadian and American military officials. The eruption of suspicious fires; the black market traffic in sugar, meat, butter, cigarettes, and lumber; a plague of venereal disease; the unrestrained expansion of prostitution; theft from army construction depots and sites; and American concerns about the quality of the provincial police were all straining relations.[71] A commitment to remove two allegedly uncooperative policemen, a further promise to increase the number of policemen, and a pledge to greater vigilance in regard to other concerns were made on behalf of the Canadians, but American military officials remained skeptical. A subsequent report concentrating solely on the availability of bootleg liquor, filed in late September 1943, indicated that because of a faulty system of permits and half-hearted attempts to control the traffic, illegal liquor was easily and openly obtained.[72]

While American military officials questioned the ability of the BCPP to keep crime in hand, local residents were, for their part, none too impressed with the behavior of the military police. In a report dated August 13, 1943, liaison officer C. K. LeCapelain detailed a variety of complaints lodged against the military police for overstepping their jurisdiction and harassing Canadian civilians. There were, according to LeCapelain, "strong feelings of resentment on the part of many Canadian citizens against recent actions of certain U.S. Army officers and military police in this area."[73] LeCapelain concluded his report in stating "that if US Military Police continue to arrest and manhandle Canadian civilians a lot of bitter resentment will arise which could easily lead to an unfortunate incident."[74] When the report was passed on to the special commissioner, Major-General W. W. Foster, he pointed out that the meetings between American and Canadian officials concluded with a decision to increase both the BCPP and American military police presence and to initiate a series of investigations by the Royal Canadian Mounted Police. In those instances in which individual Canadians had complaints, he was quite willing to have the incidents investigated but emphasized that the illicit traffic in liquor was "a serious menace."[75]

In truth and bad as it was, the unrestrained trade in liquor was but one of the problems facing local and military police. For while a number of high-profile cases suggested that Americans were the source of much disorder, the practice of local residents helping themselves to the mountain of building supplies imported for the highway construction was an even greater nuisance. Encouraged by the unwillingness of juries to convict, local residents stole from army supply depots and dumps extensively after 1942. Indeed, such pilferage was not perceived as theft at all, but was the work of "needy settlers . . . carting away lumber, doors, plumbing and electrical wire" along with truck tires, engines, and 50-gallon drums.[76] Rationalizing the practice as one that was consistent with the thrifty nature of homesteaders failed to convince the police to turn a blind eye. For according to Constable William Lumsden of the BCPP: "It makes no difference what local citizens may think of War Assets or surplus government property. The point is, any intrusion on these properties is an offense—and theft is theft, whether from the government or from widows and orphans—and we intend to prosecute all offenders to the limit."[77] Lumsden was compelled to repeat the warning one month later.[78]

These matters aside, the sense that disorder and crime were on the rise during the war years was also attributable to a number of high-profile criminal investigations. And in so far as these cases shaped public perceptions, it appeared that the American presence was accountable for a disproportionate number of serious crimes. For example, in the summer of 1944, Theresa Seline, an American civilian living in Dawson Creek on an expired work permit, was tried and eventually acquitted for murdering her husband, Roy Seline, on January 2, 1944.[79] Three months later, Guy Bradley Newton, a former employee of the U.S. government, was shot and killed during a scuffle with

Sergeant John T. Massey in the military police barracks at Dawson Creek. Why Newton, who had his travel papers for home in Minnesota, was in the barracks, and how he came to possess Massey's automatic pistol, were not explained in the sole newspaper report of the incident.[80] And then in the autumn of 1945 American Bryon Bruce Potter was tried, found guilty, and eventually hanged for murdering his lover, a married woman in Dawson Creek.[81] Although these cases represented only a small portion of those occurring during these years, they corresponded neatly with the belief that crime in the Peace, notwithstanding the rationalized theft from army depots and dumps, was not the work of permanent residents.

Specifically, two cases in the latter half of 1948 reinforced the notion that Americans were overrepresented in criminal activities. In late August 1948 local attention was drawn to the search for the body of John McComas, believed to have been killed somewhere near mile 100 of the Alaska Highway.[82] Apparently intent on starting life anew in Anchorage, Alaska, McComas and his 13 year-old daughter, Louise, responded to Gustav Weigner's newspaper advertisement soliciting companions for an automobile trip to Alaska. Other than a heated exchange between the deceased and Weigner after the vehicle became stuck outside the Nelson Reed farm in Hythe, Alberta, the trip was uneventful until the threesome stopped at a campsite near mile 100 on the Alaska Highway. It was here that Weigner shot McComas in the head with a .22-caliber rifle and in a panic fled to Bushnell, Nebraska, with Louise. After purchasing a small restaurant where he and Louise lived as brother and sister, Weigner became embroiled in another legal clash that led him to admit having shot McComas. Following a coroner's inquest and preliminary hearing in Pouce Coupé, Weigner was remanded in custody to await trial in Prince George where, in October, he was found guilty of manslaughter and sentenced to two years imprisonment in the British Columbia penitentiary.[83]

Involving as it did, Americans and a verdict delivered by a jury from outside the Peace, the response to the Weigner case provided an illuminating version of the Peace country's legal culture. When Weigner was found guilty of manslaughter and sentenced to only two years imprisonment, newspaper editor Margaret "Ma" Murray of the *Alaska Highway News* was outraged. She aimed her criticism in two directions. First, Murray touched briefly on the American angle to this and other crimes by describing Weigner as an "oily young Ohio salesman." Second, she asserted that the manslaughter verdict and the two-year sentence were "not in keeping with the traditions of the Cariboo courts." And as if to demonstrate her point, Murray then referred to the earlier Potter murder trial in which "another American at Dawson Creek killed his paramour three years ago, he got hanging and had his head wrenched from his body when dropped through the scaffold at Oakalla prison farm."[84] The inference that the accidental decapitation of Potter reflected Peace country notions of law and order was extreme speculation. Asserting that a manslaughter verdict and two-year sentence were inconsistent with legal traditions in the

Cariboo district was, however, a more interesting claim. Obviously Murray believed that the Cariboo district, and in particular the Peace country, sub-scribed to a no-nonsense approach to law and order. Where precisely she obtained this view is uncertain, especially given the cavalier attitude toward theft from the army, and a number of peculiar acquittals in cases such as the Seline murder in 1944, the Matthews murder case in 1938, and even the Jeffrey attempted murder in 1934. However, while her view of the region's criminal legal history is open to question, she was undoubtedly closer to the mark in suggesting that from a Peace country perspective, the Americans and, incidentally, their culture, had been a mixed blessing. Such a conclusion was dramatically reinforced less than a month after Weigner's trial.

Driving home to the small community of Kilkerran after watching Errol Flynn and Ann Sheridan in *Silver River* on the evening of November 12, 1948, the James Watson family was confronted by two masked bandits alongside the Alaska Highway.[85] Rather than stop in response to what was later described as a warning shot, driver Fred Watson reversed his course and sped back toward Dawson Creek. Armed with a 30–30 rifle, one of the bandits fired at the fleeing vehicle. The bullet passed through the car's trunk and rear seat, striking 62-year-old James Watson in the back. Watson died from his wound four days later in St. Joseph's Hospital in Dawson Creek.[86] When it was re-vealed during the subsequent coroner's inquest and delinquency hearing that the bandits, 11 and 13 years of age, had been reading between thirty and fifty American crime comics a week, a moral panic erupted across the Peace coun-try.[87] That which "Silent" Bill Biddle had foretold a decade earlier had come to pass.

Shock and outrage over the "comic book murder" fed into an existing de-bate over the role of American crime comics and the perceived rise in juvenile delinquency across North America and Great Britain. Led in Canada by E. Davie Fulton, a Conservative MP from Kamloops, the campaign was reinvig-orated by Watson's death.[88] Although much of the local furor over the shoot-ing resonated with language drawn on the notion of the crime-free Peace, the comments of George Murray, MP for Cariboo and part owner of the *Alaska Highway News*, were especially notable for directing blame at the Americans. Claiming to be a "humble publisher," Murray stated that "this country is deluged with filth from the publishers of the United States and no effort is made to stop this material coming past the border."[89] Although Murray's com-ments echoed similar sentiments uttered by his parliamentary colleagues, they were also consistent with the ideal of the crime-free Peace and the parallel assertion that criminality was foreign to the well-ordered and law-abiding community. Fulton's bill banning the importation of American crime comics into Canada received third reading and was passed on December 5, 1949, slightly over one year after James Watson died from the wound he received in the comic book–inspired holdup just off the Alaska Highway.[90] It might then be concluded that as far as the residents of the northeast were concerned, the peril had been vanquished and the crime-free Peace could once again rest easy.

EPILOGUE

Although the Fulton Act represented a legislative solution to the specific threat allegedly posed by American crime comics, in the Peace country Watson's murder carried much greater symbolic weight. For while the statute stemmed the tide of American crime comics, it could not address the caustic effects of over twenty years of local history and disorder on the idea of the crime-free Peace. In essence, by 1950 it was increasingly difficult to claim that the Peace was untroubled by crime. Indeed, while the specifics of Watson's murder were without parallel in the region, the possibility that such a shocking crime could occur had been demonstrated repeatedly since the early 1930s. What made the murder and the reaction it engendered such a pivotal event was that by demonizing crime comics, and thus potentially avoiding other explanations placing blame closer to home, the Peace tacitly admitted its incorporation into the broader North American culture. After all, if crime comics imperiled the entire Canadian nation and, it seemed, significant portions of the United States, the horrific events of the comic book murder could hardly reflect the true character of the Peace. Ironically, by acknowledging membership in the broader North American community, the Peace could reassert its claim to a distinctive identity as the last, best, west.

Inasmuch as this claim to a rural heritage with its attendant moral cache could be made, northeastern British Columbia was a very different place in the 1950s in comparison with the prewar homestead era. By the end of the decade, improved highway links to Alberta, the completion of the Hart Highway through the Rocky Mountains to the rest of British Columbia, and the arrival of the Pacific Great Eastern Railway swept away the final vestiges of isolation that the Alaska Highway had all but ended. The Royal Canadian Mounted Police absorbed the BCPP in 1950 and, in so doing, brought to an end a style of policing emphasizing peacekeeping and community relations as opposed to crime fighting and detached professionalism. And perhaps most important for the region's future, the gas and oil industry finally took hold and launched a fundamental transformation of the local economy, especially in the north Peace. Almost overnight Fort St. John and Dawson Creek became gas and oil boom towns with an array of consequences that were, in some instances, predictable. Described by *Vancouver Sun* columnist Jack Scott after an 18-hour visit on September 20, 1957, Fort St. John was no longer an idyllic farming community but was instead a chaotic jumble of ugly and unpainted storefronts along a muddy and pot-holed main street. "It is in short, an unwholesome mess, the agony of a boom town struggling to keep from drowning in a sea of rich oil."[91]

Yet despite the extraordinary change following the arrival of the gas and oil industry, some local residents continued to herald the "orderly," if not the crime-free Peace. And like those who subscribed to similar notions during the 1930s and 1940s, the reality of disorder, crime, and violence during the 1950s failed to match this idealized self-image. For example, in an extant police magistrate's docket book for 1950, there were 27 misdemeanors recorded; eight years later there were 1,257 misdemeanors in Dawson Creek alone.[92] Scott's column on Fort St. John claimed that "fights and brawls" were a regular feature of the community, and the police were often obliged, at their peril, to restore order. Once the content of Scott's description became known, local citizens were outraged at the grievous injury they had sustained. In response to a number of Scott's allegations, James Keddell claimed that while there "may be an occasional scuffle," he was sorry that "we can't dig up a knifing or shooting affray. Our people are still rather naïve and reckon fists are the thing to settle an argument."[93] Bristling at Scott's description, Joe German argued that at least "dope peddlers" did not trouble the Fort St. John police and that Vancouver was invited to keep such deviants because "we don't want them in our clean, orderly, civilised little town of Fort St. John." Further, street brawls occurred only once in every few months and, according to German, the "Mounties have lots of time to polish their boots." Finally, the workers in the gas and oil industry were, to a person, the cream of Canadian youth.[94] For her part, "Ma" Murray simply labeled Scott as the "Elvis Pelvis of the fourth state."[95] Yet despite the dismissal of everything Scott had offered, two weeks later Murray bemoaned the local state of affairs that required citizens to lock up their homes whereas before "civilisation caught up" to the region, such precautions were unnecessary.[96] Evidently, the arrival of so-called civilization, even one initially founded on agrarian ideals and the county-life ideology, could not maintain the mythology of a well-ordered and crime-free community.

David Garland argued that the line between acceptable levels of disorder and criminality is, like broadly conceived notions of law and order, a cultural artifact. The criminal legal history of the Peace River region of northeastern British Columbia from 1930 to 1950 reveals how, in that particular setting, these artifacts represented the stubborn determination of the region to remain true to founding aspirations while confronting a reality increasingly at odds with those ideals. Unswerving faith in the moral superiority of agrarian life endured, in part, because these ideals had assumed considerable potency for those who had escaped the southern prairie dust bowl in search of a new start in northeastern British Columbia. As such, the Peace was not merely a geographic location, it was a way that people felt about law and order which, in turn, was grounded in the very reason that settlers came to the region in the first instance. These notions quite literally were rooted in the Peace.

But as it became increasingly difficult to assert the existence of the crime-free Peace, there emerged a new construction of local identity designed to distinguish the region from the rest of the Canadian prairies and British

Columbia. Adopting a "frontier" pride in the harsh realities of farming on the northern prairies and in the free-wheeling character of the gas and oil industry, a new mythology slowly emerged celebrating hard-working and hard-drinking men who, as James Keddell noted with approval, settled disagreements with their fists. Although this adaptation rejected the older pioneer notions of the crime-free Peace, the new construction of a local identity embracing the "wild west Peace" nonetheless remained true to the proposition that regardless of the predominant culture elsewhere, northeastern British Columbia retained its own particular local identity. That such a self-image was grounded, in part, in constructions of the meaning of law, order, and criminality, bears witness to the integral role these ideas play in how communities perceive themselves and their relationships to broadly conceived regional and national identities.

NOTES

I would like to thank all the residents of the north and south Peace who have shared their recollections with me. Further, I wish to acknowledge the support provided by the University of Northern British Columbia and the research assistance provided by Erin Payne and Priscilla Phillips. Most important, I'd like to thank Jennifer, Matthew, and Thomas for their patience, support, and continuing good humor.

1. "Hudson Bay Co's. Post at Fort Nelson Held up by Masked and Armed Men," *Peace River Block News* [*PRBN*], 24 July 1936, 1; "Trapper's Story of Fort Nelson Fur Robbery," *PRBN*, 7 August 1936, 1; and "Furs Stolen from Hudson Bay Co.," *PRBN*, 14 August 1936, 1. Also see "Police Seeking Further Clues on the Fur Robbery," *Prince George Citizen* [*PGC*], 3 September 1936, 1.

2. "Hudson Bay Co's. Post at Fort Nelson Held up by Masked and Armed Men," *PRBN*, 24 July 1936, 1.

3. Gerri F. Young, *The Fort Nelson Story* (Cloverdale, B.C., 1980), 49–51.

4. "Men Charges in Fur Robbery Case Elect Tomorrow," *PGC*, 20 August 1936, 1.

5. "Hudson's Bay Stops Payments of Drafts Given in Fur Trade," *PGC*, 24 September 1936, 1.

6. "Fort Nelson Fur Robbery is Given Traverse," *PGC*, 8 October 1938, 1.

7. "Two Men Committed for Fur Robbery at Fort St. John—Colourful Scene at Preliminary Hearing," *PRBN*, 23 April 1937, 1; and "Fort St. John News", *PRBN*, 17 April 1937, 3.

8. "Two Men Committed for Fur Robbery at Fort St. John—Colourful Scene at Preliminary Hearing," *PRBN*, 23 April 1937, 1; "Fort St. John News," *PRBN*, 17 April 1937, 3; and "Acquitted in Fur Theft Charge," *PRBN*, 4 June 1937, 1.

9. "Sheffield Courvoisier Sentenced Five Years," *PRBN*, 22 October 1937, 1.

10. Ibid.

11. Ibid.

12. The newspaper argument points in the opposite direction of what Karen Dubinsky identified in her study of rape and heterosexual conflict in Ontario. She found

that the wild north and the city had a sense of immorality and danger whereas the agricultural countryside remained chaste. See Karen Dubinsky, *Improper Advances: Rape and Heterosexual Conflict In Ontario, 1880–1920* (Chicago, 1993), 143–62. On the country life ideology, see David C. Jones, "'There is Some Power About the Land'—The Western Agrarian Press and Country Life Ideology," in *The Prairie West: Historical Readings*, ed. R. Douglas Francis and Howard Palmer (Edmonton, 1992), 455–74; and David Demeritt, "Visions of Agriculture in British Columbia," *BC Studies* 108 (winter 1995–96): 47–48. Also see Cole Harris with David Demeritt, "Farming and Rural Life," in *The Resettlement of British Columbia—Essays on Colonialism and Geographic Change*, ed. Cole Harris (Vancouver, 1997).

13. R. Douglas Francis, *Images of the West: Responses to the Canadian Prairies* (Saskatoon, 1989), 107.

14. David Garland, *Punishment and Modern Society: A Study in Social Theory* (Oxford, 1990), 198.

15. Reverend George Holmes to Bishop Young, 28 May 1899, Provincial Archives of Alberta (PAA), accession A 281/149.

16. Holmes to Young, 3 June 1899, PAA, accession A 281/149.

17. See "Relief of destitute and rumoured trouble with Indians in Peace River and Lesser Slave Lake," National Archives of Canada [NAC], Record Group [RG] 18, vol. 193, file 562–00.

18. Frederick White to Clifford Sifton, 19 May 1899, in NAC, RG 18, vol. 193, file 562–00.

19. Frederick White to Clifford Sifton, 27 June 1899, ibid.

20. J. A. Macrae, Inspector of Indian Agencies, Lesser Slave Lake, N.W.T., to Frederick White, Comptroller, NWMP, 5 June 1900, in NAC, RG 18, vol. 193, file 562–00.

21. Frederick White, Comptroller, NWMP, to J. A. Macrae, Inspector of Indian Agencies, Lesser Slave Lake, NWT, 4 July 1900, in ibid.

22. For the treaty process, see Leonard, *Delayed Frontier: The Peace River Country to 1909* (Calgary, 1995), 15–33.

23. Police correspondence on the Peace River Yukon Trail is located at the Fort St. John museum, file no. 29a. These documents are photocopies of those found in the Glenbow archives in Calgary.

24. Inspector C. W. West, RNWMP, Lesser Slave Lake to Commissioner, RNWMP, Regina, 31 March 1905, NAC, RG 18, vol. 3029.

25. Report of Inspector John Richards, Fort St. John, Detachment to Officer Commanding "N" Division, RNWMP, Lesser Slave Lake, NAC, RG 18, vol. 3029, 14 October 1905.

26. "Will Open Agency in Peace River District," *Victoria Colonist*, 1 April 1909. The newspaper article names Constable Alexander McVicar as the first constable, but he was recalled in favor of Jamieson. Martin Kyllo unearthed the specifics of the BCPP appointment in his research on the history of Hudson Hope, B.C. Donna Redpath of the North Peace Museum in Fort St. John kindly brought her uncle's research to my attention.

27. "Policing the Peace River District," *Alaska Highway News* [AHN], 21 April 1949, 6.

28. *Report of the Superintendent of Provincial Police for the year ended December 31st, 1924* (Victoria, 1925), X27; ibid. (1926), S23; ibid., 3–4.

29. *Report of the Commissioner of Provincial Police, 1945* (Victoria, 1947), T35.

30. "'Scarlet Riders of the Plains' Take Over BC Police Job," *AHN*, 24 August 1950, 4.

31. "Policing the Peace River District," *AHN*, 28 April 1949, 6.

32. *Report of the Superintendent of Provincial Police for the year ended December 31st, 1924* (Victoria, 1925), X9.

33. Public address by L. W. Clay before the North Peace Historical Society, 1988: audiotape, North Peace Historical Society and Museum, Fort St. John, B.C.

34. *Victoria Colonist*, 16 January 1910.

35. Based on the County Court Plaint and Procedure Book [CCPP] 1920–29; CCPP 1930–33; and CCPP 1933–43, Dawson Creek Court House.

36. See "Re Mike Sowery," NAC, RG 13, box 1570, file cc 347. For the local newspaper reporting on the case, see "Two Found Dead at Cecil Lake," *PRBN*, 9 September 1930, 1; "Fort St. John News," *PRBN*, 30 September 1930, 1; "BC Police Search for Slayer of Two—Chase Leads to Winnipeg and Back to Lonely Settlement," *PRBN*, 21 October 1930, 1; "Babchuck Murder Case Reopened—Hythe, Alta. Man Arrested in Connection—Preliminary Hearing at Fort St. John," *PRBN*, 27 January 1931, 1; "Preliminary Hearing of Mike Sowry in Babchuck Murder Case," *PRBN*, 3 February 1931, 1; "Fort St. John News," *PRBN*, 10 February 1931, 1; "28 Witnesses Proceed to Murder Trail," *PRBN*, 12 May 1931, 1; "Sowry to Hang August 14th for Babchuck Murder," *PRBN*, 2 June 1931, 1; "Mike Sowry Executed at Oakalla Jail," *PRBN*, 25 August 1931, 1. On the news that someone had been arrested for the murder, see *God's Galloping Girl: The Peace River Diaries of Monica Storrs, 1929–1931*, ed. W. L. Morton (Vancouver, 1979), 179–80

37. "Burglaries Perpetrated at Dawson Creek," *PRBN*, 12 May 1931, 1.

38. "Police Official in Gun Battle With Desperate Character," *PRBN*, 2 June 1931, 1; and "Fort St. John News," *PRBN*, 9 June 1931, 1. In her diary entry for the week ending 30 May 1931, Anglican Church missionary Monica Storrs noted that the shooting incident had captured local attention, see Morton, *God's Galloping Girl*, at 190. "Short" Tompkins recalls Pomeroy's pursuit of Bryan since the BCPP officer stopped at the Tompkins farm to change horses: Interview with Short Tompkins, Fort St. John, 15 April 1999.

39. "Finding of Bandit Bryan Remains," *PRBN*, 3 November 1931, 1.

40. "Dawson Creek Asking For Police Protection," *PRBN*, 28 July 1931, 1 and 4.

41. "Dawson Creek Still Enjoys Night Robberies," *PRBN*, 18 August 1931, 1.

42. "Heavy Sentences Issued to Men for Breaking and Entering," *PRBN*, 13 October 1931, 1.

43. *R v JIR*, British Columbia Archives and Record Service [BCARS], GR 2235, R 91–4374–1, file 14/32; *R v JAM*, ibid., file 33/32; *R v JEM*, ibid., file 34/32; *R v WP*, ibid., file 1/33; *R v RMP*, ibid., file 2/33; *R v JWN*, ibid., file 6/33; *R v. JWS*, ibid., file 7/33; *R v ALP*, ibid., file 9/35; *R v 34/35*, ibid., file 34/35; *R v JMC*, ibid., file 43/35; *R v AC*, ibid., file 49/35; *R v GRS*, ibid., file 64/37.

44. See "Ross Jeffrey Attacks Parents with Axe," *PRBN*, 29 May 1934, 1; "Fort St. John News," *PRBN*, 12 June 1934, 4, and 19 June 1934, 4; "Ross E. Jeffry [*sic*] is Acquitted by Jury," *PRBN*, 12 October 1934, 1.

45. "Fall Assize Court Business Completed in Record Time," *Cariboo Observer*, 29 September 1934, 1, 5. I would like to thank Brian Milthrop of Quesnel, British Columbia, for unearthing this newspaper report.

46. Ibid., 5. Blanche Hipkiss, who knew Jeffrey, believes that incest may have been

a motivating factor in the outburst of violence and possibly explains the reference to the social and living conditions in the shack: Interview with Blanche Hipkiss, Fort St. John, 13 May 1999.

47. "Doe River Store is Broken into Again," *PRBN*, 17 August 1934, 1; "Convicted for Theft," *PRBN*, 12 October 1934, 1; "Suicide of Cherry Point Resident," *PRBN*, 7 December 1934, 1; "Fined for Allowing Hogs to be at Large," *PRBN*, 14 December 1934, 1; "Charged with Mail Theft," *PRBN*, 4 January 1935, 1; "Two Groundburch Men Charged with Theft," *PRBN*, 26 April 1935, 1; and "Cash Stolen from Dawson Creek Store," *PRBN*, 19 July 1935, 1.

48. "Albert Demean Brutally Murdered Near Tupper," *PRBN*, 3 January 1936, 1.

49. "Suspects are Arrested in Demean Murder Case," *PRBN*, 14 February 1936, 1; "Miller and Mueller Again Remanded," *PRBN*, 22 February 1936, 4; "Local and Personal," *PRBN*, 13 March 1936, 4; "Demean Murder Suspects Sent up for Trial," *PRBN*, 20 March 1936, 1; and "Murder Trial to be Held at Pr. George," *PRBN*, 1 May 1936, 1.

50. "Mueller and Miller receive Ten Years for Demean Death," *PRBN*, 29 May 1936, 1–2.

51. "Farmer Slays Family—Husband Succumbs Self-Inflicted Wounds—Mother and Two Children Had Throats Slashed with Razor and Beaten with Hammer," *PRBN*, 22 January 1937, 1.

52. Ibid.

53. "Morely Kier Succumbs from Injuries Received in Early Morning Fracas," *PRBN*, 10 December 1937, 1; "Inquest Held on Death of Morley Reid Kier," *PRBN*, 17 December 1937, 3, 5; "Matthews Committed for Trial on a Charge of Murder," *PRBN*, 31 January 1938, 1, 4.

54. "Belo Matthews Acquitted of Murder Charge," *PRBN*, 26 May 1938, 1.

55. Interview with Blanche Hipkiss, Fort St. John, B.C., 13 May 1999.

56. "'Does Crime Pay' asks 'Silent' Bill Biddle," *PRBN*, 5 January 1939, 1.

57. "Care and Treatment of Youthful Offenders," *PRBN*, 16 February 1939, 1, 4.

58. *"Rex v Otto Schwartz (murder)," Reports of the Commissioner of Provincial Police for the year 1939 and Inspector of Gaols for the year ended March 31st, 1940* (Victoria, 1940), 11–12. Also see "Al Hoover Shot to Death at Tupper Creek—Killer Believed to be at Large," *PRBN*, 20 April 1939, 1.

59. For example, when a picnic park in Pouce Coupé was vandalized, the *News* asserted that "the general opinion is that the perpetrators were transients as it is hardly reasonable to presume that anyone located in the district would be guilty of such an act": See "Pouce Coupé Park Maliciously Damaged," *PRBN*, 27 October 1938, 1.

60. The rumor of the highway construction hit the news in late February 1942. See "U.S. Army Engineers Hint Strongly of Alaska Military Highway Through Dawson Creek," *PRBN*, 26 February 1942, 1; and "Alaska Military Highway Through Dawson Creek Ratified by Joint Canada-US Defense Commission," *PRBN*, 5 March 1942, 1.

61. M. V. Bezeau, "The Realities of Strategic Planning: The Decision to Build the Alaska Highway," in *The Alaska Highway: Papers of the 40th Anniversary Symposium*, ed. Kenneth Coates (Vancouver, 1985), 25–38; and Kenneth Coates and William Morrison, *The Alaska Highway in World War II: The US Army of Occupation in Canada's Northwest* (Toronto, 1992).

62. "US Army Requests Larger Police Force," *PRBN*, 26 March 1942, 1. The Commissioner's report for 1942 noted that "the added responsibilities attending the con-

struction of the Alaska Highway necessitated an additional three men, and with the tremendously increased population in that area an addition to our police strength will have to be provided for next year": *Report of the Commissioner of the Provincial Police, 1942* (Victoria, 1943), 7. Seven more men were added in 1943: ibid., 1943, at W8.

63. The report for 1942 noted that the significant increase in patrol mileage in the Peace River subdivision "accounted for by the unusual conditions attending the construction of the Alaska Highway, which demanded a greater police concentration than heretofore": *Report of the Commissioner of Provincial Police, 1942* (Victoria, 1943), 10.

64. Based on statistics in *Reports of the Commissioner of the Provincial Police, 1938–1949* (Victoria, 1939–1950).

65. Coates and Morrison, *Alaska Highway in World War II*, 106.

66. See "Two Women Brutally Assaulted Here," *PRBN*, 11 February 1943, 1; and "Colored Soldier Sentenced to 15 Years Imprisonment," *PRBN*, 25 March 1943, 1. Also, see "Evans, W. (attempted rape)," in *Report of the Commissioner of the Provincial Police, 1943* (Victoria, 1945), W18–19.

67. "Evans, W. (attempted rape)," *Report of the Commissioner.*

68. Interview with Joseph Kosick on "Day Break," CBC Radio, 14 February 1992. Kosick was paid $5,500 damages for his injuries. Conversation with the author, 7 March 1999.

69. See *R v Miller Construction Company*," BCARS, GR 22335, box 2, file 53/43; See "Dawson Creek Rocked By Terrific Explosion Saturday Evening, February 13th," *Grande Prairie Herald Tribune*, 18 February 1943, 1; "Explosion and Fire Takes Five Lives—Whole Business Block Destroyed—Store Fronts Crumble, Windows Crash in Other Business Blocks from Blast"; "Coroner's Inquest Held Here—Jury Brings in Verdict"; and "List of Dead and Injured," *PRBN*, 25 February 1943, 1. For an examination of the explosion and its effect on Dawson Creek, see Catherine Mooney, "Dynamite, Death, and Destruction: The Explosion of 1943," prepared for Seminar in Local History, Fort St. John Campus, University of Northern British Columbia (November 1995).

70. Heath Twichell, *Northwest Epic: The Building of the Alaska Highway* (New York, 1992), 233.

71. "Command V.D. Control Officer, Pacific Command to Command Medical Officer, Pacific Command, SECRET," 15 July 1943, NAC, RG 36 (7), vol. 40, file 28–23, part 2.

72. W. E. Sanderson, acting Protective Security Agent, War Department, United States Engineer Office to Division Engineer, Northwest Division, Edmonton, Alberta, CONFIDENTIAL," 23 September 1943, NAC, RG 36 (7), vol. 40, file 28–23, part 2.

73. Ibid.

74. Ibid.

75. Special Commissioner, Major General W. W. Foster to R. A. Gibson, Director, Department of Mines and Resources, CONFIDENTIAL," 24 August 1943, NAC, RG 85, vol. 958, file 13439.

76. "Thieves Steal Jail at 'Alcan,' Report—Fort Alcan 'Brig' Lined with Wallboard Not Steel," *AHN*, 9 May 1946, 1. Also, see "More Scandal on the Dumphead," *AHN*, 31 July 1947, 2. See generally, Coates and Morrison, *Alaska Highway in World War II*, 204–11.

77. "At Police Court—Vagrancy, Thefts, Weapons And Dogs on the Police Blotter," *AHN*, 27 June 1946, 1.

78. "District Briefs," *AHN*, 29 August 1946, 8. For two earlier cases, see *R v David Gordon Dunn*, BCARS, GR2036, file 49/44; and *R v Alan McIntryre Moodie*, file 119/44.

79. *Rex v Theresa Seline*, Supreme Court Cause Book, Dawson Creek Court House [SCCB], vol. 1, 12/1944, and BCARS, GR 2036, box 1, file 12/1944. Also, see "U.S.E.D. Garage Superintendent Found Shot to Death in Trailer—Wife of Dead Man Charged With Murder," *PRBN*, 6 January 1944, 1; "Jury Returns Verdict in Death of Roy Matthew Seline At Inquest," *PRBN*, 13 January 1944, 1–2; "Preliminary Hearing of Seline Murder Case—Hearing Held at Pouce Coupe—Wife of Murdered Man Committed For Trial at Next Assize," *PRBN*, 1; and "Not Guilty Verdict Returned in Seline Murder Trial," *PRBN*, 22 June 1944, 1.

80. "Verdict Returned in Shooting Affair," *PRBN*, 13 April 1944, 1.

81. *Rex v Bryon Bruce Potter*, 27/1945, SCCB, vol. 1; and "Byron Bruce Potter," NAC, RG 13, box 1650, file CC 584. See "Murder Charge Is Laid When Mother Stabbed," *PRBN*, 19 July 1945, 1; "Remand B. Potter," *PRBN*, 26 July 1945, 1; "Murder Preliminary On," *PRBN*, 23 August 1945, 1; "Potter Committed to Trial," *PRBN*, 30 August 1945, 1, 6; "Potter Held for Higher Court as Evidence Completed in Preliminary Trial," *PRBN*, 6 September 1945, 1, 5; "Potter Trial Starts Oct. 1," *PRBN*, 27 September 1945, 1; "Potter Will Die on Jan 10—First To Hang in This Area," *PRBN*, 4 October 1945, 1; "Potter Hanged at Oakalla," *PRBN*, 17 January 1946, 1. A miscalculation at Potter's hanging resulted in his decapitation.

82. The following is based on "Manhunt On at Blueberry for Body of Slain Tourist," *AHN*, 26 August 1948, 1; "Murder Charge Follows Discovery of Body on Alcan Highway; Self Confessed Slayer Will Come Here for Hearing; Coroners Jury Adjourned—BC Police Will Seek Protection of Justice For Travellers on Highway," *AHN*, 2 September 1948, 1–2; "Weigner's Guilty Conscience Was His Undoing; Trigger Finger Pulled Him Into Confession of Fatal Shooting," *AHN*, 9 September 1948, 1, 5; and "Highway Murder Case to Higher Court," *AHN*, 9 September 1948, 1, 5.

83. "Sordid Shooting Case Ends; Weigner Gets Two Years," *AHN*, 14 October 1948, 1.

84. Ibid. Also, see "Big Murder Trial Will Begin Here Monday," *PGC*, 30 September 1948, 1; "Wiegner [*sic*] Faces Jury," *PGC*, 7 October 1948, 1; "Wiegner [*sic*] Gets Two Year Sentence," *PGC*, 14 October 1948, 1.

85. The following is based on "Dawson Creek Juveniles Charged with murder as 'Comic Book' Idea Backfires for Youths," *PGC*, 25 November 1948, 1; and "Two Juveniles Charged with Death of J. Watson," *PRBN*, 25 November 1948, 1. Also, see Frederic Wertham, "Murder in Dawson Creek," in *Seduction of the Innocent* (London, 1955), 274–76. A Watson family history is contained in *Lure of the South Peace* (Dawson Creek, 1981), 232–34.

86. "Kilkerran Resident Jim Watson Dies From Bullet Wound," *PRBN*, 18 November 1948, 1.

87. "Dawson Creek Juveniles Charged with Murder," *PRBN*, 13 April 1944, 1; and "Remarks on Comics in Court Session By Prosecuting Attorney and Magistrate," *AHN*, 9 December 1948, 1.

88. For a broader examination of the comic book murder, juvenile delinquency, and the campaign against American crime comics, see Jonathan Swainger, "American Crime Comics As Villains: An Incident from Northern Canada," *Legal Studies Forum* 22 (1998): 215–31. Also see Augustine Brannigan, "Mystification of the Innocents:

Crime Comics and Delinquency in Canada, 1931–1949," in *Criminal Justice History: An International Annual* 7 (1986): 111–44.

89. George Murray, Canada, *House of Commons Debates*, 21 October 1949, 1042–43.

90. The Fulton Bill would not end governmental attention on allegedly dangerous literature. See Senate of Canada, *Proceedings of the Special Committee on Sale and Distribution of Salacious and Indecent Literature 1952–1953* (Ottawa, 1952–53). For an interpretation of this investigation, see Mary Louise Adams, "Youth, Corruptibility, and English-Canadian Postwar Campaigns against Indecency, 1948–1955," *Journal of the History of Sexuality* 6:11 (1995): 89–117.

91. "Jack Scott's Field Day," *AHN*, 17 October 1957, 5, 9.

92. Police Magistrate's docket books, 1950–1960, Dawson Creek Court House.

93. "Letters to the Editor—An Answer to Scott," *AHN*, 3 October 1957, 2.

94. "Reader Answers Jack Scott," *AHN*, 17 October 1957, 2, 9.

95. "Jack Scott Must A Been All Shook Up!" *AHN*, 3 October 1957, 2. Murray blamed Elvis Presley for the incidence of juvenile delinquency in the Peace; see "Is there a Teen-age Problem?" *AHN*, 11 October 1956, 2.

96. "We Got the Feathers, Who Got the Tar?" *AHN*, 24 October 1957, 2. At the beginning of the month, local RCMP were advising citizens to lock all doors and report any missing items: "Jewellery Thieves, Thefts Figure in the Week's Police Blotter," *AHN*, 3 October 1957, 1.

CHAPTER 7

Capital Punishment and the Death Penalty in the United States: A Selected Bibliography

Compiled By Dennis Wiechman

The focus of this bibliographic work is the United States and the historical publications on capital punishment. There are some British sources, specifically the House of Commons and other English publishers. Most of the works cited are historical in nature, and some of the citations will have missing information. The works cited are mostly from a pre-1950 perspective since the source documents are from the same time period. There are a few current citations that deal with a historical content. This bibliography contains 1,078 historical sources, and the data file was created by CITATION, a software firm that will publish any file in over 1,000 styles.

Abercombie, James, M.P. *Hansard's Parliamentary Debates.* Speech in House of Commons, 29 March 1811, on the Bill to Abolish the Punishment of Death, (1811): 652.

Adams, Chester D. "Benefit of Clergy in Fayette County." *Kentucky State Bar Journal* 20 (1956): 129–32.

Adams, John Quincy. *Memoirs,* 259. Philadelphia: Lippincott, 1876.

Adams, W. H. Davenport. "Pains and Penalties." *Gentleman's Magazine,* April and May 1891.

Adelesstein, Richard P. "Informational Paradox and the Pricing of Crime: Capital Sentencing Standards in Economic Perspective." *Journal of Criminal Law, and Criminology* 70 (1979): 281–98.

Aden, M. "Bygone Forms of Capital Punishment." *Codicillus* 13 (October 1972): 20.

Akerman, John Y. *Laws and Capital Punishments in the Middle Ages.* London, 1860.

Alcock, T. *Observations on the Defects of the Poor Law and on the Causes and Consequences of the Great Increase and Burden of the Poor.* London: R. Baldwin, 1752.

Allredge, E. P. "Why the South Leads the Nation in Murder and Manslaughter." *The Quarterly Review* 2 (1942): 123.

American Almanac. *Statistics of Crime in France,* 1837.

———. *Statistics of Crime in England, Wales, and Scotland* 1837.

American Biblical Repository. "Punishment, Its Nature and Design," *American Biblical Repository* 10, (July 1843).

American Encyclopedia. "Capital Punishment." In *American Encyclopedia,* 754.

American Journal of Sociology. "Death Penalty and Homicide." *American Journal of Sociology* 16 (July 1910): 88–116.

American Law Institute and American Bar Association. Joint Committee on Legal Education. *The Problem of Punishing Homicide.* Philadelphia: American Law Institute, 1962.

American Law Reports. "Abolition Of Death Penalty as Affecting Right to Bail of One Charged With Murder in First Degree." *American Law Reports* 8 (1920): 1352.

———. "Constitutionality of Statute. Punishment Mandatory." *American Law Reports* 83 (1933): 1362.

———. "Recommendation in Capital Case." *American Law Reports* 138 (1942): 1230.

American Review of Reviews. "Does Capital Punishment Prevent Convictions?" *American Review of Reviews* 40 (1909): 219.

Amos, Sheldon. "Civilization and Crime." *Fortnightly Review* 2 (1865): 319.

Ancell, Marc. *Capital Punishment.* New York: United Nations, Department of Economic and Social Affairs, 1962.

Andover Review. "Outline Course of Study in Crime and the Criminal Classes." *Andover Review* 13 (February, April, June, and August 1890).

Andrew, J. A., Governor, Massachusetts. "Addresses to the Legislature of Massachusetts, January 1861 and 1862."

Annals of American Academy of Political and Social Science. "Crime and Capital Punishment: A Symposium." Garner, Crime and Judicial Inefficiency (601); Barrows, Legislative Tendencies as to Capital Punishment (618); Cutler, Capital Punishment and Lynching (622); Shipley, Homicide and the Death Penalty in Mexico (625). *The Annals* 29: (1907): 601.

Annals of The American Academy. (1907) Crime and Capital Punishment: Symposium. *Annals of the American Academy* 29 (May): 601–29.

Anstruther, John, Sir. *Hansard's Parliamentary Debates.* Con Bill to Abolish the Punishment of Death, 648.

Archbold, E. "Abolition of Capital Punishment." *Western Law Journal* 5 (1848): 421.

Arena. "The Crime of Capital Punishment." *Arena* I: 175.

———. "Failure of Capital Punishment." *Arena* 21: 469.

Aries, Philippe. *Western Attitudes Toward Death From The Middle Ages to the Present.* Baltimore, Md.: The Johns Hopkins University Press, 1974.

Armitage, Robert, Rev. *Essay on Capital Punishment Penscell Papers, Vol. 2.* London: Bently, 1846.

Armstrong, Lebbrus, Rev. *Origin, Tendencies, etc., of the Efforts for the Abolition of Capital Punishment.* New York, 1848.

———. *The Signs of the Times. Ten Lectures Opposing the Abolition of Capital Punishment.* New York: Carter, 1848.

Arnold, J. C. "Royal Commission on Capital Punishment." *Solicitors Journal* 18 (1952): 280.

Arnold, J. C. "Royal Commission on Capital Punishment." *Solicitors Journal* 19 (1952): 21.

Arnold, J. D. "Report on Capital Punishment." *Solicitors Journal* 20 (1954): 263.

Arnold, J. D. "Report on Capital Punishment." *Solicitors Journal* 21 (1954): 5.

Ashworth, Henry. *Capital Punishments and their Influence on Crime.* Manchester, 1861.

Atholl, Justin. *Shadows Of The Gallows.* London: John Long Limited, 1954.

Bailey, Ronald. "Facing Death, A New Life Perhaps Too Late." *Life*, 26, 27 July 1962.

Baker, T. B. L. *War With Crime.* London: Longaus, 1889.

Baldwin, Simeon E. "How to Deal with Habitual Criminals." *Journal of Statistical Society* 22 (9 September 1886).

Ball, John C. "The Deterrence Concept in Criminology and the Law." *Journal of Criminal Law, Criminal Law and Police Science* 46 (1955): 347–54.

Barbour, W. T. "Efforts to Abolish the Death Penalty in Illinois." *Journal of Criminal Law and Criminology* 9 (1919): 500.

Barkan, Irving. *Capital Punishment in Ancient Athens.* Chicago, 1936.

Barkaw, I, and J. O. Lofberg. *Sycophancy In Athens and Capital Punishment in Ancient Athens.* New York: Arno Press, 1979.

Barnes, Harry Elmer. "Case Against Capital Punishment." *Current History* 24 (June 1926): 365–70.

Barrister (England). "Capital Punishment. From a Utilitarian Point of View." In *Capital Punishment.* London: Barrister, 1879.

Barrows, Samuel J. *New Legislation Concerning Crimes, Misdemeanors, and Penalties.* Washington, D.C.: Government Printing Office, 1900.

———. Legislative Tendencies as to Capital Punishment. *The Annals* 29 (1907): 601, 618.

Barrows, Samuel June. "Legislative Tendencies." *Annals of American Academy* 29 (May 1907): 625–29.

Barry, J. V. W. " . . . Hanged by the Neck Until. . . . " *Sydney Law Review* 2 (1958): 401.

Barry, John D. "Dilemma." *Golden Book Magazine* 12 (November 1930): 90 + .

Barry, Rupert V. "Furman To Gregg: The Judicial and Legislative History." *Howard Law Journal* 22 (1979): 53–117.

Bascom, H. B., President Transylvania University. "Capital Punishment." *Quarterly Review* (October 1848).

Batcheller, George, Chairman. *Report of the Select Committee Relative to the Resolutions Upon the Subject of Capital Punishment.* Assembly Doc. No. 42. In Assembly, State Of New York, 14 April 1859.

Beasley, N. B. "Aren't We All Killers—An Interview With Henry Ford." *Collier's*, 7 June 1927.

Becarria, Cesare. *An Essay on Crimes and Punishments, With a Commentary attributed to Voltaire.* London: Newbury, 1785.

Beccari, Cesare. *An Essay on Crimes and Punishments, With a Commentary Attributed to Voltaire.* Trans. H. Paolucci. Indianapolis, Ind.: Bobbs-Merrill Co., 1963.

Beck, L. *Old Convict Days.* London: Unwin, 1899.

Bedau, Hugo Adam. "A Bibliography of Capital Punishment and Related Topics, 1948–1958." *Prison Journal* 38 (1958): 35–45.

———. "A Note on the Hauptmann Case and The Argument for Deterrence." *New Jersey State Bar Journal* 2 (1959): 255.

———. "Death Sentences in New Jersey 1907–1964." *Rutgers Law Review* 19 (1964): 1–64.

————. "Capital Punishment in Oregon, 1903–1964." *Oregon Law Review* 45 (1965): 1–39.

————. "The Issue of Capital Punishment." *Current History* (1967).

————. "The Death Penalty in America: Review and Forecast." *Federal Probation* 35 (June 1971): 32–43.

————. "Problems of Capital Punishment." *Current History* 71 (1976): 14–18.

Bedau, H. A. "A Bibliography on Capital Punishment And Related Topics—1948–1958." *Prison Journal* 38 (1958): 41–45.

Bedau, Hugo Adam. "Murder, Errors of Justice, and Capital Punishment." In *The Death Penalty in America*, edited by Hugo Adam Bedau, 434. New York: Doubleday, 1964.

————. "The Death Penalty in America." *Federal Probation* 35 (1971): 32–43.

Beggs, Thomas. "The Deterrent Influence of Capital Punishment." *Transactions of the National Association for the Promotion of Social Science.* 1865

————. *Testimony before Capital Punishment Commission. 3 March 1865.*

Beichman, Arnold. "The First Electrocution." *Commentary* 35 (1963): 410–19.

Beman, Lamar T., ed. *Selected Articles on Capital Punishment.* Handbook Series. New York: H. W. Wilson, 1925.

Bender, David L., and Leone Bruno, eds. *The Death Penalty: Opposing Viewpoints.* St. Paul, Minn.: Greenhaven Press, 1986.

Bennett, J. V. "Historic Move: Delaware Abolishes the Death Penalty." *American Bar Association Journal* 44 (1958): 1053.

Bennett, James V. "Statement on the Abolition of Capital Punishment in Delaware." *National Probation and Parole Journal* 4 (1958): 281–83.

————. A Cool Look at the Crime Crisis. *Harpers*, April 1964, 123.

Bentham, J. "Hanging Question." *New Statesman*, 26 November 1976, 743.

Bentham, Jeremy. *Principles of Penal Law.* In his *Works, vol. 1.* Edin: William Tait, 1843.

Bentley's Miscellany. "Capital Punishment." August 1864.

Bently, William G. *My Son's Execution.* London: W. H. Allen, 1957.

Bernaldo de Quiros, Constantino. *Modern Theories of Criminology.* Boston: Little Brown & Co., 1911.

Bernstein, Jerome L. "The M'Naghten Rule: Flight From Reality." *New Jersey State Bar Journal* 1 (1957): 73.

Bernstein, Theodore. "A Grand Success." *I. E. E. E.*, February 1973, 54.

Berriault, G. "The Last Firing Squad, Executioners of Utah." *Esquire*, June 1966, 54.

Berry, James. *My Experience As an Executioner (reprint).* Ed. H. S. Ward. Detroit: Gale Research Co., 1892.

————. *My Experiences as an Executioner.* London: Percy, 1891.

Best, Harry. "Capital Punishment." In *Crime and the Criminal Law in the United States.* New York: Macmillan Co., 1930.

Beyleveld, Deryck. *A Bibliography on General Deterrence Research.* Westmead, England: Saxon House, 1980.

Bierce, Ambrose. "The Shadow of the Dial." In *The Death Penalty*, 127–39. San Francisco, Calif.: A. M. Robertson, 1901.

Billson, William W. "Origin of Criminal Law." *Popular Science Monthly* 16 (1880): 433.

Bird, F. W., Chairman. *Report to the House of Representatives of Massachusetts on the Petition of Wendell Phillips and others for the abolition of Capital Punishment.* 27 April 1848. House Doc. 196.

Bishop, George V. *Executions, The Legal Ways Of Death*. Los Angeles, Calif.: Sherbourne Press, 1965.

Blackstone, William, Sir. *Commentaries on the English Law, Book IV.* London, 1783.

Blackwell, Elizabeth. *Laws Concerning Women*. London: John Chapman, 1854.

Blackwood's Magazine. "On The Punishment of Death." *Blackwood's Magazine*, June 1830.

Blake, Robert. "Law Takes Its Toll." *American Mercury* 17 (July 1929): 263–70.

Blanc, Louis. *Historical Revelations*. London: Chapman & Hall, 1848.

Bland, James. *The Common Hangmen: English and Scottish Hangmen Before the Abolition of Public Executions*. Hornchurch, Essex: Ian Henry Publications, 1984.

Bleackley, Horace. *The Hangmen Of England*. Montclair, N.J.: Patterson Smith (reprint), 1977.

Bleyer, J. Mount, M.D. *Scientific Methods of Execution*. New York, 1887.

———. (1888) Scientific Methods of Capital Punishment, No. 93. Humbolt Library.

Bliss, ed. "Death Penalty." In *New Encyclopedia of Social Reform*, 363. New York, 1908.

Block, Eugene B. *And May God Have Mercy on Your . . . The Case Against Capital Punishment*. San Francisco: Fearon Publishers, 1962.

Blom-Cooper, L. J., ed. *The Hanging Question*. London: Duckworth & Co., 1969.

Bloom-Cooper, Louis J., ed. "Selected Bibliography on Capital Punishment in Britain." In *The Hanging Question. Essays on the Death Penalty*. Published on behalf of The Howard League for Penal Reform, London: Duckworth & Co., 1969.

Blue Laws. *The Connecticut Code of 1650*. Hartford: Judd, Loomis & Co, 1836.

Boar, Roger. *The World's Most Infamous Murders*. New York: Exeter Books, 1983.

Boardman, George Dana, Rev. *University Lectures on the Ten Commandments*. Philadelphia: American Baptist Publication Society, 1889.

Bohannon, Paul, ed. *African Homicide and Suicide*. Princeton, N.J.: Princeton University Press, 1960.

Boies, H. M. *The Science Penology*. New York: Putnam's, 1901.

Bok, Curtis. *Star Wormwood*. New York: Alfred A. Knopf, 1959.

Borchard, Edwin. *Convicting The Innocent*. New Haven, Conn.: Yale University Press, 1932.

Borchard, Edwin, and Russell E. Lutz. *Convicting The Innocent: Sixty-five Actual Errors of Criminal Justice*. Garden City, N.Y.: Garden City Publishing Co., 1932.

Borchard, Edwin, and F. L. Sanville. "When Justice Goes Astray." *Prison Journal* 12 (1932): 16.

Borowitz, Albert I. "Under Sentence of Death." *American Bar Association Journal* 64 (August 1978): 1259.

Bovee, Marvin H. *Reasons for Abolishing Capital Punishment*. Chicago: Lakeside Printing Co., 1875.

Bowen-Rowlands, Ernest. *The Judgement of Death*. London: W. Collins Sons & Co., 1924.

Bowers, Duke C. *Life Imprisonment vs. the Death Penalty; Brief on Senate Bill No. 242 and House Bill No. 23*. Memphis, Tenn.: The Author, 1913.

Bowers, William J., Glenn L. Pierce, and John N. McDevitt. *Legal Homicide: Death as Punishment in America, 1864–1982*. Boston: Northeastern University Press, 1974.

Boyer, Paul. *Salem Possessed: The Social Origins of Witchcraft*. Cambridge, Mass.: Harvard University Press, 1974.

Bradford, William. "Enquiry How Far the Punishment of Death Is Necessary in Pennsylvania (in 1793)." *American Journal of Legal History* 12 (1968): 122, 245.

Braithwaite, Lloyd. "Executive Clemency in California: A Case Study in Interpretation of Criminal Responsibility." *Issues in Criminology* 1 (1965): 77.

Brasler, Fenton. *Reprieve: A Study Of A System.* London and Toronto: George G. Harrap, 1965.

Brearley, H. C. "Negro and Homicide." *Social Forces* 9 (December 1930): 247–53.

———. Firearms and Homicide." *Sociology and Social Research* 15 (May 1931): 456–62.

Brearley, Harrington C. *Homicide In The United States.* Chapel Hill: University of North Carolina Press, 1932.

Bright, John. Speech in House of Commons. In *Hansard's Parliamentary Debates,* 2092.

———. *Report of Capital Punishment Commission, Jan. 8, 1866, Recommending The Total Abolition of Capital Punishment.* House of Commons. London (1866).

Brinkerhoff, John L., et al. *Majority Report of Select Committee on the Abolition of Capital Punishment.* New York Assembly Doc. No. 133, 1 March 1848. Albany, N.Y.

Britain's Public Documents. *A Bill to Provide for the Abolition of Capital Punishment.* London: H.M. Stationary Office, 1924.

———. *A Bill to Provide for the Abolishment of Capital Punishment, and to Substitute other Punishments therefor, and for Purposes connected with Matters aforesaid.* London: H.M. Stationary Office, 1925

———. *Report of Select Committee of the House of Commons, 1929–1930.* London: H.M. Stationary Office, 1930.

———. *Capital Punishment, Cmd. 7419.* London: Home Office and Scottish Home Department; H.M. Stationary Office, 1948.

———. *Report of the Royal Commission on Capital Punishment. 1949–1953. Cmd. 8932.* London: H.M. Stationary Office, 1953.

———. *A Bill to Abolish or For a Period Suspend the Passing and Execution of the Death Sentence on Conviction of Murder and to Substitute Alternative Penalty therefor.* London: H. M. Stationary Office, 1956.

———. *A Bill to Make for England and Wales (and for Courts-Martial Whenever sitting), Amendments of the Law relating to Homicide and the Trial and Punishment of Murder, and for Scotland, Amendments of the Law relating to Homicide and the Trial and Punishment of Murder.* London: H.M. Stationary Office, 1956.

———. *Homicide Act.* London: H.M. Stationary Office, 1957.

———. *Murder Act.* London: H.M. Stationary Office, 1965.

British Journal of Crime and Delinquency. A Symposium on the Report of the Royal Commission on Capital Punishment. *British Journal of Crime and Delinquency* 4:3 (1954): 158.

Brougham, Henry, Lord. *Bentham and His Theory of Punishments. Contributions, Vol. 3.* London, 1856.

Brown v. Board of Education. 347 U.S. 483 (1954).

Brown, H. P. "The New Instrument of Execution." *North American Review* 149 (1889): 586.

Brown, Wenzell. *Women Who Died in the Chair.* New York: Collier, 1963.

Browne, J. W. *Cannibalism, the Crime Prohibited in Genesis IX.* Boston, 1846.

Browning, C. A., Dr. *The Convict Ship and England's Exiles.* London: Hamilton, Adams, 1847.

Btinn, Keith W. "First Degree Murder: A Workable Definition." *Journal of Criminal Law, Criminology, and Police Science* 40 (1950): 729–35.

Bunn, Henry. *Capital Punishment.* Birmingham: Hunt & Son, 1840.

Burbey, L. H. "History of Execution in What Is Now the State of Michigan." *Michigan Historical Magazine* 22 (1938): 443.

Bureau of Census. *Vital Statistics Rates in the United States 1900–1940.* U.S. Department of Commerce, 1943.

———. *Historical Statistics of the United States, from Colonial Times to 1957.* U.S. Department of Commerce, 1960

Bureau of the Census. *Mortality Statistics.* U.S. Department of Commerce, 1937.

Burkett, Phillip H. "Ought Capital Punishment To Be Abolished?" *Catholic Charities Review* 4 (March 1920): 75–77.

Burleigh, Charles C. *Thoughts on the Death Penalty.* Philadelphia, 1845.

Burr, Charles C., Rev. *Review of Dr. Berg's Discourse on Capital Punishment.* New York, 1845.

Bush, Francis, X. *Guilty or Not Guilty?* New York: Bobbs-Merrill, 1952.

Buxton, Thomas Fowell. "Speech on Sir James Mackintosh's motion for a Committee on the Criminal Law, March 2, 1819." In *Hansard's Parliamentary Debates* (1819) 806.

Bye, Raymond. "Capital Punishment in the United States." Ph.D. thesis, University of Pennsylvania, 1919.

———. "Recent History and Present Status of Capital Punishment in the United States." *Journal of Criminal Law and Criminology* 17 (1926): 234.

Bye, Raymond T. *Capital Punishment in the United States.* The Committee of Philanthropic Labor of Philadelphia Yearly Meeting of Friends. Philadelphia, (1919).

———. "Recent History and Present Status of Capital Punishment in the United States." *Journal of Criminal Law and Criminology* 17 (August 1926): 234–45.

Caldwell, John, M.D. "Thoughts on the Impolicy and Injustice of Capital Punishment." An Address. Louisville, Ky., 1848.

Caldwell, O. J. "Why Is the Death Penalty Retained?" *The Annuals* 264 (1952): 45.

California Assembly Subcommittee of the Judiciary Committee. *Report of the Subcommittee of the Judiciary Committee on Capital Punishment,* 1957.

Callahan, Jack. "Fingerprints Can Be Forged." *American Mercury* 47 (July 1939): 330–33.

Calvert, E. R. New York Times Book Review. In *Does Capital Punishment Really Decrease Murder?* "Review of Capital Punishment in the Twentieth Century," 3, 27 August 1937.

Calvert, E. Roy. *Memorial Lecture Series.* London: National Council for the Abolition of the Death Penalty.

Calvert, E. Roy. *Murder and the Death Penalty,* pamphlet. London.

———. *Capital Punishment in the 20th Century.* Putnam, 1927.

———. *Death Penalty Enquirer: Being a Review of the Evidence before the (Great Britain) Select Committee on Capital Punishment.* London: Victor Gollancz, 1930.

———. *After Abolition—What?* London: National Council for the Abolition of Capital Punishment, 1931.

———. *The Death Penalty Inquiry.* London, 1931.

———. "The Problem of Capital Punishment." *Prison Journal* 12 (1932): 25.

———. "Death Penalty." In *Lawbreaker: A Critical Study of the Modern Treatment of Crime*, 259–81. London: George Routledge & Sons, 1933.

———. *Capital Punishment*. London: National Council for the Abolition of Capital Punishment, 1934.

———. *The Case Against Capital Punishment*. London: The Howard League for Penal Reform, 1953.

———. *Capital Punishment in the Twentieth Century*, 5th ed. rev. (1936); *and The Death Penalty Inquiry* (1931). Montclair, N.J.: Patterson Smith, 1973.

Calvert, E. Roy, and Theodora Calvert. *The Lawbreaker—A Critical Study of The Modern Treatment of Crime*. London: George Routledge & Sons, 1933.

Campbell, Alexander, Rev. *Capital Punishment. Popular Lectures and Addresses*. St. Louis: John Burns, 1861.

Campbell, Ruth. Sentence Of Death by Burning for Women. *The Journal of Legal History* 5 (1984): 44–59.

Campion, Donald, S. J. "The State Police and the Death Penalty." In *In Canada*. Appendix F, 729–41, 1956.

Camus, Albert. *Reflections on the Guillotine*. Michigan City, Ind.: Fridtjof-Karla Publishers, 1959.

———. "Reflections on the Guillotine." In *Resistance, Rebellion and Death*, edited by Albert Camus, 173–234. New York: Alfred A. Knopf, 1966.

Canada Parliament. "Joint Committee of the Senate and House of Commons on Capital Punishment and Corporal Punishment." In *Minutes of Proceedings and Evidence*. Ottawa: Edmond Cloutier, n.d.

Canada, Joint Committee of the Senate and House of Commons on Capital and Corporal Punishments and Lotteries. *Reports*, 1956.

Canadian Bar Review. "Abolition of Capital Punishment—A Symposium." *Canadian Bar Review* 32 (1954): 485.

Cantor, Nathaniel F. *Crime, Criminals and Criminal Justice*. New York: Henry Holt & Co., 1932.

———. "Death Penalty." In *Crime and Society*, 221–25. New York: Henry Holt & Co., 1939.

Capital Punishment Commission. (1819, 1834, 1866) *Report to Both Houses of Parliament*. London.

Capote, Truman. *In Cold Blood*. New York: Random House, 1966.

Carroll, O. The Shadow of the Gallows. *The Penal Reformer* 1:4 (April 1935).

Carson, James C. L., Dr. *Capital Punishment: Is Murder Legalized!* London: Houlston & Sons, 1877.

Carter, Dan T. *Scottsboro: A Tragedy of the American South*. Baton Rouge: Louisiana State University Press, 1969.

Carter, Robert M. *Capital Punishment in California: 1938–1953*. Berkeley: University of California, 1953.

———. "The Johnny Cain Story: A Composite of the Men Executed in California." *Issues in Criminology* 1 (fall 1965): 66.

Cartwright, Henry, Capt. "Examination before the Capital Punishment Commission of July 8, 1864." In *Capital Punishment Commission of July 8, 1864* (4 March 1864).

Catherine, II, Empress of Russia. We Punish Crime Without Imitating It; The Punishment of death is rarely anything but a useless barbarity. 1768.

Catholic Law Review. "Cruel and Unusual Punishment." *Catholic Law Review* 3 (1953): 117.

Ceylon. (1962) "Commission of Inquiry on Capital Punishment, Sessional Paper XIV-1959." *The Congressional Record*, 1 March 1962, 3019.

Chamberlain, Rudolph W. *There is no Truce; A Life of Thomas Mott Osborn.* New York: Macmillan & Co., 1935.

Chambers's Encyclopedia. "Capital Punishment." London: Chambers's Encyclopedia, 1891.

Chamber's Journal. "Punishments in Good Old times." *Chamber's Journal* 31 (June 1874).

Chan, Loren B. Example for the Nation: Nevada's Execution of Gee Jon. *Nevada Historical Society Quarterly* 18 (1975): 96–106.

Chapin, Edwin H., Rev. *Three Discourses on Capital Punishment.* Boston: Temple Office, 1843.

———. *Capital Punishment Not Commanded by God.* Boston: Prisoner's Friend, 1850.

Chedieu, Emile, of France. "Examination before the Capital Punishment Commission of July 8, 1864." *Capital Punishment Commission of July 8, 1864* (11 March 1865).

Cheever, George B., Rev. *Defense of Capital Punishment.* New York: Wiley, 1846.

———. *Punishment By Death.* New York, 1849.

———. "The Death Penalty." *North American Review,* December 1881.

Chessman, Caryl. *Cell 2455, Death Row.* Englewood Cliffs, N.J.: Prentice Hall, 1954.

———. *Trial By Ordeal.* Englewood Cliffs, N.J.: Prentice Hall, 1955.

Christian Century. "Capital Punishment." *Christian Century* 53 (22 April 1936): 591–94.

———. "Kentucky Puts on a (Public) Hanging." *Christian Century* 53 (26 August 1936): 1124.

———. "Genesis and Capital Punishment." *Christian Century* (28 March 1973): 355.

Christian Quarterly Spectator. "On Penal Law." *Christian Quarterly Spectator,* September 1830.

Christoph, James Bernard. *Capital Punishment and British Politics: The British Movement to Abolish the Death Penalty 1945–1957.* Chicago: University of Chicago Press, 1962.

Cicero, Marcus Tullius. "Speech in Defense of Caius Robirius." Oration. Trans. Young. London: Bohn, 1852.

Clark, C. E. "The Death Penalty in Illinois." *Proceedings of the Illinois State Bar Association,* 1927.

Clark, John. "Criticism Criticized. On the Punishment of Death." *Eclectic Review,* February 1850.

Cogswell, Jonathan, Rev. *On the Necessity of Capital Punishment.* Hartford, Conn., 1843.

Cohen, C. "Shall We Go A Hanging?" *The Penal Reformer* 1:2 (October 1934).

Cohen, Louis H. *Murder, Madness and the Law.* Cleveland and New York: World Publishing Co., 1952.

Cohn, Haim H. "The Penology of the Talmud." *Israel Law Review* 5 (1970): 53–74.

Coke, Edward, Sir. *Epilogue to Third Institute.* London: E. & R. Brooke, 1794.

Colaizzi, Janet. *Homicidal Insanity, 1800—1985.* Tuscaloosa: University of Alabama Press, 1989.

Colquhoun, P., L.L.D. Testimony Before the Select Committee on Criminal Law. London, 1819.

Columbia Law Review. "Federal Kidnapping Act—Imposition of Death Penalty." *Columbia Law Review* 45 (1945): 797.

Combe, George. *Capital Punishment, or, the Proper treatment of criminals.* Delaware, Ohio: Wells.

Congressional Digest. "Question of Capital Punishment." *Congressional Digest* 6 (August 1927): 219–44.

Cook, Earleen H. *Death Penalty Since Witherspoon.* Montecello, Ill.: Vance Bibliographies, 1979.

Cooper, David D. *The Lesson of the Scaffold: The Public Execution Controversy in Victorian England.* Athens: Ohio University Press, 1974.

Copinger, Walter A. *An Essay on the Abolition of Capital Punishment.* London, 1875.

Corcoran, Thomas L. J. "Felony Murder in New York." *Fordham Law Review* 6 (January 1937): 43–74.

Corrections. "Contrasting Electrocutions." *Corrections,* 9 July 1937.

Cortner, Richard. *The Scottsboro Case in Mississippi: The Supreme Court and Brown v. Mississippi.* Jackson: University of Mississippi Press, 1986.

Costello, M. "Early American Views and Use of Ultimate Penalty." *Editorial Research Reports,* 10 January 1973, 30.

Cottu, Charles, Judge. *On The Administration of the Criminal Code in England.* Pamphleteer, vol. 16. London, 1820.

Coulter, E. Merton. "Hanging as a Social-Penal Institution in Georgia And Elsewhere." *Georgia Historical Quarterly* 57 (1973): 17–55.

Crime and Delinquency. "La Guillotine in 20th Century." *Crime and Delinquency* 19 (1973): 290.

Curtis, N. M., General. *Speech in Assembly, March 26, 1890.* Bill to Abolish Capital Punishment. Assembly Doc. No. 79. Albany, N.Y, 1890.

———. *Speech on Bill to Define the Crime of Murder, Provide Penalty Therefor, and to Abolish the Punishment of Death.* House of Representatives. 9 June 1892. Washington, D.C.

———. *Capital Crimes. Punishments Prescribed Therefor By Federal and State Laws and Those of Foreign Countries, with Statistics Relating to the Same. Also A Bibliography of Crimes and Punishments.* U.S. House of Representatives. 53rd Congress, 2d Session. Washington, D.C., 1894

Curvant, B. A, and F. N. Waldrop. "The Murder in the Mental Institution." *The Annals* 284 (1952): 35.

Cutler, J. E. *Lynch Law.* New York: Longmans, 1905.

———. "Capital Punishment and Lynching." *Annals of the American Academy* 29 (May 1907): 622–25.

Cutler, James E. "Capital Punishment and Lynching." *The Annals of the American Academy* 29 (1907): 622–25.

———. *Lynch-law: An Investigation into the History of Lynching in the United States.* Montclair, N.J.: Patterson Smith, 1969.

Dann, R. H. The Deterrent Effect of Capital Punishment." *Friends Social Service Series.* 1935.

———. "Capital Punishment in Oregon." *The Annals* 284 (1952): 110.

Darrow, Clarence. *Crime, Its Causes and Treatment.* New York: Thomas Y. Crowell Co., 1922.

———. The Crime of Compulsion. In *Attorney For The Damned*, edited by Arthur Weinberg, 16–88. New York: Simon and Schuster, 1957.

Darrow, Clarence, and Alfred J. Talley. *Capital Punishment; A Debate.* New York: League for Public Discussion, 1924.

Darrow, Clarence S., and R. L. Calder. "Is Capital Punishment Right? A Debate." *The Forum 80*, September 1928, 327.

Davis, David B. *Homicide in American Fiction.* Ithaca: Cornell University Press, 1957.

Davis, David Brion. "Murder in New Hampshire." *New England Quarterly* 28 (1955): 147.

———. "Movements to Abolish Capital Punishment in America, 1787–1861." *American Historical Review* 63 (October 1957): 23–46.

Davis, Harry L. "Death By Law." *Outlook* 131 (26 July 1922): 525–28.

Davis, Richard P. *The Tasmanian Gallows.* Hobart, Tasmania: Cat & Fiddle Press, 1974.

Davitt, Michael. *Leaves From a Prison Diary.* London: Chapman & Hall, 1885.

Dawes, Matthew. *Essays on Crime and Punishment.* London, 1782.

Dawtry, F. "The Abolition of the Death Penalty in Britain." *British Journal of Criminology* 6 (April 1966): 183.

De Mauley, C. F. A. C. P., Lord. *Crimes, Criminals and Punishments.* London: Macmillan, December 1873.

The Death Penalty in America: An Anthology, ed. Hugo Adam Bedau. New York: Doubleday Anchor, 1964.

Debaters' Digest. "Should Capital Punishment Be Abolished?" *Debaters' Digest* 4 (April 1930): 97–115.

Deets, L. E. "Changes in Capital Punishment Policy Since 1939." *Journal of Criminal Law Criminology* 38 (1948): 584.

Dell, Robert. "Killing No Murder." *Nation and Athenaeum* 44 (5 January 1929): 483–85.

Democratic Review. "Criticism of Wordworth's Sonnets on the Punishment of Death." *Democratic Review* 10 (March 1842).

———. "Capital Punishment." *Democratic Review* 12 (April 1843).

———. "The Gallows and the Gospel." *Democratic Review* 12 (March 1843).

———. "The Ground and Reason of Punishment." *Democratic Review* 19 (August 1846).

———. "Capital Punishment." *Democratic Review* 20 (March 1847).

———. "Capital Punishment." *Democratic Review* 20 (April 1847).

———. "The Rationale of Crime." *Democratic Review* 2 (January 1847).

Denman, George, M. P. "Testimony before Capital Punishment Commission." London, 1 December 1864.

Dent, Richard Blake. "Counting The Dead: A Profile of Walt Espy, Jr." *Southern Exposure*, 2–3 July–August 1985.

Dession, G. H. Gowers Report and Capital Punishment. *New York University Law Review* 29 (1954): 1061.

Deucher, N. D. *The Case Against Capital Punishment*, pamphlet.

Dexter, Robert Cloutman. *Social Adjustment.* New York: Alfred A. Knopf, 1927.

Diamond, A. S. *Primitive Law Past and Present.* London: Metheun, 1971.

Diamond, Bernard L. "From M'Naghtn to Currens and Beyond." *California Law Review* 50 (May 1962): 189.

Dickens, Charles. "Capital Punishment—Execution of The Mannings." *The Western Law Journal* 7 (1850): 351–52.

Dietrich, John H. *Should Capital Punishment Be Restored?* Humanist Pulpit Series. Minneapolis: First Unitarian Society, 1933.

Dike, Sarah T. *Capital Punishment in the United States: A Consideration of the Evidence.* Hackensack, N.J.: National Council on Crime and Delinquency, 1982.

Dikijian, Armie. "Capital Punishment—A Selected Bibliography, 1940–1968." *Crime and Delinquency* 15 (1969): 162–64.

Dinnerstein, Leonard. *The Leo Frank Case.* New York: Columbia University Press, 1968.

DiSalle, Michael V. *The Power of Life and Death.* New York: Random House, 1965.

Dixon, W. H. *John Howard and The World of Europe.* Jackson, 1850.

Dole, Benjamin F. *An Examination of Mr. Rantoul's report for the Abolition of Capital Punishment.* Boston, 1837.

Donlon, Edward J. "Felony Murder and the Jones Law." *St. John's Law Review* 4 (December 1929): 93–99.

Douglas, William O. *Law and Psychiatry.* New York: William Alanson White Institute, 1956.

Dow, Samuel Grove. "Capital Punishment." In *Crime and its Prevention,* edited by Samuel Grove Dow, 217–33. Ann Arbor, Mich.: Edwards Bros., 1927.

Dreiser, Theodore. *An American Tragedy.* Cleveland: World Publishing Co., 1953.

Drewery, G. "Parliament and Hanging: Further Episodes in an Undying Saga." *Parliamentary Affairs* 27 (1974): 251.

Drimmer, Frederick. *Until You Are Dead . . . The Book of Executions in America.* New York: A Citadel Press, 1990.

Drinan, Robert F. "The State and Insane Condemned Criminals." *Jurist* 12 (1952): 92–96.

Du Cane, Edmund F., Sir. *The Punishment and Prevention of Crime.* London: Macmillan, 1885.

Dublin, Louis, and Bessie Bunzel. "Homicide in the United States and Abroad." Trans. 9. In *Capital Punishment, Reference Shelf 1938,* edited by Julia A. Johnsen, 30–33. New York: W. H. Wilson Co., 1939.

Dublin, Louis, and Bessie Bunzel. "Thou Shalt Not Kill; A Study of Homicide in the United States." *Survey Graphic* 24 (March 1935): 127–31 + .

Duff, Charles. *A Handbook on Hanging.* Cayme Press, 1928.

——. *A New Handbook of Hanging.* London: Putnam, 1929.

——. *A New Handbook on Hanging.* Totowa, N.J.: Rowman & Littlefield, 1974.

Duff, L. B. *The County Kerchief.* Toronto: Ryerson Press, 1949.

Duffy, C. R, and A. Hirshberg. Testimony, in Hart Hearings, 19 (1968).

Dunn, Edward F. "Abolition of Capital Punishment." *Proceedings, Governor's Conference* 1915, 147–59.

Dunphy, Thomas, and Thomas J. Cummins. *The Gallows, Prison, And Poorhouse.* 1856.

Durant, Will. "Abolish The Death Penalty." In *Capital Punishment, Reference Shelf, 1939,* edited by Julia A. Johnsen, 106–11. New York: H. W. Wilson Co., 1939.

Durkheim, Emile. *Suicide.* New York: Free Press, 1951.

Dwight, W. T. *Discourses on Capital Punishment.* Portland, 1843.

Dygdale, Richard L. *"The Jukes."* New York and London: Putnam, 1883.

Dygdale, William, Sir. *Punishments in Criminal Cases.* London, 1866.

Dymond, Alfred H. *The Law on its Trail*. London, 1865.

Dymond, Jonathan. *Essays on the Principles of Morality*. London, 1880.

Eclectic Review. "On Capital Punishments." *Eclectic Review*. 27 (1818).

———. "On Capital Punishments." *Eclectic Review* 29 (1819).

———. "The Criminal Law of France." *Eclectic Review* 39 (May 1824) .

———. "The Punishment of Death." *Eclectic Review* 87 (1848).

———. "The Punishment of Death." *Eclectic Review* 90 (1849).

Eden, W., Lord Auckland. *Penal Law*. Dublin, 1772.

Edinburgh Review. "Review of Romilly." *Edinburgh Review 19* (February 1812).

———. "Capital Punishment." *Edinburgh Review* (July 1821).

———. "The Criminal Law of Scotland." *Edinburgh Review* (January 1825).

———. "Capital Punishment for Forgery." *Edinburgh Review* (January 1831).

———. "The Code of Criminal Law." *Edinburgh Review* (October 1879).

Edwards, J. "The Homicide Act, 1957: A Critique." *The British Journal of Delinquency* 8:1 (July 1957).

Edwards, S. W. "Death Penalty." *California State Bar Journal* 25 (1950): 98–101.

Ehrmann, Herbert B. "The Death Penalty and the Administration of Justice." *The Annuals* 284 (1952): 73.

———. *The Case That Will Not Die: Commonwealth v. Sacco and Vanzetti*. Boston: Little Brown, 1969.

Einstadter, W. J. "The Hangman's Fear." *Issues in Criminology* 1 (1965): 124.

Elder, William. "Capital Punishment." In *Essays*, 330–40. New York, 1854.

Elkington, J. A. *Lecture on Capital Punishment*. Philadelphia, 1841.

Elkins, S. M. *Slavery*. Chicago: University of Chicago Press, 1968.

Elliot, D. W. "The Homicide Act, 1957." *Criminal Law Review* 1 (1957): 282–92.

Elliot, H. R. S. "Punishment and Crime." *Nineteenth Century and After* 70 (August 1911): 306–20.

Elliot, Robert G. *Agent Of Death: The Memoirs of an Executioner*. New York: Dutton, 1940.

Elliott, Robert G. "And May God Have Mercy on Your Soul." *Collier's* 102 (24 September 1924): 9–10 + .

———. "As Humane As Possible." *Collier's* 102 (15 October 1938): 19 + .

———. "Life For A Life." *Collier's* 102 (8 October 1938): 12 + .

———. "Their Last Mile." *Collier's* 102 (1 October 1938): 12–13.

Ellis, Havelock. *The Criminal*. New York: Scribner, 1890.

Ellison, L. R, and H. E. Haas. "A Recent Judicial Interpretation of the M'Naghten Rules." *British Journal of Delinquency* 4 (1954): 128–33.

England, L. R. "Capital Punishment and Open-Ended Questions." *Public Opinion Quarterly* 12 (1948): 412–16.

England, Royal Commission on Capital Punishment. *Report*. England: H.M. Stationery Office, 1953.

England, Select Committee on Capital Punishment. *Report*. England: H.M.S.O., 1931.

Engles, Friedrich. *Anti-Duhring*. London: Lawrence and Wishart, 1943.

"English Prisons Today." In *Report of the Prison System Enquiry Committee*, 727. London, 1922.

Erez, Edna. "Thou Shalt not Execute: Hebrew Law Perspective on Capital Punishment." *Criminology* 19 (May 1981): 25–43.

Erikson, K. T. *The Wayward Puritans*. New York: John Wiley, 1966.

Eshelman, Bryon E. *Death Row Chaplin.* Englewood Cliffs, N.J.: Prentice Hall, 1962.

Espy, M. Watt, Jr. *Capital Punishment Research Project.* University of Alabama, School of Law.

———. "Capital Punishment and Deterrence: What The Statistics Can't Show." *Crime and Delinquency* 26 (October 1980): 537–44.

———. "Executions Under State Authority: An Inventory." In *Legal Homicide: Death as Punishment in America, 1864–1982,* edited by William J. Bowers and Glenn L. Pierce, 395–525. Boston: Northeastern University Press, 1984.

Evjen, V. H. "Let's Abolish Capital Punishment." *Lutheran Women,* March 1968, 218.

Ewart, William, M.P. "Speech on Bill to Abolish Capital Punishment." In *Hansard's Parliamentary Debates,* 79 (1834).

———. "Minority Report of Capital Punishment Commission, January 8, 1866, Recommending the Total Abolition of Capital Punishment." In *Parl's Papers.* London, 1866.

"Execution by Electricity." *Scientific American,* 1 March 1890, 131.

"Execution by Hanging." *The Law Times* 158 (25 October 1924): 339–40.

Fairchild, James H. "Capital Punishment" (chap. 5). In *Moral Science.*

Falletti, Marchesa Giulia. *Silvio Pellio (1788–1854).* Bently, 1866.

Fanning, C. E., ed. *Selected Articles on Capital Punishment,* 3rd ed. New York: H. W. Wilson Co., 1917.

Fanning, Clara E., ed. *Selected Articles on Capital Punishment.* Debaters Series Handbook. 3rd rev. ed. New York: H. W. Wilson Co., 1917.

Farrer, James A. *Crimes and Punishments.* London, 1881.

Ferri, Enrico. *Criminal Sociology* (English trans.). New York: Little Brown & Co., 1917.

Fido, Martin. *Murder Guide to London.* London: Gratton Books, 1987.

Filler, Louis. "Movements to Abolish the Death Penalty in the United States." *The Annals* 284 (November 1952): 22.

Fine, John. *Speech in Senate of New York on his Bill to Lesson the Severity of Criminal Punishment.* Boston: Prisoner's Friend, 6 February 1849.

Fisher, Jim. *The Lindbergh Case.* New Brunswick, N.J.: Rutgers University Press, 1987.

Fishman, Joseph Fulling. "In The Name of Parole." *Yale Review* no. 1 (September 1939): 145–63.

Fitzroy, H. W. K. "The Punishment of Crime in Provincial Pennsylvania." *Pennsylvania Magazine of History of Biographies* 60 (1936): 242.

Foltz, Clara. "Should Women be Executed?" *The Albany Law Journal* 54 (1896): 309–10.

Foote, E., Dr. *Report of Committee to Eclectic Medical Society of the State of New York,* 30 March 1892.

Forbes, Howard C. "Death Penalty From A Scientific Point Of View." *Scientific Monthly* 25 (July 1927): 80–83.

Ford, Joe. *Haunts to Hookers.* Owensboro, Ky.: Cooke and McDowell Publications, 1980.

Foreign Quarterly Review. "The Punishment of Death." *Foreign Quarterly Review,* July 1840.

Forsyth, William Douglas. *Governor Arthur's Convict System: . . . .* London: Imperial Studies Committee of the Royal Empire Society, 1935.

Fortnightly Review. "Capital Punishment, Case Against." *Fortnightly Review* LII: 322.

———. "Why Have a Hangman?" *Fortnightly Review* XL: 581.

Forum. "Capital Punishment: A Symposium." *Forum* 12 (March 1925): 436–41.

Foulhouze, J. *Inquiry Respecting the Abolition of Capital Punishment.* Philadelphia, 1842.

Frank, Jerome, and Barbara Frank. *Not Guilty.* Garden City, N.Y.: Doubleday, 1957.

Frankel, Emil. "One Thousand Murderers." *Proceedings*, 48–65. American Prison Association, 1937.

———. "One Thousand Murderers." *Journal of Criminal Law and Criminology* 29 (January 1939): 672–88.

Frankfurter, Felix. "The Problem of Capital Punishment." In *Of Law and Men.* New York: Harcourt, 1956.

Frankland, William. "Speech in House of Commons on Bill Making Alterations in the Criminal Law, March 29, 1811." In *Hansard's Parliamentary Debates*, 615 (1811).

Franklin, Benjamin. "On The Criminal Laws." In *Works.* Letter to Benjamin Vaughn, From Passey, 14 March 1785, 478. Boston: Hillyard, Gray & Co., 1785.

Fraser's Magazine. "Some thoughts on the Connection Between Crime and Punishment." *Fraser's Magazine*, vol. 20, December 1839.

———. "Capital Punishments." *Fraser's Magazine*, June 1864.

Frazier, Harriet C. "Places, Methods, and Witnesses: Executions U.S.A." Paper presented to the Academy of Criminal Justice Sciences, Orlando, 1986.

Friends, Society Of. *Capital Punishment: A Selected Bibliography (September 1966, with Addenda—August 1969).* San Francisco: Friends Committee on Legislation, 1966.

Fry, Elizabeth. *Observations on the Visiting, Superintending, and Government of Female Prisons.* London: Jno. & Arthur Arh., 1827.

Fuller, Margaret. *Life Without and Within*, 199. New York, 1860.

Fyfe, J. Hamilton. "The Spur or the Bridle! Some Thoughts on Crime and Criminals." In *Good Words.* 1863.

Gallbreath, Charles Burleigh. "Shall the State Kill?" *Friend's Intelligencer*, 6 October 1906.

Gallie, W. B. "The Lord's Debate on Hanging: July 1956: Interpretations and Comment." *Philosophy* 32 (1957): 132–47.

Gardiner, G, and N. Curtis-Raleigh. "The Judicial Attitude to Penal Reform." *Law Quarterly Review* 65 (April 1949).

Gardiner, G, E. Glover, and H. Mannheim. "A Symposium on the Report of the Royal Commission on Capital Punishment." *The British Journal of Delinquency* 6:3 (January 1954).

Gardner, Erle Stanley. *The Court of Last Resort.* New York: William Sloan Association, 1952.

Gardner, Martin R. "Executions and Indignities—An Assessment of Methods of Inflicting Capital Punishment." *Ohio State University Law Journal* 39 (1978): 96–130.

Gardner, Martin R. "Illicit Legislation Motivation as a Sufficient Condition for Unconstitutionality Under the Establishment Clause—A Case for Consideration: The Utah Firing Squad." *Washington University Law Quarterly* (1979).

———. Mormonism and Capital Punishment: A Doctrinal Perspective, Past and Present. *Dialogue* 12:1 (spring 1979): 9–26.

Garner, James W. "Infliction of the Death Penalty by Electricity." *American Institute of Criminal Law and Criminology* 1 (1910): 626–27.

————. "The Alternative Death Penalty in Nevada." *Journal of the American Institute of Criminal Law and Criminology* 2 (1911): 91–92.

Garofalo, Raffaele. *Criminology.* Boston: Little Brown & Co., 1914

"Gasocution." *Scientific American* 9 (December 1893).

George, Isaac. *Report of Select Committee on Bill Petition for the Abolition of Capital Punishment, made to the New York Assembly* (16 March 1857). Assembly Doc. No. 170. Albany, N.Y.

Gibbons, James, Cardinal. "Our Christian Heritage" (chap. 35). In *The Dangers that Threaten our American Heritage.* Baltimore: John Murphy & Co, 1889.

Gibson, E. C. S. *John Howard.* Methuen, 1901.

Gillin, John L. "Murder as a Sociological Phenomenon." *The Annals of the American Academy of Political and Social Science* 284 (1952): 20–25.

Gillin, John Lewis. *Criminology and Crime.* New York: Century Co., 1926.

Gilpin, Charles. "The Cross and the Gibbet." *Howitt's Journal* (23 September 1847).

Ginsberg, W. R. "Punishment of Capital Offenders: A Critical Examination of the Connecticut Statute." *Connecticut Bar Journal* 27 (1953): 273–81.

Glover, Edward. "Notes on the M'Naghten Rules." *British Journal of Delinquency* 1 (1950): 276–82.

————. "Psychiatric Aspects of the Report on Capital Punishment." *British Journal of Delinquency* 4 (1954): 162–68.

Goal Cradel, The. *Goal Cradel, The.* London: Isbister & Co., 1876

Goins, Craddock. "The Traveling Executioner." *The American Mercury* 54 (1942): 93–97.

Gollancz, Victor. *Capital Punishment: the Heart of the Matter.* London: Victor Gollancz, 1955.

Good, Edwin M. "Capital Punishment and Its Alternatives in Ancient Near Eastern Law." *Stanford Law Review* 19 (1967): 947–77.

Goodwin, Daniel R. "Capital Punishment." In *Biblio theca Sacra,* 270 and 435. 1847.

Gould, John Stanton, Chairman. *Report of the Select Committee on Capital Punishment, made to New York Assembly, March 5, 1847.* Assembly Doc No. 95 (1847).

Gowers, Ernest A., Sir. *A Life for a Life? The Problem of Capital Punishment.* London: Chatto and Windus, 1956.

Granger, Lester B, and Eleanor Ratner. "Sentenced To Death; Cases Closed." *Social Work Today* 5 (June 1938): 15–16.

Grant, John, Father. "Is The Electric Chair Condemned?" *The Ave Maria* 85 (1957): 8–11, 29.

Grayson, W. S. "Capital Punishment." *Southern Literary Messenger,* December 1861.

Great Britain. "Report." In *Select Committee on Capital Punishment.* London: H.M. Stationary Office, 1930.

————. *Capital Punishment.* London: Home Office, H.M. Stationary Office, 1948.

————. *Memoranda and Replies to a Questionnaire. . . .* Parliament. London: H.M. Stationary Office, 1951–1952.

————. *Minutes of Evidence.* Royal Commission on Capital Punishment. London: H.M. Stationary Office, 1953.

————. *Report.* Royal Commission on Capital Punishment. London: H.M. Stationary Office, 1953.

————. *Royal Commission on Capital Punishment. Report.* Parliament, Cmd. 8932. London: H.M. Stationery Office, 1953.

———. *Hansard's Parliamentary Debates: House of Lords (July 8 and 9, 1956)*. London: H.M. Stationary Office, 1956.

———. *Parliamentary Debates (Hansard); House of Commons (February 16 and March 12 1956)*. London: H. M. Stationary Office, 1956.

Great Britain. House of Commons. *Parliamentary Debates*. No. 24, 239–91. London: H.M. Stationary Office, 1929.

———. *Report From the Select Committee on Capital Punishment*. London: H.M. Stationary Office, 1931.

Greeley, Horace. "Death by Human Law." In *Hints Toward Reform*, 301. New York: Harper, 1850.

Green, Stanford M. *Crime, its nature, causes, treatment, and prevention*. Philadelphia: Lippincott, 1889.

Greenland, Cyril. "The Last Public Execution in Canada: Eight Skeletons in the Closet of the Canadian Justice System." *Criminal Law Quarterly* 29 (1987): 415–20.

Greenville, William W., Lord. "Speech in the House of Lords on Bill for the Abolition of Death Penalty, April 2, 1813." In *Hansard's Parliamentary Debates*, 526. London, 1813.

Grey, Charles, Earl. (1813) "Speech in the House of Lords on Bill for the Abolition of Death Penalty, April 2, 1813." In *Hansard's Parliamentary Debates*, 526. London.

Griffith, Arthur, Major. Chapter on Prison History. In *Memorials of Millbank*. London: King & Co., 1875

———. *Chronicles of Newgate*. New York: Scriber & W, 1884.

Grose, Francis F. A. S. "On The Criminal Laws of England." In *Olio*. London: Hooper & Wigstead, 1796.

Grotius, Hugo. "Of Punishments." In *The Rights of War and Peace, book no. 2, chap. 20*. Cambridge.

Guilott, Ellen E. "Abolition and Restoration of the Death Penalty in Missouri." *The Annals of the American Academy of Political and Social Science* 284 (1952): 105–109.

Haines, Edson L., Chairman. "Symposium: The Abolition of Capital Punishment." *Canadian Bar Review* 32 (1954): 485–519.

Hale, George W. *Police and Prison Cyclopedia*. Cambridge: Riverside Press, 1892.

Hall, J. W. *Capital Punishment on Trial*. Pamphlet. London: Howard League for Penal Reform, 1927.

Hall, Manley P. "Legalized Murder." In *Capital Punishment, Reference Shelf, 1939*, edited by Julia A. Johnsen, 82–93. New York: H.W. Wilson, Co., 1939.

Hand, Samuel. "The Death Penalty." *North American Review*, December 1881.

Hanley, J. Frank. "Ex Governor's Views on Capital Punishment." *American Magazine*, June 1914, 74–75.

Hargrove, A. L. "Britain and the Death Penalty." *Howard Journal* 3:2 (1931): 27–32.

Harlan, Howard. "Five Hundred Criminal Homicides." *Journal of Criminal Law, Criminology and Police Science* 40 (1950): 736–52.

Harper's Weekly. (1903) "Plato on Capital Punishment." *Harper's Weekly* L (29 December 1906).

———. "Meaning of Capital Punishment." *Harper's Weekly* L (September 1906): 1289.

————. "Should Capital Punishment Be Abolished?" *Harper's Weekly* LIII (3 July 1909).

Harris, Louis. "Punishment of Crime." In *Story of Crime*, 300–23. Boston: Stratford Co., 1929.

Hart, Hasting H. "The Reformation of Criminals." In *Biblio theca Sacra*, October 1890.

Hart, Herbert L. A. "Murder and the Principles of Punishment: England and the United States." *Northwestern University Law Review* 52:4 (September–October 1957): 433–66.

Hartmann, Raymond. "The Use of Lethal Gas in Nevada Executions." *St. Louis Law Review* 8 (1923): 164–68.

Hartshorne, Albert. *Hanging in Chains.* London: T. Fisher Unwin, 1891.

Harvey, William B. *Why Capital Punishment.* Philadelphia: Philadelphia Friends.

————. *Why Capital Punishment? Arguments for the Abolition of Capital Punishment.* Pamphlet. Philadelphia: Friends' Book Store, 1929.

Haskins, George L. "The Capital Laws of New England." *Harvard Law School Bulletin* 7 (1956): 10–11.

Haynes, Fred E. "Evolution of Penology: Capital Punishment." In *Criminology*, 214–16. New York: McGraw-Hill Book Co., 1935.

Haynor, Norman S, and John R. Cranor. "The Death Penalty in Washington State." *Journal of Criminal Law, Criminology and Police Science* 46 (1952): 101–104.

Hays, Arthur Garfeild. "The Rosenberg Case." *The Nation* 8, (November 1952).

Hayward, A. "Historical Sketch of Reforms in the Criminal Law. Judicial Tracts." *Law Magazine*, February 1835.

Hearst, William Randolph. *We Cannot Cure Murder by Murder.* Pamphlet. New York: New York American, 1926.

Hedrick, Edwin. "Hang The Dog." *Atlantic Monthly* (September 1927): 338–48.

Helie, Faustin. "The Death Penalty." In *Lalor's Cyclopedia of Political Science.* Chicago, 1881.

Hephel, F. Adamson. *The Law of Private Man.* Cambridge, Mass.: Harvard University Press, 1954.

Herapath, J. N. "Sadism In Law." *Canadian Forum* 17 (January 1938): 349.

Hibbert, Christopher. *The Roots of Evil.* Boston, Mass.: Little, Brown and Co., 1963.

Hibbert, J. T., M.P. "Speech on motion to bring in bill permitting Capital Punishments to be Carried out within the interior of prisons, March 6, 1866." In *Hansard's Parliamentary Debates* (1866).

Higgins, Henry. *Shall We Have Capital Punishment?* Massachusetts Prison Association Publication No. 69. Boston: Massachusetts Prison Association, 1925.

Hildebrand, Edward G., ed. *Death Penalty: A Literary and Historical Approach.* Mc-Gehee, William H. Boston: D.C. Heath & Co.,1964.

Hill, Matthew D. *Suggestions for the Repression of Crime.* London, 1857.

Hobart, S. C., Lord. *On Capital Punishment for Murder.* London: Parker, Son & Bourie, 1881.

Hobbes, Thomas. *Of Punishments and Rewards.* London: John Bohn, 1839.

Hoffman, Frederick L. "Murder and the Death Penalty." *Current History* 28 (June 1928): 408–10.

————. "Homicide Record of 1935." *Spectator* (*American Review of Life Insurance*) 136 (28 May 1936): 6–7.

————. "Homicide Record of 1936." *Spectator* (*American Review of Life Insurance*) 138 (29 April 1937): 6–9 +.

————. "Homicide Record of 1937." *Spectator* (*American Review of Life Insurance*) 140 (12 May 1938): 6–9.

————. "The Homicide Record of 1937." In *Capital Punishment, Reference Shelf, 1939,* edited by Julia Johnsen. New York: H. W. Wilson Co., 1939.

Hogan, John C. "Legal History—Joseph Story's—Anonymous Law Articles." *Michigan Law Review* 52 (1954): 869–84.

————. "Joseph's Story on Capital Punishment." *California Law Review* 43 (1955): 76–84.

Holdsworth, William K. "Adultery or Witchcraft? A New Note on an Age Old Case in Connecticut." *New England Quarterly* 48 (1975): 394–409.

Holland, H. R. V. Fox, Lord. "Speech in the House of Lords on Samuel Romilly's bill for Abolishing the Punishment of Death for privately stealing to the amount of five Shillings from a Shop, April 2, 1813." In *Hansard's Parliamentary Debates,* 524. London (1813).

Hollis, Christopher. *The Homicide Act.* London: Gollancz, 1964.

Hoover, John Edgar. *Youth Problem in Crime.* Mimeo. Washington, D.C.: Federal Bureau of Investigation, 1936.

Hope, Alexander J. B. *Essay on the Nature and the Extent of Punishment.* London: F. & J. Rivington, 1844.

Hopkins, Harry L. "Capital Punishment And Boys." *Survey* 32 (25 April 1913): 88.

House of Commons. Criminal Laws. Report of the Select Committee on, to House of Commons. 1819.

————. "Capital Punishment." In *Report of Select Committee of House of Commons to take Into Consideration the Present Mode of Carrying into effect Capital Punishment.* London, 1856.

————. "Report With Minutes of Evidence and Appendix." In *Select Committee on Criminal Law Relating to Capital Punishment into Felonies.* Irish University Press, 1968.

House of Representatives. *House Report 545.* Committee of the Judiciary, 53 Congress, 2nd Session. Washington, D.C., 1894.

Howard Association. *The Bible and Criminality.* London: Howard Association.

————. *Countries where Capital Punishment has been Abolished.* London: Howard Association.

————. *A Dangerous Penalty. Capital Punishment.* London: Howard Association, 1834.

————. *The Modern Jews on Capital Punishment.* Jewish World, 1877.

————. *London, American, and European Criminality and Pauperism.* London: Howard Association, 1888.

Howard League For Penal Reform. *Abolition of the Death Penalty in Denmark, Holland, Norway and Sweden.* London, England: Howard League For Penal Reform, 1925.

Howard, John. *The State of Prisons in England and Wales with some Preliminary Observations and an Account of Some Foreign Prisons.* Warrington, England: W. Eyers, 1777.

Hoyle, William. *Crimes in England and Wales in the 19th century.* London: Effingham, Wilson & Co., 1876.

Hubbard, G. W. *Capital Punishment.* New Vienna, Ohio, 1875.

Hughes, H., M.P. "Speech on bill to abolish capital punishment." In *Hansard's Parliamentary Debates*, 722 (1834).

Hugo, Victor. *The Last Days of the Condemned.* . . . London: Elder & Co., 1840.

Huie, William B. *The Execution of Private Slovik.* New York: Dell Publishing, 1970.

Hunt, George W. P. "Abolition of Capital Punishment." *Proceedings, 1915 Governor's Conference*, 130–46. 1915.

Hyde, H. Montgomery. *The Atom Bomb Spies.* New York: Athenaeum Press, 1980.

Hyde, Montgomery, ed. *Trial of Craig and Bently.* London: William and Hodge & Co., 1954.

Independent. "To Kill Or Not Kill." *Independent* 115 (8 August 1925): 143.

Ingersoll, Robert G. "Crime Against Criminals." *Proceedings of the New York Bar Association.* Albany: New York Bar Association, 1890.

Innes, Frederic M. *Secondary Punishments.* London: John Oliver, 1841.

Jacobi, A., Dr. "Report of Committee on Capital Punishment to the Medical Society of the State of New York." February 1892.

Jacoby, Susan. *Wild Justice: The Evolution of Revenge.* New York: Harper Colopom Books, 1983.

Jefferson, Thomas. *Writings*, 43–47. Note E, pages 145–62. Washington, D.C.: Taylor & Maury.

———. "A Bill for Proportioning of Crimes and Punishments." In *Public Papers*. Washington, D.C., 1985.

Jerome, Charles T. "The Death Penalty." *Potter's American Monthly*, February 1882.

Jesse, F. Tennyson, ed. *Trials of Evans and Christie.* London: William Hodge & Co., 1957.

Jessop, John, Rev. "Examination Before the Capital Punishment Commission of July 8, 1864." London, 1865.

Jester, Jean Catto. The Abolition of Public Executions: A Case Study. *International Journal of Criminology and Penology* 4 (1976): 25–32.

Jevons, Thomas. *Remarks on Criminal Law.* London: Morton, Adams & Co., 1834.

Johnsen, Julia A., ed. *Capital Punishment, The Reference Shelf, 1939.* New York: H. W. Wilson, Co., 1939.

Johnson, Julia E., ed. *Capital Punishment.* H. W. Wilson Co., 1939.

Johnson, Robert. *Condemned to Die: Life Under Sentence of Death.* New York: Elsevier, 1981.

———. *Death Work: A Study of the Modern Execution Process.* Pacific Grove, Calif.: Brooks/Cole Publishing Co., 1990.

Jolowicz, H. F, and Barry Nicholas. *Historical Introduction To The Study of Roman Law.* New York: Cambridge University Press, 1972.

Jones, A. H. M. *The Criminal Courts of the Roman Republic and the Principate.* Oxford, England: Basil Blackwell, 1972.

Jones, Ann. *Women Who Kill.* New York: Fawcett Columbine, 1980.

Jones, J. Walter. *The Law and Legal Theory of the Greeks.* Oxford: Oxford University Press, 1956.

Judaeus, Philo. *The Law Concerning Murderers (Works, Vol. 3).* London: Henry G. Bohn, 1855.

Kasel, Charles. "Recent Death Orgies; A Study In Capital Punishment." *South Atlantic Quarterly* 23 (October 1924): 295–309.

Keedy, Edwin R. "History of the Statute Creating Degrees of Murder." *University of Pennsylvania Law Review* 97 (1949): 759–77.

Kelley, James. "An Argument Against (Capital Punishment)." In *Capital Punishment*. By a Gentleman of the Bar. Doylestown, Pa., 1834

Kendall, Ben G. "Capital Punishment." *American Law Review* 43 (September–October 1909): 667–84.

Kendell, Nevin E., Rev. "The Case Against Capital Punishment." *Presbyterian Life*. 1949.

Kenny, C. S. *Outlines of Criminal Law*. Trans. J. H. Webb. New York: Macmillan, 1907.

Kershaw, Alister. *A History of the Guillotine*. New York: Barnes and Noble, Inc., 1993.

King, Frank A. "Thirteenpence-Halfpenny For the Hangman." *Justice of the Peace and Local Government Review* 122 (1958): 216–47.

Kingsly, R. "The Case Against Capital Punishment." *Los Angeles Bar Bulletin* (1957): 32.

Kingsmill, Joseph. *Prisons and Prisoners*. London: Longman, 1852.

Kingsolving, Lester, Rev. "Capital Punishment: A Reaction From a Member of the Clergy." *American Bar Association Journal* 42 (1956): 850–52.

Kirchway, George W. "The Death Penalty," 363–77. In *Proceedings of American Prison Congress*, 1922.

———. *Death Penalty*. Bulletin No. 5. New York: National Society of Penal Information, 1923.

———. "Legalized Murder." In *Capital Punishment, Reference Shelf, 1939*, edited by Julia A. Johnsen, 76–82. New York: H. W. Wilson, Co., 1939.

Kirkpatrick, Clifford. *Capital Punishment*. Monograph. Philadelphia: Philadelphia Yearly Meeting of Friends, 1925.

Klein, Norman. "Modern Crime Rates Raise The Issue Of Justice And The Death Penalty." *New York Evening Post*, 1928.

Knell, B. E. F. "Capital Punishment: Its Administration in Relation to Juvenile Offenders in the Nineteenth Century and Its Possible Administration in the Eighteen." *British Journal of Criminology* 5 (1965): 198.

Knowlton, Robert E. "Problems of Jury Discretion in Capital Cases." *University of Pennsylvania Law Review* 101 (1953): 1099–136.

Koester, Arthur. *Reflections on Hanging*. New York: Macmillan, 1956.

Koestler, Arthur, and C. H. Rolph. *Hanged By The Neck*. Harmondsworth, England: Penguin Books, 1961.

Kropotkine, P. *In Russian and French Prisons*. London: Ward & Downey, 1887.

Kunkel, Wolfgang. *An Introduction to Roman Legal and Constitutional History*. Oxford: Oxford University Press, 1966.

Lacassange, A. *Peine de Mort et Criminalit'e*. 1908.

Lake, E. H., Rev. *Objections to Capital Punishment, 2nd ed*. Haverhill, Mass., 1844.

Lamson, David. *We Who Are About To Die*. New York: Charles Scribner's Sons, 1935.

Lane, Winthorp D. "Child And The Electric Chair." *Survey* 39 (23 March 1918): 673–75.

Lang, J. D., D. D. *Transportation and Colonization*. London: A. J. Valpy, 1837.

Larrowe, Charles P. "Notches on a Chair." *The Nation* 182 (14 April 1956): 291–94.

Lathrop, S. G., Rev. *Crime and Punishment*. Joliet, Ill., 1866.

Laurence, John. *The History of Capital Punishment*. Secaucus, N.J.: Citadel Press, 1960.

Law Notes. "Capital Punishment." *Law Notes* 29 (March 1926): 221.

———. "Capital Punishment And The Pardoning Power." *Law Notes* 29 (January 1926): 181.

Lawes, Lewis E. *Man's Judgment of Death: An Analysis of the Operation and Effect of Capital Punishment Based on Facts, Not Sentiment.* New York: G. P. Putnam's and Sons, 1924.

———. *Brief History of Capital Punishment; Is Capital Punishment Necessary? Death Penalty at Sing Sing.* Pamphlet. New York: American League to Abolish Capital Punishment, 1927.

———. "Death Penalty At Sing Sing." *Survey* 59 (15 October 1927): 69–70.

———. *Life and Death in Sing Sing.* New York: Doubleday, Doran and Co., 1928.

———. "Life in Death House." *World's Work* 56 (June 1928): 159–70.

———. "Who's Afraid of the Chair?" *Collier's* 86 (12 July 1930):10–11 +.

———. *20,000 Years in Sing Sing.* New York: Ray Long and Richard Smith, 1932.

———. "Chair Is A Cheat." *Commentator* 1 (fall 1937): 52–55.

———. *Invisible Stripes.* New York: Farrer & Rinehart, 1938.

———. "A Brief History Of Capital Punishment." In *Capital Punishment, Reference Shelf, 1939,* edited by Julia A. Johnsen, 69–76. New York: H. W. Wilson Co., 1939.

———. "A Brief History of States Without the Death Penalty." In *Capital Punishment, Reference Shelf, 1939,* edited by Julia A. Johnsen, 14–19. New York: H. W. Wilson Co., 1939.

———. "Crime: A Social Cancer." In *Tomorrow in the Making,* edited by John N. Andrews and Carl A. Marsden, 241–52. New York: Whittlesey House, 1939.

———. *Is The Death Penalty Necessary?* Pamphlet. New York: League for the Abolition of Capital Punishment, n.d.

Lawson, John N., Atty. General for Ireland. Testimony before Capital Punishment Commission, 11 March 1865. London, 1865.

Leisure Hours. "Old English Modes of Punishment." *Leisure Hours* 13, 742.

Lennard, Thomas, B. "Speech on a Bill to Abolish Capital Punishment." In *Hansard's Parliamentary Debates,* 720. London (1834).

Leopold, Grand Duke of Tuscany. Edict for the Reformation of the Criminal Law, 30 November 1786. Warrington: W. Ayres, 1789.

Lewis, E. Park, Dr. Resolutions Adopted by Homeopathic Medical Society, State of New York, February 1891.

Lewis, G. K. *Elizabeth Fry (1780–1845).* Headly Bros., 1910.

Leyton, Elliot. *Hunting Humans: Inside the Minds of Mass Murderers.* New York: Pocket Books, 1986.

Liepmann, M. *Die Todesstrafe-Ein Gutachten, mit eienm Nachwort.* Berlin: I Gutentag, 1912.

Lindman, Frank T., and Donald M. McIntire, Jr. *The Mentally Disabled and the Law: The Report of the American Bar Foundation on the Rights of the Mentally Ill.* Chicago, Ill.: University of Chicago Press, 1961.

Literary Digest. "Execution By Gas." *Literary Digest* 80 (1 March 1924): 17.

———. "Intellectual Murder in Chicago." *Literary Digest* 82 (5 July 1924): 40–4.

———. "Punishment For Weak Wits." *Literary Digest* 82 (19 July 1924): 32.

———. "Rich and Poor Murderers." *Literary Digest* 82 (27 September 1924): 10–11.

———. "Abolishing The Death Penalty." *Literary Digest* 86 (22 August 1925): 29.

———. "Attacking The Death Penalty." *Literary Digest* 88 (13 February 1926): 7–8.

———. "Questions From Chapman's Grave." *Literary Digest* 89 (24 April 1926): 30–31.

———. Death Penalty: Pro and Con." *Literary Digest* 96 (4 February 1928): 13–14.

———. "Murderous America." *Literary Digest* 98 (21 July 1928): 17.

———. "U.S. Redder Than Russia." *Literary Digest* 97 (21 April 1928): 12.

———. "Executions That Do Not Stop Murder." *Literary Digest* 100 (30 March 1929): 11.

———. "Should The State Kill?" *Literary Digest* 109 (2 May 1931): 22–23.

———. "Fighting the Kidnaping Racket With the Death Penalty." *Literary Digest* 116 (12 August 1933): 6.

———. High Murder Rate in the South. *Literary Digest* 116 (16 September 1933): 15.

———. "Hauptmann Drama Marches To Last Act." *Literary Digest* 120 (19 October 1935): 7.

———. "Women Poisoners: Death Meted Out In U.S. and England Despite Opposition." *Literary Digest* 122 (25 July 1936): 30.

Livingston, Edward. *Reports of, to the House of Representatives of Louisiana, in Assembly.* New Orleans, 1822.

———. "Remarks in U.S. Senate on Introducing Bill to Abolish Capital Punishment." 3 March 1831. Washington, D.C.

———. *System of Penal Law for the State of Louisiana.* Philadelphia: James Kay, 1833.

Lofland, John. *State Executions: The Hangmen of England The Dramaturgy of State Executions.* Montclair, N.J.: Patterson Smith, 1977.

London Quarterly. "Crime and Criminal Law in France." *London Quarterly* 8 (April 1857).

Longfellow, H. W. *The Ropewalk.* Boston: Houghton, Mifflin & Co., 1887.

Longford, Joseph H. "Ilford Crime and Capital Punishment." *Fortnightly Review* 119 (fall 1923): 252–64.

Louisiana Law Review. "Cruel and Unusual Punishment." *Louisiana Law Review* 6 (1945): 298.

Lunden, Walter A. "Time Lapse Between Sentence and Execution: The United States and Canada Compared." *American Bar Association Journal* 48 (November 1962): 18.

Lushington, Stephen. "Speech at Exeter Hall on the Resolution relating to the Punishment of Death." London, 1831.

———. "Report of Capital Punishment Commission, Jan. 8, 1866, Recommending the Total Abolition of Capital Punishment." In *Report of Capital Punishment Commission.* London, 1866.

Lyon, F. Emory. "Is Capital Punishment Justified?" 193–203. Southern Sociological Congress. Nashville, Tenn., 1913.

Macauley, T. B., Lord. "Of Punishments." Chap. 2 and note A. In *Indian Law Commission. Penal Code for India.* Calcutta, 1837.

MacDonald, Arthur. "Death Penalty." *American Journal of Sociology* 16 (July 1910): 88–116.

MacDowell, Douglas S. *Athenian Homicide Law.* Manchester, England: Manchester University Press, 1963.

———. *The Law in Classical Athens.* Ithaca, N.Y.: Cornell University Press, 1978.

Mackey, Phillip English. "Capital Punishment in New Netherland." *De Halve Maen* (July 1972): 7–8.

———. "The Inutility of Mandatory Capital Punishment: A Historical Note." *Boston University Law Review* 54 (1974): 32.

———. "The Inutilitily of Mandatory Capital Punishment: An Historical Note." In *Capital Punishment in the United States*, edited by H. Bedau and C. Pierce, 32–35. New York: AMS Press, Inc., 1976.

———. *Voices Against Death*. New York: Burt Franklin Co., 1976.

MacNamara, Donal E. J. "A Survey of Recent Literature on Capital Punishment." *American Journal of Corrections* 24 (March–April 1962): 16–19.

Maconochie, Captain, R. N. *Thoughts on Convict Management and Other Subjects Connected with the Australian Penal Colonies*. Hobart, 1838.

Madison, James. *Writings*. "Letter to G. F. H. Crocket, November 6, 1823." Philadelphia: Lippincott, 1865.

Magee, Doug. *Slow Coming Dark: Interviews on Death Row*. New York: Pilgrim Press, 1980.

Mainwaring, George Boulton, Esq. "Testimony Before Select Committee on Criminal Law." London, 1819.

Maitra, Suskilkumar. "On Capital Punishment in its Relation to the Theory of the State." *Calcutta Review* (February 1926): 214–25.

Mannheim, H. "Capital Punishment: What Next?" *The Fortnightly Review*, October 1948.

Manning, L. W., Rev. *The Death Penalty Treats Human Nature With Contempt*. Boston: Prisoner's Friend, 1849.

Martin, John Bartlow. *Why Did They Kill?* New York: Ballintine Books, 1953.

———. "The Strange Boy." *Look Magazine*, 5 August 1958, 68–99.

Martin, Robert M. "Electric Shocks, Do They Really Kill?" *Popular Science Monthly* 133 (July 1938): 5 +.

Marx, Karl. "Preface to the Critique of Political Economy." In *Selected Works*, vol. 1, edited by Karl Marx and Frederick Engles. Moscow: Foreign Languages Pub. House, 1962.

Mason, Charles, Hon. *Moral Treatment of the Criminal*. Boston: Prisoner's Friend, 1849.

Massachusetts Council For the Abolition of the Death Penalty. *Abolish The Death Penalty*. Boston: Massachusetts Council For the Abolition of the Death Penalty, 1928.

Massachusetts Law Quarterly. "Proposed Resolve For A Commission To Study Capital Punishment." *Massachusetts Law Quarterly* 16 (January 1931): 97–101.

Massachusetts. Constitutional Convention, "Abolition of Capital Punishment." In *Commission to Compile Information and Data for the Use of the Constitutional Convention*. Bulletin no. 25, 245–82. Boston, 1917, 1919.

Masur, Louis P. *Rites of Execution: Capital Punishment and the Transformation of American Culture, 1776–1865*. New York: Oxford University Press, 1989.

Maude, W. C. "Shall We Abolish the Death Penalty?" *The Month*, February 1889.

McCafferty, James A., ed. *Capital Punishment*. Aldine-Atherton, 1972.

McCafferty, James A. *Capital Punishment in the United States: 1930–1952*. Master's thesis. Columbus: Ohio State University, 1954.

McCaffrey, John P. "Mass Executions." *Commonweal* 25 (11 December 1936): 176–77.

———. "Mass Executions." In *Capital Punishment, Reference Shelf, 1939*, edited by Julia A. Johnsen, 44–47. New York: H. W. Wilson, Co., 1939.

McClellan, Grant S., ed. *Capital Punishment*. New York: H. W. Wilson, 1961.

McDonald, James, M.P. "Speech in House of Commons, March 29, 1811, on a bill to abolish the penalty of death." In *Hansard's Parliamentary Debates*, 650. London, 1811.

McGautha v California. *U.S.* 402:183 (1971).

McGrath, W. T. *Should Canada Abolish the Gallows and the Lash?* Winnipeg: Stovel-Advocate Press, 1956.

McIntosh, A. C. "Manner of Inflicting Death Penalty as Cruel or Unusual Punishment." *Law Notes* 35 (September 1930): 104.

McKnight, Brian F. "Sung Justice: Death By Slicing." *Journal of the American Oriental Society* 93 (1973): 359–60.

McManners, John. *Death and the Enlightenment, Changing Attitudes to Death Among Christians and Unbelievers in Eighteenth Century France*. Oxford: Oxford University Press, 1981.

McMurdy, Robert. *The Upas Tree*. Chicago: Laird & Lee, 1915.

McNight, George H. *The Death Penalty*. The Churchman, 1893.

Medical Society of the State of New York. "Infliction of the Death Penalty by Means of Electricity; Being a Report of Seven Cases." In *Transactions*, 400–27. Carlos F. MacDonald, 1892.

Mercer, Hamilton. *Reproach: An Indictment Against Capital Punishment*. Los Angeles: Time Mirror Press, 1926.

Meredith, William, Sir. "Punishment of Death. Speech in House of Commons, May 13, 1777." In *Hansard's Parliamentary Debates*, 235. London (1777).

Methodist Quarterly. "Capital Punishment." *Methodist Quarterly*, July 1846.

Meyer, Herman. *Selected List of References on Capital Punishment*. Washington, D.C.: U.S. Government Printing Office, 1912.

Michaelis, John David, Sir. "Essay on the Nature and End of Punishment." In *Commentaries on the Law of Moses*. Appendix to Book 5. London: F. C. & J. Rivington, 1814.

Michigan History Magazine. "History Of Executions In What Is Now The State of Michigan." *Michigan History Magazine* 22:4 (autumn 1938): 443–57.

Michigan State Bar Journal. "Report of Committee on Capital Punishment." *Michigan State Bar Journal* 8 (June 1929): 278–305.

Miller, Arthur S, and Jeffery H. Bowman. "Slow Dance on the Killing Ground: The Willie Francis Case Revisited." *DePaul Law Review* 32 (1983): 1–73.

Miller, Jonas H. *Minority Report of Select Committee on Capital Punishment, To New York Assembly, March 1, 1848*. Assembly Doc. No. 133 (1848).

Mittermaier, Carl Joseph von. *Capital Punishment*. Based on Professor Mittermaier's *Todesstrafe*. Trans. J. M. Moir. London: Smith, Elder and Company, 1865.

Moak, N. C. "Capital Punishment." In *Encyclopedia Britannica, Supplement*.

Moberly, W., Sir. "Capital Punishment." *Howard Journal* 9:1 (1954).

Mogi, Torajiro. *Capital Punishment*. Ann Arbor, Michigan, 1889.

Moley, Raymond. "The Vanishing Jury." *Southern California Law Review* 2 (1928): 97.

———. "Convicts We Kill." *Survey* 62 (15 September 1929): 610.

Moley, Raymond, and Edgar Sisson. "Murder on Parole." *Today* 1 (7 July 1934): #-4+.

Monesquieu, Baron. Chap. 12 and 13. Trans. Thomas Nugent. In *Spirit of Laws*. Cincinnati, Ohio: Robert Clarke & Co., 1873.

Montagu, Basil. *Debates in the House of Commons, 1811, on the Bills of Sir Samuel Romilly For Abolishing the Punishment of Death*. London: Longman, 1812.

———. *Opinions of Differing authors on Capital Punishment*. London, 1812, 1813, 1816.

———. *An Inquiry Into the Aspersions Upon the Late Ordinary of Newgate, With Some Observation upon Newgate, and Upon the Punishment of Death*. London: Richard & Arthur Taylor, 1815.

———. His Examination by the Select Committee to Examine so Much of the Criminal Law as it Relates to Capital Punishment, March 30, 1819. *Report* July 8, 1819. London, 1819.

———. *Thoughts on the Punishment of Death for Forgery*. London: Pickering, 1830.

———. *The Opinions of Different Authors Upon the Punishment of Death*. London, 1809.

Monthly Review. "Review of Cottu on Criminal Law in England." *Monthly Review* 96 (December 1820).

———. "On the Criminal Law of France and England." *Monthly Review* 124 (August 1824).

———. "Review of Lucas on the Punishment of Death." *Monthly Review* (1827).

———. "State of Crime in France." *Monthly Review* 132 (September 1833).

Mooney, Martin. "Parole Racket." *American Magazine* 126 (July 1938): 16, 17.

———. "Paroles Over the Counter." *America Magazine* 126 (August 1938): 25-+.

More, Thomas, Sir. *Utopia*. London: Bohn, 1845.

Moreland, Roy, et al. "A Symposium on Mental Responsibility." *Kentucky Law Journal* 45 (1956–1957): 215–90.

Morris, Albert. *Homicide: An Approach to the Problem of Crime*. Boston: Boston University Press, 1955.

Morris, Edward, M.P. Speech in House of Commons, March 29, 1811, on Bill to Abolish Capital Punishment, 654. Series 1, vol. 19. London, 1811.

Morris, Norval. "The Felon's Responsibility for the Lethal Acts of Others." *Pennsylvania Law Review* 105 (1956): 50–81.

Morrison, Roderick M. Report of Select Committee of New York Assembly, May 12, 1845, on Petitions to Abolish Capital Punishment. Assembly Doc. No. 249. Albany, N.Y., 1845

Mosby, Thomas Speed "Anomaly of Capital Punishment." *Arena*, September 1907, 25–263.

Moschriker, M., Von. "Capital Punishment in the Pennsylvania Courts." *Pennsylvania Law Review* 20 (1949):178–88.

Mott, Thomas. *An Elucidation of the Ancient English Statute Relating to the Punishment of Death*. London, 1818.

Munsterberg, Hugo. *On The Witness Stand*. New York: McClure's, 1908.

Murdie, James. *The Felony on New South Wales: Being a Faithful Picture of the Romance of Life in Botany Bay*. Smith & Elder, 1837.

Nadel, E. S. "The Rationale of the Opposition to Capital Punishment." *North American Review*, January 1873.

Nash, Jay Robert. *Crime Chronology: A World-Wide Record, 1900–1983*. New York: Facts on File, 1984.

Nation. "Capital Punishment and Imprisonment for Life." *Nation* 16: 193.

———. "Capital Punishment, Arguments Against." *Nation* 16: 213.

———. "Executions: The New Sport." *Nation* 125 (14 December 1927): 676.

———. "Death Penalty." *Nation* 127 (7 November 1928): 472.

———. "Neglected Art." *Nation* 129 (16 October 1929): 402.

Nation and Athenaeum. "Capital Punishment." *Nation and Athenaeum* 32 (13 January 1923): 578–679.

———. "Coming Penal Reform." *Nation and Athenaeum* 32 (20 January 1923): 610–11.

Nation Council on Crime and Delinquency. "Capital Punishment in the United States." *Crime and Delinquency*, October 1980.

National Committee on Prisons. *Handbook on Capital Punishment.* New York: National Committee on Prisons, 1916.

———. *Handbook on Capital Punishment.* Prison Leaflets no. 38. New York: The Committee, 1916.

National Council for the Abolition of Capital Punishment. *Guilty But Insane; The Murder Trend.* Pamphlet. London: National Council for the Abolition of Capital Punishment, 1938?.

———. *Death Penalty Is Not Necessary.* London: National Council for the Abolition of Capital Punishment, n.d.

National Council on Crime and Delinquency. "Capital Punishment." *Crime and Delinquency* 15 (January 1969).

Neate, Charles, M.P. *Considerations on the Punishment of Death.* London, 1857.

———. *Minority Report of Capital Punishment Commission, January 8, 1866, Recommending the Total Abolition of Capital Punishment.* London, 1866.

Nelson, Frederic. "Executioner-Impresario." *New Republic* 55 (4 July 1928): 171–72.

Neuman, B. Paul. 'The Case Against Capital Punishment.' *Fortnightly Review*, September 1889.

Nevinson, Henry W. "Hanging." *New Statesman and Nation* 1 (14 March 1931): 97–98.

New Jersey. *Report of the Committee on Capital Punishment.* Trenton, N.J., 1908.

———. *Public Hearing on Assembly Bills Nos. 19 and 21.* Legislature. Assembly Committee on Institutions, Public Heath and Welfare. Trenton: State of New Jersey, 1957.

———. *Public Hearing on Assembly Bills Nos. 19 and 21.* Legislature. Assembly Committee on Institutions, Public Heath and Welfare. Trenton: State of New Jersey, 1958.

———. "Public Hearing Set on Capital Punishment Bills." *New Jersey Law Journal* 81 (1958): 292.

New Statesman (London). "Murderer." *New Statesman (London)* 23 (19 July 1924): 433–35.

New York Law Forum. "Symposium on Capital Punishment." *New York Law Forum* 7 (August 1961): 247.

New York Senate. *Report of the Commission to Investigate the Most Humane and Practical Method of Carrying into Effect the Sentence of Death in Capital Cases.* Albany, N.Y.: Troy Press Company Printers, 1888.

New York University Law Quarterly Review. "Felony Murder: New York Rule on Charging Degrees of Homicide." *New York University Law Quarterly Review* 16 (November 1938): 151–55.

Newman, Alan. *Criminal Executions In England, etc.* London: Steele, 1830.

Newport, John, Sir. "Speech in House of Commons 1811, on the Bill to Abolish the Death Penalty." In *Hansard's Parliamentary Debates*, 744. 1st series, vol. 19. London (1811).

Nissen, Henry N. "Examination Before the Capital Punishment Commission, of 8 July 1864" (14 February 1865).

North American. "Capital Punishment by Electricity." *North American* CXLVI: 219.

———. "Punishment of Crimes." *North American* 10: 235.

North Carolina. State Board of Charities and Public Welfare. *Capital Punishment in North Carolina*. Raleigh, 1929.

Nugent, O. *On the Punishment of Death by Law*. London, 1840.

Nugent, Richard P. T., Lord. "Address at a Public Meeting at Aylesbury, 30 April 1845, Favoring the Total Abolition of Capital Punishment." London, 1845.

Ohio State Library. "Capital Punishment." *Monthly Bulletin* 1:10 (January 1906): 3–6.

Ohio. Constitutional Convention. *Proceedings and Debate. Abolition of Capital Punishment*, 1247–62, 1268–79. Columbus, Ohio (1912, 1913).

Oldfield, Josiah. "Should Hanging End?" *Current Literature* 29 (1900): 190–92.

Oldfield, Josiah. *The Penalty of Death, or the Problem of Capital Punishment*. Bell, 1901.

———. *To Replace Hanging*. Pamphlet. London: Society for the Abolition of Capital Punishment, n.d.

Olmstead, Roger. "San Francisco and the Vigilante Style." *The American West* 7:1 (January/March 1970): 6–10.

Olson, Richard L. "Bulletin Board." *Police Product News*, August 1985, 10, 11, 44.

Osborn, W. C., Rev. *Examination Before the Capital Punishment Commission of July 8, 1864* (25 March 1865).

Osborne, S. G., Rev. *Examination Before the Capital Punishment Commission of July 8, 1864* (1865).

Oscar (Crown Prince of Norway and Sweden). *Punishments and Prisons*. Trans. A. May. London: Smith, Elder & Co., 1842.

Outlook. "Shall We Abolish the Death Penalty?" *Outlook* 114 (18 October 1916): 360–61.

———. "Murder Most Foul." *Outlook* 138 (24 September 1924): 115–16.

———. "Synder Murder Mystery." *Outlook* 146 (18 May): 74–75.

———. "Death Penalty." *Outlook* 148 (1 February 1928): 183.

———. "Nevada's Gas House." *Outlook* 155 (18 June 1930): 255–56.

O'Connell, Daniel. "Speech at Exeter Hall, June 2, 1832, in Support of Resolution Offered by Him Condemning Capital Punishment." 1832.

O'Donnell, Bernard. *Should Women Hang?* London: W.H. Allen, 1956.

O'Hagan. Thomas, Attorney General for Ireland. *Report of Capital Punishment Commission, January 8, 1866, Recommending Total Abolition of Capital Punishment*. 1866.

O'Halloran, Arthur A. "Capital Punishment." *Federal Probation* 29 (June 1965): 33.

O'Sullivan, John L. *Report to the New York Assembly, in Favor of Abolishing the Punishment of Death*. 14 September 1841. J. & H. J. Langley, 1841.

O'Sullivan, Richard. "The Case Against Capital Punishment." *Nineteenth Century and After* 143 (1948): 113–17.

Paget, R. T, Sydney Silverman, and Christopher Hollis. *Hanged—And Innocent?* London: Victor Gollancz, 1953.

Paine, Donald F. "Capital Punishment." *Tennessee Law Review* 29 (summer 1962): 534.

Paine, Thomas. "Speech in the National Convention of France, Jan. 15, 1793." *M. D. Conway's Life of Paine*. New York: Putnam, 1892.

Paley, William, Dr. "Crimes and Punishments." In *Moral and Political Philosophy*. Philadelphia: Woodward, 1836.

Palm, Andrew J. *The Death Penalty: A Consideration of the Objections to Capital Punishment*. New York: Putnam, 1891.

Palmer, Stuart. *A Study of Murder*. New York: Thomas Y. Crowell, 1960.

Pamphleteer. *Capital Punishment*, 1814.

Park, Benjamin. "The Infliction of the Death Penalty." *Forum* 3 (July 1887): 507–13.

Parker, Joel. "Law of Homicides." *North American Review* (January 1851).

Parmelee, Maurice. *Criminology*. New York: Macmillan, 1918.

Parr, Samuel, Rev. *Letters to Sir Samuel Romilly, Feb. 21, 1810. Note to the Memoirs of the Life of Sir Samuel Romilly*, P. 309. London: Murray, 1840.

Pathfinder. "Capital Punishment: Two Views." *Pathfinder*, 23 January 1926, 3–4.

———. "Shall the State Continue to Take Human Life?" *Pathfinder*, 2 July 1927, 3–4.

Paton, J. "Democracy and the Death Penalty." *The Penal Reformer* 2:1 (July 1935).

———. "An Open Letter to the Lord Chief Justice." *The Penal Reformer* 2:3 (January 1936).

———. "The Abolition Debate." *The Penal Reformer* 5:3 (January 1939).

———. "Abolition in Parliament." *The Penal Reformer* 6:1 (July 1939).

———. "Justice is Blindfolded." *The Penal Reformer* 5:1 (July 1939).

Paton, John. "Death Penalty." *Spectator (London)* 153 (28 December 1934): 996.

———. *This Hanging Business*. Pamphlet. London: National Council for the Abolition of the Death Penalty, 1938.

Peabody, Andrew P., Rev. *Review of Report on the Punishment of Death*. Ed. Rantoul Messes. Sullivan, Kendall. Boston: Christian Examiner, Charles Bowen, 1833.

Peggs, James, Rev. *Capital Punishment. Importance of its Abolition*. London: Ward, 1839.

Pelham, Camden. *The Chronicles of Crime* (2 vols.). London: Reeves and Turner, 1886.

Pennsylvania Bar Association. "Development of Modern Criminology." In *Report*, 370–85. Edwin M. Abbott, 1923.

Pennsylvania Prison Society. "Capital Punishment Poll." *Prison Journal* 32 (1952): 160.

Penny Magazine. "Statistics of Crime in England." *Penny Magazine*, vol. 5, 10 September 1836.,

Pentecost, H. O., Rev. "The Crime of Capital Punishment." *Arena* 1, (January 1890).

Pericles. "The Athian." In *Plutarch's Life of Pericles*. New York: Harper & Bro., 1851.

Perry, John H., Sergeant at Law. (1865) "Testimony before Capital Punishment Commission." 4 March 1865.

Persians (the ancient). *Herodotus*. Book 1, p. 278. London: John Murray, 1858.

Pettigrew, Thomas F, and Rosalind Barclay Spier. "The Ecological Structure of Negro Homicide." *American Journal of Sociology* 67 (May 1962): 621.

Phelps, Edith M. "Parole System." In *University Debater's Annual, 1935–1936*, 267–318. New York: H. W. Wilson, 1936.

Phelps, Harold A. "Effectiveness of Life Imprisonment as a Repressive Measure Against Murder in Rhode Island." *American Statistical Society Journal* 23 (March 1928): 174–81.

Phelps, Harold A. "Rhode Island's Threat Against Murder." *Journal of Criminal Law and Criminology* 18 (fall 1928): 552–67.

Philanthropos (Pseud.). *Essays on Capital Punishment*. Philadelphia, 1811.

Phillips, Charles. *Vacation Thoughts on Capital Punishment*. London: Ridgway, 1858.

Phillips, Wendell. *Capital Punishment (Speeches, 2nd series)*.

———. "The Death Penalty." *North American Review*, December 1881.

Pierrepoint, Albert. *Executioner: Pierrepoint*. Sevenoaks, Kent: Hodder and Stoughton, 1974.

Pike, Luke Owen. *History of Crime in England*. London, 1873.

Pillars, Isaiash, Hon. *Report to the Ohio House of Representatives, in Favor of the Abolition of Capital Punishment*. Columbus, Ohio: Nevin & Myers, 1873.

Pinel, Nicholas. *Dissertation on the Punishment of Death*. Trans. from the French. London, 1780.

Pinkerton, Matthew Worth. *Murder in all Ages*. Chicago, Ill.: A.F. Pinkerton & Co., 1898.

A Plan for the Punishment of Crime by Benjamin Rush, M.D. Ed. Negley K. Teeters. Philadelphia: Pennsylvania Prison Society, 1954.

Podgorecki, Adam. "Unrecognized Father of Sociology of Law: Leon Petrazycki." *Law and Society Review* 15 (1980): 183.

Police of The Metropolis. London: Baldwin, 1800.

Pollak, Otto. "Errors of Justice." *The Annals of the American Academy of Political and Social Science* 284 (1952): 115–23.

Pollidori, Benjamin F. *The Punishment of Death*. Pamphleteer. London, 1816.

Pollock, Frederick Sir, and Frederick M. Maitland. *The History of English Law, Vol. I and II*. Cambridge, England: Cambridge University Press, 1952.

Porter, Benjamin F. *Speech in House of Representatives of Alabama, in Favor of his Bill to Abrogate the Punishment of Death*. Tuscaloosa, Ala.: McCormick, 1846.

Potter, Charles Francis. "I Saw a Man Electrocuted." *Reader's Digest* 32 (February 1938): 70–72.

Princeton Review. "Reviews of Reports to New York and Massachusetts Legislators." *Princeton Review*, April 1842.

Prison Journal. "Capital Punishment." *Prison Journal* 12 (October 1932).

Prisoner Aid Society of Delaware. *Material: Senate Bill no. 299*, 1957.

Pufendorf, Samuel, Baron. *Law of Nations (book 8)*. Trans. Crew, chap. 3. London, 1749.

Purrington, T. *Report on Capital Punishment, made to the Maine Legislature in 1836*. Washington, D.C.: Gideon & Co. Printers, 1852.

Quaife, M. M. "Capital Punishment in Detroit." In *Burton Historical Collection Leaflet*, no. 3, 33–48. Detroit: Detroit Public Library, 1926.

Quarterly Review. "Review of Cottu on Criminal Code of England." *Quarterly Review* 22.

———. "Review of Report of Select Committee on the Criminal Law." *Quarterly Review* 24 (1819).

———. "Amendments to the Criminal Law." *Quarterly Review* (January 1828).

Quinby, G. W., Rev. *The Gallows, the Prison, and the Poorhouse*. Cincinnati, Ohio, 1856.

Radelet, Michael L, and Margaret Vandiver. *Capital Punishment in America: An Annotated Bibliography*. New York: Garland Publishing.

Radosh, Ronald, and Joyce Milton. *The Rosenberg File: A Search for the Truth*. New York: Vintage Books, 1984.

Radzinowicz, Leon. *A History of English Criminal Law, vol. 1.* New York: Macmillan, 1948.

Rantoul, Robert, Jr. Speeches, Reports, etc. In *In his Memoirs, Speeches and Writings.* Boston, 1854.

Raven, Alice. "Murder And Suicide As Marks Of An Abnormal Mind." *Sociological Review* 21 (October 1929): 315–33.

———. "Memoranda Prepared For The Select Committee on Capital Punishment." *Sociological Review* 23 (July 1931): 80–84.

Rawson, Rawson W. "An Inquiry Into the Statistics of Crime in England and Wales." *Journal Statistical Society* (October 1839).

Reader's Digest. "Execution by Lethal Gas." *Reader's Digest* 31 (December 1937): 56–59.

Redding, Cyrus. "Capital Punishment." *Colburn's New Monthly*, February and March 1866.

Reed, Thomas B. "Speech in Maine Legislature, in Favor of Abolishing the Death Penalty." *Portland Advertiser*, 19 February 1869.

Reeves, John. *An Historical View of Crime and Punishments, According to the Law of England.* London, 1779.

Reik, Theodor. *Unknown Murderer.* International Psycho-Analytical Library no. 27. Trans. K. Jones. London: Institute of Psycho-Analysis, 1936.

Reinhardt, James Melvin. *The Murderous Trail of Charles Starkweather.* Springfield, Ill.: Charles C. Thomas, 1960.

Rentoul, G., Sir. "Second Thoughts on Capital Punishment." *The Penal Reformer* 6:1 (July 1939).

Repplier, Agnus. "The Headsman." *Harpers Magazine*, 1902.

Review of Reviews. "Does Capital Punishment Prevent Convictions?" *Review of Reviews* XL (August 1909): 219–20.

———. "Does Capital Punishment Tend to Diminish Capital Crime?" *Review of Reviews* 34 (1909): 368–69.

———. "Capital Punishment." *Review of Reviews* 95 (April 1937): 18–19.

Riddell, William R. "Judicial Execution by Burning at the Stake in New York." *American Bar Association Journal* 15 (1929): 373–76.

Rigg, Douglas C. "The Penalty Worse Than Death." *Saturday Evening Post*, 31 August, 1957.

Robespierre, Maximillien, and Marie Isidore. "Against Capital Punishment." In *World's Best Orations*, Ed. David J. Brewer, 3326–69. St. Louis: Fred P. Kaiser, 1901.

Robin, Gerald D. "The Executioner: His Place in English Society." *British Journal of Sociology* (September 1964) 234–53.

Robison, Louis N. "Capital Punishment." In *Penology in the United States*, 242–56. Philadelphia: John C. Winston, 1921.

Robison, Luicius, Governor. *Report to the New York Assembly Recommending Abolition of the Death Penalty, Feb. 16, 1860.* Assembly Doc. 82. Albany, N.Y., 1860.

Rogers, L. W. "Shall Legal Murder Stop?" *Ancient Wisdom* (February 1939): 93.

Romilly, Henry. *The Punishment of Death.* London: Murray, 1885.

Romilly, Samuel, Sir. *Observations on the Criminal Law.* London, 1810.

———. "Speech in House of Commons, March 29, 1811, on a Bill to Abolish the Death Penalty." In *Hansard's Parliamentary Debates*, p. 656. London, 1811.

Ronnenberg, Harold A. "America's Greatest Mass Execution." *American Mercury* 67 (1948): 565–71.

Rosenberg, Ethel (Greenglass). *Death House Letters from Ethel and Julius Rosenberg.* New York: Jero Publishing Co., 1953.

Rowe, John G. *John Howard, Prison Reformer.* London: Epworth Press, 1927.

Royal Commission on Capital Punishment. *Report.* London: Her Majesty's Stationary Office, 1953.

Rubin, Sol. *Psychiatry and Criminal Law: Illusions, Fictions, and Myths.* Dobbs-Ferry, N.Y.: Oceana Publications, 1965.

Rudolphe, A. "Death Penalty for Children." *Saturday Review* 159 (11 May 1935): 584–85.

Ruggles-Brise, E., Sir. *Prison Reform at Home and Abroad.* Macmillan, 1925.

Rumbelow, Donald. *The Complete Jack The Ripper.* Boston: New York Graphics, 1991.

Rusche, George, and Otto Kirchheimer. *Punishment and Social Structure.* New York: Columbia University Press, 1939.

Rush, Benjamin. *Considerations on the Injustice and Impolicy of Punishing Murder by Death.* Philadelphia: The Pennsylvania Prison Society, 1954.

———. *An Enquiry into the Effects of Public Punishments upon Criminals and Society.* Philadelphia: Pennsylvania Prison Society, 1954.

———. *An Inquiry into the Effects of Public Punishment of Criminals and Upon Society.* Philadelphia, 1787.

———. *On The Punishment of Murder by Death.* Philadelphia, 1793.

Rylands, L. Gordon. *Crime, its causes and remedy.* London: Unwin, 1889.

Sabach, the Ethiopian King of Egypt. *Diodorus Siculus.* Book 1. Trans. G. Booth, chap. 5. London, 1814.

Sachs, Hanns. *Does Capital Punishment Exist?* Territet, Switzerland: Riant Chateau, 1930.

Safety Engineering. "The Death Penalty for Arson." *Safety Engineering* 67 (March 1934): 108.

Sampson, M. B. *Criminal Jurisprudence Considered in Relation to Cerebral Organization.* London: Samuel Highley, 1843.

Sampson, M. B. *The Rationale of Crime.* New York: Appleton, 1846.

Sanford, H. S., Charge D'affaires at Paris. *The Different Systems of Penal Codes in Europe; Also a Report on the Administrative Changes in France Since 1848.* Ed. Beverly Tucker. Washington, D.C.: Senate Printer, 1854.

Sanson, Henry. *Memoirs of the Sansons, 1688 to 1847.* London: Chatto, 1876.

Sanville, Florence L. "When Justice Goes Astray." In *Capital Punishment, Reference Shelf, 1939,* edited by Julia A. Johnsen, 38–43. New York: H. W. Wilson Co., 1939.

Sargent, Leonard, Governor of Vermont. "The Trial, Confessions, and Conviction of Jesse and Stephen Boorn." In *Journal Office.* Manchester, Vt., 1873.

Saturday Evening Post. "Capital Punishment." *Saturday Evening Post* 203:22 (3 January 1931).

Saturday Review. (1890) "Criminal Literature." *Saturday Review* 70 (30 August 1890).

———. (1891) "The Malady of Crime." *Saturday Review* 72 (24 October 1891).

Savitz, Leonard D. "Capital Crimes as Defined by American Statutory Law." *Journal of Criminal Law, Criminology, and Police Science* 46 (1955): 355–63.

————. "Capital Crimes as Defined in American Statutory Law." *Journal of Criminal Law, Criminology and Police Science* 46 (1956): 355–63.

Schmid, Calvin F. "Study Of Homicides In Seattle, 1914–1924." *Social Forces* 4 (June 1926): 745–56.

Schmidt, Master Franz. *A Hangman's Diary: Journal of the Public Executioner of Nuremberg, 1573–1617*. Montclair, N.J.: Patterson Smith, 1973.

Schuessler, Karl. "The Deterrent Influence of the Death Penalty." *The Annals of the Academy of Political and Social Science* 284 (November 1952).

Schuster, A. F. "Capital Punishment." *Nineteenth Century and After* 72 (October 1912): 732–44.

Schwed, Roger E. *Abolition and Capital Punishment: The United States' Judicial, Political, and Moral Barometer*. New York: AMS Press, 1983.

Science News Letter. "Domestic Quarrels Deadlier Than Gang Slaying." *Science News Letter* 35 (11 March 1939): 152.

Scongal, Francis. *Scenes from a Silent World*. Edin: Blackwood, 1889.

Scott, George Ryley. *The History of Capital Punishment*. London: Torchstream Books, 1950.

Scroggs, Joseph Whitefield, ed. *Capital Punishment: Should it be Abolished?* University of Oklahoma Bulletin. No. 345. Extension No. 94. Norman: University of Oklahoma, 1926.

Sega, J. *What is True Civilization, and, to Abolish the Death Punishment of Death*. Boston, Mass.: William Smith, 1830.

Sega, James. *What is True Civilization, or Means to Suppress the Practice of Dueling, to Prevent or Punish Crimes, and to Abolish the Punishment of Death*. Boston, Mass.: William Smith Printer, 1830.

Sellin, Thorsten. "Dom Jean Mabillon. A Prison Reformer of the 17th Century." *Journal of American Institute of Criminal Law & Criminology* 17 (1926–1927): 581.

————. "A Note on Capital Executions in the United States." *British Journal of Delinquency* 1 (1950): 6–14.

————. *The Death Penalty: A Report for the Model Penal Code Project of the American Law Institute*. Philadelphia: American Law Institute, 1959.

————. "Capital Punishment." *Federal Probation* 25 (September 1961): 3.

————. "Murder And The Death Penalty." *The Annals of the American Academy of Political and Social Science* 284 (1952): 1–166.

Sellin, Thorsten, ed. *The Death Penalty*. Harper & Row, 1967.

Sello, Erich. *Die Irrumer der Strafjustiz und ihre Urachen*. Berlin: R. von Decker, 1909.

Seymour, Thomas H., Governor. *Message to the Legislature of Connecticut*, 1850.

Shaffer, Helen B. "Death Penalty." *Editorial Research Reports* 2 (1953): 573–88.

Sharp, Malcolm P. *Was Justice Done? The Rosenberg-Sobell Case*. New York: Monthly Review Press, 1956.

Shay, Frank. *Jude Lynch, His First Hundred Years*. New York: Ives Washburn, 1938.

Shipley, Maynard. "Homicide and the Death Penalty in France." *Harper's Weekly* 51: 890.

————. "Abolition of Capital Punishment in Italy and San Marino." *American Law Review* 40 (March–April 1906): 240–51.

————. "Plato On Capital Punishment." *Harper's Weekly* 50 (29 December1906): 1903.

———. "Abolition of Capital Punishment in France." *American Law Review* 41 (July–August 1907): 561–64.

———. Homicide and the Death Penalty. *Annals of the American Academy* 29 (May 1907): 625–29.

———. "Homicide and the Death Penalty in Austria-Hungary." *American Statistical Association* 10 (March 1907): 253–59.

———. "Should Female Murders be Hanged?" *The Green Bag* 19 (1907): 234–36.

———. "Does Capital Punishment Prevent Convictions." *American Law Review* 43 (May–June 1909): 321–34.

———. "Should Capital Punishment be Abolished." *Journal of Criminal Law and Criminology* 2 (May 1911): 48–55.

Shippee, L. B. "Punishment for Murder in the State of Rhode Island. In *Legislative Reference Bulletin No. 9.*" Rhode Island State Library, 1917.

Shrady, George F., Dr. "The Death Penalty." *Arena* 1 (October 1890).

Shurter, Edwin DuBois. "Resolved. That Capital Punishment be Abolished." In *Both Sides of 100 Public Questions Briefly Debated*, 32–33. New York: Noble and Noble, 1925.

Sicker, Joseph S. *Rex et Regina vs. Lutherland (Facsimile of BLOOD WILL OUT . . . , 1691*). Woodstown, N.J.: Seven Stars Press, 1948.

Sifakis, Carl. *The Encyclopedia of American Crime*. New York: Facts on File, 1982.

Simon, Jules. *The Death Penalty*. Vol. 8. Trans. W. H. Huntington, 673–801, 1869.

Skinner, Otis A., Rev. (1849) "The Gallows Weakens the Sacredness of Human Life." *Prisoner's Friend*.

Smith, D. S. "The Case For The Death Penalty." *Los Angeles Bar Bulletin* 32 (1957): 195.

Smith, M. H. "The Shame of Capital Punishment." *The Penal Reformer* 1:3 (January 1935).

Sobeloff, Simon E. "Insanity and the Criminal Law." *American Bar Association Journal* 41 (1955): 793–96, 877–79.

Social Service Review. "Sir Samuel Romilly And The Abolition Of Capital Punishment." *Social Service Review* 5 (June 1931): 276–96.

Society for Diffusing Information on the Subject of Capital Punishment. *Tracts*. London, 1817.

Solicitor's Journal. "Death Penalty." *Solicitor's Journal* 73 (5 October 1929): 633.

———. "Capital Punishment; Report of the Select Committee (England)." *Solicitor's Journal* 75 (17 January 1931): 34–35.

Southern Quarterly Review. "The Criminal Law." *Southern Quarterly Review* (July 1842).

Spahn, Jacob. "Kemmler's Case and the Death Penalty." *The Green Bag* 2 (1890): 54–60, 107–13.

Spear, Charles. *Essays on the Punishment of Death*. Boston, 1844.

———. *Essays on the Punishment of Death*. Boston: Author, 1849.

———. The Prisoner's Friend (1849–1850).

Spectator. "Crime and Criminals. Review of DuCane." *Spectator* 59 (January 1886).

———. "The New Tenderness for Crime." *Spectator* 62 (February 1889).

———. "The Criminal Type of the Future." *Spectator* 64 (February 1890).

Sqire, Amos O. *Sing Sing Doctor*. Garden City, N.Y.: Doubleday, Doran & Co., 1935.

St. James Magazine. "The Criminal Law of England." *St. James Magazine* 11 (November 1864).

St. John-Stevas, Norman. *The Right To Life.* New York: Holt, Rinehardt and Winston, 1964.

Stace, Henry, Col. Examination Before the Capital Punishment Commission of July 8, 1864 (1865).

Stachan-Davidson, James L. *Problems of the Roman Criminal Law.* London: Macmillan, 1912.

Stedman, Edmund C. "The Gallows in America." *Putnam's Magazine* 3 (1869): 225.

Stephen, A. G. et al. "Petition Praying for the Passage of a Law Abolishing Capital Punishment." In *New York Assembly Doc. no. 59, February 13, 1843.* Albany, N.Y., 1843.

Stephen, James F. *A History of the Criminal Law of England, vol. 1.* London: Macmillan, 1883.

Stephen, James Fitzjames, Sir. *A History of Crime in England (3 vols.).* London: Macmillan, 1883.

Stern, Max. "Study of Unsolved Murders in Wisconsin From 1924–1928." *Journal of Criminal Law and Criminology* 21 (fall 1931): 513–36.

Sterne, Francis D. "Philosophy of Crime." *Fraser* 33 (February 1846).

Stetson, George R. "The Rising Tide of Crime." *Unitarian Review* 27 (May 1887).

Stevens, James F. "Variations in Punishment of Crime." *Century* 17 (May 1885).

Stewart, Dugald. "Letters to Sir Samuel Romilly." In *Memoirs of the Life of Sir Samuel Romilly, Vol. 2,* 310. London: Murray, 1840.

Stillwell, Silas M. "Report to New York Assembly, March 7, 1832, Favoring the Abolition of Capital Punishment." In *Assembly Doc. No. 187.* Albany, N.Y., 1832.

Stokes, William. *Thou Shalt Not Kill.* London: Gilpin, 1848.

Stolz, John, Dr. *The Cause and Cure of Crime. With Treatise on Capital Punishment.* Philadelphia: Trotter.

Streib, Victor L. *Death Penalty for Juveniles.* Bloomington: Indiana University Press, 1987.

Streib, Victor L., ed. *A Capital Punishment Anthology.* Cincinnati, Ohio: Anderson Publishing Co., 1993.

Stutsman, Jesse O. "Death Penalty." In *Curing the Criminal,* edited by Jesse O. Stutsman, 332–52. New York: Macmillan & Co., 1926.

Suffield, Lord. "In the House of Lords, July 18, 1834, on moving and second reading of Capital Punishment Bill." In *Hansard's Parliamentary Debate,* 90. London, 1834.

Sufrin, Ron. "Everything is in Order, Warden: A Discussion of Death in the Gas Chamber." *Suicide and Life Threatening Behavior* 6 (spring 1976): 44–57.

Summer, Charles. "Letter to Committee of Massachusetts Legislature, February 12. 1855." In *Works, Vol. 3,* 527, 1855.

Summerhays, T. F. "Capital Punishment for Murder." In *Bulletin for the Council for Social Service,* No. 163. The Church of England in Canada, 1955.

Sumner, Charles. *Against Capital Punishment.*

Sunset. "Should Capital Punishment Be Abolished?" *Sunset* 55 (November 1925): 46.

Survey. "Why The People Of Arizona Voted To Keep Their Hangman." *Survey* 33 (27 February 1915): 585.

———. "Saved By Five Hours." *Survey* 65 (15 November 1930): 127–31 + .

Sussex, Duke of. "Speech in House of Commons, Sept. 6, 1831, in Presenting Petition of Grand Jurors of Middlesex, praying for abolition of Capital Punishment." In *Hansard's Parliamentary Debate*, 1172. London, 1831.

Sutherland, Edwin H. "Murder And The Death Penalty." *Journal of Criminal Law and Criminology* 15 (fall 1925): 522–29.

Sutherland, Edwin H. *Principles of Criminology*. Chicago: J. B. Lippincott Co., 1934.

Tait's Magazine. New Series. "Capital Punishment." *Tait's Magazine. New Series*, Vol. 3, 590.

———. "The Causes of Crime in The Metropolis." *Tait's Magazine. New Series*, Vol. 17.

———. "Hanging, Past and Present." *Tait's Magazine. New Series*, Vol. 10, 233.

———. "Some Loose Thoughts on Hanging." *Tait's Magazine. New Series*, Vol. 8.

———. "Death Punishments." *Tait's Magazine. New Series*, July 1837.

Talbot, C. K. "Capitalism And Capital Punishment: A Historical Note on the Westinghouse/Edison Debate of 1890." *Crime and Justice* 6:2 (1978): 129–33.

Talleck, William. *Practical Results of the Abolition of Capital Punishment in Various Countries*. Trans. William Talleck. Nation Association Promoting Social Science, 1865.

Tannenbaum, Frank. *Osborne of Sing Sing*. Chapel Hill: University of North Carolina Press, 1933.

Tarde, Gabriel. *Penal Philosophy*. English Translation. Boston: Little Brown & Co., 1912.

Tasker, Robert Joyce. "Man is Hanged." *American Mercury* 11 (June 1927): 162–70.

Taylor, J. Sydney. *Anti-Draco; or, Reasons for Abolishing the Punishment of Death in Cases of Forgery*. London, 1830.

———. "The Punishment of Death." *Tait's Magazine*, July 1830.

———. *Punishment of Death, Selections From the Morning Herald, With Notes*. London: Hutchard & Son, 1836–1837.

———. *Selection From Writings*. London: Gilpin, 1843.

Teeters, Negley K. "Public Executions in Philadelphia." *Prison Journal* 38 (1958): 63–74.

———. "Public Executions In Pennsylvania 1682 to 1834." *Journal of the Lancaster Historical Society* (spring 1960): 86–165.

———. *Scaffold and Chair: A Compilation of their use in Pennsylvania, 1682–1962*. Philadelphia: Pennsylvania Prison Society, 1963.

———. *Hang By the Neck: The Legal Use of Scaffold and Nose, Gibbet, Stake, And Firing Squad from Colonial Times to the Present*. Springfield, Ill.: Charles C. Thomas Publishing, 1967.

Templewood, Viscount. *Shadow of the Gallows*. London: Victor Gollancz, 1951.

Terrett, Courtenay. "Hangman's Holiday." *Outlook* 148 (1 February 1928): 166–67 + .

———. "Warden Lawes and Capital Punishment." *Outlook* 148 (15 February 1928): 250 + .

Thatcher, Thomas D. "Trial By Newspaper; Hauptmann Case And The Remedy." *Vital Speeches* 2 (15 September 1936): 778–81.

The Law Times. "Death Penalty in the Army." *The Law Times* 165 (1928): 300.

The Penal Reformer. "Some Reflection on Punishment." *The Penal Reformer* 5:2 (October 1938).

———. "Abolition Moves." *The Penal Reformer* 5:4 (April 1939).

———. "The Road to Hell." *The Penal Reformer* 4:3 (January 1939).

The Police Chief. "Capital Punishment." *The Police Chief,* June 1960.

The Prison Journal. "Capital Punishment." *The Prison Journal* (October 1958).

Thomas, Paul A. "Murder and the Death Penalty." *American Journal of Corrections* 19 (1957): 16–17, 30–32.

Thompkins, Raymond S. "Notes On Hanging." *American Mercury* 25 (March 1932): 280–88.

Thompson, W. H. *Murder and the Death Penalty.* Detroit, Mich.: Phillips and Hunt, 1886.

Timlow, William. *Mr. Livingston's Strong Argument Against Capital Punishment Review.* Goshen, N.Y.: Clark & Montanye, 1850.

Titus, James H. *Reports and Addresses on Capital Punishment.* New York: De Witt & Davenport, 1848.

Tolstoy, Leo H. "I Cannot Keep Quiet." *Arena,* August 1909, 525–34.

Tolstoy, Leo. Government by Execution. *258* (1908).

Turano, Anthony M. "Capital Punishment by Lethal Gas." *The American Mercury* 29 (May 1933): 91–97.

Turner, William, Rev. *Essay on Capital Punishment (Memoirs of the Literary and Philosophical Society of Manchester).* Manchester, 1785.

U.S. House of Representatives. *Capital Crimes, House Report 545.* 53rd Congress, 2d Session. Washington, D.C.: U.S. Government Printing Office, 1894.

———. *Hearings on H.R. 8414, H.R. 9486, H.R. 3243, H.R. 193, H.R. 11797, and H.R. 12217 (March 1972).* Serial No. 29, 92nd Congress, 2d Session, 1972.

United States. *Attorney General's Survey of Release Procedures.* Washington, D.C.: U.S. Government Printing Office, 1939.

———. *National Prisoner Statistics: Executions.* Washington, D.C.: U.S. Government Printing Office, annual.

United States House of Representatives. *Report of the Committee of the Judiciary on Capital Crimes.* 53d Congress, 2d Session, H.R. 545, 14–23. Washington, D.C.: U.S. Government Printing Office.

United States v Jackson. U.S. 390:570 (1968).

United States, Library of Congress. *Selected List of References on Capital Punishment.* Washington, D.C.: U.S. Government Printing Office, 1912.

United States. Bureau of the Census. "Deaths from Homicide: 1920–1937." In *Vital Statistics—Special Reports,* no. 33, 153–56. Washington, D.C.: U.S. Government Printing Office, 1939.

Upham, T. C. *The Manual of Peace.* Boston, 1842.

Van der Elst, Violet. *On The Gallows.* London: Doge Press, 1937.

Van Horn, Burt, Chairman Committee. "Report to the New York Assembly Recommending the Death Penalty, Feb. 16, 1860." In *Assembly Doc. no. 82.* Albany, N.Y., 1860.

Van Kiekerk, S. "Name Not A Rope in His House That Hang'd Himself." *The South African Law Journal* (1971).

Vattel, E. *Law of Nations.* London: Robinson, 1797.

Vaux, Richard. *Short Talks on Crimes Cause and Cruel Punishments.*

Verax (Pseud.). *Capital Punishment.* Manchester, 1884.

Vissers (Dr. of Laws, Belgium). "Examination Before Capital Punishment Commission of July 8, 1864." 1865.

Von Hentig, Hans. *Punishment, Its Origin, Purpose and Psychology*. London: William Hodge and Company, 1937.

von Keler, M. R. "Murderer, Choose Thy Doom! Giving The Criminal A Chance To Cancel His Death." *Independent* 114 (14 March 1925): 299–300.

Wakefield, Constance. *The Prisoner's Friends: John Howard, Elizabeth Fry and Sarah Martin*. Headley Bros., 1917.

Wakefield, Edward G. *Facts Relating to the Punishment of Death in the Metropolis*. London: Ridgeway, 1831.

———. *Facts Relating to the Punishment of Death*. London, 1932.

Walker, Gerald. "Young Man be an Executioner." *Esquire* 60 (August 1963): 62–63.

Waller, George. *Kidnap: The Story of the Lindbergh Case*. New York: The Dial Press, 1961.

Wallis, J. H. "300,000 Murderers." *American Mercury* 37 (January 1936): 9–13.

Ward, Durbin. "Report of the Select Committee on the Subject of Capital Punishment, March 9, 1855." In *Assembly of New York*. Albany, N.Y., 1855.

Washington Research Project. *The Case Against Capital Punishment*. Pamphlet. C.A.L.M., Inc., 1971.

Wayland, Francis, Yale Law School. "Address on Capital Punishment." *American Journal Social Science* (1883).

Webster, Edward. *On Capital Punishment*. London: Cox & Wyman, 1856.

Wechsler, Herbert, and Jerome Michael. "Rationale of the Law of Homicide." *Columbia Law Review* (1937).

Weihofen, Henry. "A Question of Justice: Trial or Execution of an Insane Defendant." *American Bar Association Journal* 37 (1951): 651–54.

Wells, Gabriel. *On Capital Punishment*. London, 1929.

———. *On Capital Punishment*. New York: Doubleday, Doran & Co., 1929

Wertham, Frederick. *The Show of Violence*. Garden City: Doubleday, 1949.

———. *The Circle of Guilt*. New York: Rhinehart & Co., 1956.

Westminster Review. "Mr. Peel's Improvement in the Criminal Law." *Westminster Review* 7 (January 1827).

———. "Punishment of Death." *Westminster Review* (July 1832).

———. "Gnerry on the Statistics of Crime in France." *Westminster Review* 18 (April 1833).

———. On Criminal Law Reform." *Westminster Review* 21 (October 1834).

———. "Practice of the Criminal Law of Scotland." *Westminster Review* 22 (January 1835).

———. "Criminal Legislation and Prison Discipline." *Westminster Review* 61 (April 1864).

Wexley, John. *The Judgement of Julius and Ethel Rosenberg*. New York: Cameron & Kahn, 1955.

Wharton, Francis. *Philosophy of Criminal Law*. Philadelphia, 1846.

Whateley, Richard. *Defence of Transportation in Reply to the Archbishop of Dublin*. London: G. Cowie, 1835.

———. *Thoughts on Secondary Punishments*. London: B. Fellows, 1832.

———. *Remarks on Transportation*. London: B. Fellowes, 1834.

Whitbread, Samuel, M.P. "Speech in House of Commons, London 1811, on a Bill to Abolish the Death Penalty." In *Hansard's Parliamentary Debate*, 744 (1811).

White, C. *Convict Life in New South Wales and Van Dieman's Land*. Bathurst, 1889.

White, J. B. "Capital Punishment." *Southern Literary Journal* (January 1836).

White, Walter. *Rope and Faggot.* New York: Arno Press, 1969.

Whitfield, R. N. "Homicide Situation in the United States." *American Journal of Public Health* (October 1937): 981–86.

Wilberforce, William, M.P. "Speech in House of Commons, 1811, on a Bill to Abolish the Punishment of Death." In *Hansard's Parliamentary Debate*, 744 (1811).

Wilks, Helen M. "Should Women Be Hanged?" *The North American Review* 144 (1887): 211–12.

Williams, Franklin H. "The Death Penalty and the Negro." *The Crisis* 67 (October 1960): 501–12.

Williams, Glanvile. "The Royal Commission and the Defense of Insanity." *Current Legal Problems* 7 (1954): 17–32.

Williams, J. E. Hall. "Jury Discretion in Murder Trials." *Modern Law Review* 17 (1954): 315–28.

Wilson, James, Judge U.S. Circuit Court. *Charge to Grand Jury at Easton, Maryland, Nov. 7, 1791* (1791).

Wilson, John, of Edinburgh University. *On Punishment of Death. Essays (Vol. 2).* Edin, 1856.

Wilson, P. W. "Common Sense and Criminal Law." *Outlook* 138 (24 September 1924): 121–22.

Winans, James A., and William E. Utterback. "Abolition of Capital Punishment: A Classroom Debate." In *Argumentation*, 431–53. New York: Century, 1930.

Witherspoon v Illinois. U.S. 391:510 (1968).

Wix, Samuel. *Reflections Concerning the Inexpediency and Unchristian Character of Capital Punishment.* London: Gilbert & Rivington, 1832.

Wolfgang, Marvin E, and X. Cha. *Patterns of Criminal Homicide.* Philadelphia: University of Pennsylvania Press, 1958.

"Women's Right To Be Hanged." *The Literary Digest* 104:15 (March 1930): 19.

Wood, Arthur. "The Alternatives to the Death Penalty." *Annals* (1952).

Woodring, Harry W., Governor of the State of Kansas. *Capital Punishment.* Kansas Legislators, 1931. New York: American League to Abolish Capital Punishment, n.d.

Woolrych, H. W. *History and Results of Capital Punishment in England.* London, 1832.

Wordsworth, Charles, Rev. "Sermon on the Punishment of Death for Willful Murder." London, 1867.

Worley, Francis. "A Bill to Abolish Capital Punishment in Pennsylvania." *Dickenson Law Review* 60 (1956): 167–69.

Wrightson, Thomas. *On The Punishment of Death.* London: Hearne, 1837.

Wyatt, Woodrow. "Against the Issue of Capital Punishment." *New York Times Magazine*, 8 January 1956.

Wyndham, Horace. "Judgement of Death." In *Criminology.* Benn's Sixpenny Library, no. 27, 37–44. London: Ernest Benn, 1928.

Wynn, C. W., M.P. "Speech in House of Commons, 1811, on a bill to abolish the punishment of Death." In *Hansard's Parliamentary Debate*, 745 (1811).

Wyse, Thomas, M.P. "Resolution Offered in Exeter Hall, June 2, 1832, Condemning Capital Punishment" (1832).

Yale Law School. *Two Centuries of Growth of American Law.* New York: Scribners, 1902.

Younger, Evelle E. "Capital Punishment: A Sharp Medicine Reconsidered." *American Bar Association Journal* 42 (1956): 113–16.

Zaller, Robert. "The Debate on Capital Punishment During the English Revolution." *American Journal of Legal History* 31 (1987): 126–44.

Zangler, Jules. "Crime and Punishment in Early Massachusetts." *William and Mary Quarterly* 2 (1965): 471–77.

Book Review Essay

Genocide as Government through Murder: A Review of Recent Contributions

Augustine Brannigan and Kelly Hardwick

Christopher Browning, *Ordinary Men: Reserve Police Battalion 101 and the Final Solution in Poland, New Afterword*. New York: Harper Perennial, 1998. xii + 271 pp., illustrations, notes, index. $14.00.

Irving Louis Horowitz, *Taking Lives: Genocide and State Power*, 5th edition. New Brunswick N.J., 2002. xiv + 558 pp., notes, index. $59.95 hb, $29.95 pb.

Daniel J. Goldhagen, *Hitler's Willing Executioners: Ordinary Germans and the Holocaust*, revised edition. New York: Alfred Knopf, 1997. 634 pp., illustrations, maps, notes, index. $16.00.

James Turner Johnson, *Morality and Contemporary Warfare*. New Haven: Yale University Press, 1999. ix + 254 pp., notes, index. $17.00.

Iris Chang, *The Rape of Nanking: The Forgotten Holocaust of World War II*. New York: Basic Books, 1997. xi + 290 pp., illustrations, notes, index. $25.00.

Christopher Hitchens, *The Trial of Henry Kissinger*. London: Verso, 2001. xi + 159 pp., notes, index. $22.00.

Norbert Elias, *The Civilizing Process*. Translated by Edmund Jephcott and edited by Eric Dunning, Johan Goudsblom, and Stephen Mennell, revised edition. Oxford: Blackwell, 2000. xvii + 558 pp., notes, index. $36.95.

Gary Jonathan Bass, *Stay the Hand of Vengeance: The Politics of War Crime Tribunals*. Princeton: Princeton University Press, 2000. 402 pp., notes, index. $45.00.

INTRODUCTION: DOES CRIMINOLOGY HELP TO EXPLAIN GENOCIDE?

In criminal justice history we tend to view mass murders associated with armed conflict as the province of military history. The experiences of the past decade have forced us to rethink this perspective as the perpetrators of mass slaughter of unarmed noncombatants in Rwanda and Bosnia are forced to face charges before international criminal courts for war crimes including genocide. The past decade has also seen a revival of the historiography surrounding the Holocaust of European Jews, Gypsies, and other enemies of the Nazi state. Historians of the Holocaust, particularly Browning and Goldhagen, have documented the role of "ordinary" people in the mass extermination of their neighbors. As the academic debates of this were taking place in the early and mid-1990s, history repeated itself as we read in the morning papers how ordinary Serbs were committing mass murder in Srebrenica (July 1995) and ordinary Hutus were butchering their Tutsi neighbors in Rwanda (June 1994). There was a significant "bottom-up" component to mass murder in Nazi Germany, in the disintegrating Yugoslavia, and the Great Lakes region of Central Africa in the early 1990s. Since the attacks of September 11, 2001, students of crime have been contemplating the failure of criminology to tackle terrorism and genocide in the face of the suggestion that, in the twentieth century, citizens of a modern state were more likely to meet an untimely demise as a result of state-initiated murder or act of political terrorism than to die at the hands of a garden-variety murderer, and that their demise would be expedited by people who otherwise could have been trusted to mind their children. All this suggests that students of criminal justice history need to revisit armed conflict as an important venue for understanding crime. The books reviewed here merely skim the surface.

RECENT STUDIES OF THE HOLOCAUST

Browning's *Ordinary Men* is based on an examination of the judicial interviews of German policemen who were investigated in the 1960s by the Hamburg prosecutor's office for criminal activities during the occupation of Poland in the early 1940s. Browning describes how "ordinary men" became mass killers as the European Jews were deported from occupied Europe to Poland in 1940–41 and were subsequently murdered as a result of orders from the highest authorities in Germany. He reports that 75 percent to 80 percent of the victims of the Holocaust were murdered in a blitzkrieg of killing that came to a head in the fall of 1942 in "Operation Autumn Harvest" after the installation of the large gas chambers in the Polish concentration camps. The Order Police were middle-aged Germans, mostly from modest backgrounds. They were not particularly fanatical in their devotion to Nazi racial beliefs. They were involved in the protection of military targets, but became critical

in clearing the ghettoes of Jews who had been transported from all over occupied Europe. Reserve police Battalion 101 was initiated into the murder of
civilians in July 1942, but other police battalions assisted the mobile "einsatz"
units behind the front lines following the invasion of Russia in Operation
Barbarossa in June 1941. The 3,000 men assigned to the units were assisted
by the Order Police. By March 1943, when the German war on Russia was
in serious jeopardy, over 633,300 Jews had been shot.[1] Browning argues that
"the Holocaust took place because at the most basic level individual human
beings killed other human beings in large numbers over an extended period
of time" (p. xvii). "The fundamental problem is to explain why ordinary men
. . . under specific circumstances willingly carried out the most extreme genocide in human history" (p. 222).

Although Daniel Goldhagen examined the same archival records, his explanation of the events leading to the Holocaust is quite different. He attributed a specific mental frame of reference to the behavior of the policemen:
they were marked by a deeply inculcated "exterminationist antisemitism" that
was rooted in German history and culture and that fostered a hatred so intense
that ordinary Germans embraced the opportunity to kill their racial enemies
as a national project. "Demonological antisemitism, of the virulent racial variety, was the common structure of the perpetrators' cognition and of German
society in general" (p. 392). In the preface to the German translation (included
as an appendix to the 1997 edition), he adds that the conditions for the Holocaust required a fanatical anti-Semitic elite, a population that shared this
perspective, as well as a powerful army and bureaucracy capable of implementing the plans of the political elite (p. 480).

Browning reissued his 1992 edition in 1998 with an afterword to deal with
Goldhagen's criticisms of his treatment of the evidence and to set out more
formally his explanation of the Holocaust. Browning's account is "multi-
layered." He acknowledges that most policemen "did whatever they were
asked to do, without ever risking the onus of confronting authority or appearing weak" (p. 215). Four factors explain compliance at the grass roots
level: "the importance of conformity, peer pressure, deference to authority
and . . . the legitimizing capacities of government" (p. 216). He adds that "for
the most part, they did not think that what they were doing was wrong or
immoral, because the killing was sanctioned by legitimate authority" (p. 216).
This fact, if admitted, would imply that the perpetrators never had the *mens
rea* (knowledge aforethought), that they were not culpable, and that they were
collectively delusional about the nature and quality of their activities. The
evidence suggests otherwise. Browning notes that drunkenness was rife
among the executioners because a life of shooting innocent men, women, and
children was "intolerable sober," that Himmler himself was sickened by the
mass shootings he inspected in Russia, that S.S. leader Bach-Zelewski was
suffering from visions of the shootings of Jews in actions he had led (p. 25),
and that Major Trapp who led the first mass executions committed by

Battalion 101 explained the order, appearing pale and nervous "with a choking voice and tears in his eyes" (p. 2). Indeed, there was constant concern over the mental state of the executioners, which resulted in the introduction of gassing, not only to raise the efficiency of the scale of the killing, but to make it less onerous on those ordered to do it.

Even so, the photographic evidence in both Browning and Goldhagen (using many of the same pictures) shows beaming policemen who humiliated their victims and obviously undertook their duties with relish and pleasure. The record shows that policemen not "up" for the actual shootings were assigned other duties. Whatever difficulties presented at the start of the campaign where men showed evidence of scruples, the policemen could be counted on to murder on command, to move back and forth from Germany on furloughs, and to pick up where they had left off previously. The record also suggests that dominance, humiliation of the unarmed, and looting of victims were common incentives in the killing sprees.

WHAT IS GENOCIDE?

Raphael Lemkin coined the term *genocide* in 1944. Homicide is the murder of a person. Genocide is the murder of a whole genus or category of persons. He was writing in the shadow of the Holocaust and the unprecedented crimes against unarmed civilians, viz., the Jews and Gypsies of Europe. These were unarmed civilians, noncombatants, children and adults, males and females. They were selected for extermination because of their "racial" identity. A similar sentence was passed on homosexuals and, to a lesser extent, the physically and mentally disabled. The euthanasia program directed at the physically and mentally unfit was officially stopped in 1941 because of popular opposition among ordinary Germans, although it appears to have continued informally until 1945. No such common sentiments militated against the Nazi treatment of the Jews or Gypsies.

The problem with the term "genocide" is that it is not altogether clear what it refers to. We mean no disrespect to those whose lives were taken criminally by the Nazis. Lemkin meant to tag something more than "mere" murder. But what was it? And what implications does it raise for criminology? Homicide is a generic category when it comes to unlawful killing of a person by another person. Criminal codes often differentiate homicide into "murder one," "murder two," and manslaughter. They differentiate illegal killing according to the degree of culpability and identify specific penalties "measure for measure" in accordance with the culpability of the offender. Obviously, different states spell out the categories in accord with their own determination of the requirements of mens rea. Genocide is defined in the United Nations convention as acts intended to destroy in whole or in part "a national, ethnical, racial or religious group, as such." The convention identifies under this generic offense various violations that correspond to the master concept: killing members of the group, causing it "serious bodily or mental harm," inflicting conditions of life calculated to end life, controlling reproduction, and transferring children to members of other groups.[2] However, no graduated penalties are identified despite the fact that the category includes both physical elimination and mental harm under the same convention. This suggests that mass murder and "mental harm" (racist propaganda?) are the same crime, that is, genocide.

Is genocide a subcategory of murder? Or is genocide a separate crime with separate kinds of causes requiring separate legal and political theories to deal with it? Genocide studies appear to treat genocidal murders as distinct phenomena. They typologize them according to motive and historical period. Their comparative method optimizes the distinctiveness between "ideological" versus "instrumental" genocides, "international" versus "national" ones, and those occurring in classical versus modern times. Chalk and Jonassohn distinguish "genocide" as such from "genocidal massacres." This implies that the explanation of the one is different from the explanation of the other. They define genocide as "a form of one-sided killing in which a state or other authority intends to destroy a group, as that group and membership in it are defined by the perpetrator."[3] This definition would suggest that the mass murders of Tutsi civilians in Rwanda by Hutus in 1994, and Bosnians by Serbs in 1995, were not genocide inasmuch as these were not "one-sided" since both sides had a previous history of targeting each others' civilians. So these may be "genocidal massacres," but not "genocides" as such. Is this a useful distinction? Certainly, genocide scholars ought not to let U.N. conventions dictate the terms of reference of their dependent variable, but the proliferation of definitions that have been advanced to catch the essence of genocide may not be the optimum path to theoretical clarity.

The perspective of criminology we favor is to think in terms of *general* theories in which the same processes underlie diverse events. Criminological theory emphasizes the *continuity* between events, even if they vary in their particulars. The dilemma is whether we require two master concepts—*homicide* versus *genocide*—and the accompanying differentiations elaborated in specific criminal codes. This would make the study of *mass* murder versus *mere* murder two independent fields of study and would require, potentially, different theories of behavior in each case. Criminology and genocide studies would be distinct areas of study if we followed this line of logic.

IS GENOCIDE CONCEPTUALLY DIFFERENT FROM MURDER?

What is it about the murder of the European Jews and Gypsies that is qualitatively different from garden-variety murder? Is it that unarmed people were murdered—men, women, and children? No one can dispute that this occurred on a breath-taking scale in World War II and was associated with carnage unprecedented in Europe since the Thirty Years' War in the sixteenth century. This was clearly a war that repudiated the "just war" tradition described in James T. Johnson's *Morality and Contemporary Warfare*. The tradition of *jus in bello* (just war) expressly holds noncombatants immune as targets in a campaign justified in its aims and proportional in its methods. The war of total destruction carried out against Europe's Jews and the wholesale destruction of "slav" civilians as part of Nazi war policies could never meet the requirements of just war. However, the murder of the unarmed and the slaughter of innocents is already an all-too familiar historical fact. Is it that the victims are *innocent?* No one contests that in the case of either the hapless victim of robbery or of Auschwitz that the victims were innocent—the victims are not responsible for causing the crimes. So that is not the key difference. Is it that they belong to a group or category that attracts attack on the fact of mere membership? Here there is a partial lead.

We use the term *Holocaust* to refer to the mass killings during World War II, primarily of European Jews, but also of Gypsies, homosexuals, and the mentally or physically disabled. But what, for criminology, is distinctive here? Are we not *already* familiar with specific *group homicide*—murder of abortion doctors; murder of female students at the *Ecole Polytechnique;* assassination of Central American leftists, trade unionists, and community activists; elimination of political opponents in South America; rival gang killing; and so on? So the targeting of specific, innocent noncombatants, irrespective of age, gender, class, and so forth, is not of itself entirely unprecedented in the archives of criminology. Is the Holocaust different because these killings were acts of the state? Acts of state in the twentieth century have rained lethal terror on civilian populations in Europe and Japan with devastating effects on innocent, unarmed civilians regardless of age, gender, or faith. What is interesting is that we are reluctant to view such acts during wartime as crimes or to describe them as murder. They may be justified as acts of self-defense designed to terminate an aggressor's ability to continue to make war. Whether they meet the proportionality test applying only as much force as is required to meet a just end is a different question. And certainly, these acts are not covered by the U.N. definition of genocide since they are not aimed at the group "as such." Ironically, the events so conceptually similar—killing of unarmed noncombatants —in the one case (bombing cities) is not a crime at all when conducted as an act of self-defense, and in the other case (the Holocaust) it is a special kind of killing distinct from mere murder. But what makes it distinct?

The argument that removes the bombing of cities from the category of war crimes is that the bombings possess legitimate military targets whose removal will end hostilities. Their devastation is a means to an end. What differentiates the Holocaust is that the killing of the victims, noncombatants, irrespective of age or gender, is the *objective* of the state policy. These killings are not "collateral damage," but the main point of the military or police exercise. In other words, they are murders on purpose. But doesn't that return us to the original question—is the concept of genocide redundant? Is genocide simply murder in another form? If that were the case, what criminology has to say about murder might apply mutatis mutandis to genocide.

Irving Horowitz argues that genocide is a form of state-sponsored killing.[4] He notes inter alia that certain kinds of states are more prone to this behavior than others, and identifies totalitarian states as particularly so inclined. But what is a state? And what is it about a totalitarian state that motivates it to commit genocide? The concept of state action in crime suggests that there are categories of crime that are an outcome of *collective* behaviors that are institutionally *formal*, and that such acts are by definition not private but *public* acts. The concept of *state* suggests a methodological holism that is inconsistent with the most fruitful theories of crime. The control perspective in criminology[5] is situated in classical European philosophy beginning with Thomas Hobbes. Individuals determine their own courses of actions (with Marx's proviso: "but not always in conditions of their own choosing") but in ways in which they are responsible and, in the case of crime, culpable.

In the control perspective, crime is "the use of force and fraud in the pursuit of self-interest."[6] Individuals sometimes choose murder to advance their self-interests. States? Never, inasmuch as the concept of state is a reification of human actions. Hobbes recognized that behind the facade of the state there existed *a sovereign*. If the sovereign is the personification of the state, the killing of innocents as "acts of state" is, for methodological individualists, an act of the sovereign. What is it about totalitarian states that distinguishes their sovereigns? They reflect the control of the state by an elite class or core at the center of the hierarchy of power and authority. For criminology, then, genocide is the act of murder perpetrated by the elite, by the sovereign, by the class that controls the direction of public policy, that staffs the bureaucracy, and that otherwise ensures the security of the governed. In short, genocide is murder delegated by the authority structure to the ranks of underlings. The question that concerns us here is what potential role it might play in the governance of society.

SELF-CONTROL AND THE DEVELOPMENT OF WESTERN CIVILIZATION

In *The Civilizing Process* Elias describes the formation of European states in the feudal period as a process of consolidation of power among warlords. His original two volumes (*The History of Manners* and *Civilization and State Formation*) were consolidated, updated, and republished in 2000. The account he offers may be relevant to a general theory of mass murder. As the population of Europe grew during the post-Roman period and as trade integrated population centers, the empty spaces of Europe were occupied and defended by families skillful at making war, pillaging, and ruling by terror and the extraction of tribute. Kings emerged as the more powerful potentates, and lesser feudal authorities allied themselves with their military superiors to form co-alitions for the pursuit of security and prosperity. The state emerged as a political coalition in which the use of force in the pursuit of self-interest became the monopoly of the sovereign. In exchange for the use of force at the individual level, those who became subjects of the sovereign enjoyed the security of his reign. Also, rather than the use of fraud and terror to extract tribute, the sovereign enjoyed the rights of taxation. The European states were developed on the growth of the monopoly over the legitimate use of force and the monopoly over taxation.

Elias's history describes how the former warrior society was transformed into the genteel court society and how the elite class learned to suppress the immediate satisfaction of instinctual needs and impulses in favor of delayed and sublimated satisfaction. The history of manners described in Elias's first book was the education of the peasants in the habits of the elites. This "emo-tional economy" (sublimation and impulse control) is the foundation of Eu-ropean civilization. The eighteenth-century French philosophers came to describe the rights of personal security as "universal." The procurement of such rights required political suffrage, that is, representation, or the recog-nition of individual interests in the area of security and prosperity. The periods and episodes of conflict between sovereign states and between European states and their colonial extensions were frequently marked by massacres of un-armed noncombatants in the extension of sovereign authority over new ter-ritories and colonies, and in the sovereignty vacuum of stateless communities the use of force and fraud reverted to their individualistic and private form.

If genocide is a form of murder perpetrated by an elite person or group of persons, how would we interpret it in terms of criminology? Since all crime for us is the pursuit of self-interest, we ought to understand elite murder as an act of self-interest. Genocide may be the practice of politics by murder, that is, using murder as a method of governance. This may take the form of the physical extermination of political rivals, or it may take the form of cre-ating and exploiting collective fears, animosities, and threats to secure gov-ernance through the destruction of a scapegoat. The elites, according to Weber, pursue prestige, honor, and the sense of historic mission in the way they conduct political affairs. Christina Larner argues that the Scottish witch-hunts were fostered by elites who enforced the adoption of Calvinism to modernize a peasant population that still practiced druid rites alongside a superstitious Catholicism.[7] The identification of witches symbolically extir-pated primitive beliefs from a rural population facing modernization. The target of the witch-hunt was a pseudogroup. The elite governed by terrorizing the peasant class over charges of heresy and, in the result, murdering inno-cents under the ideology of destroying witchcraft. The historical record does not suggest that the controlling elite acted cynically in rooting out evil.

The Nazis exploited existing animosities against the non-"Aryans" as a way of securing their moral and political dominance. The French rulers supported the massacres during the Albigensian Crusades to advance their territorial claims to feudal France.[8] The Young Turks consolidated their political succession over the former Ottoman Empire by routing out the prominent non-Islamic, non-Turkish Armenians. The Armenian minority, which had enjoyed considerable economic success, education, and social development as the Ottoman Empire disintegrated, attracted envy and resentment. The Young Turks built their ascendancy to power through the murder of a minority whose disappearance could promote political cohesion.[9] In these instances, genocide is murder by the elites in the pursuit of their political self-interests.

The use of murder as a political strategy by an elite is not always the most expedient way to secure political authority. The situation described by Elias was one in which ideally there would emerge a balance of forces among those with competing interests, that is, the subjects would consent to be governed by the sovereign to the extent that his monopoly of force and taxation yielded satisfactory levels of security and prosperity. In a political system competing political parties would create alliances to further their individual interests and prevent the use of naked, unchecked power, that is, the use of violence and confiscation of wealth by the ruling elite. The power between sovereign states would be kept in check by coalitions of standing armies designed to guarantee diplomacy over naked force. From this perspective the explanation of state murder, that is, murder committed and directed by the elites, may be examined fruitfully in the conditions of the demise of a successful equilibrium of control. This could arise where there is competition among the elites themselves, that is, political succession through regicide and treason. However, the totalitarian states that Horowitz describes are ones in which political rivalries are ruthlessly exterminated. Power could also become unchecked by political domination of the institutions of force (the army and police), of the monetary institutions (the bureaucracy and taxation apparatus), and of the judiciary (control over the definition of crime and the rule of law). All these situations concentrate power in a small elite, and their exercise of self-interest is increasingly unchecked by the sort of countervailing interests found in Elias's "civilized" model of the state. In such states it is increasingly easy to rule through murder.

CRIME AND CRIMINALITY IN GENOCIDAL MURDER

If we accept that genocide is simply murder in which the perpetrators are members of the elite with control over the legitimate use of force (the army and police to further their interests directly), over the treasury (to finance their interests), and over the judiciary (to legitimize their choices), how sound are the parallels between genocide and "mere" murder? In control theory we typically distinguish between "criminality" (the motivation) and "crime" (the opportunity). For nonelites, the pursuit of self-interests often results in murder, rape, and robbery. For elites, the pursuit of self-interest often results (in conditions sketched above) in mass murder, conquest, and war. For no-nelites the concept of "crime" refers to a variety of conditions and situations that expedite or retard action owing to (among other things): (1) opportunities (doors unlocked, cars with keys in the ignitions, defenseless target); (2) peer facilitation (reduction of the sense of individual responsibility); and (3) facil-itation by drug and alcohol intoxication.

"Criminality" refers to the mentality or mental state of the perpetrator. Criminality is greater in males versus females, that is, males are more likely to engage in the use of force and fraud in the pursuit of self-interest. It increases during adolescence and declines with maturation. And, most im-portant, it is associated with individual differences in self-control or impul-siveness. Such individual differences are associated with failures in the social bonds between children and their parents during childhood. Persons with low self-control will exhibit delinquency early in life, will be slow to desist, and will exhibit impulsiveness in a variety of different areas—all relative to those with normal levels of impulse control. They also will be prone to elevated levels of accident and disease. The interaction between crime (opportunity) and criminality (individual differences in impulse control) produces the dif-ferences in career trajectories between criminals and noncriminals.

Does the theory of "criminality" apply to elites? We have no reason to believe that elite murder arises from failures in parental bonding among those who become totalitarian political leaders. However, if the mechanism ("crim-inality") that applies to nonelites is a function of *internal* self-restraint, it may be sufficient in the case of elites that they experience no *external* restraint. Their pursuit of self-interest is not subject to the normal systems that check the pursuit of pleasure and impose pain as a penalty following transgressions. Elite positioning by definition usually makes resort to force and fraud unnec-essary or redundant since access to symbolic and material resources comes with the territory. However, conditions may change where elites come to struggle for power, where elite structures of domination decline, and where different communities struggle for geographic domination. In the absence of such conditions, access to power is access to the means of maximizing pleasure and minimizing pain. In short, power *is* criminality.

This is consistent with the position that Christopher Hitchens outlines in *The Trial of Henry Kissinger.* This book describes how the unelected secretary of state repeatedly acted in a fashion that had landed Japanese generals in the gallows for war crimes they committed during World War II. These acts included the direction of secret bombings in Indochina during the Vietnam War that resulted in an estimated 350,000 civilian casualties in Laos and 600,000 in Cambodia. He colluded in mass murder and assassination in Ban-gladesh in 1971, and he personally suborned and planned the murder of the head of Chile's armed forces, General Rene Schneider, when the latter ap-peared willing to respect the election of Salvador Allende in 1973. The list goes on. "The current state of international human-rights legislation . . . is evolving to the point where people like Kissinger are no longer above the law" (p. 150). The fact that Kissinger will likely never face any criminal indictments emphasizes our point: The power of political elites is "criminogenic" because it puts little or no check or accountability on their actions.

If we focus on self-interest and the use of force and fraud, the idea of criminality becomes redundant in the face of the political context that controls what gets labeled as conduct requiring restraint or prevention. Control theory recognizes that certain systems of regulation check behaviors but do so differentially. The physical system will check sexual excess through disease. Body types will act similarly, with mesomorphs experiencing less resistance to assault compared with ectomorphs. Persons with strong internalized morals or religiosity will be checked by pangs of conscience and identification with (potential) victims compared with people with no moral sense. And the political system, the police, and other institutions privy to the legitimate use of force will constrain people who flout the law. With garden-variety offenders, we say that low self-control will reflect a more powerful appetite for pleasure and indifference to pain, discounting the consequences of behavior through indifference to the future, to guilt, or to both. While recognizing that these *may* be traits found among the elites, our point is that—net of these individual differences—being a member of the elite per se will be "criminogenic." In other words, history suggests that elites are more prone to the satisfaction of desires, the maximization of pleasure, and the minimization of pain simply because their location in the social structure puts them beyond the systems of political restraint.

However, going back to Max Weber, the elites are typically also caught up in political prestige systems. If the practice of politics requires respect of the elites' status and their acknowledgement by others, by their concern for history and how their memory will be honored, this system may provide a check or form of restraint. In other words, if they are to legitimize their political power, this may require that they disavow the naked use of force and fraud to secure their domination. Their self-interest may require the exhibition of self-restraint. Power may be criminogenic, but the purchase of the hearts and minds of those so governed may require the suppression of this equation of power with naked self-interest. This assumes, however, that the misconduct of elites is exposed by rivals, the press, or the international community, conditions that are obviated by a combination of secrecy, control of the press, and military dominance.

THE UNCHECKED ATTRACTIONS OF GENOCIDE AMONG THE GRASS ROOTS KILLERS

If there is merit in this concept of elites as actors whose pursuit of self-interest is unchecked by external forces, there is a similar lesson in the confrontation of unarmed, disorganized civilians by an organized, armed bureaucracy. We propose to extend the concept of the "unrestrained actor" from the elites to those acting under delegated authority in the institutions historically charged with the legitimate use of force—the police and army, that is, the organs of state security. Murders, in the accounts reported by Browning and Goldhagen, sometimes take on a gamelike quality for the perpetrators. Many of the reports suggest that the men, while following orders, often appeared to take a certain amount of pleasure in their crimes against civilians.

For example, when Police Battalion 11 arrived to dispose of the Jews of Slutsk on October 27, 1941, the shootings began immediately. Jews and White Russians were dragged from homes and places of work, pulled off their wagons, and shot on the spot. The German civil administrator tried to force the policemen out of the workshops with drawn revolvers because he wanted the action to be delayed and properly organized with regard to the economic survival of the town. What occurred was a bloodbath that "bordered on sadism" as bodies piled up on the street. "The police battalion plundered in an outrageous way . . . They took with them anything useful . . . watches were torn from the arms of Jews publicly in the streets, rings were pulled off fingers in the most brutal way".[10] Goldhagen (p. 188) describes the arrival of Police Battalion 309 into Bialystok in June 1941. The unit was barely into the city when the men swarmed out and "without any sensible case, shot up the entire city . . . They shot blindly . . . without regard to whether they hit anyone." They herded Jews into a synagogue, locked the doors, and set the building on fire, shooting at anyone who tried to escape. One of the policeman said: "Let it burn. It's a nice little fire, it's great fun" (p. 190). Seven hundred people were burned to death. When two Jews pleaded with a general for protection, he unzipped his pants and urinated on them (p. 189). The killing had a carnival atmosphere. Both Browning and Goldhagen document the "Jew hunts" in which companies of the Order Police recruited police volunteers to comb the woods for those who had run for safety and who were, effectively, hunted down and shot for sport.

One is reminded of Erasmus's characterization of war per se: "Consider [war's] instruments, I pray you: murderers, profligates devoted to gambling and rape, and the vilest sort of mercenary soldier . . . Think next of all the crimes that are committed with war as a pretext, while good laws 'fall silent amid the clash of arms'—all the instances of sack and sacriledge, rape and other shameful acts."[11] Erasmus may have been thinking of the Thirty Years' War in which armies "fighting in the name of religion, routinely targeted civilians of the opposite religion for pillage, torture, and death" (p. 121). Or the armies of the Albigensian Crusade described by Ruthven: "infantry consisting mainly of routiers or mercenaries drawn from the toughest criminal elements and lured, no doubt, by the prospect of an unlimited orgy of looting, murder and rape at God's expense."[12] But such excesses by armies using force under delegated authority are not limited to antiquity. This sort of behavior was documented at length in Iris Chang's *Rape of Nanking*.

When Japanese Imperial forces entered the city of Nanking on December 11, 1937, there followed six weeks of orgiastic slaughter. Some 300,000 civilians were murdered. Men of military age were removed by truck to the banks of the Yangtze River and mowed down with machine guns. An estimated 80,000 women were raped by the young Japanese recruits. Civilians were buried alive, set on fire with gas, and run over with tanks. Thousands of Chinese men were ritually beheaded by soldiers eager to blood their swords. Often the heads were displayed with a cigarette stuck in the lips as a joke. Thousands of men were tied to trees for "bayonet" practice and stabbed to death. The photographs show the Japanese soldiers standing in groups in the background beaming with delight at all this sport. Two Japanese sublieutenants competed with one another to determine which would first reach the mark of 100 beheadings. All these activities were captured on film by European and American missionaries, but in the absence of the Chinese army and the desertion of the civil administration, the murders went unchecked. There was no national program of propaganda in Japan to mark the Chinese as a racial threat.

There was a military tradition that held that defeated warriors had forfeited their basic human rights, but the Rape of Nanking was primarily directed against the civilian population. The crimes against civilians would not have occurred had the army's officer corps enforced discipline. Indeed, General Iwane gave explicit orders that the entry of the army into the walled city was to be "absolutely free of plunder" (p. 39). However, Iwane fell ill with chronic tuberculosis and on December 7 was replaced by Prince Asaka Yushiko, Emperor Hirohito's uncle. Almost immediately after he took command, the troops received the order to "kill all captives." The troops were effectively given license not only to murder any surrendering army units, but also to terrorize the civilian population. It was useful to the military commanders to create a terrifying reputation to guarantee capitulation to the Imperial Army—not only in Nanking but in all subsequent armed confrontations. So here we have a convergence of criminogenic forces—unchecked elites securing dominance through military victory and ordinary soldiers given a license to rape and pillage and "to live off the land."

IS DETERRENCE POSSIBLE?

The final book opens up the question of whether the legal response to criminal behavior associated with war provides a credible check on crimes associated with war. Gary Jonathan Bass examines the record of the postwar crime tribunals in *Stay the Hand of Vengeance: The Politics of War Crimes Tribunals*. He examines the disposition of Napoleon after his defeat at Waterloo in 1815, the Leipzig trials of submarine commanders for sinking civilian ships during the Great War, the Constantinople trials of leading Ottoman figures for their role in the murder of some one million Armenians in 1915, the Nuremburg trials and, finally, the U.N. International Criminal Tribunal for the former Yugoslavia (ICTY). Bass provides a compelling analysis of the tensions between a "realistic" approach to the treatment of defeated enemies and the possibility of an ideal "legalistic" approach. After World War II the political leaders of England and Russia would have been satisfied with a summary court-martial followed by swift execution for the Nazi and Japanese leadership. The United States succeeded in persuading the Allies that a trial of the major Nazi political and military elite would better serve international interests than summary justice. In his overview of the previous war trials the record suggests they were dismal failures marked by a lack of international cooperation and a process that bogged down in the political interests of the states charged with dealing with former leaders (especially at Leipzig and Constantinople).

The Nuremburg case came closest in the historical cases to meet the norms of legality that are required for the creation of a just peace, even if the process was condemned by some as "victor's justice." Indeed, Bass quotes Allied military leaders who averred that had the Axis powers won the war, many of them would have found themselves charged with war crimes. However, the idea that such trials would have been open with an independent judiciary and a strong burden of proof is highly improbable; such proceedings would have been rather novel for regimes that did not possess an independent judicial culture. As for the ICTY, Bass's account predated the apprehension of Slobodan Milosovic, and the outcome of that trial has yet to be seen. Bass is not unrealistic in the potential for the legalistic disposal of war criminals, recognizing that their conviction is not a foregone conclusion, that penalties may not meet the aspirations of the victims, and that most of the "ordinary" killers in fact never are called to give an account. However, trials along the lines of those in Nuremburg are the only morally justified option. While they may not deal with the rank and file required in genocide, they do bring accountability to those in the line of authority who are in turn capable of curbing genocidal murder, rape, and pillage at the grass roots.

NOTES

1. William L. Shirer, *The Rise and Fall of the Third Reich*, 30th anniversary ed. (New York: 1990), 1254.

2. Frank Chalk and Kurt Jonnasohn, *The History and Sociology of Genocide: Analyses and Case Studies* (New Haven: 1990), 44.

3. Ibid., 23.

4. See also his *Terrorism, Legitimacy, and Power* (Middleton, Conn., 1983).

5. Michael Gottfredson and Travis Hirschi, *A General Theory of Crime* (Stanford, Calif., 1990).

6. Ibid., 1.

7. Christina Larner, "The Witch-Hunt in Scotland," in *History and Sociology of Genocide*, Chalk and Jonassohn, 153–168.

8. Malise Ruthven, "The Albigensian Crusades," in *History and Sociology of Genocide*, Chalk and Jonassohn, 121–38.

9. Robert Melson, "Provocation or Nationalism: A Critical Inquiry into the Armenian Genocide of 1915," in *History and Sociology of Genocide*, Chalk and Jonassohn, 266–89.

10. Christopher Browning, *Ordinary Men: Reserve Police Battalion 101 and the Final Solution in Poland, New Afterword* (New York: 1998), 23.

11. Cited in James Turner Johnson, *Morality and Contemporary Warfare* (New Haven: 1999), 121.

12. Ruthven, "Albigensian Crusades," 126.

Book Reviews

Julius R. Ruff, *Violence in Early Modern Europe 1500–1800*. Cambridge: Cambridge University Press, 2001. ix + 269 pp., notes, index. $55.00 hb, $20.00 pb.

In the year following the events of September 11, 2001, journalists and sociologists alike have banded together to refocus the social lens and turn our gaze inward, magnifying the violence and savagery that suddenly seems endemic to our modern society. If the terrorism inflicted on the city of New York was perpetrated by fanatical anti-American radicals, by highlighting accounts of school-room hijackings, gun-toting patriots, unrepentant biting boxer-rapists, and depressed (and oppressed) mothers who seek salvation in the drowning of their children, American journalists have drawn attention to the fact that violence is by no means a foreign problem.

To this debate, Julius R. Ruff's latest contribution to Cambridge's New Approaches to European History textbook series offers a greatly needed breath of fresh air. Ruff reminds us that because journalists and sociologists are interested only in the events of the moment, they offer a skewed vision of society. A more *longue-durée* perspective does, in fact, demonstrate that "[o]urs are not, at least yet, the most violent of times" (p. 2). Moreover, by seeking out levels of violence in Europe's past, Ruff boldly implies there is hope for the future. If the eighteenth century was capable of diminishing its levels of violence through a conscious internalization of restraints, then so, too, might modern Americans.

As is Ruff's intention, undergraduate students should be overwhelmed by his depiction of the early modern era. Far from the gentility sometimes associated with the age of Shakespeare, the sixteenth and seventeenth centuries, as described by Ruff, were a time of ubiquitous violence. In his extraordinarily broad scope, Ruff examines daily violence in a wide variety of forms: military violence (violence inflicted on civilians by employed/discharged soldiers living in their midst), institutionalized violence (torture, execution, state arms control, policing), violence associated with extralegal dispute resolution (duels, feuds, arbitration, self-help), interpersonal violence (assault, homicide, domestic violence, rape, infanticide), group violence (the rituals of youth gangs, carnival, sports), popular protest (enclosure riots, food and tax riots), and organized crime (banditry and highwaymen). Perhaps most important, Ruff does not restrict his study to actual instances of violence; he also investigates social fears and repressions about violence, noting that "[o]ften . . . perceptions do not accurately reflect reality" (p. 9). His conclusion, that "violence was never far from the consciousness of early modern Europeans" (p. 9), suggests that early modern men and women suffered many of the same anxieties as do we today.

Nevertheless, the sixteenth century represents merely the apex of an acceleration in violence that was unsustainable. Distressed by sensationalist literature boasting graphic representations of murder and mayhem, the European aristocracy ultimately began to reform its behavior in what Norbert Elias has termed "a civilizing process."[1] Without noble support, many traditional forms of social violence inevitably fizzled out. Ruff asks important questions: Who raised the prize cock-fighters? Who imported bears for bear-baiting? (p. 179).[2] At the same time, growth in the state's control of violence through policing (particularly in France and Spain), weapons licensing, and a tighter rein on the state's military had a profound effect on communities, limiting opportunities for violence. The state's reform was complete with the withdrawal of support from torture as a means of gathering evidence and the development of a new penology, providing alternative punishments to execution. Ruff is very cautious to note, however, that these dramatic changes were not the actions of a monolithic, tyrannical state. Rather, the early modern state was too weak to impose these kinds of changes without the support of the general populace. Finally, with the decay of a popular culture grounded in violence and new expectations of social comportment enforced by the state's judicial system, both group violence and interpersonal violence receded into the background.

Ruff's book holds immense appeal for an undergraduate audience. Its gripping subject material aside, Ruff has made every effort to immerse his reader in the early modern era through a prolific and effective use of primary sources, using everything from proverbs, Punch and Judy, broadsheets, and bawdy ballads to the artwork of Hogarth. Students attempting to sympathize with early modern fears of pandemic violence can have no better image than Samuel Pepys lying in bed late at night, paralyzed with fear, perspiring until he "melted almost to water," imagining the worst of noises outside his home that turned out to be only a dog looking for a warm bed (pp. 40–41). Ruff also addresses aspects of social violence that might resonate with the lifestyles of his readers. For example, Ruff's analysis of early modern sporting events, including the tale of a particularly dedicated football player who carried the ball through the sewers of a town to win the game (p. 169), should attract a much broader readership than the typical texts used in courses about the early modern era.

Violence in Early Modern Europe 1500–1800 is not just a textbook, however. Ruff is the first historian to survey the extensive historiography of violence across Europe's vast geography and compile a comparative analysis of the manifold changes in violent behavior in this period in one single volume. In doing so, not only does he draw on the works of the best-known historians (such as Elias, Burke, Foucault, Muchembled, Stone, Le Roy Ladurie), but he also acquaints the readers with some of the more recent contributors to the debate on early modern violence (such as Joy Wiltenburg, Elaine Reynolds, Ulinka Rublack, Arne Jansson). The result is a remarkably thoughtful and insightful analysis emphasizing the similarities between national forms of violence (without dismissing the differences) and accordingly offering a much more meaningful hypothesis of why levels of violence seem to have diminished across Europe at roughly the same time. And yet, the book's strength in this respect highlights its weakness. His exposition of the eighteenth-century descent into civility is so well done that one cannot help but wonder why he is not equally interested in tracing the origins of some of these trends in violence to the period before 1500. For example, chapter 1 ("Representations of Violence") examines exaggerated fears about violence that do not appear to reflect actual rates of violence; as far back as 1979, Richard Kaeuper made the same observation about fourteenth-century England.[3] Kaeuper's comments clearly suggest that an established print culture was not, as Ruff seems to imply, a necessary instigator of widespread fears of violence. Similarly, in chapter 2 ("States, Arms, and Armies") Ruff laments that aristocrats were the greatest rivals to a state monopoly of violence and arms. If he had been willing to extend his focus back in time, John G. Bellamy's *Bastard Feudalism and the Law* might have provided valuable insight into both the rise of this predicament in the English setting and its resolution.[4] By choosing an arbitrary moment to begin his study, set only to make the text more appealing to early modern courses, Ruff is able to offer a much less comprehensive perspective of the roots of social violence.

In chapter 1 Ruff accuses early modern publishers of broadsheets and pamphlets of capitalizing on violent acts to sell their works, presenting a distorted image of the real nature of offenses (while most broadsheets focused on ghastly cases of homicide, in reality theft was far more common). And yet, at times, Ruff seems to have adopted a similar editorial approach: the more graphic, the better. For example, in chapter 3 ("Justice") Ruff examines a number of cases of feuds and personal vendettas. One case in particular stands out:

The Zambarlini [family] dismembered corpses, leaving them unburied, to be consumed by dogs or pigs, and such denial of the rites of Christian burial precluded eternal salvation. Making 'dogmeat' of victims was part of vendetta ritual in this region, and one of the leaders of the Zambarlini, Antonio Savorgnan, slain with a massive head wound by his victims' relatives six months later, was similarly left to have his brains consumed by a large dog. (82–83)

The Zambarlini certainly demonstrate the extreme nature of vendettas in the Renaissance Italian setting, but one wonders if such a graphic description (which will undoubtedly appeal to undergraduate fans of *The Godfather* and *Pulp Fiction*) was really necessary. Similarly, this same chapter has a lengthy discussion of torture and punishment on the continent. A discussion of the rise of the jury and its role in regulating violence in the English context, a much less exciting topic, is noticeably absent and will be missed by professors of English history.[5]

Given the broad scope of the book, however, omissions of this nature, while regrettable, are relatively minor oversights and do not detract from the eminently well-balanced material and fluid writing. Ruff's book has something for everyone: from gender, politics, and sports to animal rights. Professors teaching courses on the early modern era would be wise to consider such an appealing and instructive book.

Sara M. Butler
St. Mary's University, Halifax

NOTES

1. Norbert Elias, *The Civilizing Process*, trans. Edmund Jephcott, 2 vols. (New York, 1978, 1982).

2. Here, Ruff adopts the approach of Peter Burke suggesting that social élites withdrew from popular culture. See Peter Burke, *Popular Culture in Early Modern Europe* (New York, 1978).

3. Richard W. Kaeuper, "Law and Order in Fourteenth-Century England: The Evidence of Special Commissions of Oyer and Terminer," *Speculum* 54:4 (1979): 734–84.

4. John G. Bellamy, *Bastard Feudalism and the Law* (Portland, 1989).

5. For example, see Thomas Andrew Green, *Verdict According to Conscience: Perspectives on the English Criminal Trial Jury 1200–1800* (Chicago, 1985).

J. M. Beattie, *Policing and Punishment in London, 1660–1750: Urban Crime and the Limits of Terror*. New York: Oxford University Press, 2001. 491 pp., charts, notes, index. $74.00 hb., $35.00 pb.

Policing and Punishment in London brings to light the myriad elements of the modern criminal justice system already present in late-seventeenth, early eighteenth-century England. As Beattie explains in his preface, this book emerged from patterns he had noted while researching and writing *Crime and the Courts in England*. The author illustrates the key role of the City of London as a driving force in shaping significant changes in the policing and punishment of property crime during this early period. By closely examining London between 1660 and 1750, the author reveals the existence of certain elements of the modern criminal justice system, such as an increase in public funding for the policing, prosecution, and detection of crime; the growing involvement of solicitors; and a shift to more modern forms of punishment.

From the Restoration to the mid-eighteenth century, Beattie argues, there was a burgeoning population of shopkeepers, merchants, and businessmen in the City of London with a vested interest in maintaining order and reducing the amount of property crime. Their anxieties about the growth of crime and immorality put pressure on authorities to implement a new system of street lighting paid from public funds—a dramatic shift from the previous system in which private citizens were expected to place a light outside their homes at specified times. City dwellers also increasingly preferred to pay substitutes, rather than serving out their year-long unpaid appointment as constables, creating a group of full-time salaried constables. At the same time, with the advent of a new Whig government willing to use the public purse to combat crime, there were increased incentives for prosecution and detection, with unprecedented reward money. Along with creating a prominent group of career thief-takers, these rewards also motivated the victims of theft to engage solicitors. Defendants eventually gained permission to involve lawyers as well, though the author is unable to explain exactly how or why this came about.

Beattie also shows that modern forms of punishment were emerging during this period. While Michael Ignatieff traced the origins of the modern penal system from 1750, Beattie shows that criminal punishment already was retreating from the public eye well before that date. He describes the decline of hanging, branding, and public whipping in the City in the early eighteenth century. However, while the modern move toward punishing the soul over the body stemmed from modern ideals of order and civility, the early eighteenth-century movement away from corporal punishment was driven by much more pragmatic considerations. Constantly testing which forms of punishment would have the most deterrent properties, City officials even went from branding thieves on the thumb to the cheek, but discovered that cheek brands made it impossible for convicts to find honest work and turned them into career criminals. Public whipping, the author argues, probably was abandoned initially because it drew disorderly crowds and disrupted trade for the London shopkeepers, whose opinion mattered so much in the administration of criminal justice.

Indeed, Beattie stresses that very little, if any, of the reforms of policing, prosecution, and punishment under the criminal law were consciously modernizing or idealistic. He presents an image of each change as a more or less isolated response to an immediate problem. According to Beattie these changes were highly experimental and often adjusted when the experiment went wrong. Nevertheless, the roots of the modern system of criminal justice were laid during this period, and the movement was driven largely by the actions and interests of the City of London.

Policing and Punishment is a superb reference source for administrative history. Beattie lays out the unique court system of the City with the meticulous detail that characterizes all of his work. He places the Old Bailey firmly within the metropolitan legal system and outlines its distinctness from the country as a whole. He explains the functions of all of the various officials that administered the law in the City between 1660 and 1750, from watchmen to the recorder of London. As a reference manual for these elements of local government, *Policing and Punishment* serves as a much-needed supplement to Sydney and Beatrice Webb's *English Local Government*. Unlike the Webbs, Beattie does not present a bleak image of an urban administration riddled with corruption. While he recognizes venality as a problem, he represents it as only a small element of a legal system genuinely concerned with reducing crime.

William Thomson, recorder of London between 1715 and his death in 1739, is presented as one of the most prominent examples of a public-minded official. The author devotes a chapter to Thomson, tracing his active involvement in creating new legislation governing transportation and controlling its implementation at the Old Bailey. As an individual, Thomson single-handedly shaped the way that petty thieves were treated in the early eighteenth century. Beattie stresses the importance of Thomson's personal enthusiasm and idealism. Thomson was not dissuaded from transporting individuals even when their dependents may be a burden on the poor rates. Rather than glorifying Thomson, however, the author uses him to illustrate the strong reform efforts that could exist in the period before the Fieldings, and the tremendous influence that the recorder of London could have from the Old Bailey Bench to the King's cabinet meeting.

Because *Policing and Punishment* is so strong as an administrative history, it is somewhat weaker as a social history. Although Beattie wishes to show that wider anxieties about a growth in crime and immorality shaped the development of policing and punishment in the first half of the eighteenth century, those who voiced such anxieties remain very much in the background. The active role of Londoners as prosecutors and petitioners in shaping the changes the author describes is largely lost—we rarely hear their names or even the words of their complaints or anxieties. Nevertheless, this is due largely to the dearth of such sources, and Beattie has been able to offer some very interesting insights on seemingly dry administrative occurrences—such as his theory on the "social snobbery" behind the exclusion of metropolitan magistrates from the Old Bailey. *Policing and Punishment* proposes that the City's mayor, aldermen, sheriff, and recorder—and their wives—did not wish to have Middlesex or Westminster magistrates added to the commissions of jail delivery because the City officials' wives did not wish to associate with the metropolitan justices' wives in the galleries reserved for them during the sessions.

Wherever possible, the author has supported his conclusions with quantitative data. He includes 30 tables and 2 graphs, based on sources ranging from the Old Bailey Sessions Minute Books to parliamentary legislation. Many of the graphs are based on a one-third sample from the former, where he has taken the records of property offenses from the City for every third session of the court, thus including a complete cycle of the sessions every three years. Beattie provides very convincing figures on the increasing use of substitute constables and the growing selectivity of judges in issuing hanging sentences during the period. He uses tables for small-scale analyses as well. His tables on the lord mayors' magisterial activities, for example, offer a comprehensive summary of the contents of the Lord Mayors' Charge Books. They will be invaluable for historians interested in assault and morality offenses, as well as property crime, who need only a quick digest of this source. The book's extensive quantitative material is clearly laid out and firmly buttresses Beattie's conclusions.

Policing and Punishment brings the City and its criminal law courts to life and reveals the years between 1660 and 1750 to be a very significant period in the history of modern London.

Jennine Hurl-Eamon
Carleton University

Peter Oliver, *"Terror to Evil-Doers": Prisons and Punishments in Nineteenth-Century Ontario*. Toronto: Osgoode Society/University of Toronto Press, 1998. xxvi + 575 pp., illustrations, bibliography, notes, index. Can$47.

Ontario, Canada's largest and wealthiest province, set the standards for criminal justice policy and institutions. The Auburn-styled Kingston Penitentiary opened in 1835. Yet as this detailed study indicates, prisoners in nineteenth-century Ontario were very much "out of sight, out of mind." County jails, which always housed the bulk of individuals in custody, remained cramped, dingy, and neglected into the 1960s and beyond.[1]

Peter Oliver examines imprisonment and punishment principally from the point of view of judges, magistrates, prison officials, politicians, and a small number of late-Victorian prison reformers. He leaves to others detailed examinations of crime in general and of juveniles. His thesis is that changes in the justice system, such as the penitentiary, "were made primarily in response to elitist views and influenced only indirectly by economic change and class tensions."

The author subjects his evidence to a nuanced, balanced analysis. Ontario, he argues, did not experience moral panics over crime in the nineteenth century, possibly because as late as 1891 it was 65 percent rural. Yet the prevailing attitude toward those in the clutches of the law was punitive, and many suffered in local jails, from both poor physical conditions and loss of livelihood.

The discussion of punishment in early Upper Canada makes the interesting observation that offenders before the quarter sessions were not stigmatized as "criminals" but viewed as individuals. Criminality had yet to become associated with class. The pillory and stocks, abolished by statute in 1841, along with whipping were little used. Half of the 115 felons sentenced to death from 1800 to 1869 were executed.

The birth of the penitentiary must be understood in relation to criminal law reform and attempts to improve a growing jail system. The latter, because of political and financial neglect, suffered despite periodic attempts at improvement. Elite Tories such as Chief Justice John Robinson had limited expectations of individual reform, but they valued criminal justice as a cornerstone of the political and social order and supported an expanded role for the state within the framework of the rule of law. Crime, for the Tory elite, was not a threat so much as a constant that could be countered with deterrence and institutions such as the penitentiary. Tories, we are reminded, "were never utopians." This contrasted with radical reformers such as Charles Duncombe, implicated in Upper Canada's Rebellion, who believed that society should prevent crime by rescuing and saving the poor.

Kingston Penitentiary, modeled on the less coercive and less costly Auburn system, was not an isolated reform but part of a larger package. Again "social malaise" or fear of crime, according to Oliver, was not a major factor. Unlike local jails, the penitentiary was characterized by isolation, strict rules, harsh labor, and the lash. Rehabilitation was never taken seriously as convicts, unlike short-term jail guests, soon became regarded as pariahs and their home a school of crime.

Until 1851 the warden worked under the legal authority of unpaid amateur inspectors. Although there were no escapes, discipline in a congregate institution with a rule of silence was a problem. One convict received roughly twelve hundred lashes in the space of seven years, and boys between 8 and 12 years old were lashed, placed in the torturous "box" or the dark room, or placed on bread and water. The 1849 commission that investigated abuses simplistically heaped blame on Warden Henry Smith who, ironically, for years had pointed out many of the external and internal constraints that impeded a more humanitarian policy. The real villain, Oliver reveals, was "general government debility."

Kingston was hardest on three inmate subcategories: the insane, women, and children. Officials, faced with the cost of inmate care, experimented with prison labor, setting off initial protests from local mechanics. Convict labor was geared more toward cost-recovery than training prisoners for civilian pursuits. Contract labor, always controversial, was ended in the 1880s. Over the years there were minor reforms in the disciplinary system; the most outstanding was the achievement by statute in 1883 of earned remission.

Lost in the shadows of the historiography, the jails were on the front lines of the criminal justice system. Upper Canada's jails (there were 31 by 1859) often housed more debtors than criminals and periodically were condemned by provincial inspectors as "boarding houses." Up to one-third of their inmates were women and children under 16. For provincial prison inspectors, the real criminal class was recidivists, many of them vagrants and prostitutes, who filled these local dungeons. The solution seemed to be district prisons on quasi-penitentiary lines, complete with hard labor. In 1877, the year federal legislation authorized chain gangs for indictable offenders, more than thirteen thousand were committed to Ontario jails. Many were victims in a transition away from agricultural and artisanal employment to urban industrial production.

Municipal bylaws governing morality and public order, and the expansion of urban policing, put pressure on traditional detention facilities. But late-nineteenth-century experiments in specialized facilities for medium-term offenders took place against a backdrop of falling crime rates (based on convictions). Ontario's Central Prison (1874) was not created because of jail overcrowding and, unlike the famous Elmira Reformatory, it was not aimed at first offenders between the ages of 18 and 30. The Central Prison was for intermediate male offenders, a majority of whom from 1874 to 1900 were sentenced for property crimes. Drunks and vagrants composed more than one-fifth of the total number of inmates, most of whom served six months or less.

Oliver argues that, at least for prison officials, problem criminality was categorized in terms of class, not ethnicity, race, or religion, although he does offer one intriguing quotation on an overrepresentation of Blacks and shows that Roman Catholics were more likely than Protestants to end up in custody. It would be interesting to contrast this class-based view with that of other knowledge brokers such as journalists and politicians, particularly in the context of a late Victorian Protestantism that produced "reform" movements such as the Equal Rights Association.

The aim of the Central Prison was not rehabilitation but punishment. Although it had a milder reputation, the Andrew Mercer Reformatory for women (1880) also was based on punishment of a mostly working-class clientele. Mercer did not follow the American model of differential treatment in terms of indeterminate sentences; like the Central Prison it soon filled with recidivists who were guests of Her Majesty for six months or less. Two-thirds of Mercer inmates were morals or public-order offenders, and half of them were illiterate. All the same, the absence of a formal disciplinary code and the evidence of humaneness on the part of Warden Mary Jane O'Reilly and a small number of volunteers indicates, for Oliver, that Mercer was not as harsh as others have suggested.

The final chapter discusses the limited reach of volunteer aftercare organizations in an age when Canadian society held harsh attitudes toward inmates and ex-convicts. The Prisoners Aid Association attracted elite evangelical Protestants but not much public interest. Reform energies were monopolized by the "child saving" movement that produced the provincial Children's Aid Act (1893) and eventually the federal Juvenile Delinquents Act (1908).

In conclusion, the author credits the architects of institutionalization of criminal offenders with only partial success. Deterrence and punishment continually stifled genuine rehabilitation, and the local jails continued to operate on their own logic. Although the dreaded Central Prison closed in 1915, and juvenile probation and limited adult parole began in the 1910s, the "nineteenth-century punitive equation" left a lasting imprint on Ontario.

Punishment in Ontario moved away from shaming and the lash in the early colonial period toward fines and imprisonment. As early critics of the penitentiary had predicted, a custodial sentence, especially to Kingston, the Central Prison, or Mercer Reformatory, became a life-long mark of shame.

The focus of *"Terror to Evil-Doers"* is intellectual, political, and administrative; in a sense the social history of the penitentiary, jail, and reformatory prison is a separate subject. Oliver gives us hints of inmate subculture when he discusses petitions for early release, discipline, the convict barter system, the absence of riot and disorder, and the infrequency of escapes. Sources are admittedly the chief challenge. But perhaps the history of "everyday prison life" in Canada will someday find its historian.

Greg Marquis
Halifax, Nova Scotia

NOTE

1. From 1791 to 1840 Upper Canada was a distinct colony. In 1841 it became half of the United Canadas, which in 1867 joined the Dominion of Canada as the province of Ontario. With Confederation, penitentiaries became a federal responsibility.

Clive Emsley, *Gendarmes and the State in Nineteenth-Century Europe*. Oxford: Oxford University Press, 1999. xii + 288 pp. £57.50, $90.00.

This important new book is one that could only have been given to us by Clive Emsley. Twenty years ago, and largely before the onslaught of major new studies on the early history of modern English policing by David Philips, Robert Storch, and others, Professor Emsley gave us *Policing and Its Context, 1750–1870* (1983), a pioneering effort to delineate the differing paths toward modern policing practices pursued in England and France from the eighteenth century onward. Now he has put scholars further in his debt by this ambitious new survey of one of the most conspicuously neglected features of the history of nineteenth-century European peacekeeping: the emergence throughout most of western Europe of military-style gendarmeries for maintaining law and order in rural hinterlands. Given that the majority of Europeans lived outside urban areas down to (and in many cases, beyond) the outbreak of the First World War, the local gendarmerie was likely to be the most common sort of police force to be encountered by the common people of the continent.

The central narrative of this book is the dissemination of the gendarme model of policing as a legacy of the Napoleonic empire, so Emsley inevitably focuses the bulk of his narrative on developments in France during the tumultuous century that followed the collapse of the Ancien Régime. Established in 1791, the Gendarmerie Nationale essentially followed the model and function of its predecessor, the *maréchaussée*, only the new force's peacekeeping function was now expressed as a manifestation of an impersonal rule of law rather than, as previously, the will of an absolute monarch. In either case, however, provincial authorities and local imperatives often proved difficult to override. The size of the gendarmerie would have to be boosted several times before the disintegration of Napoleon's empire, no mean accomplishment in light of the constant drain on manpower and resources produced by a generation of total warfare. The particular role of the gendarmes in enforcing conscription and pursuing deserters made these armed and uniformed forces particularly unwelcome in many parts of the realm, and Emsley estimates that in 1801 they suffered an average of two assaults per day (p. 71). Yet despite the inevitable tensions and often violent disorders that followed in the wake of war, the gendarmerie commanded sufficient respect to be maintained and repeatedly expanded and reorganized after 1815. Indeed, Emsley emphasizes that, despite the gendarme's associations with political surveillance—which was indeed one of his centrally emphasized roles—as well as the inevitable tensions that arose with his often annoying and intrusive regulatory tasks, the vast bulk of the nineteenth-century gendarme's time was spent in the more prosaic and routine tasks of patrolling country roads and filing reports on usually minor criminal incidents. We should not be misled by the dramatic collapse of several French regimes into believing that the gendarmerie was solely the tool of paranoid and ultimately unstable political orders. Most of its day-to-day work in fact bears a striking resemblance to the sorts of policing practices now well known to historians of the English model.

Equally surprising perhaps was that Napoleon's former enemies subsequently proved so willing to adopt his model of policing. The Hapsburgs did not create their own gendarmerie until after the violence of 1848, but their stubborn resistance to the "French" innovation was the exception rather than the rule. Most major German states had adopted the model even before Waterloo, though many of them preferred to compare their forces with the Italian Carabinieri rather than the example of their old enemy. The Carabinieri seemed a particularly striking success, partly in light of the contrast with the corrupt and extortionate *sbirri* it had replaced, and partly given both its rapid spread as a result of Italian unification and its significant successes in suppressing widespread brigandage in the remoter parts of the new nation. Emsley notes variants in several other nations, too, but again emphasizes that the central theme in most European experiences of the gendarmerie was not the absolutist political policing so feared by continental liberals and reviled by English observers, but rather the widely perceived need to tackle the basic problems of suppressing crime and maintaining the public peace. In this again, Emsley concludes, the purposes and legacy of the gendarmes were not so divergent from those of English police forces as we might be inclined to believe.

All these important arguments are managed within a short space and enlivened with narratives drawn from personal recollections and archival material. Many readers, perhaps especially those familiar with the now extensive literature on English police history, will undoubtedly find that this book does not provide them with as many details of policy and practice as they might wish. But this should not detract from the scale of Professor Emsley's accomplishment. He has drawn together a wide range of foreign-language documentary sources and the findings of many unpublished or untranslated theses and produced a coherent and fluent narrative. His book is an outstanding starting point for a more detailed and sustained comparison of the history of policing throughout Europe as a whole.

Simon Devereaux
University of Queensland, Australia

David Philips, *William Augustus Miles (1796–1851): Crime, Policing and Moral Entrepreneurship in England and Australia*. Melbourne: History Department, Monograph Series #30, University of Melbourne, 2001. 216 pp., index. $22 AUS; electronic copies by RMIT Publishing: informit.com.au.

This book is no. 30 of the University of Melbourne History Monograph series, an outlet for publishing research undertaken by the staff, postgraduate students, and research associates of the University's History Department. It is a biography of a man who contributed significantly to the debate on the nature of policing and the treatment of offenders in England and who ended his career as police commissioner in Sydney.

The early chapters cover Miles's childhood and his father's career, the possible circumstances of the births of both Miles and his father (also called William Miles) and the various theories behind their claims to royal blood, the disgrace of Miles's expulsion from the East India Company's college of Haileybury, and the death of Miles Senior. One cannot help sharing the author's frustration at not being able to discover precisely the nature of the dishonorable or possibly criminal charges that led to Miles's expulsion from Haileybury, nor being able to pinpoint the character flaw that made Miles not entirely acceptable in respectable society.

The middle chapters show the patronage system at work. At a time when there was an increasing number of paid government posts in areas of social policy and reform, Miles was able to use his claims of royal blood to obtain employment. His work for the Select Committee on Gaols, the Constabulary Force Commission, and the Charity Commission was thorough and influential. It is interesting to break through the near anonymity of an early proto–civil servant and become familiar with the man behind the reports. The picture is not very flattering. The substantial extracts of Miles's letters to his patrons the Duke of Richmond, Lord Melbourne, and Lord John Russell illustrate Miles's use and possibly overuse of patronage. The letters also contain in them the reasons he ended up in Australia—from which his letters took six months to reach his weary patrons.

The final chapters cover Miles's time in Sydney. His appointment was not welcomed, and he arrived at a difficult period in the colony's development. Philips illustrates the complexities of a convict colony's attempts to take control of its affairs while being bound to accept appointees from the mother country, but never being given sufficient money to do what was required.

Although Miles appears to have had poor management skills, he did initially have some success in his new post, despite being caught up in the power struggle between the colony's governor, the Legislative Council, and the newly incorporated Sydney City Council. However, he always remained an unpopular figure, suspected of both financial corruption and drunkenness.

In his acknowledgments, Philips admits to becoming "hooked on the mystery of Miles." His enthusiasm for his subject, as well as the detective work necessary to piece together his subject's life, comes over very clearly. The extracts from the letters are interesting and illuminating, but the repetition of facts, statements, and more particularly quotes—some of which are quite substantial—is unnecessary and becomes increasingly irritating. In Philips's own opinion, Miles did not have a successful career. Having written this biography sympathetically, the author is being kinder to Miles than were most of Miles's contemporaries.

Mary Clayton
Institute of Historical Research

Maurice A. Martin, *Urban Policing in Canada: Anatomy of an Aging Craft*. Montreal and Kingston: McGill-Queen's University Press, 1995. xiv + 240pp., notes, bibliography, index. $18.95 hb.

Philip Rawlings, *Policing: A Short History*. Uffculme Cullompton: Willan Publishing, 2002. v + 274 pp., notes, bibliography, index. £17.99/U.S.$27.50 pb, £45.00/U.S.$59.95 hb.

Rob C. Mawby, *Policing Images: Policing, Communication and Legitimacy*. Uffculme, Cullompton: Willan Publishing, 2002. ix + 214 pp., notes, index. £30.00/U.S.$55.00 hb.

Approaching the policing environment as a multifaceted milieu, Maurice A. Martin has selected what he considers important issues facing urban police forces in Canada. His study takes as its common denominator the urban environment, in which he concludes modern policing was born. The book covers seven chapters, ranging from an introduction of themes and topics and conventional views of law, order, and the community, to the roots of policing, the order maintenance functions of the police, and their accountability and competence. He concludes with an epilogue that sets out a unique challenge for police organizations.

Martin argues that the police have failed to keep abreast of urbanization, which he defines as a "shifting mix of attributes." Furthermore, police departments and personnel traditionally have been reactive and monolithic in nature, instead of proactive and preventive in approach to crisis in the urban environment. Martin suggests that police tend to pursue their traditional mission rather than explore the possibilities of transforming it. Indeed, changing ingrained and "deeply rooted subcultural standards" founded on an "experienced-based occupation" is part of the revitalization of police organizations through in-service "professionalisation." As he points out, change must come from within. Martin's recommendations in the epilogue are instructive. This portion of his book provides an engaging, readable conclusion when juxtaposed to the inordinately long, dry, laborious, and seemingly randomly arranged extracts on urban development.

For scholars of policing in Canada and the United States, determining what stimuli exert the most profound influence(s) on the policing environment is a formidable task. The collecting, correlating, quantifying, and qualifying of the evidence, both from primary and secondary sources, and the prioritizing and substantiating conclusions on the relative importance of these variables, are crucial to the process. Martin's apparent reliance on published secondary sources does little to create or contribute to a new or formative body of original knowledge. Disparate themes emerge from the chapters, which in turn reveal the lack of a focused, incisive, analytical methodology throughout the book. Although the epilogue effectively summarizes his thoughts, he fails to provide a convincing discourse to defend his selection of crucial issues. His conclusions, therefore, do not dissect adequately the anatomy of an aging craft.

Philip Rawling's *Policing* is part of the "Policing and Society Series" edited by Les Johnston, Frank Leishman, and Tim Newburn. In the first five chapters of this book, Rawlings condenses twelve hundred years of English legal history (600–1800) into early "police history." That includes a short chronology and historical summary of the systems of private justice and the blood feud, the tithing man, sheriff, keepers and sergeants of the peace, watchmen, the hue and cry, parish constables, and justices of the peace. The evolution of these disparate institutions supports the inevitable growth of a "New Police" establishment. The remaining three chapters offer a brief glimpse into specialized policing duties, the police union, the role of women police officers in England, police and politics, and modern policing, and then concludes with a short summary.

The underlying theory is that laws are an imposed vehicle of social control, and that it was the codification of unwritten Anglo-Saxon customs that provided the impetus for ad hoc law enforcement by local authorities. In that regard English constitutional history supported a fragmented and decentralized enforcement system that thwarted any form of centralized police establishment as being too continental, French, and militaristic, and thus repugnant to English sensibilities. Rawlings concludes, however, that it was the reluctance of English communities and crime victims to engage in policing duties that finally gave rise to a central and institutionalized form of policing. This required "professional experts," and it was the emergence of Robert Peel's London police in 1829 that provided the impetus for the new model of law enforcement. The police on patrol would be visible, and their presence would prevent crime, ensure the security of people and property, preserve public tranquillity, and assist in apprehending and arresting offenders. The community was now to be "subjected to policing" as opposed to the old model of direct participation in policing. He opines that "The idea of policing [w]as a route into the state's involvement in policing"(p. 6). Unremarkably, the momentum of English history gave rise to the new model of policing.

Rawlings's arguments are not dramatic, and scholars familiar with policing history will not be impressed with his hypothesis. Previous interpretations remain unchallenged. Throughout the book, Rawlings's continual use of mid-sentence references badly impedes the narrative flow of his review. There is also an unexpected historical gap between the end of the nineteenth century and World War II (chapters 6 and 7), and insufficient attention is given to the effects of the two world wars and the rise of new police investigative techniques.

English police historiography has been well documented, and the author's bibliography is extensive with a tidy compendium of English policing history. His primary document section, however, is largely devoted to the twentieth century. Finally, Rawlings suggests "one of the main reasons for writing this book was to take a longer view of the question of what it is that the modern police are meant to be doing" (p. 6). Although his "short history" retraces the rise of English policing, it does not address adequately the impact of what the police are meant to be doing today.

If there is one issue with which modern police organizations have been overconcerned, it is their image: how they are perceived by society. In Rob Mawby's *Policing Images*, the way the police systematically construct and communicate that image is fully examined. Moreover, as the publisher suggests, the book is "the first systematic analysis of the way the police in Britain have constructed and projected their own image." In that regard, Mawby's theory is that a positive police image legitimizes police work itself.

There is nothing more ignominious than observing policemen involved in overt violence, whether directed at an individual or groups. Whether the incident is a legitimate crime in progress calling for the police use of justifiable force or a media-contrived event meant to sensationalize police actions, those images can irrevocably destroy the trust society has in them. Consequently, as Mawby argues, "police image work has always existed," and when scrutinized, the police will attempt to influence or control the interpretation of a specific event and situate themselves in a positive light.

Mawby's book is based on his Ph.D. dissertation and is divided into eight chapters that variously discuss and analyze the history of police image work, professionalization, legitimacy, proactive promotion of the police image, and a case study of the South Yorkshire Police that examines their diverse attempts at image creation and control. He theorizes that there is an overt and conscious effort by operational policemen to portray themselves in a positive light, and there are also concerted efforts by image management professionals to place the police organization in a larger, positive light. Mawby concludes that police image work ensures that the police are held accountable for their actions, which also enhances their legitimacy. However, he also concludes that image work might also be deployed as a vehicle to disguise legitimation.

Overall, the book is rather rigid reading and thesis-like in construction and content, laden with numerous midsentence references and acronyms that seriously impede its smooth reading. To his credit, Mawby integrates his research from firsthand encounters with the South Yorkshire Police and argues that the chief constable's annual reports are "obviously promotional" and meant to mask "images of incompetence and deceit projected through television programs such as *Hillsborough*." For the police historian, it provides another interpretation into a previously undocumented aspect of police organizations: managed image control.

Rod Martin
University of Calgary

Ideology, Crime and Criminal Justice: A Symposium in Honour of Sir Leon Rad-zinowicz; edited by Anthony Bottoms and Michael Tonry. Portland and Cullompton, U.K.: Willan Publishing, 2002. xxiii + 184 pp., bibliography, notes, index. $55.00

The six commissioned papers in this collection, delivered at a symposium in 2001, reflect Sir Leon Radzinowicz's commanding presence in the twentieth-century study of the theory and history of criminal justice, the making and implementing of criminal justice policy, and the development of criminology as a program of study in British universities. A celebration of Sir Leon both as a person and as a scholar, this symposium testified to the continued vitality of his ideas and accomplishments. Each contributor in the print version expands on or challenges Radzinowicz's ideas in the light of present practice, theory, and research. All seem to recognize the humaneness that permeated his views on criminal justice. However, several authors thoroughly challenge his notion of progress. I remember as a graduate student rather pompously pronouncing anathema on his "Whiggish" presentation of history: the idea that things in the past were bad, so things in the present must be better, because the best possible choices had been made to institute reform. The first contributor imaginatively allows Sir Leon to change his mind about the smooth upward course of progress.

David Garland, in "Ideology and Crime: a further chapter," invents a final lecture, in Sir Leon's "aphoristic, broad-brush style," to bring Radzinowicz's 1965 Columbia University lectures [the basis for *Ideology and Crime: A Study of Crime in its Social and Historical Contexts* (1966)] up to date. Examining the changes in penal ideology that have occurred since then, Garland argues that the penal-welfare model that encouraged the rehabilitation and societal re-integration of the prisoner, a model supported by Sir Leon, has been replaced by a model that permanently stigmatizes the offender and brings the victim of an offense to the forefront while hardening the walls between the prisoner and society. Garland concludes that Sir Leon would counsel that "there is no . . . Whig story of penal progress. . . . that the practices of the present day should not be regarded as our destiny. . . ." Perhaps the real Sir Leon might agree, given the changes in criminal justice that he had witnessed.

In a rather jargon-laden sociological presentation, Anthony Bottoms in "Morality, Crime, Compliance and Public Policy" celebrates Radzinowicz's belief that there is "a close interrelationship between criminology and public policy." His argument seems to be that criminologists should understand more about societal morality, how it changes, and how that morality informs people's compliance to laws and rules. He then argues that criminologists should be critical moralists, making sure that criminal justice agencies do not use just "technical and managerialist approaches to tackling crime," but recognize that there should be an element of morality both in the treatment of offenders and, he implies, in the prevention of crime.

Seán McConville and Clive Emsley contribute two papers, "Gentlemen convicts, Dynamitard and paramilitaries: the limits of criminal justice," and "The English Police: a unique development," both excellent examples of the sort of historical writing Radzinowicz cherished—clear analysis based on empirical research. McConville's paper examines the treatment of "conscionable offenders" convicted of treasonous or seditious acts, using as examples Irish rebels, and shows how the government treated them as ordinary criminals in prisons, often, as a consequence, increasing public support for those so treated. Emsley's paper continues his brilliant work on the comparative establishment of police forces in Europe, arguing that Radzinowicz's "Whiggish" police history ignored the effectiveness of some ways England policed itself before the formation of organized police forces, and challenging the view that continental police forces were so completely the master tools of absolutism.

The final two papers, "A 'liberal regime within a secure perimeter'?: Dispersal prisons and penal practice in the late twentieth century" by Alison Liebling and "Criminology and penal policy: the vital role of empirical research" by Roger Hood, touch on areas in which Radzinowicz had made enormous contributions—prisons and criminological studies. Each author shows how Sir Leon's original ideas have been changed or neglected. Liebling writes a historical study of dispersal prisons, "dispersing or absorbing the highest security prisoners among the general population of a number of prisons with very secure perimeters." This practice came about in the late sixties following on the recommendations of a committee chaired by Radzinowicz. Liebling traces the failure and reorganization of such dispersal prisons, using, among other evidence, the number of fights and escapes and the power of prisoners over the guards. He concludes that Radzinowicz would approve the new more rigorous regime.

Hood decries the fact that the empirical research carried out by criminologists in academia has had little effect on public policy. He criticizes both academic criminologists for carrying out short-term research projects that do little to advance the knowledge of crime control and prevention and the government for its lack of support of long-term research. Hood seeks "a revitalized and transformed" criminology that would have strong "social influence," opining that without criminology having such a role, "Sir Leon would really turn in his grave."

This collection brings together important scholars whose work would most certainly persuade Radzinowicz that the future of criminal justice history and criminology was in good hands. They do him great honor.

Mary Beth Emmerichs

John Phillip Reid, *Patterns of Vengeance—Crosscultural Homicide in the North American Fur Trade*. Pasadena, Calif.: Ninth Judicial Circuit Historical Society, 1999. 248 pp., bibliography, notes, index. $40.00

Questions of language loomed large in relations between Euro–North American explorers and the diverse indigenous peoples of the New World. The difficulty was not merely that of miscomprehension in the absence of a shared dialect but, even when newcomers and indigenous peoples *were* using the same words and phrases, that use did not always translate into shared meaning. And it is here, at the intersection between language and meaning, that John Phillip Reid builds his argument in *Patterns of Vengeance—Crosscultural Homicide in the North American Fur Trade*. Reid contends that left largely to their own devices, the trappers and mountain men of the transboundary North American West gradually adopted what they understood to be indigenous responses to violence and, specifically, to homicide. Although he acknowledges that this adoption was, for various reasons, flawed, Reid nonetheless contends that in employing indigenous phrasing and a willingness to exact vengeance, the trappers and traders were acting in a principled way that was consistent with their environment. An intriguing and well-presented argument to be sure, but we are left with doubt, not the least of which is rooted in the question of whether behavior informed by misunderstanding of a principle is, nonetheless, principled.

Reid's argument turns on a series of connected points. Using direct anthropological and historical evidence from the indigenous peoples of the Northwest in concert with parallels from other nations across North America, Reid identifies two distinct approaches to homicide. The first was that framed by the dictates of domestic homicide, that being, a homicide in a specific community. An appropriate response was determined by the social structure of that community and who, within the extended family of the deceased, had the right and responsibility of responding to the death. This was a privileged responsibility in that a second homicide answering for the first was not ground for further revenge. That said compensation could be accepted for the initial death as a bar to further bloodshed. But again, the right to accept compensation was privileged.

The second approach was that dictated by an international homicide—that being the death of an individual caused by someone from outside the community. Unlike domestic homicide, there was no privileged right of response and, indeed, exacting vengeance on a manslayer (or his or her family) outside the community carried great risk of igniting a series of mutually deleterious reprisals. Circumstances such as this required a measure of diplomacy in arriving at a solution that answered to the victim's family while avoiding aggravating a potential ally or trade partner.

Although Reid is able to document that the mountain men and trappers witnessed these responses to homicides, there is little question that while recording the varied responses, the non-Natives really did not appreciate the factors shaping what was, and was not, an appropriate response in a given situation. Rather, the accounts suggest that most of the trappers and traders combined domestic and international practice to conclude that all homicides entailed a privileged and, all too often, a disproportionate right of response. In effect, they drew on indigenous practice to rationalize their own use of violence in response to violence.

Reid is at his best here in drawing our attention to the inequities of importing legal notions and the language bearing those notions into a world that subscribed to its own categories of law, order, recompense, and punishment. An early and compelling example is that of "horse stealing"—a notion and phrase assuming Anglo-American norms of private property, the appropriation of that property and indeed, the moral assumptions underpinning the response to such behavior. Pointing out that such language says nothing about how the indigenous peoples perceived horses or the meaning of taking horses, Reid captures a striking example of how foreign legal notions were impressed onto northwestern North America. A similar point related to accusations of "murder"—a charge firmly rooted in Euro–North American conceptions which, in practice, did not conform to the contextual factors framing homicide in the indigenous world. Reid's advice here deserves our attention; we err in applying norms from one society onto another as if a universal truth governed all communities.

Arguably, Reid's footing is less steady when he moves beyond words and action toward possible meanings. The most striking example of his difficulty opens chapter 4, titled "Principled Vengeance." In making the point that narrow anthropological definitions and distinctions can hamper our understanding of law and law ways in the indigenous world and beyond, Reid states that "there is no need to make a fuss over words" (p. 67). For a scholar arguing that we ought not to refer to all homicides as murders and that horse taking is not necessarily horse theft, the dismissal is rather odd. Indeed, Reid's evidence demonstrates that we must "fuss" for the very reason that words uttered from one perspective do not embrace a singular meaning for all parties to an event. This peculiarity points to another difficulty with Reid's argument although, admittedly, it turns on a question of interpretation. Reid argues that in measuring out vengeance and violence in the manner they did, trappers and mountain men were exacting principled vengeance because the policy was informed by what Euro–North Americans *believed* was indigenous practice. The key to such an argument is, as Reid admits, based on a misunderstanding of homicide in the indigenous world. Still, Reid argues the trappers and mountain men acted in a principled way. The claim is difficult to credit: the Euro–North Americans did not appreciate the context, structure, or meaning of the "rules" they allegedly were applying and, when they did apply them, they did so in a manner that often violated the principles at play. But because they thought or, more likely, chose to believe they were acting in a manner corresponding to indigenous practice, Reid claims the practice was principled. In the very least, the argument asserts that two wrongs do make a right.

Still, there is no question that Reid has written an intriguing book that deserves a wide audience. Indeed, for the very reason that his argument most certainly will generate lively discussions, *Principles of Vengeance* could certainly find a place in upper division courses in which students have the opportunity and aptitude to engage intellectually with a work. The writing is crisp, and even if one might not agree always with Reid's conclusions, the argument is interesting and worthy of serious consideration. For anyone whose interests touch on the interaction of diverse peoples and their legal worlds, it can be argued safely that Reid offers valuable insight for any intersection of people, language, and laws.

Jonathan Swainger
University of Northern British Columbia

Index

For general subjects, see Corrections, Courts, Crime, Crimes and offenses, Criminal law, Criminal law—procedure and process, Economics, Government, Human condition, Law, Police and policing, Professions, Religion, Society, Violence, and War.

Abbott, Jack, magistrate, 132
Abishabis, Small Eyes, 78
Acadian Recorder, 10–11, 13, 16
Acheson, T.W., 16
Ada County, Idaho, 69
Africa, Central, Great Lakes region, 196
Akins, Thomas B., 5
Alaska: 131; Highway, xvii, 140, 144–45
Alaska Highway News, 144–45
Alberta, southern, district court of, 114
Albigensian Crusades, 203, 206
Allende, Salvador, 204
Allies, the, 208
Ambrose R., Mrs., 115
America, Central, 200
America, North: xi–xx; fur trade in, 229–31; northern Rockies, 69; Western Frontier of, 53–74
America, South, 200
Anchorage, Alaska, 144
Andrew Mercer Reformatory for Women, 219–20

Angus, Robert, 11
Arco, Idaho, 68
Armenians, 203, 208
Armstrong, Frank, 68
Askamekeseecowiniew, 88
Auburn Penitentiary, New York, xviii, 37
Auschwitz, Poland, 200
Australia: 222–23; Charity Commission, 223; Constabulary Force Commission, 223; governmentality in, xii; Legislative Council, 223; Select Committee on Gaols, 223; violent crime in, xiii

Babchuck, Annie, 136
Babchuck, John, 136
Bach-Zelewski, SS leader, 197
Backhouse, Constance, 124
Bangladesh, 204
Bannock City, Idaho, 57
Barncard, J.Z., 42–43
Bass, Gary Jonathan, 207–8

Battleford, Northwest Territories, 82, 85, 93
Beattie, John M., xv, 215–17
Beck, N.D., prosecutor, 93
Behan, G.P., watch captain, 20
Bellamy, John G., 213
Berry, judge, 90
Bialystok, Russia, 206
Biddle, Bill, 139, 145
Big Bear, Cree band of, 82
Bingham County, Idaho, 68
Binney, Stephen, 15, 16
Blackfoot, Idaho, 67–68
Boise, Idaho: 58; Overland Hotel, 67; territorial prison, 65
Boise City, Idaho, 59, 61
Boise County, grand jury, 59
Boise News, 55–58
Bonaparte, Napoleon, 207, 221
Bosnia, massacres in, xx, 196, 199
Bottoms, Anthony (Tim), xix, 227–28
Brannigan, Augustine, xx
Bright, David, xvi
Bright Eyes, 82–83
Britain (Great): xx, 145; British Army, 134; Parliament, 78; Royal Navy, 4, 20
British Columbia: government, 134; Peace region, 131–54; penitentiary, 144; Provincial Police, 142–43, 146
British Empire, xv
Brockway, Zebulon, xviii, 32, 34, 44
Brown, Richard Maxwell, 53
Browning, Christopher, 196–98, 206
Bunn, governor, 68
Burke, Edmund, 213
Bushnell, Nebraska, 144
Butler, G.D., sergeant, 134
Butler, Sara, xi

Calgary, Alberta: xvi; Bow River, 120; CPR tracks, 118; district court of, 114; Elbow Park, 119; Lowery Gardens, 124; Mewata Park, 119; Nose Creek Hill, 118; Pat Burns meat packing plant, 115; Prince's Island, 120; Prudential Assurance Company, 121; Rideau district, 120; Riley Park, 119; Salvation Army Hostel, 118; sexual assault in, 105–29; Sunnyside, 120; Variety Theatre, 113; Victoria Park, 119, 124; St. George's Island, 120
California, correctional officials in, 41
Calverley, C. Cromptom, 87, 89
Cambodia, 204
Campaign Station, Idaho, 65
Campbell, F.C., 136
Campbell, Sir Colin, 14
Campbell, William, 85
Canada: Department of Indian Affairs, xv; policing in, 224–26; violent crime in, xi–xx
Cariboo district, 144–45
Cariboo Observer, 137
Caribou Lake, Manitoba, 86
Cashman, constable, 91
Cashman, William J., 87
Castonguay, Charles, 137
Cat Lake, Ontario, 82
Cecil Lake, British Columbia, 136
Central Prison, Ontario, 219
Chalk, Frank, 198
Chandler, W.L., 43
Chang, Iris, 207
Chapman, Terry, 105–6, 113–14; 116; 123; 125
Charlebois, Cree indian, 82–83
Chesapeake, United States, Blacks of, 4
Children's Aid Act, 220
Chile, 204
Choi, Kock Wah, 67
Chop, Ah, 61
Chuckachuck, 83–85
City of London, 215–17
Clark, Tommy, 132
Clarke, James Stewart, 19
Clay, L.W., constable, 135
Clayton, Mary, xvi
Coeur d'Alène Weekly Eagle, 55, 58
Coffin, Walt, 67
Cohen, Daniel, xvii
Cold Spring Station, Idaho, 64
Constantinople, trials, 208
Coray, John, 58
Cornwallis, governor, 2

Corrections: Bertillon system, 37; borstals, 139; branding, 215; bridewells (houses of correction), 3–7, 12, 16, 20, 27, 39; capital punishment, xiii–xv, xvii, xix, 55–58, 61–67, 77, 81, 83–85, 87–88, 90, 94–95, 137, 144, 159–94, 212, 215, 217–18, 228; Criminal Evidence Act, 116; fines, 5–6, 8, 12–13, 16–17, 23, 28, 36, 142, 220; hard labor, xiii, xviii, 66, 118, 142, 218–19; indeterminate sentences, 36–39, 44, 51, 219; jails, 4–7, 13, 16, 20–21, 39, 46, 56, 58, 81, 96, 218–20; pardons, 39, 62, 85, 92–93, 96, 160, 176; parole, 32–33, 37, 41–45, 50–51, 168, 179–80, 220; pillory, 218; poorhouses, 5, 20; prisons and prisoners, 11; prisons and prisoners, escapes, xviii, 40, 45, 78, 220; prisons and prisoners, xviii–xix, 8–9, 12, 20, 22, 31–45, 56, 64–65, 67–69, 78, 82–85, 91–92, 96, 132, 138, 144, 180, 183, 186, 217–20; reform of, xii, xviii–xix; reformatories, 28, 31–45, 219–20; rehabilitation, 139, 219–20; rehabilitation, xii, xviii–xix, 172; torture, 206, 212; transportation, 216; whipping, 5, 118, 138, 215–16, 218, 220

Cotter, Garrett, marshall, 21

Courts: appeals, 66, 68, 81, 99, 142; bail, 2; circuit (or assize), 132, 217; coroners inquests, 11, 40, 135, 144–45; court records, xiii, xv, 6, 13, 17–18, 80–82, 107, 119, 121–24, 147, 197, 217; district, 65, 114; fees of, 12–13; military, 7, 142, 160, 190, 208; Old Bailey, 216–17; police, xv, 2–3, 5–7, 15–20, 114; Quarter Sessions, 3, 5–7, 10, 13–14, 17, 218; Supreme Courts, xiv, 5–7, 11–12, 14, 17, 66; territorial, xvii, 53–70, 83, 93. *See also* Professions

Courvoisier, Henry, 131–32

Cree, communities, 95

Cree Indians: xiv; spirit world of 75–103

Crime: and criminal statistics, xii, xiv–xv, xvii, 6, 17–18, 23, 54–55, 67, 78, 107, 109, 117–18, 122, 124, 136, 141; deterrance, xviii–xix, 157–58, 187, 215, 218; deviance, 4, 19, 28, 33, 45, 147; juvenile delinquency, xxiii, 28, 32–33, 39–41, 44, 46, 116, 145, 153, 204, 218, 220; recidivism, xii, xviii, 22, 27–28, 39, 48–49, 219; retribution, xiii, 17, 174, 227, 229–30; social control, xvi, xviii, 31–33, 37, 44–45, 204–5, 218, 225, 228

Crimes and offenses: abduction, 123; abortion, 200; abusive language, 2, 7, 17–18, 39; adultery, 173; against the peace, xiii, xv, 2–5, 7, 10, 16–19, 147, 222; arson, xvii, 45; assassination, 200, 204; assault, xiii, 2, 7, 10, 16–17, 20, 23, 33, 36, 40, 54, 59, 109, 137, 139, 147, 212; assault and battery, 16; bastardy, 7; begging, 17; break and enter, 1; burglary, xvii, 40, 47, 137; counterfeiting, 47; desertion, xvi, 7, 221; drugs (illegal), xiii, 147, 204; forgery, 47, 161, 167, 180; fraud, 35, 137, 201–2; genocide, xx, 195–209; gross indecency, 107; homicide, xiv–xv, xvii, xix–xx, 1, 10–11, 54–70, 75–96, 137, 139, 143–45, 195–209, 211–14, 229–30; indecent assault, 47, 106–8, 113, 116, 118–19, 121; indecent exposure, 106–9, 120; infanticide, 212; libel, 11, 13; xiv–xv, 36, 47, 61, 65, 75, 81, 83–84, 89–90, 138, 144, 198; misdemeanors, 4, 10, 35, 147; nuisances, 3, 16; perjury, 89; poisoning, 177; prostitution, xiii, xvi–xvii, 20, 23, 106, 142, 219; rape, xii, 36, 47, 106–25, 142, 148, 204, 206–7, 211–12; receiving, 7; regicide, 203; rural, xvii–xviii, 53–70, 75–96, 104, 131–48, 218–22; sedition, 228; sexual, xv–xvi, 7, 36, 47, 118, 105–25, 142, 148, 173, 204–7, 211–12, 217; smuggling, 45; sodomy, 118; suicide, xvii–xviii, 40, 45, 61, 87, 94, 138, 140, 159, 185; theft, xvii, 1–2, 7, 11–12, 16–18, 20, 23, 33, 36,

38–39, 47, 54, 131–33, 137–38, 142–43, 145, 204, 213, 215, 217, 221, 230; threats, 2, 7, 78, 108; treason, 203, 228; trespass, 76; urban, xii–xiii, xv–xvii, 1–24, 105–25, 215–17, 224; vagrancy and vagrants, xv, 2, 4–5, 7, 12, 14, 18–20, 23, 28, 35, 219

Criminal law: acquittals, 11, 13, 17, 63, 82, 84, 132, 137, 139, 143; benefit of clergy, 155; confessions, 94, 117; Criminal Code, 107–9, 114, 117; evidence, xv, 11–12, 58, 60–61, 79–81, 84–85, 87–88, 90, 93–94, 96, 105, 113–18, 137; juries and jurors, xvii, 3–4, 9, 12–14, 56, 59–61, 63–64, 80–81, 84, 89–90, 93–94, 102, 137, 143–44, 175, 179; prosecutions, xiii–xv, xvii, 2, 5–6, 17–21, 23, 58–64, 75, 77, 79–90, 105, 112, 115–16, 120, 124, 137, 141–43, 207–8, 215–16; reform of, xx, 13–14, 20–24, 32–45, 216–18; sureties (recognizances), 49–50, 61, 132; warrants, 5, 10–11, 13, 20; 11, 61, 79–80, 82–84, 86–87, 89–90, 93–94, 96, 113–14, 132

Cromartie, John, 78

Crowley, Margaret, 17

Curtis, E.J., governor, 62

Daisy, James, 67

Dawson Creek, British Columbia: 135–37, 139, 142–47; Carlsonia Theatre, 139; military police barracks, 144; St. Joseph's hospital, 139, 145

Delorie, Nora, 138

Delorie, Stella, 138

Delorie, Stephen, farm of, 138

Delorie, Steven, 138

Demean, Albert, 138

Devereaux, Simon, xvi

Dollard, Julia, 17

Donohue, Hugh, 58

Dooley, Pat, 43

Dressy Man, 82–83

Dubinsky, Karen, 105, 108, 110, 113–14, 116, 124–25

Duncan, G.J., inspector, 135

Duncombe, Charles, 218

Dunn, Michael, 61

East India Company, Haileybury College, 223

École Polytechnique, Montreal, Canada, xiv

Economics: agriculture, xiii, 123, 132, 138–40, 147–48, 219; charities (philanthropy), 5, 19–20, 223; corporations, xii, xviii, 32; debt, 14, 132, 219; enclosure, 212; fishing, 76, 86; fur trade, xvii, 78, 86–87, 91, 95, 131–32, 229–30; {the} gold rush, xvii, 134; hunting, 76–78, 86, 92, 94–95, 135; husbandry, 16; industry, 106, 120, 219; markets, 4–5, 12; mining, 64–56, 61, 64, 68–69, 133; oil and gas, 146–48; poor laws, 216; poverty, xii, 4, 8, 13, 19, 23, 86, 123, 139, 173, 218; property, xii–xiii, 2, 8–9, 15, 17, 22, 38, 66, 77, 137, 207, 215, 217, 225, 230; rent, 5, 12, 15; rewards, 68, 215; trade, transportation and communication, xiv, xviii, 16, 86, 106, 120, 131, 143–44, 146, 223; trade unions, 200; unemployment, xii, 118; wages, 10–15, 21, 23; work, 13–14, 21–22, 33–36, 38, 42, 64

Edmonton, Alberta, 83, 94, 132, 133; Fort Edmonton, 95

Elias, Norbert, 201–3, 212–13

Eliza, a Cree, 83–84

Elmira Reformatory, New York, xviii, 32–34, 36, 38, 44–45, 219

Emmerichs, Mary Beth, xix–xx

Emmettsville, Idaho, 68

Emsley, Clive, xvi, xx, 220–22, 228

England: 208, 222–23; policing, 221, 224–26

Entominahoo, 83–84

Erasmus, Desiderius, 206

Europe: 196, 200–3; *Ancien Régime*, 221; Early Modern, violence in, 211–14; *Gendarmerie Nationale*, 221;

Gypsies of, 198–200; *maréchausée*, 221; nineteenth-century, 220–22; policing in, xvi; police forces, 228; post-Roman period, 201; prison reforms, xix; Thirty years' War, 199; violent crime in, xi, xiii

Evans, Charles, 69

Falkland, governor, 15
Fallon, Mary, 17
Fiddler, Adam, 86
Fiddler, Jack, 85–92, 95
Fiddler, Joseph, 85–92, 95
Fiddler, Mrs. Thomas, 89
Fiddler, Robert, 86
Fiddler, Thomas, 87
Fielding, Henry, 216
Fielding, Sir John, 216
Fingard, Judith, 17, 105, 107 124
Fitz Gibbons, Thomas, 58
Flynn, Errol, 145
Foo, Ah, 66
Ford, Henry, 123
Forrester, Thomas, 15
Fort Lapwai, Idaho, 56
Fort Nelson, British Columbia, 131–32, 138
Fort St. John, British Columbia, 132–38, 146–47
Fort Saskatchewan, 83
Fort Severn, Ontario, 78
Foster, W.W., major-general, 143
Foucault, Michel, 31, 36–38, 44, 213
Fowler, magistrate, 116–117
France: 202–3, 212; policing, 221
Franklin, Idaho, 66
Fraser, Donald, watch captain, 20
Friedman, Lawrence, xix
Frog Lake, Northwest Territories, 82
Fulton, E. David, 145

Garland, David, xvii–xx, 38, 41, 133, 147, 227
Gauthier, magistrate, 3
Geeshingoose, 82
German, Joe, 147
Germany: 196–98; Holocaust, 197–200,

202; Nazi State, 196; Nazis, 198–202; Operation Barbarossa, 197; Order Police, 196–97, 206; Police Battalion No. 101, 197–98; Police Battalion No. 11, 206; Police Battalion No. 309, 206

Gillard, Bob, 131
Girard, Philip, 3, 15
Goffman, Erving, 38
Goldhagen, Daniel J., 196–98, 206
Goldman, Mike, 63
Gordon, Ira, 137
Government: xix–xx; attorney-general, 15, 134, 139; bureaucracy, xviii, 23, 197, 201, 203; of Canada, 91; Canadian, Department of Justice, 82; colonial, xiv, xvi, 1, 13, 97, 202, 223; concentration camps, 196; corruption, xvi, 12, 223; Department of Justice, 93; Dominion, 134; education (and schools), xviii, 32–33, 35–37, 47, 93, 109, 120, 203, 211; elections (and voting), 15–16, 22, 202; Fulton Act, 145; Immigration Department, 132; Indian Act, 93; Indian Department, 80–82, 90–91, 93, 134; Justice Department, 82, 91, 93; legislatures and legislation, xii, 4, 9, 16, 22, 33, 39, 41, 44–45, 59, 62, 66–67, 78, 93, 105–25, 131–48, 145–46, 205, 219; licenses, 12, 14, 16, 19–20, 22; local communities, xii–xiii, xv–xvi, 1–24, 41–44, 56–69, 76–96, 105–25, 131–48, 224–26, 229–30; Middlesex Justices Act of 1792, 3; Ministry of Justice, 91; municipal, 1–24, 105–25; patronage, 223; sheriffs, 56–58, 67, 69, 215, 217; taxes, 12–13, 202–3, 212; treaties, 82, 93–95, 134; United Nations, 199–200, 208

Great Slave Lake, 93

Hailey, Idaho: 65–68; jail, 66
Haileybury, college, 223
Halifax, Canada: xv; 1–29; city and police courts, 22; Exchange Coffee House, 11; incorporation bill, 15;

Police Court, 6, 17; Revolutionary
crisis of 1775, 8; Rockhead Farm,
prison, 20, 23; Sessions of the Peace,
3, 5, 9–10, 13–15; Waterloo Tavern,
19
Hall, Johnny, 66
Hamburg, Germany, 196
Hamilton, Canada, 23
Hapsburgs, the, 221–22
Hardwick, Kelly, xx
Harker, Lloyd, 137
Harring, Sidney, xiv
Hart Highway, British Columbia, 146
Healy, Leonard, 139
Hill, P.C., mayor, 21–22
Hillsborough, 226
Himmler, Heinrich, 197
Hinckley, Joel, 66
Hirohito, Emperor, 207
Hitchens, Christopher, 204
Hobbes, Thomas, 201
Hogarth, William, 212
Holmes, Reverend George, 133–34
Hood, Roger, xix, 228
Hoover, Al, 139–40
Horowitz, Irving Louis, 201, 203
Houlton, William, 34, 40
Howe, Joseph, 11–13, 15
Hudson's Bay Company, 78, 85, 91, 95,
131–32
Human condition: cannibalism, 76,
88–91, 94, 160; class, xv, xviii, 1,
16–18, 23, 125, 219; discipline,
41–44; drunkenness, xiii–xvi, 4, 7,
9–10, 12, 16–19, 22–23, 33, 35–36,
47, 61, 64, 67–68, 135, 139, 142–43,
197, 204, 219, 223; family, xv, 9, 37,
68, 76–77, 84–86, 92, 94–95, 112,
115–16, 137–38; gambling, xiii, 1,
10, 206; gender, xiii, 1, 16, 110, 125,
200; insanity, xix, 80–81, 94, 97, 163,
166, 181, 188, 192–93, 198, 219;
morality, xiii, 12, 36, 65, 67, 125,
133, 140, 146, 178, 205, 216, 230;
nudity, 108; population, 2–4, 106,
132–33, 136, 140–41, 201–2, 228;
prejudice, 112; race, xviii, xx, 1,
16–17, 125, 197–99, 219; refugees, 4;

sexuality, 36, 40, 45, 94, 105–25, 148,
198, 200, 205; slavery, 4; spirits, xv,
9, 75–96; temperance, 20–22. *See also*
women under Society
Hurl-Eamon, Jennine, xv
Hutt, Lew, sergeant, 21
Hythe, Alberta, 144

Idaho: Middle Boise River, 55; Moore's
Creek, 55; North Boise River, 55
Idaho City, Idaho: 58, 61; gambling
house, 64
Idaho Territory, xvi, 53–74
Idaho Tri-Weekly Statesman, 62–68
Idaho World, 58–61
Ignatieff, Michael, 215
Indians (Natives): Crane band, 86, 89;
Cree, 94, 133; Denne-za band,
133–34; Ojibwa, xiv, 75–103; Slave
band, 92; Sucker band, 85–88, 90–91
Indochina, 204
Ireland: xx; Charitable Irish Society, 4;
rebels, 228
Island Lake, Ontario, 85–87
Italy: Carabinieri, 222; Renaissance,
214; *sbirri*, 222
Iwane, General, 207

Jamieson, Thomas, constable, 135
Jansson, Arne, 213
Japan: 200, 208; Imperial Army, 207
Jeffrey, Ross, 137, 138
Jenness, Diamond, 76, 77
Johnson, James Turner, 200
Johnson, Mark, 67
Jones, James, 68
Jonnasohn, Kurt, 199
Joyce N., 116
Juvenile Delinquents Act, 220

Kaeuper, Richard, 213
Kamloops, British Columbia, 145
Kate H., 117
Keddell, James, 147, 148
Kelly, Dr. M.A., 57
Kenora, Ontario, 82
Kerr, J.K., lawyer, 81
Ketchum, Idaho, 68

Kier, Morley Reid, 139
Kilkerran, British Columbia, 145
King, James I and VI, 11
Kingston Penitentiary, xviii, 217–20
Kissinger, Henry, 204–5
Klondike, Yukon, gold rush, xvii, 133
Klumpenhouwer, Richard, 114
Knafla, Louis, 105, 114
Knickerbacker, D. H., 42–43
Kosick, Joseph, 142
Kunuksoos, 84

Lake of the Woods, Ontario, 79
Langford, H., prosecutor, 79, 80
Laos, 204
Larner, Christina, 202
Laudry, Josephine, 92, 94
Law: arbitration, 212; customary, xv,
    61, 75–96, 98–99; equity, 4; mercy 3,
    22, 66, 90–91, 93; ordinances, 3, 13,
    16, 18. See also Criminal law; Profes-
    sions; pardons and parole under
    Corrections
Le Roy Ladurie, Emmanuel, 213
LeCapelain, C. K., captain, 143
Lee, William, 34, 35
Lefoin, Michel, 92
Leipzig, trials, 207
Lemkin, Raphael, 198
Lepine, Marc, xiv
Lesser Slave Lake, NWT, 133–34
Lewiston, Idaho, 56
Liddell, John, 11
Liebling, Alison, 228
Lindberg, O.A., 43
Little Slave Lake, Alberta, 83
London, England: xv, 3, 215–17; con-
    stabularies in, 14; Lord Mayors'
    Charge Books, 217; police, 225; St.
    Paul's, 5
Loon Creek, Idaho, 64
Lower Post, British Columbia, 135
Lumsden, William, 143

McBride, judge, 60
McCarty, Denis, 67, 68
McComas, John, 144
McComus, Louise, 144

McConville, Seàn, xix, 228
Machekequonabe, 75, 79–83, 89–90
McKerchar, D.W., lawyer, 87–89
Macleod, Rod, 124
McMartin, Oliver, 131
Macrae, J.A., inspector, 134
Magruder, Lloyd, 55, 56
Malad, Idaho, district court of, 65
Manitoba, Canada, northern, 78, 95
Manitoba, northeastern: 86; Upper Bay
    River, 85
Marie, a Cree, 83
Marquis, Greg, xv–xvi, xviii
Martel, Charles, 92
Martin, Maurice A., xvi, 26
Martin, Rod, xvi
Marx, Karl, 201
Maryland, 4
Massachusetts: xviii; Reformatory,
    33–34
Massey, John T., 144
Matthews, William, 139, 145
Mawby, Rob C., xvi, 224–26
Mayasksaysis, 83
Mayer, George, 64
Meekis, David, 88
Meekis, James, 88
Meekis, Joseph, 88
Meekis, Lucas, 88
Melbourne, Lord, 223
Mellick, Mary Ann, 17
Menewaseum, 88
Mettray Reformatory, 37
Michigan: xviii; reformatory prison,
    33–34
Middlesex, England, 217
Midnapore, Alberta, 108
Mihkooshtikwahnis, 84
Miles, William, senior, 222–23
Miles, William Augustus, xvi, 222–23
Miller, George, 138
Milosovic, Slobodan, 208
Miner, Franklin, 35
Minnesota Reformatory, Red Wing,
    xviii–xix, 31–51
Minnesota State Prison, Stillwater,
    32–34, 39, 41–42
Monkkonen, Eric, xix, 107

Montreal, Canada: constabularies in, 14; École Polytechnique, 200; World Trade Organization, xiv
Mooney, Michael, 66
Moostoos, 83–85, 93
Morning Chronicle, 22
Morning Post, 10, 14
Morning Sun, 20
Morris, Aaron, 68
Mount Idaho, Idaho, 67
Mowat, Oliver, 81
Muchembled, Robert, 213
Mueller, Chris, 138
Murdoch, Beamish, 10
Murray, George, MP, 145
Murray, Margaret, "Ma," 144, 147
Muskwa, British Columbia, 135
Myers, D.E., superintendent, 34–35, 37

Nanking, Rape of, xx, 207
Napaysoosee, 83–85
Napoleonic Empire, xvi, 221
Narrows Lake, Ontario, 86, 91
Natives. *See* Indians
Natland, Nels, 131
Nelson, George, 77
Netsena, 131–32
New England, towns in, xvii
New York, 3, 6; 11 September 2001, 211
New Zealand: governmentality in, xii; violent crime in, xiii
Newton, Guy Bradley, 143, 144
North America, British, 1
North-West Mounted Police, 114, 134–35
Northwest Rebellion, 85
Northwest Territories, 87, 92
Northwest Uprising, 82
Norway House, Manitoba, 85–87, 91
Nova Scotia, Canada: xiii, xv, 1–29; Dartmouth, 10; Hammond's Plains, 10; House of Assembly, 8; Society of Tradesmen, 13; Spryfield, 10
Nova Scotian, 9–10, 15–16
Noyce, Bill, 65
Nurenburg, trials, 208

Oakalla prison, British Columbia, 144
O'Callahan, Dr. E.J., 67
O'Connor, T.J., counsel, 113, 115
Ohio State University Press, xix
Ojibwa: xiv; communities, 95; Crane band, 86; Crane band, 89; Saulteaux, Sucker clan, 85–88; spirit world of, 75–103
Old Bailey Sessions Minute Books, 217
Oliver, Peter, xviii, 217–20
Ondler, O.R., 43
O'Neil, constable, 86
Ontario, Canada: xiii–xiv, xviii; Legislature, xiv; nineteenth-century, 217–20; rape in, 116; sexual assault in, 108
O'Reilly, Mary Jane, warden, 220
Ottoman Empire, 203, 208

Pacific Great Eastern Railway, 146
Panopticon Prison, England, 37
Parry Sound Reserve, Ontario, 76
Parsons, T.W.S., commissioner, 142
Parton, John, 17
Patterson, Ferdinand, 60, 61
Paupanakiss, Reverend Paul, 89–90
Payoo, 83–85
Peace Region, Canada, xvii
Peace River Block News, 131–32, 136–40
Peel, Robert, 225
Pelletier, inspector, 91
Pennsylvania: xviii; Industrial Reformatory, 33–34
Pepys, Samuel, 212
Perry, Aylesworth Bowen, commissioner, 87, 89–91
Pesequan (Norman Rae), 87
Peskawakeequic, 80
Philadelphia, Pennsylvania, 2, 6, 23
Philips, David, xvi, 221–23
Phillips, Jim, xix, 19
Phyllis F., 123
Picket, James, 64
Pierce City, Idaho, 64
Pierson, George, 66
Pinkham, Sumner, 60

Pisciotta, Alexander, xviii
Placerville, Idaho, 58
Pocatello, Idaho, 68
Poland, 196
Police and policing: xi, xiv–xvi, xx,
  2–24, 43, 91, 113, 118–22, 124,
  134–37, 140–42, 196–98, 203, 205–6,
  212, 215–17, 219, 221–26, 228; British Columbia Provincial Police, 135;
  Canadian NWMP/RCMP, 85–87,
  91–92, 94–96, 101, 124, 132, 134,
  143–43, 146–47; *carabinieri*, 222;
  gendarmes, xvi–xvii, xx, 220–22;
  maréchaussée, 221; military, 142–43;
  sbirri, 222; stipendiary magistrates,
  87, 94, 132; thief-takers, 215; watchmen, 6, 8–9, 18–21, 23, 225. *See also*
  sheriffs under Government
Pomeroy, A.J., constable, 137
Port Arthur, Ontario, 80
Portland, Oregon, 56
Potter, Bryon Bruce, 144
Pouce Coupé, British Columbia, 132,
  135–36, 144
Pratt, John, xii
Prince George, British Columbia,
  131–32, 139, 144
Prisoners Aid Association, 220
Professions: anthropology, 75, 230;
  constables, *see* Police and policing;
  criminology, xx, 51, 196, 199, 201,
  205, 211, 227–28; doctors, 8, 83–84,
  89, 100, 115, 117, 135; journalists
  and the press, xiii–xiv, xvii, 5, 10, 12,
  20, 53–70, 108, 132, 136–38, 144,
  146, 211–13; judges, xiii, 37, 46, 83,
  90–91, 93–94, 203, 217; justices of
  the peace, xiii, xv, 1–24, 114, 217,
  225; lawyers, 9–10, 13, 16, 22, 37,
  83, 87, 90, 93, 116, 132, 137, 215;
  penologists, 31–45; trades (skilled),
  9–11, 13, 123, 219. *See also* Police
Pryor, Henry, 22
Pulp Fiction, 214
Punch and Judy, 212
Pyke, John George, 4
Pyke, magistrate, 8, 12

Quebec, Canada, xiii–xiv
Quebec City, Canada: constabularies in,
  14; Summit of the Americas, xiv
Quesnel, British Columbia, 137

Rabbit Creek, Yukon, 133
Radzinowitz, Sir Leon, xix–xx, 227–28
Rae, Angus, 86–91
Rae, Elias, 88
Rae, Norman, 86–88
Randall, Frank, 34, 38–39, 42–43
Rat Portage (now Kenora), Ontario, 79
Rawlings, Philip, xvi, 224–26
Regina, Manitoba, 87
Reid, John Phillip, xvii, 229–31
Religion: xviii, xx; Calvinism, 202;
  clergy, 8, 36; Cree, 78, 80; Crusades,
  203, 206; evangelical, 20; Islam, 203;
  Lord's Day Act, 16; missionaries, 90,
  101, 133–34, 150, 207; prayer, 56,
  83; preaching, 92; Protestants, 20,
  219–20; Puritans, 167; Roman Cath-
  olic, xix, 19, 202, 219; Sabbatarians,
  12; salvation, 214; sin, 1, 4–5, 16, 36;
  sorcery, 76, 95; witchcraft, 76, 159,
  173, 202. *See also* Crimes and of-
  fenses; Human condition
Restoration, the, 215
Reynolds, Elaine, 213
Richardson, magistrate, 94
Richmond, Duke of, 223
Ridgway, Samuel, 66
Robert B., inmate, 35
Robinson, John, chief justice, 218
Rocky Bar, Idaho, 64, 69
Rolla, British Columbia, 136
Ronald J., 123
Rose, judge, 81, 89
Rothman, David, xviii, 31
Rouleau, Charles, judge, 83, 85, 93
Royal Canadian Mounted Police,
  85–87, 94–96, 132, 143, 146–47
Royal North-West Mounted Police,
  124
Rublack, Ulinka, 213
Ruff, Julius R., xi, 211–214

Russell, Alexander, 1
Russell, Lord John, 223
Russia: xiii, 208; invasion of, 197
Ruthven, Malise, 206
Rwanda: 196, 199; Hutus, 196, 199;
   massacres in, xx; Tutsi, 196, 199

Sabascon Lake, Ontario, 79
Sabourin, Joseph, 94
Sabourin, Paul, 92–95
Saint John, New Brunswick, 16, 21
St. Paul, Minnesota, 42
Sanders, Colonel Gilbert, 108, 113–14
Sandy Lake, Ontario, 86
Saskatchewan, Canada, 137
Saunders, C.E., superintendent, 87
Savorgnan, Antonio, 214
Sawyers, William, 13
Schall, Carl, 138
Schneider, General Rene, 204
Schwartz, Otto, 139–40
Scotland, witch-hunts, 202
Scott, alderman, 19
Scott, H.K.W., 34
Scott, Jack, 146–47
Scully, John, watchman, 21
Seattle, United States, globalization
   talks, xiv
Seline, Roy, 143
Seline, Theresa, 143
Serbia, 196, 199
Shakespeare, William, 212
She Wills, 82
Shea, William, 138
Sheffield, Bert, 131–32
Sheridan, Ann, 145
Sifton, Clifford, 134
Silver City, Idaho, 61, 68
Silver River, 145
Simon, Jonathan, 41
Sing Sing prison, California, 139
Slusk, Russia, 206
Smandych, Russell, xix
Smart, James, 93
Smith, Daisy, sergeant, 85, 86
Smith, Henry, warden, 218
Society: Afro-Americans, 8, 10, 19, 114,
   160, 183, 193, 219; apprentices, 1,

4–5, 7–8; children, xix, 4–5, 14, 19,
   50, 57, 83–84, 93–94, 108–12,
   115–20, 123–25, 138–39, 196–99,
   204, 211, 218–20; Edwardian, 96;
   elites, xi, xviii, 1–2, 4, 12–14, 114,
   197, 201–5, 207–8, 212–13, 218,
   220; ethnic minorities, xii–xiii, xvi–
   xvii, xix–xx, 1, 8, 111, 114, 198, 219;
   gypsies, 196, 198–200; Jews, 114,
   196–200, 206; merchants, 4–5, 9, 18,
   215; middle class, 2, 10, 13–14, 23,
   107, 215–16; Natives (Aboriginals),
   xii–xv, xvii, xix, 64–65, 67, 75–96,
   131, 133–36, 229–20; Victorian, 96,
   107; wendigo, 75–103; women,
   xii–xv, xviii–xix, 1, 19, 23, 34, 46, 53,
   57, 68, 77, 82–83, 85, 94, 105–25,
   138, 144, 160–62, 168, 177, 188,
   193, 197–99, 204, 211, 217, 219;
   working class, xii, xviii, 2, 8, 18, 28,
   34, 38, 42–43, 107, 120–23, 133,
   219. *See also* Human condition;
   Professions
Soda Springs, Idaho, 68
Sodom and Gomorrah, 20
Son, Ah, 61
Spain, 212
Srebnick, Amy, xvii
Srebrenica, Yugoslavia, 196
Star, Idaho, 69
Steinberg, Allen xv, 2, 6
Stone, author, 213
Stony Mountain Prison, Manitoba, 85,
   91–93, 92, 96
Storch, Robert, 10, 221
Sues, Willliam, 67
Sutherland, David, 3, 13, 15
Swainger, Jonathan, xvii
Sweden, prison reform, xix
Sweet Grass, Montana, 132
Swift Runner, 92–95
Sydney, Australia, 222–23; City Coun-
   cil, 223
Sykes, Gresham, 38

Tambiago, an Indian, 65
Taylor, H.C., lawyer, 93
Teicher, Morton I., 78

The Godfather, 214
The Idaho Tri-Weekly Statesman, 54–55
Thomson, William, 216
Thorner, Tom, 105
Tonry, Michael, xix, 227–28
Toronto, Canada, xiv, 124
Trapp, major, 197
Tucher, Andie, xvii
Tufts, Gardiner, 33
Tupper Creek, British Columbia, 138–39
Tushwegeh, 81–82, 92

United Kingdom, governmentality in, xii
United Nations: 198–200; International Criminal Tribunal, 208
United States: 22, 208; Army, xvii, 140–43; governmentality in, xii; Military Police, 143; policing in, 224–26; prison reform in, xix, 31–51; Supreme Court, xii, xiv; violent crime in, xi–xx
Upper Canada: 218–20; Rebellion, 218

Vancouver, British Columbia, 147; APEC conference, xiv; young offenders rehabilitation center, 139
Vancouver Sun, 146
Victoria, Australia, prison reform, xix
Violence: banditry, 212; brigandage, 222; domestic, xii–xiii, xvii–xix, 212, 229; duels, 212; feuds, 212, 214, 225; Holocaust, xx, 196–97, 200, 206; lynching, xvii, 58, 164; riot and rebellion, xiii–xiv, 2, 7, 12–13, 16, 20, 38, 212, 218, 220; terrorism, xii, xx, 196; vigilantes, xvii, 53, 57–59. *See also* Corrections; Crimes and offenses; War; Weapons
Virginia, 4

Wahsakapeequay, 87
Waite, Robert, xvi–xvii
Waldrep, Christopher, xiii
Walkowitz, Judith, 125
Walter, Simeon, 61
War: army (and soldiers), 4, 13, 36, 58, 134, 140–41, 206–7, 212; Battle of Waterloo, 207; conscription, xvi, 8; {the} military, 6, 19, 36, 56, 58–59, 134, 140, 143–44, 200–2, 206–7, 212, 221; militia, 2, 5, 8, 137; navy (and sailors), 8, 13, 18–20, 207–8; Thirty Years' War, 199, 206; Vietnam War, 204; War of 1812, 3, 8; World War I, 106, 115, 120–121, 123–25, 208, 221; World War II, xvii, 106, 135, 140–45, 195–209, 225. *See also* desertion under Crimes and offenses
Warlick, Theodore, 67
Wasakapeequay, 85
Wasawpscopinesse, 79–80
Watson, Fred, 145, 146
Watson, James, 145
Watson, Neil, 105
Weapons: axes, 17, 55, 83–84; chains, 83; clubs, 8; cudgels, 9; guns, xiv, xxii, 17, 38–39, 53–54, 57–59, 61–66, 77, 79–80, 82, 92, 108, 133, 138–40, 143–44, 147, 197–98, 206, 211; knives, 17, 84; sabers, 82; swords, 11
Weaver, John, 23, 105
Webb, Beatrice, 216
Webb, Sydney, 216
Weber, Max, 205
Weichman, Dennis, xix
Weigner, Gustav, 144
Wendigo, killings, xiv, 75–103
West, C.W., inspector, 135
West Point, cadets, 36
Westminster, England, 217
White, Frederick, 134
White Pine, Idaho, 63
Whittier, F.A., 42
Whittier, H.B., 42
Wilkie, William, 12, 13
Wilkins, Martin, 15
William H., inmate, 35
Wiltenburg, Joy, 213
Wink, A.S., lawyer, 80, 81
Winnipeg, Manitoba, 85
Wismer, Gordon S., 139
Wohl, Anthony, 107
Wood, George, 17

Wood River News-Miner, 67
Wood River Times, 65
Wood River Valley, Idaho, 68
Woodburn, E.D., counsel, 137

Yangtze River, China, 207
York Factory, Ontario, 78

Yorkshire, South Yorkshire Police, 226
Young, A. McB., lawyer, 132
Young Turks, 203
Yugoslavia, 208
Yukon, 134
Yushiko, Prince Asaka, 207

Zambarlini, family, 214

About the Editor and Contributors

AUGUSTINE BRANNIGAN is a professor of sociology at the University of Calgary. He has conducted extensive investigations of street crime, including prostitution and delinquency. In recent years he has focused on the problems associated with defining and explaining genocide and similar acts of mass murder committed by states and their political elites. He has recently published with William Gemmell, David Pevalin, and Terrance Wade "Self-Control and Social Control in Childhood Misconduct and Aggression," *Canadian Journal of Criminology* 44:2 (April 2002): 119–42; "Criminology and the Holocaust: Xenophobia, Evolution and Genocide," *Crime and Delinquency* 44:2 (April 1998): 257–76; and has an article in press with Zhiqiu Lin, "The Implications of a Provincial Police Force: The Case for Alberta and Saskatchewan."

DAVID BRIGHT is an assistant professor of history at the University of Guelph. He has published on labor, crime, and society in western Canada and is the author of the Canadian Historical Association's prize-winning book, *The Limits of Labour: Class Formation and the Labour Movement in Calgary, 1883–1929* (1998). He is currently completing a study of vagrancy, the work ethic, and moral regulation in Alberta before World War II.

SARA M. BUTLER is a Social Sciences and Research Council of Canada postdoctoral fellow at St. Mary's University, Halifax, Nova Scotia. Her recent publications include "Spousal Abuse in Fourteenth-Century Yorkshire: What can we learn from the Coroners' Rolls?" *Florilegium* 18 (2002) and "Lies,

Damned Lies, and the Life of Saint Lucy: Three Cases of Judicial Separation from the Late Medieval Court of York" in P. Romanski's and A. Sy-Wonyu's *Falseness, Forgeries and Counterfeits* (Rouen, forthcoming). She is also in the process of completing her book-length study titled *The Language of Abuse: Marital Violence in Later Medieval England.*

MARY CLAYTON is a private scholar at the Institute of Historical Research, University of London. Her dissertation (M.Phil.) is titled "Elections and Electioneering in Haslemere, 1715–80" (Royal Holloway College, University of London, 1993). She has written articles titled "Electioneering and Voter Choice in Haslemere, 1715–80," *Southern History* 17 (1995); "Voter Choice in a Patronage Borough: Haslemere, 1754–80," *Parliamentary History* 15:2 (1996); "A Contemporary Electoral Map: Occupation and Votes in Mid-Eighteenth Century Haslemere," *Parliamentary History* 16:3 (1997); and "The Wealth of Riches to be found in the Court of Chancery: Chancery Pleadings and the Equity Database Project' Archives" (forthcoming). She is preparing an article on infanticide for the Old Bailey Online 1674–1834 conference (March 2004), for which she was a researcher, on women's use of Chancery, and the career of a prostitute and pickpocket in the 1780s.

SIMON DEVEREAUX is in the School of History, Philosophy, Religion and Classics at the University of Queensland, St Lucia, Australia. He has published "The City and the Sessions Paper: 'Public Justice' in London, 1770–1800," *Journal of British Studies* 35 (1996); "In Place of Death: Transportation, Penal Practices and the English State, 1770–1830," in *Qualities of Mercy: Justice, Punishment and Discretion*, edited by Carolyn Strange (1996); and "'The Fall of the Sessions Paper': The Criminal Trial and the Popular Press in Late-Eighteenth Century London," in *Crime, Punishment, and Reform in Europe*, vol. 18 of *Criminal Justice History* (Westport: Greenwood Publishing Group, 2002). He is currently completing a book titled *The Home Office and the Administration of Criminal Justice in Great Britain, 1760–1806.*

MARY BETH EMMERICHS is an assistant professor of history at the University of Wisconsin–Sheboygan, a campus of the University of Wisconsin Colleges. A member of the Criminal Justice/Legal History network of the Social Science History Association, she has published articles on the investigation of homicide and trials of women for homicide in nineteenth-century England, the most recent of which is "Getting away with Murder? Homicide and the Coroners in Nineteenth-Century London," *Social Science History* 25:1 (spring 2001). The first books she read about legal history as an undergraduate were those written by Sir Leon Radzinowicz.

KELLY HARDWICK is a senior research associate at the Canadian Research Institute for Law and the Family. He recently completed his doctoral dissertation at the University of Calgary titled "Unraveling 'Crime in the Making': Re-Examining the Role of Informal Social Control in the Genesis and Stability of Delinquency and Crime" (2002). He also teaches advanced courses in criminology at the University of Calgary. He has rekindled interest in the classic Glueck and Glueck longitudinal study of delinquency and has identified its relevance for reconciling differences in contemporary explanations of misconduct.

SIDNEY HARRING is a professor of law at the City University of New York School of Law. He is the author of *Crow Dog's Case: American Indian Sovereignty, Tribal Law, and United States Law in the Nineteenth Century* (1994) and *White Man's Law. Native People in Nineteenth-Century Canadian Jurisprudence* (1998), and he has an article in press titled "'There Seemed to be No Recognized Law': Canadian Law and the Prairie First Nations." He has studied the constitutional relations of peoples in Namibia, and the Epupa Dam project near the Angola border, as well as Malaysian law, and has also taught at the faculties of law at the universities of Saskatchewan, Namibia, and MARA Institute of Technology at Selangor Danul Ehsan. He has examined First Nations people and colonial law for more than a decade.

JENNINE HURL-EAMON is an assistant professor of history at Trent University. She completed her doctoral work in history at York University, Toronto, in 2001, and held a Social Sciences and Humanities Research Council postdoctoral fellowship at Carleton University, Ottawa, where she was also a lecturer. She published articles on women, crime, and litigation in Restoration and eighteenth-century England in the *Journal of Family History* and *The London Journal*, and her doctoral dissertation titled "Voices of Litigation; Voices of Resistance: Constructions of Gender in the Records of Assault in London, 1680–1720" has been accepted for publication at the Ohio State University Press. Her teaching specialty is early modern Britain and Europe, and her current project is a study of the wives of soldiers and sailors who remained at home in eighteenth-century London while their husbands served abroad.

LOUIS A. KNAFLA is professor emeritus of history at the University of Calgary. He has written *Kent at Law 1602: The County Jurisdiction* (1995), and he has co-edited with Susan Binnie, *Law, Society, and the State: Essays in Modern Legal History* (1995); with Clive Emsley, *Crime Histories and Histories of Crime* (Greenwood 1996); and with Rick Klumpenhouwer, *Lords of the Western Bench: A Biographical History of the Supreme and District Courts of Alberta 1876–1990* (1997). His most recent book chapters are "Britain's 'Solomon': King James and the Law," in *James VI and I: A Reappraisal*, edited by Dan Fischlin and Mark Fortier (2002) and "Mr. Secretary Donne: The Years with Sir Thomas Egerton," in *John Donne*, edited by David Colclough (2003). He is currently working on the Star Chamber and equity courts in the late-sixteenth and early seventeenth centuries, a biography of Lord Chancellor Ellesmere, and the legal history of Western Canada.

GREG MARQUIS teaches Canadian and criminal justice history in the Department of Politics and History at the University of New Brunswick, Saint John. He is the author of *Policing Canada's Century: A History of the Canadian Association of Chiefs of Police* (1993), *In Armageddon's Shadow: The Civil War and Canada's Maritime Provinces* (1998), and several articles on the policing of Canadian cities. A current article is in press titled "Policing Two Imperial Frontiers: The Royal Irish Constabulary and the North-West Mounted Police." His current research interests are alcohol policy and society in twentieth-century Canada and historical commemoration.

ROD MARTIN is a former member of the Royal Canadian Mounted Police who served 24 years in a variety of positions in Alberta. He retired from the force and is now a Ph.D. candidate in legal history at the University of Calgary, where he is writing his dissertation on the history of the North-West Mounted Police as judicial magistrates and teaching the history of crime at the University of Calgary and Mount Royal College, Calgary. He has written several submitted articles, including "The Common Law and the Justices of the Supreme Court of the North-West Territories: The First Generation, 1887–1907."

ALEXANDER W. PISCIOTTA is a professor in the Department of Criminal Justice at Kutztown University, Pennsylvania. He has published a number of articles on the history of punishment and social control. His book, *Benevolent Repression: Social Control and the American Reformatory-Prison Movement* (New York University Press), received the Outstanding Book Award (1997) from the Academy of Criminal Justice Sciences.

JONATHAN SWAINGER is an associate professor of history at the University of Northern British Columbia, Prince George. He has published numerous articles on extradition in nineteenth-century Canada; lawyering in Red Deer, Alberta; and crime and criminal justice in the Peace River country of Alberta and British Columbia. He has recently published *The Canadian Department of Justice and the Completion of Confederation 1867–78* (2000), is co-editor of *People and Place: Historical Influences on Legal Culture* (2003) and *Studies in the Legal History of the Northwest Territories and Prairie Provinces* (2004), and is currently writing a history of crime in the Peace River area.

ROBERT G. WAITE is in the office of Special Investigations, Criminal Division, Washington, D.C. He specializes in the history of law enforcement and crime in the United States and Germany. His articles on nineteenth-century American prison reform and the German view of crime in America during the 1920s and 1930s appeared in the 1991 and 1992 volumes of *Criminal Justice History*. He has articles in press in German-language journals titled "Rudolf Hess and Anti-Germanism in Criminological Texts" and "The American Legal Profession and War Crimes Trials in Germany 1943–1947." He is also writing papers on German sentiment in Latvia 1942–44 and abortion in Germany 1914–45, and he is completing a book on juvenile delinquency in Nazi Germany. He continues to work on his larger study of the Idaho penitentiaries.

DENNIS WIECHMAN is professor emeritus of criminal justice at the University of Evansville in Indiana. He has published more than thirty articles and presented many more papers in national and international journals on capital punishment and comparative justice, including works concerning Singapore, the European Community, and Islamic Courts and Corrections. He has also been a consultant to various criminal justice agencies in Indiana, Kentucky, Missouri, Iowa, and Illinois on traffic, police administration, program review and evaluation, police selection, and promotion testing, and he has taught law enforcement and corrections education.